OMNIVM LVX CIVIVM

BOCCACCIO
AND
FIAMMETTA

I les amoureux cueurs des
treslouuale poures z diseur
de liesse et de tout plaisir souffre
teur qui continuellement lan

Janet Levarie Smarr

BOCCACCIO
AND
FIAMMETTA
THE
NARRATOR
AS
LOVER

UNIVERSITY OF ILLINOIS PRESS

Urbana and Chicago

Publication of this work was supported in part by a grant
from the Andrew W. Mellon Foundation.

This book is printed on acid-free paper.

Frontispiece showing Boccaccio presenting the *Teseida* to Fiammetta is
reproduced from Eduard Chmelarz, "Eine Französische Bilderhandschrift
von Boccaccios Theseide," *Jahrbuch der Kunsthistorischen Sammlungen
des Allerhöchsten Kaiserhauses* 14 (1893).

Library of Congress Cataloging-in-Publication Data

Smarr, Janet Levarie, 1949–
    Boccaccio and Fiammetta : the narrator as lover.

    Bibliography: p.
    Includes index.
        1. Boccaccio, Giovanni, 1313–1375—Characters—Women.
I. Title.
PQ4291.A3W78 1986   858'.109   85-20499
ISBN 0-252-01224-0 (alk. paper)

To Larry

CONTENTS

ACKNOWLEDGMENTS

I would like first and foremost to acknowledge Robert Hollander and Robert Durling, who read and commented extensively on various stages of this work. Judith Kates, Victoria Kirkham, and Larry Smarr also undertook the burden of reading critically through my first draft. My more general thanks extend to Thomas P. Roche, from whom I learned to ask some of the questions which led me to this study.

I received financial support for these researches from the American Association of University Women, the Southeastern Center for Medieval and Early Renaissance Studies, a Harvard Mellon Faculty Fellowship, and the Research Board of the University of Illinois. Publication of this work was supported in part by an anonymous contribution from a friend of scholarship in the humanities.

Quedam vero, et si natura sui forsan sint lucida, tanto sunt fingentium artificio palliata, ut egre etiam quis possit ingenio verum ex illis excerpere sensum, ut persepe inter nubila conditum solis pregrande corpus etiam doctissimi queant astrologi, qua celi vagetur in parte, comprehendere punctaliter oculorum intuitu. Et ex his esse non nunquam vatum poemata non inficior.

Boccaccio, Genealogia XIV.12

[Some things, in truth, even if perhaps they are clear by nature, are so cloaked by the art of fiction-makers that scarcely anyone could by his wit derive from them their true sense; as often the immense body of the sun when hidden among clouds cannot be accurately located by the eye of even the most learned astrologers, who seek in what part of the sky it is wandering. And that the poems of prophetic poets are sometimes of this sort, I do not deny.]

Introduction

This study attempts to investigate several of Boccaccio's techniques as a writer of fiction: chiefly, his introduction of readers and narrators within the text, the narrator's recurrent pose as a lover, and the reappearance from work to work of the beloved Fiammetta in changing roles. Such an investigation necessarily involves other issues as well: how these fictions should be read, how Boccaccio is making use of borrowings from Dante and other writers, how Boccaccio's works relate to one another, and how his techniques relate to his ideas about the function of poetry in general. To these larger issues I cannot hope to do justice, but I do endeavor to suggest some thoughts about them which may help in an understanding of Boccaccio's methods.

The problem of the narrator as lover has been discussed by Robert Hollander in his study *Boccaccio's Two Venuses;*[1] in his view the nature of this role is always the same: the narrator consistently loves in a cupidinous fashion and consistently misunderstands his own texts. Moreover, by focusing on the *sententia* of these works, Hollander ends up seeing them all as quite similar; Boccaccio seems to be saying the same thing over and over again. I would like to suggest that the case is not so simple. Sometimes the narrator appears to be consciously taking on the pose of lover after some wiser introductory remarks, i.e., his own self-presentation sometimes changes within a given work. In some books the image of the "author" is suddenly split into two distinct persons, raising questions about which one means what and how intelligently the second is copying from the first. Furthermore, the situation from book to book is not exactly the same, and the

I

beloved Fiammetta may or may not have strong celestial associations depending on which book we are looking at. By considering some of these matters at greater length, I hope to begin to trace certain lines of development in Boccaccio's methods as a writer. After all, if one is thoughtful about one's work, one's thoughts and emphases are likely to change in time, especially given the changes in Boccaccio's external situation and audience. The old Boccaccio is not like the young; but I do not mean by this to follow the line of many other scholars who have seen in the young Boccaccio a poet of amorous self-expression and in the older a sudden rejection of love. Rather I find in him, as I intend to show, a growing sense of the difficulties of both moral and literary pursuits, a growing distrust of the power of reason and thus an increasing wariness of love's potential to lead to good, and a concomitant need to speak more clearly or directly. One can study these developments through the changing roles of Fiammetta, who appears both as a reader and as an object of the poet's love.

Since the troubadours, centuries of poets have presented themselves as lovers. So when Boccaccio started his literary career in the pose of a lover, he had already a long literary tradition behind him. Love, however, means different things to different persons; and the poet as lover could treat a large variety of themes, including religious, moral, aesthetic, and political ideas. Within his poems, the lady could exist as a vivid personality or as a vague ideal, an object of physical passion or a symbol of unworldly goals.

Boccaccio slowly developed his own uses for the tradition he inherited. As early as his first work, the *Caccia di Diana*, Boccaccio used the story of an amorous narrator to frame the rest of the text.[2] The lady remained unnamed ("la bella donna il cui nome si tace") and the narrator too. In the *Filostrato*, where Boccaccio repeated this framing device, the narrator and lady took on names: Filostrato and Filomena. Finally in the *Filocolo* Fiammetta's name appeared for the first time. The story of the poet's love for Fiammetta continued into the *Teseida*, *Comedia delle Ninfe*, and *Amorosa Visione*, and Fiammetta told her own story of love in the *Elegia di Madonna Fiammetta*. In the *Decameron* and *Corbaccio*, however, the narrator fell out of love; and though Fiammetta appears in a diminished role as one of the ten storytellers in the *Decameron*, the widow in the *Corbaccio* is once again unnamed. Boccaccio has reverted to the abstract figure of woman.

It is easy to relate Boccaccio's love for Fiammetta to Dante's for Beatrice or Petrarch's for Laura; yet the three ladies are very different. Boccaccio wrote that according to the account of a reliable person Beatrice was a real historical woman and a daughter of Folco Portinari.[3] Boccaccio also wrote that Laura was purely the invention of her author: "Et quamvis in suis quampluribus vulgaribus poematibus . . . se Laurettam quandam ardentissime demonstravit amasse, non obstat nam prout ipsemet bene puto, Laurettam illam allegorice pro laurea corona quam postmodum adeptus, accipiendam existimo"[4] [And however much in his many vernacular poems . . . he demonstrates that he ardently loved Lauretta, for that is no objection as I see it, I think that Lauretta is to be taken allegorically for the laurel crown which soon he attained]. Which way are we to take Boccaccio's own Fiammetta?

At the turn of this century a number of scholars devoted their efforts to reconstructing the biography of Boccaccio and, taking both his prefaces and his narratives at their word, believed Fiammetta to be his long-loved lady Maria d'Aquino, an illegitimate daughter of King Robert of Naples.[5] With painstaking research they pieced together the history of their love; it is a romantic account, for its sources are poetry and fiction. The test of such an approach would be its self-consistency, for we should see the fixed set of historical events as a recurring story. Yet the biographers had to struggle to make the pieces fit and disagreed among themselves about the history supposedly revealed.[6]

The debate about the historicity of Fiammetta began contemporaneously with the research on her affair, but for a long time it did not succeed in dissuading those scholars in search of the real romance. Tiraboschi first bravely suggested that Fiammetta was a fiction, supporting his suggestion by pointing to the contradictions about her from work to work.[7] His thesis was attacked by both Baldelli and Renier, each convinced that they had satisfactorily answered his objections.[8]

The doubts about Fiammetta's reality nonetheless grew with time. As Hauvette admitted, the records of Naples and of the Anjou family show no sign of a Maria d'Aquino.[9] Moreover, as Symonds remarked, Boccaccio would have been in no position to write openly about an adulterous affair with a daughter of the king.[10] Billanovich continued this line of attack, reviewing the contradictions in the account and commenting: "arrischiò il fantasioso scolastico di comporre una favola di cui al re poteva spiacere la sconvenienza? Ma quanto più improvvida e ingiuriosa la divulgazione di reali penosi misteri, sulla nascita e sulla dissoluta vita della nobilissima: per il re, la potente famiglia di Maria e il potente marito"[11] [did the fanciful scholar risk composing a fable whose impropriety could have displeased the king? But how much more improvident and injurious to divulge the painful royal mysteries on the birth and dissolute life of the very noble lady: for the king, the powerful family of Maria and her powerful husband]. Battaglia warned that historical elements which have been transformed into parts of a work of art should never be believed too literally.[12]

Replacing the search for the real Fiammetta with a study of literary and rhetorical sources for Boccaccio's writings, Billanovich and Branca finally put an end to the old autobiographical approach. The dedicatory letters to Boccaccio's early works are "non, come vedremo, gelose confessioni di avvenimenti reali, ma escercitazioni retoriche intessute su schemi convenzionali e preordinati. Persino la romantica narrazione amorosa della *Mavortis miles extrenue* non ha che il valore di un'abile ripetizione di paradigmi letterari"[13] [not, as we shall see, jealous confessions of real events, but rhetorical exercises woven on conventional and prearranged schemes. Even the romantic narrative of love in the *Mavortis miles extrenue* has no value other than a skillful repetition of literary paradigms]. The details of the *Elegia* are drawn from Ovid's *Heroides* and the tragedies of Seneca.[14] The parentage of Boccaccio and Fiammetta in the *Filocolo* picks up elements from the enclosed romance of royal children.[15] For the enamorment in church König supplies a whole array of literary precedents.[16]

The studies of Billanovich, Branca, and König are excellent and important because at last scholars acknowledged the literary background to Boccaccio's fictions. Now as a result of their work new questions are raised, or rather the old question "Who was Fiammetta?" must be posed with a new meaning. We need to ask not who she was among the real women of Naples, but who she is within Boccaccio's fictions, what roles she plays in his works, and why, if Boccaccio's love for her is a fiction, he chose to use this particular fiction as a frame for book after book—for Fiammetta appears in texts as different as an elaborately rhetorical prose epic, a twelve-book epic in verse, a pastoral allegory in mixed verse and prose, a dream vision in terza rima, a *Heroides*-like complaint with detailed psychological observation, a collection of diverse short tales, and scattered sonnets and canzoni. Moreover, the image of the beloved lady is refracted into multiple images seen through the eyes of characters, narrator, and real author. Thus we cannot simply excerpt the passages in which Fiammetta occurs, as earlier critics so often did;[17] instead we must study them within the context of the books by which their meaning is defined.

As Boccaccio began to develop his own ideas about how to use the traditional lover-poet role, he took both Dante and Ovid simultaneously as models. From Ovid came the complaining lover and the playful author behind him. Ovid's poet, like Boccaccio's narrators, writes in order to win his lady:

> at facie tenerae laudata saepe puellae,
> ad vatem, pretium carminis, ipsa venit (*Amores* II.1)

> [but if the face of a tender girl is praised often, / she herself comes to the poet, the reward for his song].

Dante does not try to persuade his lady to come to him; rather he is the one who must be moved, and she the one who comes to draw him toward herself and toward God. The two poets represented for Boccaccio the polarities of worldly and holy love, and also the two simultaneous goals of Boccaccio's writing: to seduce and to educate, to draw the soul toward pleasure and toward truth. Dante, of course, was not the only poet to mix religious language and ideas with love poetry; he had inherited a tradition reaching back into Provençal and Sicilian lyrics. But from the beginning Dante was Boccaccio's clearly acknowledged master and model, as well as the clearest example of how such a mixture can serve the most serious ends.

In order to understand Boccaccio's writings, we need to sort out the various rhetorical levels or stances within them. First of all, there is usually a narrator who refers to himself in the first person and occasionally tells us some of his own story as well as the story he is recounting. This persona, whether or not he is involved as an actor in the main narrative, is analyzable as a fictional character in his own right, and his remarks about himself must be viewed in relation to the fiction which they frame. In some works, such as the *Filocolo* or *Comedia delle Ninfe*, we find mentioned the actual writing of the text at hand; I refer in these cases to the "authors" (in quotation marks) as distinguished from the real author Boccaccio. Sometimes, indeed, Boccaccio presents not one but two quite different "authors" for a single text, so different that they cannot possibly intend the same interpretations or uses for their book. The lover-poet who says "I," and who has therefore often been identified with Boccaccio, is only one of these two "authors." The existence of two such different "authors" suggests that there are at least two possible sets of intended meanings to the text—three if neither of the two is identifiable with Boccaccio himself. In other cases, we are presented with a disagreement between two characters within the fiction about the meaning of events in which they are involved. I refer to these characters as "speakers." The "voices" we hear addressing us can come from any of these levels. In the *Amorosa Visione*, for example, one of the speakers is the first-person narrator, who is also the main actor within the story.

Besides the doubling of "authors" and speakers, Boccaccio involves himself in a whole series of narrative levels. The "I" of the *Filocolo* is translating a text written by Ilario, who heard the story told by Florio; and that tale in turn includes other stories told by sundry characters such as Idalagos. The *Decameron*'s "I" describes ten narrators, who in turn often tell stories about characters telling stories.[18] In the *Comedia delle Ninfe Fiorentine* the "I" is writing down the same events narrated by Ameto, who is transcribing the tales told by the nymphs; among the nymphs' narrations, Fiammetta's includes the story told to her by Caleone. If we identify Caleone with the original "I" as critics have done, then the loop becomes closed and one of the characters is telling about her own "author." The nesting of narrators within narrators is undoubtedly an imitation of Ovid's technique in the *Metamorphoses*. As one is continually reminded of the act of telling or writing in Boccaccio's works, each narrator is in turn a character whose words must be judged in the light of his situation. There is no reason for this to stop—and every reason for it to continue—when we reach the outer layer, the "I" of the book.

The problem of finding our way among these various voices is connected for Boccaccio to the problem of the narrator's relation to his readers, who, like the narrators or "authors," exist both inside and outside the text and undergo a similar multiplication. On one hand, Boccaccio could assume that his audience was Christian; on the other hand, he chose to write for people who would rather hear a good story than a sermon or a treatise. This audience must be pleased but also educated, that is, drawn into thought beyond the surface of the tale. The problematic nature of the author's task in regard to such an audience is reflected in the frequency of Boccaccio's address to at least two sets of readers: the lady, and other lovers (including us). The lady is not in love and must be wooed, but the other readers are already lovers and must be reading for a different purpose. When Fiammetta herself becomes narrator, she too speaks to two different audiences: Panfilo whom she hopes to reseduce, and other women whom she hopes to warn away from passion.

The use of multiple rhetorical stances on both the narrating and receiving ends of the text invites our acknowledgment of ambiguities and ambivalences. Thus Boccaccio is neither the absolute moralist, as Hollander paints him, nor the champion of nature and the rights of the flesh, as asserted by Scaglione.[19] Hollander tends to explain *away* the erotic aspects of Boccaccio's fictions in order to focus on their moral meanings; while these meanings are there and Hollander's book is important in pointing them out, nonetheless the dominant effect of these fictions seems to me precisely the doubleness of aspect, the attempt to join the erotic with the moral, the Ovidian with the Dantean. The *Comedia delle Ninfe*, where tales of seduction signify the operation of the virtues, is the most blatant example of this kind of forced conjunction of opposites, but it appears in subtler ways in other works as well.

The multiplications of author and audience manifest a self-conscious literariness on the part of Boccaccio which bids for attention quite as loudly as any autobiographical elements might do. Curiously, critics who have studied the ironies of Chaucer's writings have often assumed that Boccaccio was much less complex than his English admirer. Thus, for example, Root says of Chaucer's "Troilus and Criseyde," "It is in this spirit of a wise and thoughtful irony that Chaucer has conceived and executed his poem, a spirit poles assunder from the tender sentiment and ardent passion which inform the *Filostrato*."[20] Meech, making the same comparison, also considers the *Filostrato* much simpler and more literal than Chaucer's poem because he takes literally Filostrato's preface as the remarks of the real author.[21] Thus while recognizing in Chaucer's work a treatment of broad issues, such as fortune and providence, or free will and necessity, he is content to call Boccaccio's poem a narrower love tragedy without such philosophical considerations. Similarly Ruggiers in a chapter entitled "The Italian Influence on Chaucer" writes that Chaucer "is not driven by so intensely personal a motive as Boccaccio's anguish over his terminated love affair . . . with the philosophical inspiration provided by Boethius and Dante, he is more thoughtful and detached."[22]

It is time to call attention to some of the ironies involved in the pose of Boccaccio's narrators, to map out some of the distance between narrator and author, and to consider in which ways that distance and those ironies affect our understanding of the meaning of his works. Chaucer undoubtedly understood what Boccaccio was doing and learned from him many of the tricks of his trade for which he is rightly admired.

Although each of his writings stands by itself, Boccaccio alludes from one to another as if suggesting that we view each in the context of the others. Thus, for example, the *Comedia delle Ninfe Fiorentine* mentions Idalagos from the *Filocolo;* the *Amorosa Visione* mentions Florio and Biancifiore of the *Filocolo* and also Lia and Ameto of the *Comedia delle Ninfe;*

the *Decameron* alludes to Troiolo and Criseida of the *Filostrato* and to the Theban knights of the *Teseida;* the beginning of the dream in the *Corbaccio* echoes the opening of the *Amorosa Visione*.

While the methods of writing change considerably from text to text as Boccaccio modifies his techniques, I am led to conclude that Boccaccio's basic ideas about the purposes of literature did not greatly change during his life. For, despite what most critics have said, the love stories written in the first half of Boccaccio's career are not devoid of the moral and religious concerns of his later years.[23] The "lovers" addressed by the younger Boccaccio must be taught in an indirect and alluring manner. But to speak indirectly is to risk misintepretation. The sophistication of Boccaccio's techniques required sophisticated readers. What did change as Boccaccio grew older was his relation to the audience, whom he trusted less and less, therefore both moralizing more openly and also withdrawing into the humanist notion of writing for the intellectual few.

Moreover, in order to defend the claims—asserted all along—that literature, even pagan literature, is a moral teacher, Boccaccio later felt obliged to abandon as too dangerous the love poetry of Ovid, which he had earlier attempted to "save" not by allegorizing it but by setting it within a context of Christian wisdom that would make evident the limits of Ovidian eloquence. Thus in later works Boccaccio stops writing as a lover and begins to write as someone who has fallen out of love.

I

Before Fiammetta

The earliest works of Boccaccio do not mention Fiammetta; nonetheless, they do refer to a beloved lady whom scholars until recently identified with her. Although this strict identification was an error, the early writings certainly offer a prototype for the story of the poet and his love.

The *Caccia di Diana*, Boccaccio's earliest work (probably 1334–35), celebrates an unnamed lady in a list of other women. The rhyme scheme shows Boccaccio starting his literary career as an eager disciple of Dante, and the *Caccia* is apparently a long imitation of the "serventese" of beautiful women mentioned by Dante in the *Vita Nuova* 6.[1] Beatrice was miraculously ninth in Dante's list of sixty women, and Dante commented on the relation of her number to the Trinity (*Vita Nuova* 29). Boccaccio's lady is thirty-third in a list of fifty-nine, though if one adds Diana (or Venus), one reaches Dante's sixty. Is the poem, however, a parody of Dante's writing or a serious imitation? Boccaccio's choice of the number thirty-three may have Christian resonances[2] or may be a doubling of the Venerean three.

The title *Caccia di Diana* partly refers to the hunt by ladies of the Neapolitan court who are presented as nymphs of Diana; but, as Hollander has pointed out, the title also means the chasing-away of Diana. It is Boccaccio's lady who leads the nymphs' rebellion to drive Diana away and who summons Venus to take over instead. The ambiguity of the title reflects the problematic nature of the whole poem, which has evoked two quite opposite readings.[3] Victoria Kirkham has argued that the Venus here represents Christian love, which causes the metamorphosis of the hunted beasts into men, converting them, that is, from vice to virtue and from bestial lust to Christian love. She notes the strong echoes of the *Vita Nuova,* and also relates the men's bathing in a stream to Dante's baptism in the earthly paradise and to the similar baptism of Ameto in Boccaccio's *Comedia delle Ninfe,* where Venus clearly represents God. Diana and Venus are thus seen as working together: Diana leads the hunt of virtues against vices, and then is replaced by Venus who "must represent something better than chastity, and that could hardly be wanton lust." She notes that Venus offers the ladies "grazia" (XVII.32–34) and that the lover ends his poem with the hope of obtaining "salute." One could add to these arguments with parallels from the *Filocolo.* For example, the rebelling nymphs crown themselves with laurel, a symbol of immortality which crowns the Madonna-like Fiammetta-Maria of the *Filocolo.* Furthermore Venus appears in a little white cloud; Hollander has noted that in the *Filocolo,* after the Venus of lust has appeared either nude or partially veiled in purple, the proper Venus descends in a white cloud after the marriage of Florio and Biancifiore.[4] The *Caccia*'s young men, however, are mantled in crimson and the nymphs in purple, clothing colors associated with the lusty Venus as easily as with *caritas.* To support the idea of the men's baptism, Kirkham recently pointed out a dream clearly significant of baptism and conversion in *Filocolo* II.3, where a lion cub and white deer cross a stream and emerge as a human pair, i.e., the hero and heroine of the tale.[5] However, the animals in the *Caccia* are metamorphosed not in the stream but in the flames of a sacrifice to Venus.

There are other problems with this reading as well. First, Venus seems to be in opposition to Diana, who is "turbata" at being replaced. Diana has bid the ladies sacrifice their prey to Jove, a deity suggestive of the Christian God. In revolt against Diana, the ladies choose to dedicate their sacrifice to Venus instead.[6] Nor is it clear that the "virtù" for which the ladies pray to Venus is "moral strength" rather than the power of love, or that their prayer

> Deh, fa sentire a noi quanto piacenti
> sieno gli effetti tuoi, e facci ancora,
> alcuno amando, gli animi contenti (XVII.25–27)

> [Ah, let us experience how pleasant are your effects,
> and make us also, by loving someone, of happy mind]

signifies a prayer for "spiritual happiness." Kirkham herself points out the resemblance to Troiolo's prayer in the *Filostrato* (III.74), where he praises Venus's "virtute" and thanks her for bringing him "salute"; but Troiolo is sadly mistaken about his condition, as we will discuss later in this chapter.

Hollander's reading is negative. For him, the Venus here represents lust, and the ladies thus rebel on behalf of physical pleasure. The antithesis between Diana and Venus is reinforced by Boccaccio's reversal of the Actaeon myth: as Diana turned Actaeon into a stag, so Venus counters Diana by turning a stag into a man. Despite the narrator's remarks about his new rational condition, the animals have become human only to satisfy the ladies' prayer for lovers. Thus the metamorphosis is no more ennobling than that of Cimone in the *Decameron*, who learns how to dress well and speak with polish but remains a lustful and violent brute. Hollander notes that if the lady drives away pride, sloth, avarice, and wrath from her lover (XVIII.34), she still leaves him with lust, gluttony, and envy. The poem becomes an ironic comedy, a satire on life at the court of Naples. The stilnovistic language must serve, in this case, to mark the parodic divergence of this poem from its model. This reading too is problematic, however, for the fifty-eight named ladies, some of whom are married, are real and identifiable women of Naples.[7] If Hollander's reading is correct, then this poem not only fails to celebrate these ladies but, indeed, insults them and the honor of their families.[8] How could Boccaccio have written such a poem, and why and for whom?

Other key elements of this poem only add to the puzzle. Let us consider, for example, the narrator and his lady. Are we to emphasize the narrator's change from animal to human, implying the need for a parallel shift in our reading from carnal to spiritual? Or are we to remark that the narrator has, surprisingly, been an animal all along until the end, recalling that Boccaccio in the *Corbaccio* identifies the animal voice as the voice of irrational lust? When the *Caccia* opens, the narrator is already in love:

> sol pensando mi stava che riparo
> potessi fare ai colpi che forando
> mi gian d'amor il cuor con duolo amaro (I.4–6)

> [I was alone, thinking what remedy I might make for the blows
> with which love was piercing my heart with bitter pain.]

Then he hears a voice summoning Diana's court to assemble. His desire for "riparo" from love may be answered by the assembling forces of Diana. And yet the nymphs' wounding, killing, and kindling of their hunted victims seem clearly, from lyrical tradition, to represent the effects of love. Are the ladies killing bestial vices, or instilling a love quite inappropriate to Diana? At the end of the poem, the narrator is still in love and writes as an act of service to Amore. His bitter pain has turned to hope, but is the nature of his love any different from before? It seems that "riparo" means not shelter from love but the hope of its satisfaction.

The unnamed lady is introduced (I.46–51) as the possessor of supreme virtue who increases and encourages the virtue of the other nymphs

> e per salute
> dell'altre, quasi com'una guardiana,
> avanti gio per guidarle tute

> [for the safety (or salvation) of the others, almost like a guardian, went ahead to guide them safely].

On the other hand, it is "Amore" who honors her above the rest for her "somma virtute"; what, then, is this "virtue"? Is it the same as the Venerean "virtù" for which the ladies pray (XVII.22–24)? And how can Amore's honoring be appropriate to the leader of Diana's nymphs? The narrator's lady leads her band of hunters to the south, while three other groups go off in the other directions. Branca notes that south is a direction associated with love.[9] It is she alone who instigates the revolt against Diana's commands and suggests Venus as the proper deity for the nymphs' devotions. Venus says nothing to the newly metamorphosed men about living virtuously; she commands them only to serve their ladies until such time as they may merit "vittoria . . . con pietate" (XVII.50–51). For all the stilnovistic language with which the narrator describes his lady—calling her angelic, surely descended from heaven, a delight even to her Creator—her two chief virtues, emphasized at the end of the final canto, are her beauty and her "pietate," a word associated less with piety here than with the pity which will ultimately allow her lover "victory" in love.

Meanwhile, he and the other newly metamorphosed men are content to contemplate their ladies and to gather flowers from the meadow:

> givan cogliendo diversi fioretti,
> tutti aspettando li promessi doni (XVII.57–58)

> [they went gathering various flowers, / all awaiting the promised gifts].

Is this a Matelda-like flower-picking of active moral virtue? Kirkham associates the narrator with Dante in the earthly paradise, and observes that he claims to have been not turned but returned to human form (XVIII.23) as if, like Dante, he had temporarily strayed from the right way and had been called back to it by his lady. But could his activity not be just as well the

Roman de la Rose flower-plucking of erotic consummation, here presented as a metaphor whose realization the lovers are hopefully awaiting? For the gifts promised by Venus, which they think of as they amuse themselves in the meadow, are at least as likely to be sexual as spiritual "vittoria" and "salute." Then is the echo of Dante in the following canto meant seriously or parodically?

> Il più parlar omai qui non mi piace,
> però che in parte più di lode degna
> serbo di dir con laude più verace
>   quella biltà. (XVIII.49–52)

[Now I wish to speak no further here, / for I am waiting to express that beauty / with truer praise in a more praiseworthy place.]

Is the allusion subverted by the preceding scene? Do not the narrator and his lady both have a purely carnal goal in mind? Is this animal-turned-poet not a foolish imitation of the sublime Dante?

Possibly Boccaccio is trying to have it both ways: to write a poem which can be read either as a celebration of erotic love or as an exhortation to human rationality and moral virtue. In the first case, it might even be a gallant celebration of the ladies who inspire such devotion. The ladies hunt "per l'altrui danno e per la lor difesa" (II.57) [for harm to others and their own defense]; the latter phrase suggests that the men who are wounded by them with love will not receive satisfaction but be met by the ladies' defense of their honor. So far the ladies have inspired men with love and hope but have not yielded to their desires; thus they can be praised in the lyric manner as both lovable and chaste. Branca has suggested that the work is a gallant rather than stilnovistic compliment to the ladies.[10] Nonetheless, the ladies' desire for lovers sounds hardly chaste; the lovers have good reason to be hopeful.

The identity of the narrator's lady remains extremely vague. Although the other ladies are historically identifiable, "La bella donna il cui nome si tace" (IV.1) [the beautiful lady whose name is unspoken] is presented "senza che una sufficiente riflessione le abbia riposatamente attribuito origine, vicende, superbie e travagli; perchè la stessa sua vantata anonimia è solo comodo mantello, che tenta maestosamente di nascondere che, frettolosamente preparata, la bella testa di bambola non è legata a un corpo"[11] [without sufficient reflection to have calmly attributed to her an origin,

circumstances, haughtinesses and torments; because her own vaunted ano-
nymity is only an easy cloak which tries majestically to hide the fact that
the beautiful doll's head, prepared in haste, is not attached to a body]. The
nonidentity of this lady who is ringleader in summoning Venus and ban-
ishing Diana may allow Boccaccio to avoid blatantly dishonoring some real
Neapolitan woman with the attribution of lustful wishes.

Ultimately this poem remains for me a puzzle unresolved. The problems it raises for the reader are much the same as those in subsequent writings: to what extent can we trust a narrator who confesses himself in love?
Does *he* mean something spiritual through his words about love? Or are *we*
to understand such a meaning despite his own more carnal view? If there is
some spiritual significance, can the erotic aspects thus be explained *away*,
or are we not rather forced to confront a combination of the moralizing
and the erotic, a conjunction of opposites? And what of Boccaccio's relation to Dante? The imitation of Dante here is manifold: the use of terza
rima, the writing of a sirventese to pretty women with the poet's own lady
in a numerically noteworthy position on the list, the many verbal echoes.
Is this an imitation of Dante or a parody, and if the latter, is that parody
intended to mark the subversion of Dante's ideas or of Boccaccio's—or
merely the humility of the young apprentice-poet? [12]

Some of these questions can be answered more easily—and in a way
which may shed some light on the *Caccia*—for another of Boccaccio's earliest works, the *Filostrato*, which has been dated 1335, very close to the *Caccia*.[13] The *Caccia* was written about but not to the narrator's lady; the *Filostrato* is the first work addressed specifically to a lady by the poet-lover. The
woman for whom it is supposedly written is named Filomena. Certainly
this is not the real name of a Neapolitan but rather a reference to classical
mythology. Filomena, the tuneful nightingale, is readily recognizable as
the metamorphosed victim of Tereus's rape, the singer of her own sorrowful history.[14] The nightingale's song is inspired by pain. To some extent,
then, the name Filomena projects Filostrato's own role. As he says in his
Proemio, he has chosen to write as a way of expressing some of his anguish
lest it kill him. His cause of sorrow, however, is the opposite of the Ovidian
Filomena's; for whereas he suffers from his lady's absence and apparent
lack of interest, Filomena suffered from the illegitimate and uncontrolled
passion of Tereus. Thus she is a perennial rebuke to men in danger of being
carried by their passions into violence.

Boccaccio, using the name Filomena, has apparently not yet met or conceived of Fiammetta.[15] Moreover, when later prefaces address Fiammetta, the speaker is not given another name, such as Filostrato, but remains, either explicitly as in the *Amorosa Visone* or else by our assumption, Boccaccio. The *Filostrato*, then, is doubly outside the Boccaccio-Fiammetta system.[16] Yet its Proemio sounds remarkably like the other prefaces within the system. If the names had not yet been fixed, nonetheless the general idea for the narrator's situation and for the relation of his story to the main narrative was already established.

Filostrato, like the narrators of the *Teseida* and *Elegia*, claims to be presenting a tale parallel to his own; and the meaning of the name "Filostrato," explained in the title, applies to the hero Troiolo as well as to himself: "Filostrato tanto viene a dire quanto uomo vinto e abbattuto d'amore" [Filostrato is as much as to say a man conquered and beaten by love]. It was precisely the similarity in structure between this book and others which led many scholars to assume that Filomena and Fiammetta were the same. This double structure of Proemio and narrative forces us to consider separately what the story of Troiolo and his love Criseida represents to Filostrato and what to us, how the narrator views his own love affair and how we are made to view it despite his bias.

To Filostrato, Troiolo is a serious and noble lover like himself. But the growing ironies of Troiolo's position in our eyes point up the limitations of the narrator's view. Troiolo is a standard lover, whose falling in love follows step by step the description set forth by Andreas Capellanus:

> For when a man sees some woman fit for love and shaped according to his taste, he begins at once to lust after her in his heart; then the more he thinks about her the more he burns with love, until he comes to a fuller meditation. Presently he begins to think about the fashioning of the woman and to differentiate her limbs, to think about what she does, and to pry into the secrets of her body, and he desires to put each part of it to the fullest use. Then after he has come to this complete meditation, love cannot hold the reins, but he proceeds at once to action; straightway he strives to get a helper to find an intermediary. He begins to plan how he may find favor with her, and he begins to seek a place and a time opportune for talking; he looks upon a brief hour as a very long year, because he cannot do anything fast enough to suit his eager mind. It is well known that many things happen to him in

this manner. This inborn suffering comes, therefore, from seeing and meditating. Not every kind of meditation can be the cause of love, an excessive one is required; for a restrained thought does not, as a rule, return to the mind, and so love cannot arise from it.[17]

Troiolo sees Criseida and takes supreme pleasure in staring at her fixedly (I.28). Then he goes home and, sitting alone on his bed, begins to recall the pleasure he had that morning from seeing her, and reconsiders her beauties detail by detail. Disposed to follow love (36), he decides at first to keep it secret, but finally confesses to his friend Pandaro who can serve as a go-between. Capellanus suggested that the meditation with which love begins is "excessive." Even if one chooses not to read Capellanus's *De arte honesti amandi* as a work of irony, Boccaccio's text introduces plenty of clues to set Troiolo's love in a critical perspective.

Troiolo first sees his beloved in the temple of Pallas, the Trojan equivalent to a Christian church. There could be a complication here, as this is a place of pagan worship, a wrong and empty religion in Christian terms; but Boccaccio does not mention anywhere the false nature of the pagan gods—as he does quite pointedly in the *Filocolo*. He does, however, refer to the role of Pallas in the fall of Troy:

li Troian padri al Palladio fatale
fer preparare li consueti onori (I.18)

[the Trojan fathers prepared for fatal Pallas the customary honors].

He is probably considering her, as in the *Teseida*, the goddess of wisdom and reason. This might have explained to Boccaccio her enmity to the Trojans. Pandaro suggests in IV.64 that Troiolo steal away Criseida as Paris did Helen. Thus the Trojan cause represents the same service to Amore as Troiolo's private situation. Pallas and her temple are "fatale" to both. Certainly her temple is an ironic background for Troiolo's subjection to the irrational forces of love.

The religious setting is being used, as in the *Elegia*, to establish a contrast between religious devotion and devotion in the religion of love. Troiolo pays little if any attention to Pallas and chooses to worship Criseida, to whom he addresses a profusion of religious language. In his very first glimpse of her, he marvels at her face "adorno di bellezza celestiale" [adorned with heavenly beauty], "gli occhi lucenti e l'angelico viso" (I.27, 28) [her lucent eyes and angelic face]. He prays to Amore:

da quei occhi ti priego impetri la salute
dell'anima (I.39)

[from those eyes, I pray you obtain the salvation of my soul].

He is not sure whether love has given him to a woman or to a goddess
(I.38), "e Criseida come suo Iddio / con gli occhi della mente ognor vedea"
(V.42) [and Criseida as his God he saw at every moment with the eyes of
his mind]. In the *Filostrato*, as later in the *Elegia*, the love service is shown
as an idolatry opposed to the religious service. The phrases of religious devotion become part of an attempt to seduce.

Pandaro is, moreover, the counselor who leads astray, unlike the *Elegia*'s virtue-counseling nurse. When Troiolo naively reflects that Criseida's
acceptance of his love ought to satisfy him,

ma l'appetito cupido vorrebbe
non so che più, sì mal son regolati
gli ardor che'l muovon (II.87)

[but my eager appetite wishes I don't know what more, so badly
regulated are the ardors which move it],

Pandaro knows what is wanted and urges Troiolo on to an affair, offering
to seduce his own cousin on Troiolo's behalf:

. . . parmi per partito
poter pigliar, che ciaschedun amante
possa seguir il suo alto appetito,
sol che sia savio in fatto ed in sembiante,
sanza vergogna alcuna di coloro
a cui tien la vergogna e l'onor loro.

Io credo certo ch'ogni donna in voglia
vive amorosa, e null'altro l'affrena
che tema di vergogna; e s'a tal doglia
onestamente medicina piena
si può donar, folle è chi non la spoglia (II.26–27)

[it seems to me / that I can take the side (which says) that each
lover / may follow his lofty appetite, / as long as he is wise in his
action and in his appearance, / without any shame to those /
who care about their shame and their honor. / / I believe surely
that every woman / lives in desire for love, and nothing holds her

back / but the fear of shame; and if a thorough medicine / can honestly be given for that complaint, / he is a fool who doesn't strip her].

When Troiolo answers that he has no intention of doing anything dishonorable to Criseida, Pandaro laughs.

Pandaro is certainly not speaking for Boccaccio when he utters such sentiments as these. Repeatedly Boccaccio emphasizes the immoral nature of the whole enterprise by using the phrases of the three main characters to reassert the moral code that they are breaking. Thus, for example, Troiolo apostrophizes Criseida, "Or foss'io teco una notte di verno, / cento cinquante poi stessi in inferno" [If I were with you one winter's night, I would then spend a hundred and fifty in hell]. And Pandaro answers, "Sempre son succinto / a far non sol per te ciò che conviene, / ma ogni cosa" (II.88 and 89) [I am always ready to do for you not only what is proper but anything]. Criseida again and again protests that Pandaro is asking her to do things contrary to her honor; each time she yields saying that she is only trying to please Pandaro. Similarly Pandaro passes on the responsibility to Troiolo, saying he felt sorry for him. When all the arrangements have been made, Pandaro urges Troiolo to maintain secrecy:

> per te gittato ho'n terra il mio onore,
> per te ho io corrotto il petto sano
> di mia sorella . . .
>
> Tu sai ch'egli è la fama di costei
> santa nel vulgo

[for you I have thrown to the ground my honor, for you I have corrupted the healthy breast of my sister . . . you know that her reputation is holy among the crowd].

Ironically he adds to urge home the importance of discretion: "tu vedi ben che'l mio priego è onesto" (III.6,8,10) [you see well that my request is honest]. Troiolo swears secrecy and ridiculously offers to return Pandaro's favor: perhaps Pandaro would like something arranged with Polissena or another of Troiolo's sisters.

Troiolo also feels the need to defend himself against criticism.

> Il che avvegna che alcun riprenda,
> poco men curo, ch'el non sa che dirsi;
> Ercole forte in questo mi difenda,
> che da Amore non poté schermirsi,

avvegna ch'ogni savio il ne commenda.
E chi con frode non vuol ricoprirsi,
non dirà mai ch'a me sia disdicevole
ciò ch'ad Ercole fu già convenevole. (III.80)

[If it happens that anyone blame it, / little I care, for he doesn't know what he's saying; / Hercules the strong defends me in this, / who could not shield himself from Love, / and every wise man praises him for it. / And whoever does not want to cover himself with lies, / will never say that it is unsuitable to me / what was once suitable to Hercules.]

The defense is so weak that it reinforces the sense of Troiolo's folly. For Hercules's passion for Iole was never commended by the wise as "convenevole." Fiammetta in the *Filocolo* points to Hercules as a prime example of the destructive and debasing powers of love, to be avoided.[18]

Ultimately Boccaccio will make his own comments directly. As Troiolo and Diomede attack each other in battle, he remarks how they are "vendendosi caro / insieme molto il loro amor non sano" (VIII.26) [selling dear to each other their unhealthy (or mad) love]. When Troiolo is killed by Achilles, the narration concludes:

Cotal fine ebbe il mal concetto amore
di Troiolo in Criseida, e cotale
fine ebbe il miserabile dolore
di lui al qual non fu mai altro eguale;
cotal fine ebbe il lucido splendore
che lui servava al solio reale;
cotal fine ebbe la speranza vana
di Troiolo in Criseida villana.

O giovinetti ne' quai con l'etate
surgendo vien l'amoroso disio,
per Dio vi priego che voi raffreniate
i pronti passi all'appetito rio,
e nell'amor di Troiolo vi specchiate,
il qual dimostra suso il verso mio;
per che, se ben col cuor gli leggerete
non di leggieri a tutte crederete. (VIII.28–29)

[Such an end had the ill-conceived love / of Troiolo for Criseida, and such / an end had his wretched misery / which never had an equal; / such an end had the bright splendor / which reserved him for a royal throne; / such an end had the empty hope / of Troiolo in base Criseida. / / O youths in whom / amorous desire surges with your age, / for God's sake I pray you that you rein in / the steps which readily follow wicked appetite, / and mirror yourselves in Troiolo's love, / which my verses demonstrate above; / because, if you read it well and with your heart, / you won't believe too lightly in every woman.]

If a young woman is fickle and vaingloriously measures her beauty in the number of her lovers, the narrator goes on to suggest that an older woman may make a better, more appreciative lover (30–31). But now we are faced with a text given two incompatible meanings and thus with the familiar problem of distinguishing between voices,[19] for that follow-up is clearly comic, yet Filostrato presents his work as a tragedy.

On the one hand Criseida's allure and fickleness imply the allure and fickleness of all of fortune's goods; it is that combination of qualities which makes those goods so perilous. This view of Criseida is supported by her identification with Filomena. According to the *Ovid Moralisé* of the late thirteenth or early fourteenth century, Tereus is the body married to Procne the soul, and Philomena is

> Amour decevable et faillie.
> C'est li faillibles biens du monde,
> Que diex, en cui tous biens habonde,
> Fist pour humaine creature
> Soustenir a sobre mesure

> [deceitful and failing love. / It is the fallible goods of the world, / which God, in whom all good abounds, / made in order to sustain the human creature within sober measure].

Tereus is punished for his gluttonous lechery,

> Et le delis li vait fuiant
> Plus tost que rosseignols ne vole,
>
> . . .
>
> Le delit vain et muable
> Devienent rosseignols volable.[20]

> [And delight flies from him sooner than the nightingale flies away . . . vain and mutable delight becomes the winged nightingale.]

Troiolo is presented, like Fiammetta in the *Elegia*, as a mirror or example to warn the reader from similar folly.[21]

On the other hand, the lesson about the allure and deceit of fortune's goods is not what Filostrato means to demonstrate by his tale. He hopes that the book will win a favorable response from Filomena, that she will have for him the same compassion which Criseida felt for her suffering lover. His seductive intention is stated explicitly in the Proemio:

> Da esse (parole) potrete comprendere quanti e quali siano i miei disii, dove terminino e che cosa più ch'altro dimandino e se alcuna pietà meritino. Ora io non so se esse fieno di tanta efficacia che a voi, leggendole voi con alcuna compassione, possano toccare la casta mente, ma Amore ne priego che questa forza lor presti.

> [From them (words) you will be able to understand how great and of what sort are my desires, what end they seek and what they ask for more than anything else and whether they merit any mercy. Now I do not know if they will be so efficacious that they can touch your chaste mind when you read them with some compassion, but I pray Love that he lend them such force.]

In short, he thinks of the story as an example of what to imitate, not what to avoid.

This double purpose can be seen more clearly if we look at Boccaccio's use of allusions to Dante. Thanks to Branca's excellent notes on the *Filostrato*, we can see easily that echoes of Dante appear throughout Boccaccio's poem. By examining the contexts of these echoed phrases in the writings of both Dante and Boccaccio, I am drawn to the conclusion that these passages are not merely the random borrowings of a young poet from his most admired precursor, but rather that they form a network which reveals in the *Filostrato* (as in the *Caccia?*) a major element of parodic inversion of Dante's works about Beatrice, the *Vita Nuova* as well as the *Commedia*.[22]

The echoes begin to occur in Boccaccio's Proemio. Filostrato's claim that he is writing to release some of the grief which otherwise would kill him has been linked by Branca to *Vita Nuova* 31, where Dante expresses the same idea: after his eyes had grown weary of weeping, he tried with words to release some of his life-destroying sorrow. The canzone which follows contains the declaration of Beatrice's death and ascent to heaven among the angels, leaving mere mortals behind her. Dante explains that she was summoned by God who desired her because of her virtue and humility, and calls her "full of grace": "piena di grazia l'anima gentile." The death of Beatrice is almost an Assumption.[23] But what is the case for Filostrato? His lady Filomena has gone to Sannio, a province in the Kingdom of Naples, because it is springtime and she wanted to get out of the city. The cause is so much less, the grief so much more, that one wonders whether Boccaccio did not see this as humorous. Filostrato, who used to sing love songs and speak speeches full of fiery love, now spends his voice "in chiamare il vostro nome di grazia pieno" [in calling your name full of grace]. The religious setting of Dante's canzone has been turned into the religion of love which is Filostrato's. This is the merely graceful "grazia," not the divine one.

The "pace" for which Filostrato prays is also quite different from Dante's, for his desires "appena in me reggere li posso che non mi tirino, posta giù ogni debita onestà e ragionevole consiglio, colà dove dimorate; ma pur vinto dal volere il vostro onore più che la mia salute guardare gli raffreno" [I can hardly govern them in me so that they don't pull me, all proper honesty and rational counsel laid down, there where you dwell; but overcome by the wish to safeguard your honor more than my well-being (or salvation), I hold them back]. The double meaning of "salute" makes even clearer the substitution of one religion for another. Boccaccio repeats the word at the end of his Proemio, praying to "colui che nelle vostre mani ha posto la mia vita e la mia morte, che elli nel vostro cuore quello disio accenda che solo può essere cagione della mia salute" [him who placed my life and my death in your hands, that he may kindle in your heart that desire which alone can be the cause of my salvation]. The well-being of the lover satisfied by his woman is played off against his spiritual salvation.

In the immediately preceding chapters of the *Vita Nuova*, that is, in 30 and also in 28, we find Dante's quotation from the Lamentations of Jeremiah, "Quomodo sedet sola civitas" [How doth the city sit solitary]. The same quotation from Jeremiah is picked up by Boccaccio as part of Filostrato's complaint. Filostrato has been wandering all through the city and noticing the places where he used to see his lady. Again phrases of religious significance are being twisted for another sort of use in the religion of love.

Now the tale of Troiolo gets underway. Troiolo has confessed to Pandaro his love for Criseida; and Pandaro speaks to Criseida, encouraging her to accept Troiolo's love. Pandaro's persuasive speeches are echoed by Boccaccio from Dante's *Inferno* II, where Lucia urges Beatrice to help Dante, who loved her and is in peril of death:

Ché non soccorri quei che t'amò tanto

. . .

Non odi tu la pietà del suo pianto?
Non vedi tu la morte che 'l combatte? (103, 106–7)

So Pandaro tells Criseida how he overheard Troiolo calling for death in his anguish:

Deh, dilmi, starai altera,
e lascerai colui che sé non cura
per amar te, a morte tanto fera
venire? (II.64)

[Ah, tell me, will you remain haughty, / and will you let him who has no care for himself / because of his love for you, come to such a cruel death?]

Filostrato too in the Proemio declares himself "assai vicino a disperata morte" [quite close to desperate death]. Troiolo will end up dead indeed despite or even because of the progress of his love. Whereas Beatrice is sent to remove Dante from the danger of his soul's eternal death, Filostrato hopes, on the contrary, to lure Filomena into a state like his own. So too Pandaro, unlike Lucia, urges Criseida to respond in kind to Troiolo, rather than to help him recover his liberty.

When Pandaro returns to the timid Troiolo to report his success, Boccaccio uses a simile:

Quali i fioretti, dal notturno gelo
chinati e chiusi, poi che'l sol gl'imbianca,
tutti s'apron diritti in loro stelo,
cotal si fé di sua virtute stanca
Troiolo allora

[As the flowers, bent and shut by the nocturnal chill, when the sun shines on them, all open upright on their stems, so then did Troiolo with his tired courage].

This simile too comes from *Inferno* II (127ff.).[24] There Vergil has brought Dante word from three heavenly women and comes to rescue Dante from his misery with a glad promise of help. Dante, aroused, exclaims his thanks at this heavenly aid. He is ready now to follow Vergil into Hell; the very next words are "Per me si va nella città dolente." Troiolo, who thanks the

heavenly aid of Venus in place of Beatrice, is heading for Criseida; she
seems like a paradise, but he will find himself in hell sooner than he
imagines.

As Pandaro urges Criseida to allow Troiolo to visit, he tells her not to
hesitate in giving but to be generous at once:

> Assai fa mal chi può far ben nol face,
> e perder tempo a chi più sa più spiace (II.135)

> [He does enough evil who can do good and does not do it, and
> the loss of time displeases most the one who knows most].

The second line here is an echo now from the *Purgatorio* (III.78) as Vergil
asks some shades the way up Mount Purgatory—the way to Beatrice—so
that he and Dante can ascend without losing time:

> sì che possibil sia l'andare in suso;
> ché perder tempo a chi più sa più spiace.

This advance from the *Inferno* to the *Purgatorio* shadows perhaps Troiolo's
progress from misery to the hope of better things to come. But again the
progress toward Criseida's bed is contrasted with Dante's progress in the
purgation of sins and his advance upward ("suso") toward God. Who is
Pandaro's "a chi più sa"? Is he suggesting that God is impatient with
Criseida for not accepting Troiolo as her lover? But Pandaro is pagan; and
any reference to divine will and knowledge surely undermines his argument, at least for the reader, by bringing in the moral and religious context
for Criseida's actions.

The success of Troiolo's endeavors calls for a new invocation:

> Fulvida luce, il raggio della quale
> infino a questo loco m'ha guidato
> com'io volea per l'amorose sale,
> or convien che'l tuo lume duplicato
> guidi lo'ngegno mio, e faccil tale,
> che'n particella alcuna dichiarato
> per me appaia il ben del dolce regno
> d'Amor, del qual fu fatto Troiol degno. (III.1)

> [Shining light, whose ray / has guided me up to this point / as I
> wished through the chambers of love, / now it is fitting that your
> doubled light / guide my intellect, and make it such / that in

some little part appear declared by me / the goodness of the sweet realm / of Love, of which Troiolo was made worthy.]

The echo this time is from the beginning of *Paradiso* (I.13ff.) where Dante prays to Apollo for divine aid in describing the blessed Kingdom:

O buono Appollo, a l'ultimo lavoro
fammi del tuo valor sì fatto vaso,
come dimandi a dar l'amato alloro.
Infino a qui l'un giogo di Parnaso
assai mi fu; ma or con amendue
m'è uopo intrar ne l'aringo rimaso.

. . .

O divina virtù, se mi ti presti
tanto che l'ombra del beato regno
segnata nel mio capo io manifesti

[O good Apollo, for this last labor / make me such a vessel of your might / as you demand in order to give the beloved laurel. / Up to here one peak of Parnasus / was enough for me, but now with both / it is necessary that I enter the remaining wrestling-ground . . . O divine power, if you may lend yourself to me / so much that I may make manifest the shadow of the blessed realm / signed in my head].

Troiolo thinks himself in paradise, thanking Pandaro "che d'inferno e di peggio, / in paradiso posso dir m'hai tratto" (III.16) [that from hell and worse into paradise I can say you have drawn me]. To this "sommo diletto" (III.3)[supreme delight], this "regno d'Amor" [kingdom of love] "rado pervenire / vi si puo bene" [one rarely is able to arrive well]. The phrase continues to draw from *Paradiso* I (28) as Dante hopes for the laurel crown which "rade volte, padre, se ne coglie" [one rarely gathers, father]. The sharp split between the "regno beato" [blessed kingdom] and the newly sung "regno d'Amor" [kingdom of love] is clear. Moreover, the "lume" which Filostrato addresses is not Apollo but Filomena, the "splendido lume della mia mente" (Proemio) [splendid light of my mind]. This substitution repeats the first invocation in part I (1–2):

Alcuni di Giove sogliono il favore
ne' lor principi pietosi invocare,
altri d'Apollo chiamano il valore;

io di Parnaso le Muse pregare
solea ne' miei bisogni, ma Amore
novellamente m'ha fatto mutare
il mio costume antico e usitato,
po' fui di te, madonna, innamorato.

. . .

tu mi se' Giove, tu mi se' Apollo,
tu se' mia musa. [25]

[Some are wont to invoke the favor of Jove / in their pious beginnings, / others call on the might of Apollo; / I used to pray to the
Muses of Parnasus / in my needs, but Love / has newly made me
change / my old accustomed habit, / since I fell in love with you,
my lady. . . . you are Jove to me, you are Apollo to me, / you are
my muse.]

Dante is certainly one of the poets whose invocations are replaced here.
Filostrato is explicitly substituting his own idolized "dea" for the heavenly
aids invoked by Dante. The new muse helps him sing of the only kind of
paradise that she knows how to offer.

Troiolo's prayer to Venus in Book III begins "O luce etterna" [O eternal light], Dante's words directed to God in *Paradiso* XXXIII (124). Boccaccio himself would later use the same phrase in a sonnet to the Virgin Mary
(*Rime* CXVIII). Peter Dronke has referred to Troiolo's prayer as Boccaccio's hymn to cosmic love, pointing out how it draws from traditional concepts.[26] The passage in *Paradiso* that begins "O luce etterna" ends with
Dante's will and desire moved by "l'amor che move il sole e l'altre stelle"
[the love which moves the sun and the other stars]. He experiences the
unifying of his own motive energy or love with that of the cosmos. Troiolo's prayer, however, turns aside from the "amore onesto" which binds
heaven and earth to "amore per diletto" which is what really interests him.
Boccaccio's Troiolo includes "Iddio" [God] in his thanks (85), but it is to
Venus that he addresses the words by which Dante, in the famous fifth
canto of the *Inferno*, referred to God: "si puote ciò / che si vuole" [who
can do whatever he wills]; Troiolo beseeches Venus to maintain Criseida's
love for him "che se' tu dessa, dea, che far lo puoi, / sol che tu vogli"
(III.87) [because it is you, goddess, who can do it if only you will to]. The
fact that his hope is deceived says something about the consequences of his
addressing the wrong deity.

At the height of his felicity, Troiolo seeing Criseida

si rifaceva grazioso e bello,
come falcon ch'uscisse di cappello (III.91)

[made himself gracious and handsome again, like
a falcon that is unhooded].

The words refer once more to Dante's *Paradiso* (XIX.34):

Quasi falcone ch'esce del cappello
    move la testa e con l'ali si plaude,
    voglia mostrando e faccendosi bello,
vid'io farsi quel segno, che di laude
    de la divina grazia era contesto,
    con canti quai si sa chi là sù gaude.

[As the falcon, being unhooded, / moves his head and beats his
wings, / showing his will and making himself handsome, / so
I saw that sign do, which was woven / of the praise of divine
grace, / with songs which he knows who rejoices up there.]

Perhaps it is significant—at least it is appropriate—that Troiolo's ascent on
the wheel of fortune ends with reference to the image of divine justice. For
although Troiolo's prayer of thanks for Criseida's love is filled with liturgical elements, reflecting how Troiolo feels divinely blessed, a mere few
stanzas later the narrator pronounces the brevity of envious fortune's
goods.[27]

While Dante's paradise ends with his sight of God, Troiolo's worldly
paradise soon turns to a hell worse than his original lovesickness. And
so too the references to Dante now come once again from the *Inferno*.
Troiolo in his sorrow at Criseida's forced departure from Troy rages like an
animal.

Né altrimenti il toro va saltando
or qua or là, da poi c'ha ricevuto
il mortal colpo, e misero mugghiando
conoscer fa qual duolo ha conceputo,
che Troiolo facesse. (IV.27)

[Nor otherwise does the bull go leaping / now here now there,
when he has received / the mortal blow, and by his wretched bellowing / makes known what pain he feels, / than did Troiolo.]

The echo is of the minotaur's "ira bestial" [bestial wrath] in *Inferno* XII.22ff.:

> Qual è quel toro che si slaccia in quella
>> c'ha ricevuto già 'l colpo mortale,
>> che gir non sa, ma qua e là saltella.

[As that bull who breaks loose when / he has just received the mortal blow, / who does not know how to go but leaps here and there.]

Both are "in furia." The minotaur bites himself as a sign of self-consuming rage. Troiolo, like a denizen of hell, curses the gods and beats himself, calling for his own death; for with Criseida his "salute" has been taken away. The lines that follow soon after in Dante's canto offer a comment on Troiolo's changed estate:

> Oh cieca cupidigia e ira folle,
>> che sì ci sproni ne la vita corta,
>> e ne l'eterna poi sì mal c'immolle! (49–51)

[O blind cupidity, and mad wrath, / that thus spurs us in our short life, / and in the eternal life afterwards drenches us so badly!]

In this part of hell are the sinners who have done violence to others, including Nessus who died for the beautiful Deianira (67–68). Troiolo spends three stanzas wishing for the death of Calcas, who has caused Criseida's departure. Ultimately he will hurl himself into battle, hoping both to revenge himself and to die. The echoes here bode ill for the state of his soul.

In his letter to Criseida after her departure, Troiolo writes,

> . . . e non cheggio
> ammenda, fuor vedere il tuo bel viso,
> nel quale è sol tutto il mio paradiso (VII.69)

[and I ask for no amends other than to see your beautiful face, in which alone is all my paradise].

In *Paradiso* XV (35–36) Dante looks at Beatrice and feels that he is touching paradise with his eyes:

io pensai co' miei occhi toccar lo fondo
de la mia gloria e del mio paradiso.

But the first thing he hears is "Benedetto sia tu . . . trino e uno" [Blessed
are you . . . triune and one]. Later (XVIII.16–21) as he gazes at "'l piacere
etterno, che diretto / raggiava in Beatrice, dal bel viso / mi contentava col
secondo aspetto" [the eternal pleasure which radiated straight into Beatrice, from her beautiful face contented me with a secondary aspect], Beatrice warns him, "Volgiti e ascolta, / che non pur ne' miei occhi è paradiso"
[Turn and listen, for not in my eyes is paradise]. Dante's love for Beatrice
must always, with her guidance, be directed on through her toward God.
Troiolo's love ends in Criseida who is his god, but a fickle one; for the Love
which he had called "signor verace" (I.39) [true lord] is the god of false
love. The entire process of heavenly intercession on behalf of Dante and
the progress toward Beatrice, God, and his own salvation, has been turned
into the self-destructive process of Troiolo's love for a fickle woman of this
world.

In *Inferno* XV Brunetto Latini prophesied to Dante:

Se tu segui tua stella,
     non puoi fallire a glorioso porto. (55–56)

[If you follow your star, you cannot fail to reach the glorious
port.]

At the very beginning of his narrative Filostrato announces (I.2):

tu se' la tramontana stella
la quale io seguo per venire a porto;
ancora di salute tu se' quella
che se' tutto 'l mio bene e 'l mio conforto

[you are the northern star / which I am following in order to
come to port; / anchor of salvation you are, / who are all my
good and my comfort].

The narrator's words are a dangerous echo of Troiolo's to Criseida (III.29):

. . . Donna bella,
sola speranza e ben della mia mente,
sempre davanti m'è stata la stella
del tuo bel viso splendido e lucente.

[Beautiful lady, / only hope and good of my mind, / always before me has been the star / of your beautiful face, splendid and shining.]

Troiolo as he says these words is about to cast anchor in Criseida's bed, a port toward the like of which Filostrato is also headed.

Having become aware of Criseida's deception, Troiolo cries out with a phrase from *Purgatorio* VI.118–20: "O sommo Giove . . . son li giusti occhi tuoi rivolti altrove?" (VIII.17) [O supreme Jove . . . are your just eyes turned elsewhere?] For Dante, this is half of a pair of alternatives, the other half continuing:

O è preparazion che ne l'abisso
del tuo consiglio fai per alcun bene
in tutto de l'accorger nostro scisso?

[Or is it a preparation which you are making in the depth of your counsel for some good completely cut off from our awareness?]

Troiolo ignores the possibility that this catastrophe might be meant as a lesson for his own good and instead merely calls for Criseida's punishment, indeed for her damnation—"né più la fate degna di perdono" [nor make her worthy any more of pardon]. His hope to see Diomede's ghost "nelli regni bui," while plain enough within the pagan context, suggests in Christian terms that Troiolo too will be in hell. The fact that he is quoting from the *Purgatorio* adds to the implication that he is ignoring the possibility of turning events to his own education and salvation.

Filostrato's final plea that Filomena come back to him or he will die is the same plea that Troiolo sent in vain in his letter to Criseida. But the narrator has learned nothing from the ultimate disaster of his hero. Finished with his book, which he hopes will win Filomena's compassion and return, he offers her as his muse "quelle grazie . . . che render dee il grato pellegrino, / a chi guidati n'ha" (IX.4) [those thanks . . . which a grateful pilgrim ought to render to one who has guided him]. Thus at the end comes the final pointer back to Dante's work, to the "pellegrino" [pilgrim] led and guided by his beloved Beatrice.

The parody of Dante's love journey was possibly inspired by Dante's own similar parody of Augustine in his *Inferno* V. There the act of reading which led in one case to salvation leads in the other to lust; so too, although the purpose of Dante's *Commedia* is to lead his readers toward salvation, Filostrato sends his book to Filomena to kindle a return of passionate love in her hitherto chaste mind. Augustine needed to read no farther, for God's message had already reached his heart and turned it from its old lusts. Francesca and Paolo, by not reading farther, miss the tragic ending of the Lancelot story which should provide a warning to them. Filostrato finishes his narrative but misses its application to himself. He is seemingly unconscious of his allusions to Dante or at least of their effect.

The final echo of Dante in the Envoy returns to the *Vita Nuova*. Perhaps Boccaccio is thereby suggesting that Filostrato is in the same condition as before despite the intervening tale. Filostrato tells his book:

Ma guarda che così alta ambasciata
non facci sanza Amor, ché tu saresti
per avventura assai male accettata.

[But see to it that you do not make such a high embassy without Love, for you might be by chance rather badly received.]

Significantly, the reference is to *Vita Nuova* 12, in which Dante has lost Beatrice's "salute" and hopes to regain it by sending his ballata to her:

ma se tu vuoli andar sicuramente,
retrova l'amor pria,
ché forse non è bon sanza lui gire;
però che quella che ti dee audire,
sì com'io credo, è ver di me adirata

[but if you want to go securely, / first find Love, / for perhaps it is not good to go without him; / because she who ought to hear you / is, as I believe, truly angry at me].

While there are several allusions to the *Vita Nuova* in Filostrato's Proemio, the references in the main body of the narrative come from the *Commedia*. Filostrato's Envoy brings us back to the *Vita Nuova*. It seems that Boccaccio was reading the *Vita Nuova* as a promise of a tale rather than as the tale itself. Filostrato is associated with Dante's love for the mortal Beatrice but not with his new transformed vision of that love. That is, the Proemio and Envoy where Filostrato tells his own story are related to Dante's autobiography but stop short of the vision of Beatrice in glory and the lesson which Dante must learn from her in the earthly paradise. There, in fact, she criticizes Dante's love for the world's "cose fallaci" (XXXXI.56) [deceitful things], saying that her death should have taught Dante not to put his faith in mortal things. In the light of her remarks we can understand Criseida's deceitfulness as an example of the deceitful and ultimately unsatisfying nature of temporal things. Filostrato, to mirror his own frustration, has picked a hero from pagan times who cannot learn the Christian answer to his loss.[28] Thus Filostrato's echoes from the *Vita Nuova* emphasize only those moments when Beatrice has angrily withdrawn her "salute" or has died. Dante ends his *Vita Nuova* with a new vision of Beatrice and a glimpse of her new role in his life. But Filostrato remains at Dante's Chapter 12, praying for "salute" from a lady who has left him in order to enjoy herself elsewhere.

The idea of framing *Commedia* allusions with allusions to the *Vita Nuova* had occurred to Boccaccio already in the *Caccia*.[29] Echoes of the *Vita Nuova* appear in the *Caccia*'s cantos I and XVIII while a dozen citations from the *Commedia* are found in cantos II through XVII.[30] The circularity of reference is underlined in the *Caccia* by a return in canto XVIII to the very same *Vita Nuova* passage already cited in canto I: the promise of praising his lady more adequately in some later writing. For Dante, this final promise is linked with a vision which reveals Beatrice as more than an object of worldly love. If the *Caccia* narrator is like Filostrato, however, he has no such transcendent understanding. Despite his use of religious phrases to describe his lady, he remains a lover in the purely worldly sense without any effort to convert that horizontal, human love into a vertical, divine perspective.

The result can be interpreted either as a conscious rebellion against Dante's kind of love, or else as an ironic comment on Boccaccio's poet-lover. In the *Caccia* we cannot perhaps be entirely sure which is meant, but the *Filostrato* seems to me to point toward the latter interpretation. In the *Caccia* we see the poet set himself within an unfinished sequence of events, but in the *Filostrato* the poet's complaint frames a completed tragedy which threatens to repeat itself for him. In either case, the device of associating the framing situation with the *Vita Nuova* as set against the *Commedia* suggests that Boccaccio's poet has not yet achieved the vision or understanding appropriate to his own enclosed text.

The technique of framing Dante's text written after the vision of Beatrice in glory with Dante's text written supposedly before that vision is comparable to the framing technique which we will notice in the *Filocolo*, in the *Comedia delle Ninfe* (Part I.i), and especially in the *Teseida* (II.ii): there a text with moral or Christian meanings is enclosed by the remarks of a narrator who seems to understand only its literal significance. It is a remarkably sophisticated device, whereby we are asked as readers to judge the validity of our informant's views by measuring his comments against our own perceptions of the story he recounts.

This particular kind of playfulness is one of the important lessons learned by Chaucer from his much-imitated master. For Boccaccio, in turn, the idea may have come from Ovid's *Metamorphoses*, where the series of narrators within narrators confuses the issue of who is responsible for a specific tale. He may also have developed the idea from Dante or Augustine by reversing their double perspective in which an older and wiser writer describes his earlier incomprehension. If my interpretation of the *Filostrato* is correct, then Boccaccio is by no means rejecting Dante's moral and religious vision, but is using that vision as a norm against which to evaluate his own this-worldly narrative. Yet there is a divergence as well, for Boccaccio is writing a tragedy of destructive love, not a comedy of the love that blesses and saves. Moreover, the difference between Filostrato's final understanding and Dante's may signify Boccaccio's reluctance to follow Dante's prophetic role, a role requiring considerable self-assurance. Boccaccio in the *Filostrato* does not claim to have seen the ultimate Truth but only to have seen the consequences of certain errors. He humbly leaves it to Dante to supply the corrective context. Perhaps this is Dante's role in the *Caccia* as well; Boccaccio's parody in that case may be asking us to amend its erotic goal with a better one, to recognize its foolishness in the light of Dante's wisdom, and to praise the ladies of Naples in a more proper way, "con laude più verace."

II

Filocolo

The *Filocolo* was a tremendously ambitious enterprise undertaken in Boccaccio's hopeful youth. It is a complicated—not to say scrambled—mixture of all the great literature which Boccaccio wanted to imitate: a Vergilian epic, an Ovidian *Metamorphoses*, and a French romance all rolled together and, moreover, allegorized. The story tells of Florio's search for the captured Biancifiore, their happy marriage, and the conversion to Christianity of Florio and his friends.

The book opens with an imitation of the *Aeneid* as Juno once again plots to overcome the Trojans who have by now settled in Italy. This time Jove consents to their defeat, "però c'ha preso isdegno, veggendo . . . che più a' sacrifici di Priapo intendono che a governare la figliuola d'Astreo, loro debita sposa" [because he has become angry, seeing . . . that they attend more to the sacrifices of Priapus than to the government of Astreo's daughter, their proper wife]. Thus Jove has allowed the house of Anjou to conquer Naples, where Boccaccio lived while composing the book. In this manner Boccaccio can justify the rule of King Robert, tracing its causes to divine will and translating the glory of ancient epics to contemporary history, just as Vergil himself used the Trojan heroes to glorify Rome.[1]

The *Aeneid* was commonly read for moral lessons, and Boccaccio's reference to Astrea and Priapus shows that he too is using it this way. The rhetorical cloak of pagan epic and chivalric romance parts almost at once to reveal a body of scriptural history. Jove becomes "sommo Giove" or the Christian God (I.1). Within the first pages we find an account of the fall of the angels and man and of Christ's redemptive mission. God or "Giove" is described as a powerful king whose son frees the prisoners of war taken by their enemy. Satan is "Pluto" and an exile from the kingdom of Giove. Christ, "figliuolo di Giove" [son of Jove], fights "varie battaglie" with "nuovi cavalieri entrati contra Pluto in campo" [sundry battles . . . new knights entered in the field against Pluto] and miraculously transports to Spain on a floating marble sarcophagus St. James, "uno de' suddetti prencipi" (I.3) [one of the above-mentioned princes].

Meanwhile all of this is addressed to youths and ladies who are in love (I.2). The book offers to show them how fortune has tossed ancient lovers, yet finally allowed them repose; these examples will console the readers for their own troubles and encourage their efforts by the hope of reward. Whereas on one page the terms of romance-epic refer to God and Christ, on another page "signore" is Amor and "salute" the erotic goal of lovers; and the illustrious line of Anjou, agent of Jove's justice and Juno's wrath, brings forth the narrator's beloved Maria.

This peculiar mixture of secular and religious narrative is the result of the work of not one but two fictional authors besides the real Boccaccio. One is the lover who writes as a labor of love at the request of his lady Maria. His task is to write down with appropriate elegance a story preexisting in the "fabulosi parlari degli ignoranti" [fabling speeches of the ignorant]. The other and, according to the fiction, the original author of the history is a hermit named Ilario, who within the story converted Florio and his companions to Christianity (V.96–97). The existence of these two writers implies two different intentions for the same narration. On one hand, the lover seeks to earn his lady's regard: "il suo priego in luogo di comandamento mi riputai, prendendo per quello migliore speranza nel futuro dei miei disii." [I considered her request as a command, taking from it better hope for the future of my desires.] This narrator offers to educate young and gentle readers in the art of "perfect" love exemplified by Florio and Biancifiore (I.2). On the other hand, the hermit who taught Florio the love of God ("accesi del celestiale amore" V.58) writes down Florio's history to educate future readers in this holy love. He hopes, no doubt, that the story will serve as did the tales of Roman conversions in Augustine's *Confessions*, i.e., as examples to inspire imitation. Thus the story of Florio and Biancifiore is exemplary in both cases, but exemplary of very different things. The text is meant to inspire love, but two quite different kinds of love: human and divine.

This doubleness of the text—almost a duplicity, for Boccaccio wittily waits until the end to inform us of Ilario's writing[2]—persists throughout every aspect of the work. Priapus and Astrea, lover and monk, classical epic and Christian allegory, the pairs multiply until the entire structure of the *Filocolo* is based on dualities. Besides moments of stark polarity, however, there are also moments of conversion or new understanding. Most startling, perhaps, is our recognition that the story of Christ which Ilario tells Florio is a story like Florio's own: the son of a king has left his kingdom and undertaken sufferings in order to rescue his beloved servant from captivity. Thus the Ovidian narrative about young lovers who fall in love reading the *Ars amatoria* is paired with the story of Christ's incarnation and redemption of man. In this way Book V provides an explanation for the initial narration of Christ's mission in epic-romance terms.

The book's polarities blur not only because of the merging of romance and Christian history but also because the lover's—and not Ilario's—text is the only one we really see, and it includes a large quantity of obviously Christian material, especially in Books I and V. The question arises, then, whether the narrator's amatory preface and envoy are to be taken as limiting his role, with the suggestion that he does not understand the implications of the Christian material "copied" from Ilario, or whether he does fully understand the Christian meaning of his text and is somehow playing with his readers. In the latter case, there is little need to distinguish the narrator from Boccaccio, but we do need to ask why he might present himself in this particular way; why, that is, he is introducing himself as a lover and what kind of love is really involved here. These questions cannot be answered without some attention to the story he tells.

The romance describes a double journey. Florio, urging his friends to accompany him in his search for Biancifiore, quotes Dante's lines from *Inferno* XXVI (119–20):

Fatti non foste a viver come bruti,
ma per seguir virtute e canoscenza.

[You were not made to live as brutes but to follow virtue and knowledge.]

The speaker in Dante's work is Ulysses, another wanderer, whose journey, in contrast to Dante's, was the wrong kind and ended in destruction.[3] One journeyed in the world, the other toward God.[4] There are several journeys going on in the *Filocolo* too, undoubtedly in imitation of Dante. One is Florio's actual sea voyage in search of Biancifiore. There are similarly the metaphorical sea voyages of other lovers: the readers, who have set the sails of their minds to catch the wind from Cupid's wings and are sailing eagerly through amorous seas toward their "porto di salute" (I.2), and Caleone, who later loses the star that was guiding his ship "a salutevole porto" and is tossed in the middle of a stormy sea of passions (V.30).[5] In these cases the "porto di salute" is the state of bliss to be attained in the arms of the beloved. There is, however, another "salute" as well toward which both Florio and Caleone journey by means of their learning about and converting to Christianity.[6] Florio's self-description is ambiguous, allowing the reader to connect his two journeys: "Io povero giovane e pellegrino, statomi dato del mio padre etterno esilio dalla sua casa, vo ricercando una giovane a noi per sottile ingegno levato, la quale s'io ritrovo, licito mi fia alla paternale casa tornare." (IV.76) [I, poor youth and pilgrim, having been given eternal exile by my father from his house, go seeking a young lady taken from us by subtle plot, whom if I find, I will be allowed to return to my father's house.]

The "etterno esilio" is an echo of his earlier, bitter complaint: "si troverà la prima madre per lo suo ardito gusto essere stata cagione a sé e a' discendenti d'etterno esilio de' superiori reami" (III.35.2)[7] [one will find that the first mother through her bold taste was the cause to herself and her descendants of eternal exile from the superior realms]. Moreover, the phrase harks back to Dante's *Inferno* XXIII.126, and *Purgatorio* XXI.18, where it clearly signifies damnation.[8] The latter example, referring to heaven as a court, fits in with Florio's exile from and hope to return to his father's palace. Florio is addressing Fiammetta, who is named Maria after the Virgin Mary, "per cui quella piaga, che il prevaricamento della prima madre aperse, richiuse" [through whom that wound was closed which the disobedience of the first mother opened]. The "prevaricamento" again alludes to the fall of Adam and Eve as recounted in I.3: "il precetto del loro creatore miserabilmente prevaricarono" [they wretchedly disobeyed the commandment of their creator]. Thus Florio, in exile because of Eve's sin, equated with the loss of Biancifiore, addresses the Fiammetta-Maria who offers a possible redemption from that sin and so the hope of finding Biancifiore and returning home. Florio's final journey is in fact a Christian pilgrimage, a realization of the metaphorical journey toward God, just as his search for Biancifiore is a realization of the metaphorical sea-voyage of lovers in general.

Florio's scene with Fiammetta is worth observing in detail. There are, in fact, two women named Maria and called Fiammetta: one the author's beloved, the other a character within the story, which is supposedly set in early Christian times; yet the two Fiammettas are very much alike. When Florio comes upon Fiammetta in the famous garden scene in Naples (IV.16), she is described consistently with the other Fiammetta (I.1) as the daughter of the king of the region, i.e., Naples ("figliuola dell'altissimo prencipe sotto il cui scettro questi paesi in quiete si reggono"). She is herself the "donna" or *domina* of the group in the garden. Among the young men and ladies who accompany her is Caleone, who is especially enamored of her. Thus, as has often been pointed out, he mirrors the narrator's love for his own Fiammetta.

As the narrator first saw Fiammetta in church, so too Caleone introduces Fiammetta with a number of religious resonances. Caleone explains to Florio that the group is harmoniously united by love under her leadership. His phrase "ci mosse e tiene" [she moved us and keeps us] suggests that she is in some mysterious way a source of the kind of love which binds together both the cosmos and human society, and which she herself will describe in this scene (IV.44). She contains every virtue (16), and the group crowns her queen with a laurel crown, the symbol of immortality, because she is "d'ogni grazia piena" (18)[9] [full of every grace]. As she sits in the garden, "vestita d'umiltà" (43) [clad in humility], she resembles a Madonna of Humility, a theme newly popular in the fourteenth century, in which the Virgin sits on the ground in a *hortus conclusus* that represents herself.[10] She offers an alternative kind of love to Eve's "ardito gusto," recalling the alternative offered in the introduction between Priapus and Astrea. If she is truly a divine representative, suggesting the beloved of no less than God, her answers to the questions about love are worth heeding.

She prays for divine guidance in answering the questions but also declares that she will answer lightly as befits a game (18). The game is interrupted, however, and she is forced to delve more deeply ("cercare le profundità") by Caleone's question, the seventh and central question of the game.[11] Just as it is his turn to ask, a ray of light reflected from the pool in their midst plays like a flame on Fiammetta's head, "forse qual fu già quella da Tanaquila veduta a Tulio piccolo garzone dormendo" (43) [perhaps like that which once was seen by Tanaquil on the little boy Tulio while he was asleep]. Boccaccio had referred to that marvelous event in II.58, where he calls it a manifest sign of future triumph. Thus it reinforces the meaning of Fiammetta's laurel crown. In I.3.8, Boccaccio writes that at Christ's birth the earth gave "allegri e manifesti segni di futura vittoria"—a phrase very close to his comment on the flaming head. Indeed, Boccaccio tells us that this garden scene takes place while the sun is in Gemini (IV.12), possibly on the very day of Pentecost, when the Holy Spirit descended in flames on the heads of the apostles.[12]

Caleone recites the song which he hears the flame singing on Fiammetta's head:

> Io son del terzo ciel cosa gentile,
>
> . . .
>
> e'n questa mia fiammetta con effetto
> mostro la forza de' dardi divini,
> andando ogn'uom ferendo
> che lei negli occhi mira, ov'io discendo
> ciascuna ora ch'è piacer di lei,
> vera reina delli regni miei. (IV.43)[13]

> [I am a gentle thing from the third heaven . . . and in this my flamelet / I show effectively the force of the divine darts / which go striking every man / who gazes into her eyes, where I descend / any time that pleases her, / true queen of my kingdoms.]

The "vera reina" at the end of the song reinforces the association with the Virgin Mary. The "fiammetta," of course, refers to the lady as well as to the miraculous flame. Thus the song implies that she too is a miracle sent from the heaven of the celestial Venus as a demonstration of divine love, the holy alternative to Cupid's "dardi."

Fiammetta's eyes mirror the divine light to all who observe her and thus spread *caritas*. Similarly Beatrice reflects the light of God to Dante before he has dared to look directly at the source. In *Purgatorio* XV Virgil discusses the mirrored amplification of love. There, like Caleone, Dante is dazzled by a light

> Come quando da l'acqua o da lo specchio
> salta lo raggio a l'opposita parte (16–17)

> [as when from the water or from a mirror a ray leaps to the opposite direction]

and Vergil explains what it is:

> "Non ti maravigliar s' ancor t'abbaglia
> la famiglia del cielo," a me rispuose:
> "messo è che viene ad invitar ch'om saglia." (28–30)

["Do not wonder if the family of heaven still / dazzles you," he answered me; "he has been sent, / who comes to invite man to ascend."]

The intensification of Fiammetta's association with a heavenly kind of love prepares for her answer to Caleone's question (IV.43): is it better for a person, for his own good, to be in love or not? She sighs before she answers: "Parlare ci conviene contra quello che noi con disiderio seguiamo." [We must speak against that which we follow with desire.] Following Aristotle,[14] she explains that there are three kinds of love. One is "amore onesto" [honest love], the good, direct, and loyal love which binds together the Creator and his creatures. It maintains the heavens in their order and also the governments of the world. Through it alone we can deserve to inherit the heavenly kingdom. Without it we have no power to do anything good. This seems to be the kind of love by which Fiammetta has bound the youthful group in harmony. Obviously it is better to be in love if one is talking about this kind of love.

Amore onesto is in fact related to Astrea, with whom Fiammetta has already been connected; as is written in the _Aeneid_ commentary attributed to Bernard Silvester (p. 9), "Legitimam Venerem dicimus esse mundanam musicam, id est equalem mundanorum proportionem, quam alii Astream, naturalem iustitiam vocant. . . . Impudicam autem venerem et petulantie deam, dicimus esse carnis concupiscentiam que omnium fornicationum mater est."[15] [We call the legitimate Venus the music of the world, i.e., the just proportion of worldly things, whom some call Astrea, or natural justice . . . . But the unchaste Venus, goddess of wantonness, we call the concupiscence of the flesh which is the mother of all fornications.] Here is clearly another case of Astrea versus Priapus.

There is a second kind of love, "amore per utilità" [love for utility], which is the kind most commonly found in the world. It is tied to fortune and disappears when fortune changes. As it aims only to make use of others without regard for their good, it would rationally speaking be better named hate than love. It is the cause of much evil and obviously better done without.

The third is "amore per diletto" [love for pleasure], "al quale noi siamo suggetti" [to which we are subject], says Fiammetta, including herself, and yet to which, truly, no one who desires to follow a virtuous life ought to submit himself. "Viva chi può libero." [Let him who can live free of it.]

Caleone protests with a series of arguments very familiar from the "courtly love" tradition (IV.45). Love makes the avaricious liberal, as Medea to Jason; the fierce humble, as Mars to Venus. It makes men aspire to noble deeds, for example, Paris and Menelaus. It adorns the speech and manners and produces poetry. Thus it leads to good and not to evil.

"Molto t'inganna il parer tuo" [your opinion is much deceived], replies Fiammetta (IV.46). Lovers judge falsely because they have lost the light of the eyes of the mind and have chased away reason as their enemy.[16] "Questo amore niun'altra cosa è che una irrazionabile volontà, nata da una passione venuta nel cuore per il libidinoso piacere che agli occhi è apparito, nutricato per ozio."[17] [This love is nothing other than an irrational will, born from a passion which entered the heart through the libidinous pleasure which appeared to the eyes, nourished by leisure.] Its pretended humility is really a presumption aimed at claiming that to which the lover has no right.

Caleone's examples are all double-edged. What he called liberality was destructive prodigality. Mars's gentleness was adultery. Paris was inspired not to honorable achievement but to crime, which Menelaus revenged out of regard more for honor than for love. Amore is the source not of virtues but of vices. Fiammetta's counterexamples include Phaedra, Tireus, Pasiphae, and Hercules made "vile" by his service to Iole. Love, sums up Fiammetta, leads its followers into every evil; and if by chance they perform some virtuous deeds, which happens rarely, they only do it in order to arrive the sooner at the wicked end wished for by their obscene will (46).

The correct behavior is to nip love in the bud. If it is discovered too late, and we are already trapped in the snare, we must continue helplessly "infino a tanto che quella luce, la quale trasse Enea de' tenebrosi passi, fuggendo i pericolosi incendii, apparisce a noi, e tiraci a' suoi piaceri" [until that light which drew Aeneas from his dark steps, fleeing the perilous fires, appears to us and draws us toward its pleasures]. Quaglio's note mentions that it was Venus who appeared luminous to Aeneas and that she symbolizes Christian love.[18] In *Aeneid* II.588ff., just as Aeneas, enraged, is preparing to kill Helen, glimpsed in the light of the flames that she has caused, Venus appears as a clear, pure light:

non ante oculis tam clara . . .
et pura per noctem in luce refulsit
alma parens, confessa deam qualisque videri
caelicolis (589–92)

[never before so clear to the eyes . . . / and through the night in a pure light shone / the nourishing mother, manifestly goddess and such as she is seen / by the dwellers of heaven].

She bids Aeneas quit the battle, and declares that she is protecting him from the flames. As Aeneas has just spoken of the "ultricis flammae" [vengeful flames] which burn his soul at the sight of Helen, it would be easy for medieval readers to see in this Venus a protection against one's own inner passions. Her pure and heavenly light is also a clear opposite to the fires of Troy, caused by Paris's burning lust.[19] She appears again, indirectly, at the end of Book II as the morning star which beckons Aeneas's party to leave Troy behind and set forth on their long journey toward the divinely promised land.

The game of love questions, which all deal with the third kind of love, can only be continued by the players' reestablishing the assumptions that have just been broken down. Thus the questioner who follows Caleone begins: "O nobile reina, voi avete al presente determinato che alcuna persona questo nostro amore seguire non dee, *e io'l consento*, . . . Però al presente lasciando con vostro piacere la vostra sentenza, terrò che licito sia l'innamorarsi, *prendendo il mal fare per debito adoperare*. (my emphasis) [O noble queen, you have at present determined that no person ought to follow this love of ours, and I agree; . . . Yet at present leaving aside your statement, if you please, I will consider it permissible to fall in love, taking evildoing for proper practice.] Boccaccio has chosen to interrupt the horizontal flow of the *questioni* with the vertical shaft of Fiammetta's moralizing, which sets the game into a wholly new perspective. Thus it prepares for Florio's vertically ascending vision of the virtues and divine love, immediately following this scene.

Despite the unambiguous nature of Fiammetta's reply to Caleone, there are nonetheless certain problems with her position. At the start of her sermon, she confesses that she herself is in love and is speaking contrary to her own desires (IV.44). She is, moreover, involved in a game of debate which forces her to make an extreme case in opposition to Caleone's. So far the *Filocolo* has offered a series of polarities: Eve versus Mary, Priapus versus Astrea, etc.; but Fiammetta defines *three* kinds of love. *Amor per diletto* is clearly somewhere between the obviously good and obviously evil kinds; yet Fiammetta's argument with Caleone attempts to classify it on one side or the other, ignoring the idea of a middle ground. Is she, then, entirely correct in her assessment or is she failing to acknowledge the possibility that such love can lead to good?

We have, after all, the example of Florio and Biancifiore. Although they fall in love over the *Ars amatoria* like Paolo and Francesca over the story of Lancelot, and although Venus sends Cupid to them in disguise "come già nella non compiuta Cartagine prendesti forma del giovane Ascanio" (II.1.5) [as before in uncompleted Carthage you took the form of Ascanius], the negative implications of both these models are transmuted by the innocence of Boccaccio's young couple: "si porgeano semplici baci, ma più avanti non procedeano, però che la novella età, in che erano, non conoscea i nascosi diletti" (II.4.7) [they gave each other simple kisses, but further they did not proceed because the young age at which they were did not know the hidden pleasures]. When Florio is finally reunited with Biancifiore, they do not rush to seize "the wicked end wished for by their obscene will" as Fiammetta had said, but stop instead to perform a marriage ceremony, exchanging vows and rings before the statue of an unblindfolded Cupid, who, Biancifiore says, "nostro Imeneo, elli la santa Giunone e Venere ci sia" (IV.20.4)[20] [may he be for us Hymen, holy Juno, and Venus]. Florio repeats Biancifiore's assertion, "Tu sii nostro Imineo, tu in luogo della santa Giunone guarda le nostre facelline e sii testimonio del nostro maritaggio" and he prays, "questa giovane con indissolubile matrimonio cerco di congiungermi" (IV.121.2–3) [May you be our Hymen, you in place of holy Juno keep our torches and be witness to our marriage . . . I seek to join to myself this young girl with indissoluble marriage]. The *Filocolo* celebrates their marriage as a relation that can reconcile virtue and chastity with sexual desire. Venus and Diana, the motivating deities of much of the *Filocolo*'s action, join forces for the marriage of Florio and Biancifiore, as they will do again in the *Teseida*.

The narrator promised (I.2.4–5) that his book would teach young lovers to love only one person, as is pleasing to Amore. This repeats Cupid's command in the *Roman de la Rose* (ll. 2239–44), which does not refer in any way to marriage. However, in his commentary on *Inferno* V, Boccaccio wrote about *lussuria*: "Alla cui troppa licenzia reprimere nostro Signore primieramente instituì il matrimonio, nel quale, non dando più che una moglie ad Adam né ad Eva più che un marito, mostrò di volere che uno fosse contento d'una, e una d'uno." (V.alleg.61) [To keep down their too great lust our Lord first instituted marriage, in which, not giving more than one wife to Adam nor to Eve more than one husband, he showed his will that one man be content with one woman and one woman with one man.] This puts the command of love in a totally different light. Fiammetta lectures on the importance of marital fidelity in her answers to several questions in the garden (IV.34 and 52). The perfect lovers whom the narrator offers as examples to his readers interrupt the "festa" of their reunion to say: "né credere che io sì lungamente aggia affannato per acquistare amica, ma per acquistare inseparabile sposa, la qual tu mi sarai" (IV.120.3) [do not believe that I have travailed so long in order to acquire a lover, but to acquire an inseparable wife, which you will be to me].

The "affanni" of their separation, moreover, are providently designed to maintain the purity of the protagonists (II.9.8):

Ma che si può dire, se non che il benigno aspetto, col quale la somma benivolenza riguarda la necessità degli abandonati, non volle che il nobile sangue, del quale Biancifiore era discesa, sotto nome d'amica divenisse vile, ma acciò che con matrimoniale nodo il suo onore si servasse, consentì che le pensate cose sanza indugio si mettessero in effetto?

[However, what can one say but that the kind aspect with which the supreme benevolence watches over the need of the abandoned, did not wish that the noble blood from which Biancifiore was descended should become base under the name of lover, but in order that her honor should be preserved with the knot of matrimony, he consented that the plots without delay be put into effect?]

This concern for marriage before lovemaking is new with Boccaccio's revision of his sources. There are two French versions of the story from the twelfth century and an Italian one close in time to Boccaccio's own;[21] but although Boccaccio shares many elements with all three, not one includes the exchange of rings and vows until after the couple has been caught in bed and then pardoned.

The earlier versions of the tale also include a gold cup which King Felice receives from the merchants as part of the payment for Biancifiore and which Florio takes with him on his wanderings, using it finally to bribe the guard of the emir's tower. This gold cup is decorated in one version with the three goddesses that appeared to Paris, Paris's abduction of Helen, and the Trojan War. In this text the story of Paris is made to sound similar to that of Florio; like Florio, Paris sailed to find the woman he loved (p. 24). When Florio has reached the emir's tower and is afraid to pursue his venture, he gazes at the cup with envy for Paris, who is shown taking Helen by the hand (pp. 39–40). The other French text gives the cup somewhat less emphasis. It seems to show only Paris's abduction of Helen. The scene of Florio's envious gazing is absent. The Italian text says simply that the cup shows "tutta la storia di Troia" [the whole story of Troy].

Boccaccio mentions in passing that the king received in exchange for Biancifiore a rich cup of gold, on the stem and foot of which was enameled with subtle workmanship the ruin of Troy (III.45.5). All that is left of the Trojan story is the monitory ending—an aspect of the story not emphasized in the sources. Moreover, Boccaccio uniquely takes the trouble to contrast the love of Florio and Biancifiore to that of Paris and Helen. Thus, for example, Florio protests to his father that he is wise to love the local Biancifiore unlike Paris who carried Helen away from another's kingdom, thus causing the destruction of his own (II.13.6). Again the abduction of Helen is immediately connected with its destructive consequences. Later in Book II (26.12) Florio compares himself to Menelaus, fearing that his absence from Biancifiore may lead to the success of rivals. He is thinking of himself already in the role of husband, for he wants to marry Biancifiore, and it is in fact his desire to marry her, not merely his love for her, that worries his father the king.[22]

Paris receives further negative commentary in III.18.23, where Florio, anxious still about losing Biancifiore to rivals, recalls how Paris abandoned Oenone for Helen. Thus Paris, whom Caleone cites as an example of the ennobling inspiration of love, is not a faithful lover at all. The final and most explicit blow to the image of Paris comes from the mouth of Fiammetta in answer to Caleone: "Paris fu sollecito alla sua distruzione, se'l fine di tale sollecitudine si riguarda" (IV.46.7) [Paris was solicitous to his own destruction, if you look to the end of such solicitude].

Fileno, bitter from his unrequited love for Biancifiore, speaks similar ill against "la lascivia di Elena, la quale, abandonando il proprio marito, e conoscendo ciò che dovea della sua fuga seguire, anzi volle che il mondo perisse sotto l'armi che ella non fosse nelle braccia di Paris"(III.35.6) [the lasciviousness of Helen, who, abandoning her proper husband, and knowing what would have to follow from her flight, wished rather that the world should perish in arms than that she not be in the arms of Paris]. He associates Helen with Clytemnestra, Medea, Mirra, Biblis, and other evil women, whereas Biancifiore will counter his antifeminist statements in person as the example of female fidelity that opposes Helen's "lascivia."

In sum, everything is being done to legitimize the relation of Florio and Biancifiore in contrast to the illegitimate and destructive love of Paris and Helen, who in the earlier romance are a parallel example. Florio and Biancifiore not only marry before they make love, they also see themselves as a faithfully married couple all along.

Moreover, their secular love has religious implications which relate the couple to Fiammetta, raising questions about the heavenly or earthly nature of her role as the narrator's beloved. Florio and Biancifiore are both born "nel giocondo giorno eletto per festa de' cavalieri, essendo Febo nelle braccia di Castore e di Polluce insieme" (I.39) [on the joyous day elected as a festival for the knights, Phoebus being in the arms of Castor and Pollux together] and are named in honor of the day (I.44). The holiday during the period between mid-May and mid-June, when the sun is in Gemini, is Pentecost; Boccaccio has written a riddle for the holiday named clearly in the earlier versions of the tale. Pentecost was known as "pascha rosata" or "paque fleuri," and in Italy included the custom of dropping a flurry of roses from the vault of the church to signify the descent of the Holy Spirit. Hence the flower names of the protagonists, and Florio's arrival to Biancifiore in a basket of roses. Biancifiore's orphaned state may furthermore be connected to Christ's promise in John 14:18, "Non relinquam vos orphanos" [I shall not leave you as orphans], regularly read during the Pentecost service.

The hymn "Veni creator spiritus" sung for Pentecost has in its text the prayer, "Infunde amorem cordibus" [Pour love into our hearts]; and a homily of St. Gregory regularly read for the occasion says: "Hodie namque Spiritus Sanctus repentino sonitu super discipulos venit, mentesque carnalium in sui amorem permutavit, et foris apparentibus linguis igneis, intus facta sunt corda flammantia; quia dum Deum in ignis visione susceperunt, per amorem suaviter arserunt. Ipse namque Spiritus Sanctus amor est."[23] [For today the Holy Spirit with a sudden sound came over his disciples, and changed the minds of the carnal to his love, and as tongues of flame appeared outwardly, inwardly their hearts were set aflame; because while they received God in the vision of fire, they burned sweetly with love. For the Holy Spirit himself is love.] Moreover, the reading, from Acts 19, describes the resistance to the new religion by the Ephesian worshipers of Diana. Florio and Biancifiore are truly born for love, and the anger of Diana at having been slighted is, according to Boccaccio, the cause of their troubles. The day of their birth provides a fitting background for their story. Ilario's account to Florio of the life of Christ ends with the events of Pentecost (V.54). The descent of the Holy Spirit in tongues of flame is certainly also part of the significance of the miraculous flame that flickers on the head of Fiammetta in the garden. All three characters are thus linked with Pentecost, the manifestation of the Holy Spirit, and the conversion of carnal love to holy love.

The idea that human love can actually lead to Christian love without our needing to reject the former is further supported by Florio's vision immediately following the scene of the love debate with Fiammetta. As Florio is waiting to set sail from Naples, he has a sudden vision of a ship at sea. It carries seven ladies, who are the cardinal and theological virtues, as their attributes make clear (IV.74). The four in the prow look familiar to Florio, but the three in the stern are beautiful strangers; for Florio as the son of a pagan king and queen does not recognize the theological trio. Among the seven ladies appears the image of Biancifiore held by a youth and weeping. As Florio runs toward her, however, the sea swells in a sudden storm. When it has calmed again, Biancifiore is among the four cardinal virtues, while a man with a golden crown introduces Florio to the three new ladies. Desirous of learning more about them, Florio sees the sky open; a lady dressed in white washes him with the contents of a golden phial and disappears. Florio seems to see more clearly than ever both worldly and divine things, "e quelle amare ciascuna secondo il suo dovere" [and to love each according to its due]. Biancifiore is now among the theological virtues. The object of Florio's affection is thus at once the same and altered. It is still Biancifiore but in a new context. As the three virtues lead Florio up the mast, he seems to enter the holy region of the gods and to see inestimable glory streaming from the face of Jove. And as he exclaims, "Oh felice colui che a tanta gloria è eletto!" [O happy he who is elected to such glory!], he suddenly finds himself seized by his traveling companions, who call him back to earth. Their boat is ready for sailing.

The fact that the vision corresponds in part to the reality of Florio's external situation while it is also an allegory for his inner condition provides a link from the external events to the internal significance of the story. Florio's horizontal love for Biancifiore is suddenly verticalized, as Biancifiore becomes the lure which draws Florio toward virtue and grace. The fact that Biancifiore is herself a Christian helps connect Florio's love for her with the love inspired by his revelation. Biancifiore, held weeping in the arms of a mysterious young male figure and then reappearing among the seven virtues, is clearly modeled after Beatrice, and Florio the pilgrim thus becomes a sort of Dante. Florio's exclamation is indeed taken from the beginning of Dante's *Commedia* (*Inf.* I.129), where Vergil offers himself as a guide but tells Dante that if he wishes to ascend to the realm of the blessed, a worthier soul than Vergil's—i.e., Beatrice—will lead him there. It is Vergil who wistfully cries out, "o felice colui, cui ivi elegge!" And Dante responds by begging Vergil in the name of the God he did not know to lead him as far as he can out of the present evil:

> E io a lui: "Poeta, io ti richeggio
> per quello Dio che tu non conoscesti,
> a ciò ch'io fugga questo male e peggio,
> che tu mi meni là dov' or dicesti. (130–33)

Florio, like Vergil, does not yet know about the Christian God; but like Dante he has a chance to learn and be among the blessed. His pursuit of Biancifiore brings him toward, not away from, that heavenly goal.[24]

Biancifiore is herself the child of Christianized descendents of Scipio. Thus her own family history leads from Scipio's moral virtues to the additional theological virtues of the later generations. Scipio is, furthermore, an example of mediation between the pagan and Christian realms, for he is a "good" pagan particularly celebrated in Christian literature. As Boccaccio knew nothing yet of Petrarch's *Africa*,[25] his reason for choosing Scipio probably comes from Dante's use of the Roman hero, for Dante mentions him in all three parts of the *Commedia* as well as in other writings. Georg Rabuse, tracing Dante's Scipio back to Macrobius, comments that Dante saw in him an embodiment of Providence hovering over the empire.[26] From Dante's references to a Scipio who is "benedetto" [blessed] (*Convivio* IV.5), "di gloria erede" [heir of glory] (*Inf.* XXXI.116), and triumphant under "il sacrosanto segno" [the sacred sign] (*Par.* VI.32 and 53), Boccaccio easily drew his Laelius Africanus, who adds the new revealed knowledge to the old classical virtues and represents the conversion of the Roman empire to Christianity. The combined names of Scipio and Laelius come undoubtedly from the exemplary friends of Cicero's *De amicitia;* thus they point appropriately to the good kind of love which unites virtuous persons. If Laelius's acceptance of the new faith illustrates not only an individual conversion but also the historical conversion of the pagan world, and if the completion of his interrupted pilgrimage by Florio and Biancifiore and their large-scale conversion of others illustrates the persecution and ultimate triumph of the church in the world, such a theme would justify Boccaccio's expansion of a romance into a lengthy prose epic with classical epic trappings. As it leads from the false pagan gods to the true Christian one, so too it leads from the epic of pagan myth to the epic of Christian history. The point is, once again, that we are dealing not with unbridgeable dichotomies but with a process of transition.

If Biancifiore can truly act for Florio as Dante's Beatrice, then it is possible that the scene of the narrator's enamorment with Fiammetta in church is similarly a serious rather than subverted imitation of Dante's love. Is the narrator, like Dante, in love with a truly heavenly being who can be his Beatrice, or is he, like Petrarch—whose personal Laura myth Boccaccio probably did not yet know—choosing the holiday that celebrates God's incomparable love for man as the day on which to turn away from Christ and take Cupid as "signore"? We need to consider closely the narrator's own story.

Fiammetta's birth is introduced by the history of Naples, in which the house of Anjou is divinely elected to restore Naples from the worship of Priapus to that of Astrea. Robert of Anjou inherits the kingdom, which he rules with the aid of Pallas or wisdom. But before his coronation he produces an illegitimate daughter from a noble lady at the court, whose honor is protected by the king's discretion.[27] Thus Fiammetta's last name is that of an assumed (and unidentified) father; but the king gives her her first name: "lei nomò del nome di colei che in se contenne la redenzione del misero perdimento che avenne per l'ardito gusto della prima madre" (I.1)[28] [he named her with the name of her who contained in herself the redemption of the wretched loss which came about through the bold taste of the first mother]. Despite her own illegitimacy, the description of her name as a remedy of Eve's (and her own mother's?) sin fits in with the remedy provided by the house of Anjou for the cult of Priapus. Her beauty and virtuous deeds make her seem more the daughter of God than of man; thus she lives up to her name.

The narrator first sees her on Easter Saturday in the Franciscan church of San Lorenzo. There are several details to note here. First, the day is Saturday, not Friday as for Petrarch,[29] and Boccaccio tells us that the service that day was celebrating the harrowing of hell: "il glorioso partimento del figliuolo di Giove degli spogliati regni di Plutone." Whereas Petrarch associates his enamorment with the death of Christ, almost as if he were responsible for that death by his own birth of desire, Boccaccio instead chooses the day of Christ's victory over hell and the salvation of—among others—Eve. His love marks the Easter weekend while Florio and

Biancifiore are related to Pentecost or the end of the Easter season. The Fiammetta-Maria of Book IV is also associated with Pentecost rather than with Easter; the two Fiammettas frame the Easter season.

Two chief events occur during the service on Easter Saturday.[30] One is the blessing of the baptismal water, the renewal of baptismal vows by the congregation, and the sprinkling of the congregation with blessed water. This seems relevant to the *Filocolo* story, which ends with the baptism not only of Florio and his companions but also of whole city populations, including the entire population of Florio's kingdom. The blessing of baptismal water is accompanied by recitations of the Litany, beginning with a triple invocation of Maria, petitioning for her intercession.

The other main event of the service, which precedes the baptismal blessing, is the renewal of the year by kindling a new flame. The church is dark at the beginning of the service. From a newly struck spark, the Paschal candle is lit and blessed. As a symbol of the pillar of fire which led the Jews from Egypt to the promised land, it is clearly appropriate to Christ's harrowing of hell as well as to the significance of the whole Easter weekend, for the Exodus is the Old Testament parallel to Christ's liberation of the human race from sin. From the Paschal candle the clergy members light their own candles, and then in turn the members of the congregation light candles which have been distributed among them in advance. Finally lights are lit throughout the church. Christ's statement "Ego sum lux mundi" [I am the light of the world] is read, and thus the spreading of light from the Paschal candle signifies Christ's illumination of the faithful. The kindling of a flame is certainly relevant to Fiammetta's name. The narrator, in describing her, emphasizes the light of her eyes from which a flaming arrow comes to pierce his heart: "i lucenti occhi della bella donna sintillando guardarono ne' miei con aguta luce, per la quale luce una focosa saetta, d'oro al mio parere, vidi venire" (I.1.22). Entering his heart, it "v'accese una fiamma" [kindled a flame]. The narrator is set on fire like a candle from the luminous Fiammetta. The idea of this spreading of flame within the hearts of those present in church just as from candle to candle is expressed in the reading for the service: "Deus itaque qui dixit de tenebris lumen clarescere, clarescat in cordibus nostris, ut aliquid intus simile faciamus, quale in domo hac orationis accensis luminaribus fecimus." [And so may God, who told the light to shine from the darkness, shine in our hearts, so that we may do within something similar to what we have done in this house of prayer with kindled lights.] The association with light and flame which kindles love in others connects this Fiammetta to the other one, as the spreading flame of Christ on Easter Saturday corresponds to the descending flame of the Holy Spirit on Pentecost. Fiammetta's name seems to have been chosen with these two holy days in mind. As the song in the garden reveals, the Fiammetta of Book IV, like that of Book I, is a flame sent to earth to kindle holy love.[31]

Of course, the narrator's phrases also invoke the golden arrow of Cupid and the age-old topos of the fires of love, thus opening a possible conflict between the narrator's erotic perception and its religious context. However the religious setting is clearly appropriate to a reading *in bono* of Fiammetta's name; moreover, since the Virgin Mary herself was addressed in amatory terms, the use of traditional love-words does not necessarily undermine a more religious reading of the situation.

The evening service on Easter Saturday includes a reading about the three Marys coming to Christ's tomb. Saturday is anyway a day generally devoted to the office of the Virgin Mary, and therefore a suitable day for initiating the cult of a Maria. Dante, in *Vita Nuova* 5, sees Beatrice in church during a service to the Virgin, although he does not mention which day of the week it is. The psalter to the Virgin Mary compiled by St. Bonaventure in the thirteenth century includes in its psalms several phrases which closely resemble the *Filocolo* narrator's.[32] There is repeated reference to the Madonna's beauty and to the splendor and light of her face. The person praying is referred to frequently as a lover, "amante," of Mary. He prays to her to light him with the ray of her understanding and to burn him with her flames of charity, "Con *raggio* d'intelligenzia riverbera il cuore mio, e con *fuoco* di tua carità *infiamma* la mente mia." "L'amore superno *accendi* nelli cuori nostri" (my emphases) [kindle supernal love in our hearts]. He prays to her to lead his soul "a porto di salute"; similarly the narrator addresses young lovers who are eager to reach "a porto di salute" [to the port of salvation]. The final hymn praises her: "Tu sei mediatrice tra Dio e l'uomo: tu amatrice dei mortali . . . illuminatrice dei fedeli. . . . Tu sei Madonna del mondo e del cielo regina, e dopo il Signore unica nostra speranza." [You are the mediator between God and man: you are the lover of mortals . . . the illuminator of the faithful. . . . You are Lady of the world and queen of heaven, and after the Lord our only hope.] If the narrator's Maria is at all like her namesake, then she must be closely related to the other Fiammetta-Maria of Book IV, whose Marian attributes have already been noted. The narrator, in I.1, treats his Maria within a context of churches and religious awe, and with very little subversively erotic suggestion.

His choice of the specific church in which he sees her first may also be significant. Partly there are historical reasons for it: Boccaccio actually lived near San Lorenzo,[33] and Casetti notes that the church was one of the noblest monuments of Naples, attracting members of the court on holidays.[34] But the saint is also fitting to Boccaccio's literary theme, for his story as told in the *Legenda Aurea*[35] contains a long discussion on the many meanings of the flames of his martyrdom;[36] it concludes: "Item esse salvatoris ignem fervorem fidei legimus in Evangelio: ignem veni mittere in terram." [Similarly we read in the Gospel that the fervor of faith is a fire of the savior: I have come to set a fire in the lands.] As a flame sent from heaven, might Fiammetta represent faith? She could in this regard be compared to the *Comedia delle Ninfe*'s Lia, a nymph who represents faith and is the beloved of the central character, Ameto.

Seeing Fiammetta in church, the narrator says to Amore: "tu hai dinanzi agli occhi miei posta la mia beatitudine" [you have set before my eyes my beatitude]. Boccaccio here conflates two passages from the *Vita Nuova* (2 and 5): Dante's seeing the lady in church and Love's saying to him, "Apparuit iam beatitudo vestra." The conflation is suggested by Dante's own repetition in chapter 5 of the phrase from chapter 2: "ed io era in luogo dal quale vedea la mia beatitudine" [and I was in a place from which I could see my beatitude]. Numerous echoes from both chapters pervade Boccaccio's scene. From chapter 2 he drew the phrase, "Ella non parea figliuolo d'uomo mortale, ma di deo," which becomes in the *Filocolo* (I.1.16) "facea pensare a molti che non d'uomo ma di Dio figliuola stata fosse." He seems also to have borrowed from this same chapter the use of astronomical periphrasis for establishing the date. The obvious borrowings from the *Vita Nuova*, taken together with the references to the Easter ritual and to the Virgin Mary, strongly suggest that Fiammetta may be, like Beatrice, a truly celestial lady.[37]

Another echo refers not to Fiammetta but to the book which she bids the narrator write; previously, says Fiammetta, the story of Florio and Biancifiore has not been properly honored in writing but left only to the "fabulosi parlari degli ignoranti" [fabling speeches of the ignorant]. Dante, at the end of *Vita Nuova* 2, remarks that his own "soprastare a le passioni e atti di tanta gioventudine pare alcuno parlare fabulose" [rising above the passions and acts of such youth may seem to some a fabling speech]. This identifies Dante's love with that of Florio and Biancifiore, similarly young and pure. As it is Fiammetta who urges the writing of their story, we have added reason to connect Fiammetta with their good and innocent love, just as the other Fiammetta is connected with their Pentecostal associations through the tongue of flame descending on her head.

Moreover, like the couple in her story, Fiammetta too is backed by a combination of Venus and Diana. The narrator first sees her at the beginning of the fifth hour on Saturday, an hour governed by Venus, according to a common astrological scheme which he explains in the *Genealogia* (I.34) and alludes to here as well: "un giorno, la cui prima ora Saturno avea signoreggiata" [a day whose first hour Saturn had governed]. During Venus's hour, then, the lover addresses Amore and speaks of the flaming arrow of love which has struck him. On the second occasion he sees Fiammetta in another church, "nel quale sacerdotesse di Diana, sotto bianchi veli, di neri vestimenti vestite, cultivavano tiepidi fuochi divotamente; là dove io giungendo, con alquante di quelle vidi la graziosa donna del mio cuore stare con festevole e allegro ragionamento" (I.1.23) [in which priestesses of Diana, under white veils, dressed in black garments, devoutly cultivated tepid fires; there where I arrived, I saw the gracious lady of my heart in merry and joyful conversation with some of them]. Furthermore, if this second church, which Boccaccio says is named for the prince of the angels, is truly the convent of Sant'Arcangelo dedicated to Gabriel, as Quaglio's notes suggest, then the second church through the Annunciation relates to the Maria name just as the first church, through San Lorenzo's flames, relates to the Fiammetta name. The Fiammetta name may partly be associated with the Venerian flames of love,[38] while Maria has a long iconographic tradition of association with Diana.[39]

At the end of this chapter the narrator, for aid in accomplishing the assigned task of writing this book, invokes not Amore or his lady as in the *Filostrato* but "o sommo Giove," the Christian God, in one more phrase borrowed from Dante (*Inf.* XXXI.92 and *Purg.* VI.118). He prays to God to sustain his writing so that it may be "degna essaltatrice del tuo onore" and "in etterna laude del tuo nome" [worthy exalter of your honor . . . in eternal praise of your name]. This states a Christian intent on the part of the lover-writer quite apart from Ilario. As Boccaccio was, in fact, studying canon law at the time and refers to these labors in his invocation, the narrator is identified with the real Boccaccio in the context of a Christian pursuit.

The narrator's role as lover, then, may be twofold. One, he presents himself as a lover in the *Vita Nuova* manner, a lover of some real but miraculous lady who can mysteriously become a representative of Christ and a means to his salvation. Thus for him, as for Florio and Biancifiore, human love properly pursued becomes a way toward and not away from God. Two, the narrator in the following chapter addresses his book to lovers and, by identifying himself with them, may entice them to read his book, which will teach them, he says, not to pursue lust like the rabbits but to maintain "debita fede" [due faith] in love and to find consolation for the permutations of fortune.[40]

Besides Florio, or even more than Florio, there are two other characters in the *Filocolo* analogous to the narrator: Caleone, who loves Fiammetta-Maria, and Idalagos, a poet who loves a backwards Mary named Alleiram. These two characters, whose stories are told chiefly in Book V, map out certain alternatives which may help to shed some light on the position of the narrator, his affections, and his intentions as a writer.

Florio had first met Caleone in the garden at Naples where Fiammetta answered a series of questions on love. There Caleone seemed to be especially in love with Fiammetta, sitting directly across from her in the circle of questioners, and prefacing his question with an expression of contemplative wonder at her miraculous, heavenly nature. Florio later finds Caleone alone and wretched at the loss of his guiding star Fiammetta. Truly desirous of "la futura sua salute," he is comforted by Florio "che già tali mari avea navicati" (V.31) [who had already sailed such seas]. Florio makes him the governor of a new town, following the theory that love is nourished by idleness and that, as Ovid, master of love, has advised, activity drives Cupid away.[41] The *Ars amatoria* which Florio was reading when he fell in love now gives way to the *Remedia amoris* as he advises Caleone on how to free himself from passion.

Actually, Caleone's governorship is more than mere busywork, for the city is frequently a symbol for the psyche.[42] Caleone by learning to govern something external to himself learns to govern himself as well. The theme of ruler ruling himself or conqueror conquering himself is a common one throughout the following centuries, and we can see it again in the *Decameron* (X.6) where King Charles overcomes his own lustful inclinations. The town which Caleone founds is none other than Boccaccio's Certaldo, identified by the "cerreto" or oak grove (IV.1 and 13; V.33 and 42–43). It is dedicated, as the trees might suggest, to Giove, indeed to "sommo Giove" (V.49). Shortly before, we have heard Florio pray to "sommo Giove, governatore dell'universo con ragione perpetua" (V.34)[43] [supreme Jove, governor of the universe with perpetual justice (or reason)]. Not only is this Jupiter the Christian God, but also among the planetary gods Jupiter represents temperance and rationality. Boccaccio in the *Genealogia* (II.2) describes this planet's influence as temperate, modest, and honest, producing wise men, doctors of law, just judges, divine worship, etc. Caleone names the new town "Calocepe" from καλο-χηπος or beautiful garden, Branca suggests. The transformation of Certaldo from a wilderness into a garden and of its population from savage beasts to men reflects the reestablishment of rational order within Caleone. Thus Certaldo is, at least in this instance, a town of Jovial temperance and rationality.

In contrast to Certaldo, Naples seems to be for Boccaccio the special place of love. Billanovich suggests that this is largely in homage to Ovid,[44] rather than to Boccaccio's adolescence there, but both are possible at once. Ovid's poems to Baia, imitated by Boccaccio, contribute to the lascivious atmosphere of the region.[45] Another connection is the Ovidian "Mirteo mare" (*Filoc.* IV.73 and V.5) which name Boccaccio mistakenly derives from the myrtle abundant on its shores.[46] Boccaccio probably found further support for the Venerian quality of Naples in *Paradiso* VIII, for the discussion of the history of Naples and Sicily takes place in Venus's heaven. Here we find the account, repeated in *Filocolo* I.1, of how the house of Anjou overcame the heir of Frederick II and took possession of the region. As Boccaccio's King Robert, governing with the aid of Pallas, is backed by the gods who wish to turn people from the worship of Priapus to the service of Astrea, the history of Naples reveals a plot of conversion parallel to that of lovers and pagans in the book.

While Caleone learns eventually to replace his passion with reason, another character, Idalagos, changes in reverse. Whereas Caleone comes from Naples, where he is in love, and ends up in Certaldo, learning to govern his own passion and turning the inhabitants of the area from animals into men,[47] Idalagos comes from Certaldo (V.8), a town which we have noted as a symbol for temperate reason, travels to Naples, and there falls in love.

If Florio and Biancifiore's joy in marriage demonstrates the reward of proper love, the metamorphoses of Idalagos and Alleiram illustrate the wretched results of the wrong kind of love. Idalagos's love for Alleiram has been seen as a retelling of Boccaccio's love for Maria.[48] But the Alleiram whom Idalagos loves is really a reversal of Maria not only in name.[49] While Maria is associated with the Madonna of Humility and explicitly "vestita d'umiltà" [clad in humility], Alleiram is chiefly characterized by pride. Her vaunted resistence to Cupid is a lie with which she feeds this pride. For while she rejects faithful love, in a barren frigidity which her final metamorphosis to stone merely concretizes, she does not reject lust, recounting how her lover "divenuto d'ardire piu copioso ch'alcuno altro che mai mi amasse, s'ingegnò di prendere, e prese, quello ch'io con sembianti gli volea negare" (V.20) [having become more bold than anyone who ever loved me, endeavored to take, and took, what I feigned to want to deny him]. Whereas Maria clearly defends true *caritas* against the self-deluding vanity of concupiscence, Alleiram flagrantly seeks only self-aggrandizement from her lovers, using them as objects of that "amore per utilità" which is better called hatred than love (IV.46). Indeed, Alleiram actively seeks to give Idalagos pain as a proof of her own powers. Whereas Fiammetta, through her nickname and through the miraculous flame in Book IV, is associated with fire, the element that ascends highest toward heaven, Alleiram ends up converted by Venus into a stone, the heaviest element, sinking farthest from grace. The names of all four cruel ladies are backwards versions of the names significant of grace: Maria, Mariella, Giovanna, Agnese. In their attempt to make themselves like gods, they are identifiable with the Eve side of the Eve-Maria opposition. The sunless grotto in which they are eternally condemned is a miniature hell in which, as in Dante's *Inferno*, the punishments fix the criminal state of the soul perpetually.

Idalagos, like Florio another "pellegrino d'amore" (V.20) [pilgrim of love], is moving in the wrong direction. Deriving Idalagos's name from ιδη (forest), Crescini interprets it to mean inhabitant of the forest.[50] The forest which Caleone converts into a garden-city symbolizes animal-like living ruled by appetite.[51] Idalagos inhabits the forest of appetite, not the city of reason, and his metamorphosis into a tree reverses Caleone's conversion of the forest dwellers to rational city folk.

The pine tree, which Idalagos says represents his state, is particularly significant, for it is associated throughout medieval literature with concupiscence. A pine grows above Narcissus's well in the *Roman de la Rose*. Phyllis and Flora sit by a pine tree debating on the relative merits of clerics and soldiers in an anonymous twelfth-century poem ("Anni parte florida, celo puriore"). The same debate takes place in Old French between Florance and Blanchefleur, who seek out Cupid's palace and dismount there under a pine.[52] In the *Teseida* Venus's temple is surrounded by pines (VII.50) because, as Boccaccio's gloss explains, doctors say that the fruit of the pine is aphrodisiac. Arcita in the *Teseida* lies under a pine tree dreaming of Emilia, and Emilia later gives Palemon, Venus's protégé, a shield with a pine tree painted on it. Idalagos, imprisoned in his pine tree by Venus, suffers from desires to which he has yielded completely. He is trapped by his own passion, and the immobility that comes with his new shape ("mi sentii non potermi avanti mutare" V.8) is an outward manifestation of his soul's despondency.

A dismal set of allusions accompanies his transformation, for Boccaccio borrows several lines from the scene of Piero della Vigna in *Inferno* XIII and mentions Polydorus from *Aeneid* III.[53] Like Polydorus, Idalagos has been betrayed by someone that he trusted, and like Piero he has caused his own destruction by despair, "in tribulazione disperato rimasi" (V.8). Ironically, he claims that his evergreen needles illustrate a never-dying hope. Nonetheless, in concluding bitterly he offers himself as an example of "quanta poca fede le mondane cose servino agli speranti, e massimamente le femine" [how little faith worldly things hold for those who hope in them, and especially women]. Biancifiore hastens to correct his anti-feminist pessimism by her own example.

Now Idalagos is not only an unfortunate lover, he is also a poet; and through him Boccaccio raises the issue of poetry's powers to persuade for good or evil. Idalagos's tale really begins with the story of his father, who piped his songs in order to seduce the French princess. Cupid, descended from Parnassus, inspired him to play better and better in order to please his lady (V.8.8). Finally Eucomos exchanged the piping, by which he had literally led her astray, for words which lied to her, falsely pledging fidelity. Eucomos, then, is the Ovidian seducer-poet par excellence. Opposed to him, in one more pair of terms, stands Calmeta who, using the same instrument ("sampogna"), describes the movements of the heavens, a subject matter which Boccaccio uses repeatedly to represent the lofty poetry of those who are wise as well as eloquent.[54] He is the Dantean poet, singer of heavenly things.

Idalagos, the son of one, becomes a pupil of the other. Inspired by Calmeta, he tries for a while to follow wisdom ("seguitar Pallade") but, subverted by love as his father had been,

> abandonate le imprese cose, cominciai a disiderare, sotto la nuova signoria, di sapere quanto l'ornate parole avessero forza di muovere i cuori umani: e seguendo la silvestre fagiana, con pietoso stile quelle lungamente usai, con molte altre cose utili e necessarie a terminare tali disii (V.8.36)

> [having abandoned the things which I had undertaken, I began to desire, under a new lord, to know how much force ornate words might have to move human hearts: and following the pheasant of the woods, I used those words for a long time with a

pity-seeking style, with many other things useful and necessary for bringing such desires to their end].

Quaglio, relating Idalagos's story to Boccaccio's life, glosses "le imprese cose" [the things undertaken] as "Forse, la mercatura"[55] [perhaps the commercial trade]; but the allusion is undoubtedly to the studies necessary for true, wise poetry.

Possibly the lines imitate Dante's letter to Moroello. Having fallen in love, Dante changes his manner of writing, for Amor "Occidit ergo propositum illud laudabile, quo a mulieribus suisque cantibus abstinebam, ac meditationes assiduas quibus tam coelestia quam terrestria intuebar, quasi suspectas, impie relegavit" [killed then that laudable proposal, that I abstain from women and their songs; and the attentive meditations by which I was contemplating heavenly as well as earthly things, as if suspect, he impiously put away]. Similarly Idalagos has ceased using poetry as a means to wisdom and has turned instead to the use of its sweetness as a means of seduction. Whereas Eucomos was successful in deceiving, Idalagos is himself deceived by his lady. His example combines a warning about love with a warning about literature. Toying with the power of words to persuade the heart, Idalagos creates illusions which trap him in the end.

Idalagos has clearly made a number of wrong choices and is paying for them. Not only is his lady in a sort of hell, but Idalagos's own imprisonment in a tree is linked to the sufferings of suicides in Dante's *Inferno*. One might note that Piero della Vigna was a writer too, who used his pen to advocate a quasi-religious cult of the emperor Frederick. Perhaps, then, we are dealing in both these cases with the rhetoric of false religions, Cupid in the *Filocolo* in this case being the rival to Christ.[56] Now Boccaccio, like Idalagos, had in fact made the journey from Certaldo to Naples, the region of Ovid, and his narrator presents himself as a lover writing to win his lady, which was exactly Idalagos's goal. The narrator's Fiammetta, however, is a Maria, not a backwards version. Moreover, although she is an inhabitant of Naples, she is the daughter of King Robert, who is praised as having converted his kingdom from the worship of Priapus to that of Astrea. If Fiammetta's role is similar to that of the Maria for whom she is named, then she is a mediator between human and divine love and, like her father, offers restoration from the fall of Eve. We cannot, then, identify the narrator entirely with the mistaken love of Idalagos. On the other hand, we cannot identify him too closely with Caleone either, although some scholars have seen in Caleone's words the expression of Boccaccio's own passion.[57] Ca-

leone is shown at the end as happily freed from passion; and although this
is what his Fiammetta had urged, it is hardly appropriate to the narrator's
efforts at writing as an act of love. The narrator, in sum, seems to belong
to neither of these alternatives, destructive love or the rejection of love.
Rather he can be more closely related to his chosen hero, Florio, especially
as regards his final comments on his models as a writer.

Despite the epic elements scattered throughout the book and despite
the highly inflated rhetoric, the narrator classifies his work finally (V.97) as
belonging to the low style, in prose and in the vernacular language which
Dante had labeled appropriate for writing to women about love. The narrator lists Vergil, Lucan, and Statius as authors unlike himself. The two
writers whom he does claim to follow are Ovid, "delle cui opere tu se' confortatore" [of whose works you are the comforter], and Dante, "il quale
tu sì come piccolo servidore molto dei reverente seguire" [whom you, like
a little servant, must follow very reverently]. Dante is really set in both
classes at once, a model for Boccaccio to imitate humbly and also one of
the authors who deserve much more honor and readers of more excellent
intellect. Although Dante too wrote of love and in Italian, the narrator
begs that his prose not be compared to Dante's measured verses.[58] Only
Ovid, then, is left as really close to the narrator's style. Yet while the narrator says to his book, "a te è assai solamente piacere alla tua donna" [for
you it is sufficient only to please your lady], he adds: "E a' contradicenti le
tue piacevoli cose, dà la lunga fatica di Ilario per veridico testimonio" [and
to those who speak against your pleasant things, give the long labor of Ilario as a witness of the truth]. On the one hand this is, for the lover, a mere
pretense of historicity to justify his amatory subject.[59] On the other hand it
is also a reminder to the reader that there are several viewpoints from
which to read the text. The puzzling phrase "confortatore" of Ovid's works
may mean that Boccaccio, like Dante, is turning love stories to an ultimately Christian use, thus "saving" the pleasures of Ovid's poetry in both
senses of the word: preserving them and transforming them for Christian
readers.[60]

One can understand this attempt better in the light of a similar attempt by Dante. Battaglia, comparing Dante's first-person narrator with
Augustine's, has noted that whereas Augustine felt obliged by his conversion to reject Vergil's poetry as a pagan distraction from the Christian
truth,[61] Dante, imitating Augustine's intellectual process with his own
journey from the state of misery to the state of grace, reinstated Vergil as a
prophetic teacher within the Christian providential scheme.[62] Vergil's guid-

ing power is appropriately limited, as one who cannot know the whole truth; nonetheless he leads at least in the right direction, toward faith, not away from it as Augustine had feared. Thus Statius can even say dramatically to Vergil, "Per te cristiano" [through you (I became) a Christian] (*Purg.* XXII.73).

Similarly Boccaccio gives Ovid a limited place within a larger Christian context, in this way allowing the sweetness of his poetry to be imitated while alerting the reader clearly to the ways in which the ancient masters have been surpassed by the newer Christian knowledge. The love Ovid teaches becomes a step toward, not away from, Christian love. Thus Florio and Biancifiore, who fall in love over Ovid's text, marry instead of having an affair and even add to their human love a new Christian zeal. Thus too the image of Biancifiore can appear to Florio within a vision of the seven virtues and the gift of grace. Thus too Florio's romance and rescue can be seen as an analogy—though not an outright allegory—for Christ's love and salvation of man.[63]

The use of human love to lead toward divine love was, of course, already Dante's idea. It is Dante's "antica fiamma" for Beatrice which motivates his ascent of the Purgatorial mountain; and ironically, Vergil can hold out Beatrice as the lure that draws Dante through the flames which purge lust. Boccaccio will imitate this aspect of the *Commedia* even more clearly in his *Amorosa Visione*, where the Vergil-like guide uses the narrator's erring love as a means to entice him to make the ascent toward heaven. The radical act on Boccaccio's part is to try to rescue Ovid's *Ars amatoria* as the text which will serve him the way the *Aeneid* served Dante; it takes the place of Dante's reference to Dido.

The lesson Florio learns from his vision in Book IV is that one must "conoscere e le mondane cose e le divine . . . e quelle amare ciascuna secondo il dovere" (IV.74.17) [to know both worldly and divine things . . . and to love each of them according to its due]. The lesson is not that worldly things are to be rejected, but that they are to be loved appropriately within the perspective of the Christian religion. The narrator can attempt to educate his audience without alienating them or appearing presumptuous to his superiors by suggesting that it is he himself who, like Florio, needs educating[64] and that his audience, summed up in the noble Fiammetta, is able to teach him.

III

Teseida

The *Teseida* is not only Fiammetta's next appearance, but it is also, like the *Filocolo*, an epic addressed to her and dealing with a love that ends in marriage. Having in the *Filocolo* developed an elaborate presentation of Fiammetta—including her background and her speeches as a character in the book—Boccaccio does very little with her in his next major work. She is addressed in a separate preface as the recipient of the *Teseida*, but given almost no description either of background or of her own person and excluded altogether from the narrative. Indeed, if not for Boccaccio's naming her in the preface, we would have little reason to think this book addressed to the same woman as before. He does, however, state that he is writing for her as he has done in the past, a story of the kind that previously pleased her:

> ricordandomi che ne' dì più felici che lunghi io vi sentii vaga d'udire e tal volta di leggere una e altra istoria, e massimamente l'amorose, . . . come volonteroso servidore, il quale non solamente il comandamento aspetta dal suo maggiore, ma quello, operando quelle cose che crede che piacciano, previene, trovata una antichissima istoria . . . in latino volgare e per rima, acciò che più diletasse, e massimamente a voi che già con sommo titolo le mie esaltaste, con quella sollecitudine che conceduta mi fu da l'altre più gravi, disiderando di piacervi, ho ridotta (p. 246)

> [recalling that in those days more happy than long I perceived that you desire to hear and sometimes to read one or another

story, and especially ones about love, . . . as a willing servant, who not only awaits his superior's command but anticipates it, doing those things which he believes will please, . . . desiring to please you with all the solicitude allowed me by other graver cares, I, having found an ancient story, turned it into the Latin vernacular and into rhyme, so that it might be more delightful, and especially to you who previously exalted my stories with highest title].

This time the narrator has chosen the story himself. It is possible, then, that he and Fiammetta may have different views on what this story indicates for its reader. For, unlike the *Filocolo* preface, the preface to the *Teseida* does not state any clearly Christian intention. The narrator's assertion that his book is written with "chiuso parlare" [closed (or secret) speech]—although true in a number of ways [1]—seems to refer for the narrator only to his concealment of his own love history in the tale, a ruse necessary to "coprire ciò che *non è onesto* manifestare" (p. 247, my emph.) [cover what it is not honest to reveal]. The implication here is quite different from the religious implications of the *Filocolo* introduction. The narrator's hope that his book will be held "in quelle dilicate mani nelle quali io più non oso venire" [in those delicate hands into which I no longer dare to come] sounds much like the narrator's wish at the *end* of the *Filocolo* and suggests a similarly erotic attitude. [2] Here that attitude is counterbalanced not by the introduction of a second and religious "author" but by the definition of Fiammetta as a reader of exceptional intelligence who may be able to open up more closed meanings than the narrator expects.

> E che ella da me per voi sia compilata, due cose fra l'altre il manifestano. L'una si è che ciò che sotto il nome dell'uno de' due amanti e della giovane amata si conta essere stato, ricordandovi bene, e io a voi di me e voi a me di voi, se non mentiste, potreste conoscere essere stato detto e fatto in parte. . . . L'altra si è il non avere cessata né storia né favola né chiuso parlare in altra guisa, con ciò sia cosa che le donne sì come poco intelligenti ne sogliano essere schife, ma però che per intelletto e notizia delle cose predette voi della turba dell'altre separata conosco, libero mi concessi il porle a mio piacere. (pp. 246–47)

[And that it was composed by me for you, two things among others make clear. One is that what is recounted as being under the name of one of the two lovers and the beloved girl, if you

remember well, you would be able to recognize as having in part
been said and done to you by me and to me by you, unless you
were lying. . . . The other is that I have not held back either history or fable or closed speech in any way, since women, being of
little intelligence, are usually bored by them; but because I know
you to be separate from the crowd by your understanding and
knowledge of things, I put them in as freely as I pleased.]

One obvious question is to what extent it is helpful for reading the *Teseida*
to know about Fiammetta's character and role in the earlier work. My conclusion is, briefly, that although it is not necessary to transfer any information about her from the *Filocolo*, nonetheless her previous role additionally
supports my interpretation of her situation here.

The narrator's remarks tell the reader nothing about who Fiammetta
might be historically. From the manner in which the poet addresses her, we
can assume that Fiammetta has a higher social rank than he, as consistent
with the situation established in the *Filocolo* and with the lover-poet tradition in general.[3] However, she is neither named Maria nor associated with
either King Robert or the Aquinas family as in other writings. We know
only that she once seemed to favor the poet's attentions "e già fece contenti
con gli atti suoi gran parte de'nostri ferventi disii" [and once made content
with her actions a large part of our fervent desires] and now has turned
from pleasing to angry, "di piacevole sdegnosa siate tornata" (Proemio).

The situation calls for a specific rhetorical response, and the letter to
her neatly follows the advice in the *Rhetorica ad Herennium* and Cicero's
De inventione. The audience is hostile; therefore the case is a "difficult"
one. The purpose is "conquestio" or the arousal of pity.[4] Cicero suggests
that such a plea begin with a commonplace about the general weakness of
humanity, so that the auditor, considering his own weakness, may be disposed to pity; he suggests secondly that the speaker contrast his past pros-
perity with his present plight. He goes on to advise a detailed description
of misfortunes, followed by a complaint that they have come contrary to all
expectation, from someone who ought to have behaved differently, and
that the speaker is helpless, alone, and undeserving of his troubles. He advises finally that the speaker declare his patience in suffering and entreat
humbly for mercy. Boccaccio pulls every one of these stops.

Boccaccio begins according to Cicero's recipe with a familiar topos:
"Come che a memoria tornandomi le felicità trapassate, nella miseria ve-
dendomi dov'io sono, mi sieno di grave dolore manifesta cagione, . . ."
[Although recalling to memory the past happinesses, seeing myself in the

misery in which I am, is evident cause to me of great pain]. Once again Boccaccio is borrowing terms from Dante in order to address his beloved; this time, however, he is not using Dante's love for Beatrice as his source. Instead, the line is taken from the beginning of Francesca's speech in *Inferno* V. Thus Boccaccio is identifying himself with a famous lover damned for her love.[5] In short, the letter not only is highly rhetorical, a feature which Billanovich takes as evidence of its untruth,[6] but also has the effect of separating the real poet from the poet-lover by presenting the latter in a critical light. Francesca's will was overwhelmed by passion when she read the romantic adventures of Lancelot. Boccaccio now sends another book of romantic adventures to Fiammetta in hopes of arousing a similar passion in her "sdegnosa" heart.

Although the *Teseida*, which is much more tightly unified than the *Filocolo*, does not directly concern itself with Fiammetta's actions, nonetheless, as in the *Filostrato*, the poet claims to have chosen the ancient story as a veiled way of writing about his own love for Fiammetta. Thus the epic, in one sense complete within itself quite apart from the story of the poet and Fiammetta, is in another sense a clue to our reading of that other story, the poet's love. Conversely, the framing narrative may offer information about how to read the epic, for the framework sets up a poet and a reader within the fiction. In the beginning the poet is allowed a few words about his intentions; at the end we will find, more briefly, the reader's response. We need to understand what the poet thinks his work is telling Fiammetta, what she may understand it to mean as far as we can surmise, and whether or not the poet is aware of its full message. In the meantime we can begin by investigating for ourselves what the epic is saying apart from its frame.

Both Vergil's *Aeneid* and Statius's *Thebaid*, which Boccaccio used as models for his epic, were read in the medieval schools as moral allegories; so it is not surprising that Boccaccio should have chosen to imitate them in this regard as well as in others. Boccaccio himself offers a reading of the fourth book of the *Aeneid* in his *Genealogia* (XIV.13), declaring that Vergil's purpose

quod sub velamento latet poetico, intendit Virgilius per totum opus ostendere quibus passionibus humana fragilitas infestetur, et quibus viribus a costanti viro superentur. Et cum iam non nullas ostendisset, volens demonstrare quibus ex causis ab appetitu concupiscibili in lasciviam rapiamur. . . . Et sic intendit pro Dydone concupiscibilem et attractivam potentiam, oportunitatibus

omnibus armatam. Eneam autem pro quocunque ad lubricum
apto et demum capto. Tandem ostenso quo trahamur in scelus
ludibrio, qua via in virtutem revehamur ostendit, inducens Mer-
curium, deorum interpretem, Eneam ab illecebra increpantem
atque ad gloriosa exhortantem. Per quem Virgilius sentit seu
conscientie propriae morsum, seu amici et eloquentis hominis re-
dargutionem a quibus dormientes, in luto turpitudinem, excita-
mur, et in rectum pulchrumque revocamur iter, id est ad gloriam.
Et tunc nexum oblectationis infaustae soluimus quando, armati
fortitudine, blanditias, lacrimas, preces, et huius modi in contrarium trahentes, constanti animo spernimus, ac vilipendentes
omittimus

[concealed within a poetic veil, was to show with what passions
human frailty is infested, and the strength with which a steady
man subdues them. Having illustrated some of these, he wished
particularly to demonstrate the reasons why we are carried away
into wanton behavior by the passion of concupiscence. . . . So he
represents in Dido the attracting power of the passion of love,
prepared for every opportunity, and in Aeneas one who is readily
disposed in that way and at length overcome. But after showing
the enticements of lust, he points the way of return to virtue by
bringing in Mercury, messenger of the gods, to rebuke Aeneas,
and call him back from such indulgence to deeds of glory. By
Mercury, Vergil means either the remorse, or the reproof of some
outspoken friend, either of which rouses us from slumber in the
mire of turpitude, and calls us back to the fair and even path to
glory. Then we burst the bonds of unholy delight, and, armed
with new fortitude, we unfalteringly spurn all seductive flattery,
and tears, prayers, and such, and abandon them as naught].

Here we find Boccaccio interpreting allegorically a scene which he will imitate in the *Teseida* (II.3–7).

Padoan has pointed out that the *Thebaid* as well as the *Aeneid* was
subject to allegorical readings. The commentary by "sancto Fulgencius
episcopus" derives Theseus from "theos" and explains his war with Creon
as "quando humilitate docetur a deo vinci superbia; . . . tanto autem
vitiorum conflictu Thebe, id est humana anima quassata est quidem, sed
divine benignitatis clementia subveniente liberatur" [when pride is taught
by God to be overcome by humility; . . . moreover the great conflict of

vices at Thebes, that is the human soul torn by them (vices); but it is freed by the intervening mercy of divine goodness].[7] Bernard's *Commentum super sex libros Eneidos* (VI) also derives Theseus from "theos enim deus, eu bonus. Per hunc intelligimus rationalem et virtuosum"[8] [for *theos* is god, *eu* good. Through this we understand the rational and virtuous man]. Padoan's article is an intriguing effort to explain Dante's christianizing of Statius; but it is equally helpful for a reading of the *Teseida*. Indeed, ever since Prudentius, the Christian attempt to write epic seems to have required allegory, a spiritual heroism and an inward-turned meaning of external events.

Within the twelve books of the *Teseida*, Boccaccio has carefully shaped the pattern of events. The full title includes the word "nozze" [wedding], and the poem deals with marriages at both the beginning and end. Book I begins with the violation of marriage, the story, told by Statius, of how the Amazon women murdered their husbands and established a female regime in which marriage was outlawed. Boccaccio describes their action consistently as "follia" and "crudeltà" [madness, cruelty].

Ipolita is allowed a stirring speech to her women in which she says:

> per voler virile animo mostrare,
> contro a Cupido avete presa guerra,
> e quel ch'a l'altra più piace fuggite,
> uomini fatti, non femine ardite. (I.24)
>
> . . . a servitù vi dilibraste;
>   . . .
> cacciando ogni atto feminil da voi. (I.25)
>
> Non fa mal que' che s'aiuta
> per raver libertà, se l'ha perduta (I.27)

[to show a virile spirit you have made war against Cupid, you flee from that which most pleases another woman, having become not fearless women but men. . . . you have liberated yourselves from slavery; . . . chasing from you every feminine action. . . . He does no ill who helps himself to regain liberty if he has lost it].

The appeal to liberty is strongly persuasive, but Boccaccio omits Statius's account of the men's neglect of their role of husband, an account which would have added some justification to the women's action. The Amazons' desire to deny their female nature and make themselves men is futile. Their liberation has not only been achieved through cruel means but is also in itself a "dismisura" (13) [excess], which Teseo compares to the giants' revolt against Jove. The insurrection is thus seen as an act of pride and over-stepping, and Teseo writes to Ipolita that he has come to put down her pride as well as to avenge their killings.

Marriage was commonly an emblem for the proper hierarchic order-ing of the soul, the government of the appetites and passions by reason. This, for example, is how the *Glossa Ordinaria* interprets Adam and Eve, their fall being an upsetting of that governing order. Boccaccio himself was to make use of this idea several times in the *Decameron*,[9] and in the *Ge-nealogia* he interprets Pasiphae as a woman passionate beyond the ability of her husband Minos, i.e., human reason, to control (IV.10).[10] Very similar is Boccaccio's own *Corbaccio*, in which the dead husband and the widow rep-resent reason and lust.[11] In this light the insurrection of the Amazons can be interpreted as an insurrection of the passions against the control of rea-son. Ipolita herself acknowledges that the gods have sided with Teseo (116–17), who as ruler of Athena's city is a perfect figure for the governing wisdom. Boccaccio underlines the point by explaining in his gloss to I.60 that the ancients considered Minerva the goddess of wisdom and honored her in Athens above all other gods.

Book I ends with a restoration of proper order. The Amazons change their dress and reappear happily as women. Ipolita marries Teseo and many of her women marry other Greeks. The temple of Venus is reopened and Imeneo assists at the marriages, to the satisfaction of the women as well as of the men.[12]

The moral problem is not securely solved forever by these marriages. Alertness is required even by Teseo lest he yield up too easily his responsi-bilities of government. In the beginning of Book II he is in danger of sub-jecting himself to the love of a woman, like Hercules or Aeneas, and is re-proached by a heavenly messenger:

E stando entra la turba feminile,
la tua prodezza, la qual già sapeva
ciaschedun regno, hai messo in oblio
d'Ipolita nel grembo e nel disio? (II.5)

[And lingering among the female throng, / have you forgotten your valor, / which once every kingdom knew, / in the lap and desire of Ipolita?]

Here is an imitation of the passage from Vergil that we have seen allegorically interpreted by Boccaccio himself. Teseo realizes that the message must have come from some god who is charitably watching over his honor (II.7). The danger is clearly from within, as this brief episode reminds us, and the proper government of one's soul requires constant effort.

Book I in several ways sums up the epic as a whole. It begins with violence and ends with marriage. It begins with a revolt by the passions against the government of reason and ends with a restoration of the proper order. It begins with women who have dedicated themselves to Diana and ends with their entering the temple of Venus for a wedding ceremony.

Book I also forms a pair with Book II. Both books begin with the report of a disruption and the decision of Teseo to set things right. In Book II, as in Book I, the disruption is described as an act of cruelty and pride which Teseo again promises to put down (II.38.61).[13] Moreover, although this is not immediately evident, Creon's crime is, like the crime in Book I, an offense against Juno, for he has forbidden wives to bury their husbands and it is these wives who appeal to Teseo for help. Arcita and Palemon complain throughout the epic that Juno has always held a special grudge against Thebes because of Jove's adulteries with Semele and Alceste (e.g., III.66; IV.16–17). Thus the curse on Thebes results at least partly from broken marriage vows and manifests itself in Creon's interruption of the wives' final duties.

III.1 starts "Poi che alquanto il furor di Iunone / fu per Tebe distrutta temperato" [when the anger of Juno had been somewhat tempered by the destruction of Thebes] and includes a gloss explaining Juno's long hatred of the Thebans. Significantly, when Arcita has died, Palemon builds a temple to Juno on the site of his pyre (XI.69); and when Palemon has married Emilia, Juno is invoked to bless the wedding chamber. The enmity of Juno (as in the *Filocolo*) is an echo from the *Aeneid*, which also tells about the rivalry of two men for a bride. Whereas Vergil ends with the promise of a marriage to follow Turnus's death, Boccaccio includes the marriage as the final book of his epic.

Books I and II as a pair balance Books XI and XII in a kind of chiasmus. In I we find marriage forbidden; in XII we find marriage celebrated, even by a former Amazon. In II funeral rites are forbidden in Thebes; XI is entirely devoted to the funeral of the Theban Arcita. Thus Books XII and XI describe in detail the elaborate rites and ceremonies denied altogether in Books I and II. The forms prescribed by society to contain human life and death reassert their functions in the maintenance of social order. And this social order represents by analogy the reestablishment of psychic order as well. Whereas the initial transgressions take place in Scythia and Thebes,[14] the reestablished rites are performed in Athens with Wisdom's king in charge.

Within this framework unfolds the tale of Palemon and Arcita. Besides being noble youths from Thebes, these two characters are identified with the two passions, concupiscence and irascibility. The announced themes of love and war are an externalization or a kind of metonymy for the theme of these two passions. Both are socialized by Teseo: *ira* in the tournament and *concupiscentia* in marriage; the ceremonies of burial and wedding are their results. Boccaccio himself provides the glosses to the temples of Mars and Venus where Arcita and Palemon respectively worship:[15] "è da sapere che come di sopra, dicendo Marte consistere nello appetito irascibile, così Venere nel concupiscibile" (VII.50) [it is to be known, as above, that as we said Mars consists in the irascible appetite, so Venus consists in the concupiscible]. There is other evidence for their identification as well. When Arcita and Palemon appear at the tournament, Arcita is compared to a lion (VII.115) and Palemon to a boar (VII.119). Statius's *Thebaid* recounts in Book I how Tydeus and Polynices met, one wearing a boar skin and the other a lion skin, thus fulfilling the prophecy of Adrastus. Helpfully, Boccaccio explains in his *Genealogia* XIII.1 that the lion symbolizes *ira* and the boar *concupiscentia*. These identifications undoubtedly derive from Boethius's *Consolation of Philosophy* IV.prose 3: "Irae intemperans fremit? Leonis animum gestare credatur. . . . Foedis inmundisque libidinibus immergitur? Sordidae suis voluptate detinetur."[16] [The man who is ruled by intemperate anger is thought to have the soul of a lion. . . . the man who is sunk in foul lust is trapped in the pleasures of a filthy sow.]

Teseo as tempering reason seeks to govern the passions properly, not to do away with them. Boccaccio's interpretation of Admeto's chariot with its yoked boar and lion (*Gen.* XIII.1) comes very close to Plato's image of the charioteer:

Admetus anima rationalis est, cui tunc Alchista, id est virtus, nam alce Grece, Latine virtus, iungitur, dum a leone et apro, id est ab appetitu irascibili et concupiscibili currus eius, id est vita qui circumitionibus consumatur, trahitur, id est agitatur. Virtus enim non ob aliud iungitur, nisi ut ab ea passiones frenentur, et sic pro salute anime adversus passiones virtus se ipsam opponit.

[Admetus is the rational soul, to whom then is joined Alchista, that is virtue, for "alce" in Greek is "virtus" in Latin, while by a lion and a boar, that is by the irascible and concupiscible appetites, his chariot, that is the life which is consumed as it rolls along, is drawn, that is, is stirred. For virtue is joined (to it) for no other purpose than that by her the passions may be reined in, and thus for the safety of the soul virtue opposes herself to the passions.]

Although the *Phaidros* was unknown to Boccaccio and his contemporaries, the notion of the passions as animals to be driven or ridden was common;[17] Bernard Silvester even mentions Plato in this context: "Unde Plato et alii philosophi cum de anima et de alio theologico aliquid dicunt ad integumenta se convertunt, ut Maro in hoc opere. FRENA revocamina. STIMULOS incitamenta."[18] [Whence Plato and other philosophers, when they talk about the soul or other theological matters, turn to (fictive) coverings, as Maro in this work. REINS what holds us back. SPURS what urges us on.] The important thing is to guide and restrain the passions, which have a necessary function in the soul.

The *Genealogia* provides not only a myth of the two passions as yoked animals but also a tale about Theseus as a master over passion in its wildest state (IV.10). Pasiphae, a beautiful woman, marries Minos or human reason "que suis legibus eam habet regere atque in rectum iter dirigere. Huic inimicatur Venus, id est appetitus concupiscibilis, qui sensualitati adherens semper rationis est hostis" [who ought to rule her with his laws and direct her on the right way. Venus is his enemy, that is the concupiscible appetite, which always adhering to sensuality is the enemy of reason]. The bull, dedicated to Jupiter but loved by Pasiphae, is

mundi huius delitias prima facie pulchras et delectabiles a Deo rationi concessas, ut ex eius moderamine certo vite nostre oportuna ministret; nam dum his debite utimur, rite ex eis Deo sacrum conficimus; sane dum eis iudicium sensualitatis sequentes abutimur aut abuti desideramus, in bestialem concupiscentiam devenimus

[the delights of this world, beautiful and delightful at first glance and granted to the reason by God so that from them, with a certain moderation, it may provide the things necessary for our life; for while we use them properly, we duly effect with them the

sacrifice to God; but while we abuse or wish to abuse them following the judgment of the senses, we fall into bestial concupiscence].

The Minotaur is this vice of bestiality, and the labyrinth in which he lives is
the human breast "infandis desideriis intricato"[19] [tangled with unspeak-
able desires].

Teseo, representing the governing reason, both marries and fights
wars; but lust and wrath, as opposed by Boccaccio to married love and
righteous anger, are both classified as "furore."[20] Boccaccio's gloss to the
Temple of Venus (VII.50) distinguishes between the legitimate Venus of
marriages and the illegitimate Venus of lust, fornication, and adultery. Teseo
marries Ipolita in a temple of the legitimate Venus at the end of Book I.
Similarly, although Boccaccio does not mention a legitimate Mars in his
gloss to VII.30, the Temple of Mars in which Teseo celebrates his victory
over Creon at the end of Book II is clearly a temple of righteous anger.[21]
The Temple of Mars in which Arcita worships is under clouds to demonstrate that wrath darkens the counsel of reason, signified by the rays of the
sun, which are reflected away from the temple (VII.30 gloss).

Although Arcita seeks the patronage of Mars and Palemon of Venus,
nonetheless the two overlap to some extent; for lust and anger are closely
allied and equally destructive. The falling in love of Arcita and Palemon is
described as a serpent's bite which slowly swells the entire body with poison (cf. *Elegia* I). Like the crimes in Books I and II it is evidently "dismisura." It is also "furore"; for rivalry in love leads to wrath. Tesifone, the
same fury that in association with Venus impels Fiammetta in the *Elegia* to
self-destruction, in the *Teseida* (V.13) arouses strife between the two youths,
as between the brothers in the *Thebaid*.

> E sì come Tesifone, chiamata
> dal cieco Edippo nella oscura parte
> dov'elli lunga notte avea menata,
> a'due fratei del regno con su'arte
> mise l'arsura, così a lui [Arcita] 'ntrata
> con quel velen che'l suo valor comparte,
> d'Emilia aver, dicendo, "Signoria
> né amore stan ben con compagnia."[22]

[And just as Tesiphone, called / by blind Oedipus in the dark
place / where he had led a lengthy night, / set fire to the two
brothers of the kingdom with her art, / so to him (Arcita) she

entered / with that poison which spreads her power, / (wanting) to have Emilia, saying, "Neither lordship / nor love go well with company."]

In his commentary on *Inferno* IX, Boccaccio cites Fulgentius's derivation of Tesifone from Tritonphones or voice of wrath. In the *Genealogia* III.6–8 he repeats the derivation and interprets the Furies as perturbations of the mind, born from Night or mental blindness, and rejecting reason. When Arcita's horse, startled by another fury summoned by Venus, plunges out of control and crushes him, it is not difficult to interpret the cause of his death as uncontrolled passion.[23] Arcita is implicitly compared to Turnus,[24] to whom a fury brings the augury of his imminent doom. That fury was sent by Jupiter, because Aeneas's imperial destiny demanded Turnus's defeat. Arcita's fury is sent by Venus because it is love which has brought him to his end.[25] The appearance of furies to both Theban knights makes clear the "furore" of their love as opposed to the rational implications of Athens and its king. One comment by Macrobius would serve well as a gloss to the *Teseida*'s plot:

> motus enim eius [animae] est quicquid irascimur et in fervorem mutuae collisionis armamur, unde de paulatim procedens rabies fluctuat praeliorum, motus est quod in desideria rapimur, quod cupiditatibus alligamur, sed hi motus si ratione gubernentur proveniunt salutares, si destituantur, in praeceps et rapiuntur et rapiunt (II.xvi.25)

> [for its (the soul's) motion is whenever we become angry and take arms in the heat of mutual antagonism, whence, proceeding little by little, the madness of battles tosses us; its motion is that we are seized by desire, bound by cupidities, but if these motions are governed by reason they lead to health, if they are left alone they are carried away and carry us away headlong].

The "praeceps" becomes literal in Arcita's fall.

In their prison, peering out through the little window at Emilia, the two knights are emblematic of the passions in the body stirred by something pleasant transmitted through the eye. The epic model for passions imprisoned in the body is no less than the *Aeneid* VI.733–34, where Anchises explains to Aeneas the life of the soul in the body:

> hinc metuunt cupiuntque, dolent gaudentque, neque auras
> dispiciunt clausae tenebris et carcere caeco

[here they fear and desire, grieve and rejoice, nor do they catch sight of the sky, shut in darkness and in a blind prison].

The bodies stained with passions must suffer purgation in Hades. Scipio in the *Somnium Scipionis* also talks about the prison of the body and the life after death: "hi vivunt, qui e corporum vinclis tamen a carcere, evolaverunt"[26] [these live who have escaped from the bonds of the body as from a prison]. Macrobius comments that the prison of the body with its binding passions is like hell itself: "aliud esse inferos negaverunt quam ipsa corpora, quibus inclusae animae carcerem foedum tenebris horridum sordibus et cruore patiuntur" (I.10.9) [they say hell is nothing other than the body itself, in which the enclosed soul suffers in a filthy prison horrible with darkness, dirt, and blood].

Boccaccio, in the *Genealogia* I.14, elaborates the identification of hell with the passions:

Circuitur seu inundatur Herebus a quattuor fluminibus, ut per hoc sentiamus, quia hi qui se ratione deiecta ab inceptis concupiscentiis trahi permittunt, primo recti iudicii perturbata letitia Acherontem transeunt, qui carens gaudio interpretatur, et sic pulsa letitia ut eius occupet mestitia locum necesse est, ex qua ob bonum letitie perditum persepe vehemens nascitur ira, a qua in furorem impellimur, qui Flegeton est, id est ardens, ex furore etiam in tristitiam labimur, que Stix est, et ex tristitia in luctum et lacrimas, per quas Cocitus accipiendus est quartus Inferni fluvius. Et sic miseri mortales angimur ceca concupiscibilis appetitus opinione seducti, intraque gerimus quod in visceribus terre a poetis stolidi arbitrantur inclusum.

[Erebus is surrounded or flooded by four rivers, by which we may understand that those who, throwing down reason, permit themselves to be dragged by concupiscences which have started up, the happiness of right judgment being disturbed, first cross the Acheron, which means "lacking joy," and as joy has been driven out it is necessary that sorrow take its place, whence on account of the loss of joy vehement wrath often arises, by which we are driven into madness, which is Phlegethon, that is "burning," and from madness we fall into sadness, which is Stix, and from sadness into deep grief and tears, which is to be understood by Cocytus, the fourth river of Hell. And thus we wretched mortals are troubled, seduced by the blind opinion of the concupis-

cible appetite, and we bear within us what the foolish think has
been shut by the poets into the bowels of the earth.]

Arcita, demonstrating all the well-known symptoms of love, looks like a
creature from hell (IV.29).

For both young men love is a religion with Emilia as its goddess.
Their cult, however, is by no means Boccaccio's own ennobling of love.
The temple of Venus, both text and gloss, makes manifest what kind of love
this is.[27] The temple is made of copper, explains Boccaccio, because it looks
like gold and is a base metal. The inner sanctum where Venus lies is
guarded by Ricchezza. Her lying down signifies the idleness of the lustful.
She holds in her hand the apple of discord that Paris awarded her in order
to demonstrate the foolish choice of those who prefer such a life to every
other. Boccaccio sketches briefly the story of the apple and how the judgment of Paris brought about the downfall of Troy.[28] In the temple Gentilezza is accompanied by Van Diletto [empty pleasure], and Cortesia is
"smarrita in tutto" [completely lost].

> E in quel vide Priapo tenere
> più sommo luogo, in abito tal quale
> chiunque il volle la notte vedere
> potè quando ragghiando l'animale
> più pigro destò Vesta, che'n calere
> non poco gli era e'nver di cui cotale
> andava. (VII.60)

> [And he saw therein Priapus hold / the highest place, dressed the
> way / anyone could have seen him who wanted to on the night /
> when the lazy beast with its braying / woke Vesta, for whom he
> cared / not a little and toward whom he was heading.]

Boccaccio's gloss explains the story and adds: "e vuole per questo dise-
gnare quale sia la cagione alle femine da amare, con ciò sia cosa ch'egli nel
descrivere della forma di Venere mostri l'affezione degli uomini" [and he
wants by this to describe what is the cause of women's love, just as in describing the form of Venus he shows the affections of men]. Palemon's solemn devotions are rendered ridiculous by the setting.

His prayer itself is humorous, though not to his own ears. He addresses the "bella dea, del buon Vulcano sposa" [beautiful goddess, wife of
good Vulcan], praying to her by the love which she bore for Adonis
(VII.43).[29] As Boccaccio's gloss distinguishes between the Venus of cupid-

inous love involved here and the holy Venus of marriage (VII.50 gloss), it is clear to which one Palemon is praying.

The virtue of Arcita's love is similarly undercut. His wanderings in exile and his constant pangs of love have rendered him as thin as Erisitone, who, the gloss informs us, was starved to death as a punishment for his disrespect to Diana (IV.27). That is, of course, the goddess of chastity whom Emilia serves. When, returning to Athens in disguise, he sees Emilia again,

> Maggior letizia non credo sentisse
> allor Tereo quando li fu concesso
> per Pandion che Filomena en gisse
> alla sua suora in Trazia con esso. (IV.54)

[I do not think that Tereus felt greater joy when he was allowed by Pandion that Filomena go with him to her sister in Thrace.]

Boccaccio's gloss reminds the reader that Tereo raped Filomena on the way home. A few stanzas later, lying under a pine tree such as abound in Venus's temple grove, Arcita prays to Amor and then

> . . . sentendo Filomena
> che si fa lieta del morto Tereo,[30]
> si drizza (IV.73)

[hearing Filomena (the nightingale) that rejoices at the death of Tereus, he got up].

The comparison bodes ill for Arcita, who prays that he may not perish through excessive love, "per soverchio amore." The prayer is, in fact, not granted, for his epitaph states:

> a chiunque ama, per esemplo lui
> pigli, s'amor di soverchio l'accende;
> perciò che dicer può: "Qual se', io fui;
> e per Emilia usando il mio valore
> mori': dunque ti guarda da amore" (XI.91)

[let whoever loves take him for an example, / if excessive love burns him; / because he can say: "As you are, I was; / and using my valor for Emilia, / I died: therefore guard yourself from love"].

There is an opposite extreme, however, which Boccaccio wants also to avoid. The Amazons, after all, were as wrong to reject Venus as Erisitone was to spite Diana. Emilia must be persuaded to set aside her dedication to the virgin goddess and to enter into marriage. When Emilia and Palemon marry, the worship of Diana and Venus are combined, as in the *Filocolo*, for marriage combines love with chastity and avoids both destructive extremes of isolation and uncontrolled lust.[31] Palemon, consenting to the wedding, invokes both "sacra Diana e Citerea" (XII.35).

As Palemon's marriage to Emilia combines Venus with Diana, so Palemon's submission to Teseo's rule and the death of Arcita cause the old Mars and Venus pair to be replaced with a new pair, Venus and Jupiter. Mars and Venus, connected through the two knights, are not only a famous example of adulterous lovers but also an astrological combination of planets signifying adultery and fornication:[32]

> ex Marte et Venere . . . homines apti ad passionem suscipiendam secundum corpoream dispositionem producuntur. (*Gen.* IX.4)

> E di questo dice Ali nel comento del *Quadripartito* che, qualunque ora nella natività d'alcuno Venere insieme con Marte partecipa, avere questa cotale partecipazione a concedere a colui che nasce una disposizione atta agl'innamoramenti e alle fornicazioni. (*Esposiz.* on *Inf.* V)

> [from Mars and Venus . . . are produced men apt to take up passion according to their bodily disposition.

> And Aly speaks about this in his commentary on the *Quadripartito* that, whenever in someone's nativity Venus participates together with Mars, such a (joint) participation gives to the one who is born a disposition suited to love affairs and fornications.]

On the other hand, the combination of Venus with Jupiter, the planet of temperance and reason, produces legitimate love and friendship, such as can exist only among the virtuous:

> Amorem Iovis et Veneris fuisse filium omnes volunt, quod ego non hominum credam sed planetarum. Sunt enim ambo complexione similes, . . . ex his amorem gigni, et eum potissime quo convivimus, quo amicitias iungimus, fictum est, ut intelligamus quoniam ex convenientia complexionum et morum inter mortales amor et amicitia generetur. Que quidem, vera preter inter

virtuosos esse non potest, ut clare demonstratur Tullius ubi *De
amicitia*. . . . De concupiscibili autem amore satis supra dictum
est. (*Gen.* XI.5)

[everyone says that Love was the son of Jupiter and Venus, which
I believe means not of men but of the planets. Both (planets) are
of similar complexion . . . it has been feigned that from them
springs love, and especially that love by which we live together,
by which we join in friendships, so that we may understand that
from the harmony of complexions and manners among mortals
love and friendship is born. Which indeed cannot be except
among the virtuous, as is clearly demonstrated by Tully in *On
Friendship*. . . . But about concupiscible love enough has been
said above.]

Cupid is the offspring of Venus and Mars. Another attribute of their
alliance is the net, whose hidden bonds Boccaccio interprets as lascivious
thoughts and delights that trap the soul (*Gen.* IX.3); this net is opposed to
the "matrimonio, id est indissolubili vinculo" [marriage, that is the indissoluble bond] by which Venus is bound to her husband Vulcan. Arcita and
Palemon are caught and bound in the net of passion: "gli teneva d'amor
nella rete" (III.43); "Io mi sento di lei preso e legato" (III.24).

E' si credevan, mirandol bene,
saziar l'ardente sete del disio
e minor far le lor gravose pene:
e essi più dal valoroso iddio
Cupido si stringean nelle catene. (III.32)

[And they believed that by gazing thoroughly / they could satisfy
the burning thirst of desire / and lessen their grave pains: / and
drew the chains of the mighty god / Cupid more tightly around
themselves.]

Unlike the readers whom Boethius summons to cast off "the foul chains of
that deceiving lust which occupies earth-bound souls" ("Quos fallax ligat
improbis catenis / terrenas habitans libido mentes"),[33] Arcita and Palemon
for all their complaints prefer captivity to freedom:

Né era lor troppo sommo disire
che Teseo gli traesse di prigione. (III.37)

[Nor did they have much desire that Teseo take them out of prison.]

This statement gains meaning when one considers Teseo as a Jupiter figure, for Jupiter is the planet of temperance and reason.[34] The knights are in no hurry to be released from passion by reason.

The combination of Venus and Mars involves one more portent, the furies (*Gen.* III.22):

> Quod Furias in domo Martis hospitata sit et eis familiaris effecta, hanc ob causam dictum reor. Sunt enim inter signa celestia, ut dicebat venerabilis Andalo, duo que Marti ab astrologis domicili loco attributa sunt, aries scilicet, et scorpio, in quam harum domorum illas Venus duxerit non habemus. Sed si in arietem duxerit, initium veris per arietem designari credo, cum tunc ver incipiat quando sol arietem intrat, circa quod tempus animalia cuncta in concupiscentiam inclinatur, et, ut dicit Virgilius: In furias ignesque ruunt.

> [That she receives the Furies in the house of Mars and is similar to them in effect, I think is for this reason. For among the heavenly signs, as the venerable Andalò used to say, are two signs which astrologers call the houses of Mars, that is Aries and Scorpio; in which of these houses Venus led the Furies we do not know. But if she led them into Aries, I think the beginning of spring is meant by Aries, since spring begins then when the sun enters Aries, around which time all animals are inclined to concupiscence and, as Virgil says: They rush into furies and fires.]

These then are specifically furies of love; "que quidem excitatio, nisi frena rubor iniceret, verti in furiam videretur" [which excitation, indeed, unless a strong rein is imposed, is seen to turn into fury (or madness)]. But not only spring connects the furies to love.

> Si in scorpionem duxisse velimus, quoniam venenificum atque fraudulentum est animal, intelligo non nunquam amantum amaritudines anxias modice mixtas dulcedini, ob quas sepissime miseri adeo vexantur ardentes, ut in se ipsos gladio, laqueo, precipitioque furentes vertantur.

> [If we want (to say) that she led them into Scorpio, as the animal is poisonous and deceitful, I understand by it the frequent anx-

ious bitternesses of lovers mixed somewhat with sweetness, on account of which very often the burning wretches are so vexed that they turn upon themselves the sword, the noose, and the headlong fall, in their madness.]

Palemon and Arcita are clearly suffering from the Martian Venus, and the beginning of their love is "lor primo furore" (III.38).

The knights' prayers to Venus and Mars in the middle of the epic are replaced at the end by Palemon's prayer to Jupiter:

> O Giove pio, che con ragion governi
> la terra e'l cielo e doni parimenti
> a ciascheduna cosa ordini etterni,
> volgi gli occhi ver me e sii presente
> e con giustizia il mio voler discerni,
> il quale ora si fa consenziente
> a quel del mio signor: (XII.34) [35]

[O holy Jove, who with reason governs / the earth and heaven and gives equally / to each thing eternal orders, / turn your eyes to me and be present / and with justice judge my will, / which now accords itself / with that of my lord.]

The rebellious lover accepts the rule of reason, which in turn brings about the marriage he desires. The lust of Venus and Mars is transformed into the virtuous love of Venus and Jupiter; Priapus yields to Astrea.

From the dedicatory letter to Fiammetta, one can see that Boccaccio's narrator is not reading the epic at all as I have suggested. However, we have been warned from the very first line to be suspicious of his remarks. For Boccaccio has identified him as someone who is in love in a dangerous way; the helpless whirling of Francesca demonstrates the loss of self-direction to overwhelming passion. Describing in Book III the sufferings caused by love, the poet writes that only those who have been captured by love can know what the knights were feeling, and appends the gloss "che sono io" [as I am] (III.35).

He identifies himself in the Proemio with one of the two knights but refuses to reveal which one, telling Fiammetta that she will be able to figure it out. Scholars have argued for one or the other identification.[36] I suspect, however, that the poet is carefully identifying himself with neither one nor the other; or rather, his identification depends on the outcome of his love. For the two Theban knights present an alternative: a resubordination of passion to the government of reason, including literally and meta-phorically the control of passion within marriage, or increasing madness leading to self-destruction. Boccaccio playfully suggests which course is more likely to be his; the narrator announces in his letter that "d'amore, giovane d'anni e di senno, mi fece suggetto" [to love, young in age and in judgment, I subjected myself]. The lack of "senno" is both a humorous touch by which Boccaccio undercuts his narrator and also an appropriate overture to the theme of the *Teseida*, the relation between reason and passion.

Like both young men, the narrator deifies his lady and addresses to her the language of religion: "più tosto celestiale che umana figura" [rather a heavenly than a human figure], "la mia beatitudine" [my beatitude]. His worship of the lady is a conscious pose, however, for he serves in hope of "guiderdone" [reward], and the goal of his desires is apparent.[37] He asks her to accept the book, confessing, "Io procederei a molti più prieghi . . . ma però che io del niego dubito con ragione" [I would proceed to many more prayers . . . except that I have reason to fear your refusal] and ends with a prayer that Amor "se in lui quelle forze sono che già furono, raccen-dendo in voi la spenta fiamma, a me vi renda" [if he still has the powers which he used to, rekindling in you the extinguished flame, may return you to me]. The poem, in short, is meant to kindle her passion so that she will reward his desire. Ironic, in that case, is the statement earlier in the letter that perhaps she likes to read love stories so that boring and idle times not cause her more harmful thoughts.

Having identified himself with the passionate knights, the poet prays for inspiration to Mars, Venus, and Cupid, i.e., to a combination of deities that represent illegitimate lust. These are the right gods to pray to for the effect that the poet hopes to produce by his book. When he sends the epic to Fiammetta, however, asking her to give it a title, she responds with a reference to marriage or legitimate love, calling the book *Teseida delle nozze d'Emilia* [Teseida of the wedding of Emilia]. Moreover, she associates that marriage with the achievements of the Jovian Teseo, naming the book for him rather than for the Theban lovers. Her title, contained in the muses' sonnet at the end of the book, is the only evidence we have for her reading of the poem.

Further support for this position, however, comes from Boccaccio's prefatory remark that Emilia in part represents Fiammetta. For example, just as Fiammetta's lover invokes the same Mars and Venus worshiped by the two Thebans, so Emilia's contrasting devotion to Diana may suggest that Fiammetta is similarly chaste and devout in contrast to her lover. Francesca's line, quoted by the narrator at the beginning of his preface, is in turn an echo of Aeneas's opening remark in Book II as he begins his story; it has the effect of kindling Dido's love, the same effect that the *Teseida* narrator hopes his book will achieve. But Emilia is an anti-Dido. Hunting in Book V.77−79, she resembles both the Diana whom she worships[38] and also Dido setting out on her famous hunt of *Aeneid* IV. Dido too had previously been compared to Diana with her quiver (I.498−504); but, a victim of Venus's plotting, she is about to consummate her love illicitly whereas Emilia is offered by Teseo *in marriage* to one of the two knights. Furthermore, Emilia, as Hollander has noted, is described in terms from the *Vita Nuova*, "d'umiltà vestuta" (III.29; *Vita Nuova* 26).[39] This echoes not only the *Vita Nuova* but also the description of Fiammetta in the *Filocolo* garden (IV.43), thus adding to the Emilia-Fiammetta connection and suggesting that the *Teseida* Fiammetta too may be a representative of proper and holy love. In both the narrative and gloss of the *Teseida*, that holy love is defined by Boccaccio as one which leads not to a heavenward ascent but to marriage. Perhaps, although she no longer appears as an educator within the narrative and although, according to the final sonnet, the book has succeeded in rekindling her love, "di fiamma d'amor tututta accesa," she is trying to point out to the poet the meaning of his own poem as a way of answering his plea.

The *Teseida* in several ways resembles the *Filostrato*. Both works are written in ottave; both are set in the times of ancient Greece; both make use of an ignorant and erring lover-poet who presents the narrative as a reflection of his own love story but fails to understand the lesson it should teach him. The concern of both works, given their pre-Christian setting, is moral rather than religious, although their morality lies within a context of Christian assumptions.[40] But whereas the *Filostrato* illustrates only the tragedy toward which the narrator too may be headed, the *Teseida* offers a happy solution as well as a possibly tragic end. So too the *Filostrato* presents only one reading within the fiction, i.e., that of Filostrato, while the *Teseida* offers us two, the poet's and Fiammetta's. Fiammetta, as the book's first reader, is a model for us, its other readers.

This view of her role in both the *Filocolo* and *Teseida* certainly alters the image of a fickle and passionate Fiammetta, derived by some scholars from the poet's complaints about her leaving just when he "almost" had everything he wanted. Indeed, nothing in the *Teseida* preface suggests that she has abandoned the narrator for someone else, as most of the biographical critics assumed. She is more likely offended at his having gone too far. Torraca suggested that as Fiammetta was a married woman—this information is taken from the later *Comedia delle Ninfe* and *Elegia di Madonna Fiammetta*—she had to be careful; therefore she turned "sdegnosa" when her lover became too insistent. Boccaccio, he says, wrote for her in order to reingratiate himself; "pensò che il miglior modo di rientrarle in grazia fosse l'offerta di una storia d'amore. . . . E scrisse la *Teseida*."[41] One can see, however, how absurd it is to think that the *Teseida* with its emphasis on reason and marriage could have been devised by the real Boccaccio as the most effective way to seduce a married woman. Indeed, if the *Teseida* implicitly praises the virtue of Fiammetta through the complaints of a foolish lover and through her own response within the work, the reality of such a patroness at the Neapolitan court becomes much more likely than if she is seen as the poet's adulterous lover. Meanwhile, however, Branca has argued that the *Teseida* was not written in Naples at all but rather after Boccaccio's return to Florence.[42] Thus the dedicatory letter would be completely unreal, and intended simply to establish the poet's persona as a humorous reflection of the lovers within the poem.

It is also inaccurate to consider the Fiammetta of the *Filocolo* and *Teseida* a representative of "quel mondo prezioso e cortese . . . che riduce il sapere 'a raffinato edonismo intellettualistico' e propone 'un' arte senza grossi impegni di vita (politici, morali, religiosi)'"[43] [that precious and courtly world . . . which reduces knowledge 'to a refined intellectual hedonism' and proposes 'an art without great engagements of life (political, moral, religious)']. Although she is certainly presented in the *Filocolo* as a member of aristocratic Neapolitan society, she demonstrates more concern for morality than for hedonism in both works, especially in the *Filocolo* where we know more about her and witness her long answer to Caleone. In the *Teseida* we are dealing with a writer who pretends to miss the point of his own book while Fiammetta provides a proper answer to the narrator's erotic hope.

IV

Comedia delle Ninfe Fiorentine

In the *Filocolo*, Book IV, Boccaccio set side by side a scene in which noble men and ladies talk about love in a garden and a vision of the seven virtues in which the ascent toward divine love is foreshadowed for Florio. In the *Comedia delle Ninfe Fiorentine* (1341–42) he combined the two scenes into one. The noble ladies who gather in a *locus amoenus* form the same kind of "court" with an appointed ruler to choose the speakers and with a set topic on which everyone speaks by turn; but now they are the seven virtues themselves. The nymphs who seem to love "per diletto," as Venus offers them handsome lovers outside their marriages, despite and even through this erotic love represent love of a very different and religious kind. This is the problem which Boccaccio set for himself in his *Comedia* and which, critics agree, he failed to solve completely.[1] For the doubleness of the situation as established by Boccaccio leaves us with the sense of two quite separate scenes superimposed one on the other. Appropriately, there turn out to be, as in the *Filocolo*, two different "authors" for this text. The first, as before, is a lover; the other, again, a character within the fiction, none other than Ameto, who listens to the nymphs' stories just as Ilario listened to Florio's tale.

Boccaccio declares in chapter I that he will sing of a love the effects of which keep the heavens in perpetual motion and give eternal law to the stars: "i suoi effetti tengono in moto continuo li piacevoli cieli, dando etterna legge alle stelle e ne' viventi potenziata forza di bene operare" (I.8). This is the "amore onesto" of the *Filocolo* garden, the source of our ability to do good. The poet will sing the victories of his prince, "delle quali il

83

cielo e la terra sono pieni" [of which heaven and earth are full]. The liturgical phrase bears out the holiness of the love meant here. Yet the poet explains that he will follow this lord, the Christian God, not directly but
rather "per donna" [through woman] and that this mediation is pleasing to
the lord as well as to the poet.[2] When Boccaccio presents himself "con voce
convenevole al mio umile stato, sanza paura di riprensione, non poeta, ma
piuttosto amante" [with a voice appropriate to my humble state, without
fear of blame, not a poet but rather a lover], the humility appropriate to
religious song is transferred to the humility of a lover before his lady, an
indirection meant in part to protect the poet from criticism ("riprensione") for trying to be too bold.[3] The lady is to represent the gracious
view of God's treasures, revealed on earth to the unworthy poet: "la
graziosa vista de' suoi tesori, a me indegno mostrati in terra, racconterò nel
mio verso";[4] for, as the poet declares, no other work of nature or art has
ever equaled female beauty.

Notwithstanding his declaration of allegorical intent in chapter I, the
verses of invocation in chapter II are addressed to Cupid. The Venus who
will appear at the end of the book will announce herself thus:

> Io son luce del cielo unica e trina,
> principio e fine di ciascuna cosa (XLI)

[I am the light of heaven, one and triune, beginning and end of
all things].

Ameto recognizes her; she is not "quella Venere che gli stolti alle loro disordinate concupiscenzie chiamano dea, ma quella dalla quale i veri e giusti
e santi amori discendono intra' mortali" (XLII) [that Venus whom the
foolish call goddess of their disordinate concupiscence, but she from
whom the true and just and holy loves descend among mortals]. But in the
invocation of chapter II, Venus is the adulteress of Mars; mother of pious
Aeneas but also adulterous wooer of the incestuously begotten Adonis, the
son of his own sister Mirra ("che figliuol fu di Mirra sua sorella"). Her
heavenly house, the astrological sign of Taurus, is called the animal "ch'Europa ingannò con falso gioco" [who deceived Europa with false play]. In
sum, despite his promise to sing of divine love, the poet prays in his invocation to a Venus totally different from the one who will descend at the end
of the book. He seems to be praying to the goddess of erotic, passionate,
and even illicit love. We can understand from this that the poet, having explained in chapter I that he will write "non poeta ma piuttosto amante"

and "per donna," has then donned his role as lover and begun his veiled or masked writing. But why the mask? Why write as a lover?

An answer lies in the condition of the readers to whom Boccaccio is directing his book. He is writing to offer good hope (Fiammetta's virtue) to those who feel love as a weight, "che gravoso il sostengono." His readers are those "chi per conforto e qual per diletto cercando gli antichi amori, un' altra volta *col concupiscevole cuore* transfugano Elena, raccendono Didone," etc. (my emphasis) [who for comfort and who for pleasure seeking out the ancient loves, once again with concupiscent heart steal Helen away, rekindle Dido]. The *Comedia delle Ninfe* is written for those who love not "onestamente" but "per diletto" and are already feeling the frustrations of such love. Using the figure of "donna," the poet hopes to draw the readers through responses which they naturally feel for a beautiful woman toward the recognition of an ultimately happier kind of love and higher object. "E però chi ama, ascolti; degli altri non curo" [And therefore let him who loves listen; I don't care about the others]. By dismissing from his audience anyone not in love, he implies that human love is a necessary prerequisite for the lesson he wishes to impart. Perhaps he is thinking of a sentiment such as: "He that loveth not his brother whom he hath seen, how can he love God whom he hath not seen?" (I John 4:20). Ameto, as someone who is successfully lured *through* erotic desire to a new understanding and faith, sets an example for the reader.

The name Ameto refers to a hero of classical mythology who was to be delivered from death on the condition that someone would volunteer to die for him. His wife volunteered and was subsequently brought back from Hades by Hercules. Obviously Boccaccio is translating this tale into a Christian allegory. Ameto is saved from spiritual death by Christ's voluntary self-sacrifice. Boccaccio's Ameto is, in a sense, any Christian, whose faith, Lia, leads him to salvation.[5] The main narrative recounts Ameto's Dante-like progress from the "selva" [woods] through the seven virtues to baptism and a vision of the Trinity.

Although the book is introduced by the lover, one begins to think of Ameto as the narrator before one is really aware of what is happening. First Ameto's thoughts are revealed directly. Then, as Ameto understands better what has passed, he speaks of wanting to write down what he has learned "sì che si possa, / sì come io, d'esse inamorare" (XLVII.47–48), so that his readers may fall in love with the nymphs as he has done—the very purpose set forth in the introductory chapter by the other narrator. Ameto even speaks of the hoped-for preservation of "le mie carte" (51); he is writing, not just singing. In a clever joke, the original narrator suddenly reveals in chapter XLIX that he has been hiding in the bushes all along and watching the events he has described.[6] He confesses envy for Ameto (43),

> e con quel cuor che io pote' sostenni
> vederlo a tanta corte presidente
> parlar con motti e con riso e con cenni (46–48)

> [and as well as I could I bore to see him preside at such a court speaking with jests and laughter and nods.]

Although he claims to feel the same effect of love waking in his soul which he calls "disio movente omo a salute" (70) [a desire moving man toward salvation], his envy of Ameto seems to be based on a concupiscent desire for the nymphs, in whom he declares "compiute / le delizie mondane" (72–73) [complete worldly delight]. Whereas in the *Filocolo* a tale about lovers is revealed in the end to have had a religious author, the joke here is that just when the reader has accepted the allegorical explanations and Christian message, we are suddenly reminded of the carnal, literal vision with which we started out.

We see the fruits of the lover-poet's mistaken love as he contrasts Ameto's happy society of beauty, "gentilezza," virtue, and love with the home to which he himself must return, full of "malinconia e etterna gramezza," dark, silent, and inhabited by an ugly, avaricious, cold old man (74–84). The passage has usually been understood as a contrast between Boccaccio's life at the court of Naples and his life back in Florence with his father. This is undoubtedly part of the meaning, for Boccaccio portrays his father as avaricious also in the *Amorosa Visione*. Calling Ameto's happier society the sum of worldly delights suggests the literal and physical pleasures of the Neapolitan court. Yet the words suggest as well a literal reading on the poet's part; for what Ameto has learned is that the joy and beauty offered by the nymphs are not "mondane" and not physical. One can read this passage, in keeping with the rest of the allegory, as a contrast between the new man and the old man in the Pauline sense. The new man, Ameto, has "put on God"; the old man is without God, therefore so dark and mute and bitter. The poet's longing to return to a better life, the reference to his present life as an inn, and his calling for death as the way to freedom all fit traditional Christian themes appropriate to the meanings of the work, if not to the narrator's intentions. What the poet wants is his "real" lady; but even this separation can be read, from Ameto's new perspective, as an alle-

gory "per donna" of his distance from virtue and the life of true felicity.
The Venus-trinity had promised:

che chi mi segue non andrà giammai
errando in parte trista o tenebrosa (XLI)

[whoever follows me will never go wandering in a sad or dark
place].

Obviously the poet is not following that deity; instead he is praying to that
other Venus "che gli stolti alle loro disordinate concupiscenzie chiamano
dea." Like Idalagos, the lover-poet of the *Comedia delle Ninfe* ends up in
misery and despair; he is literally in the dark, and figuratively ignorant or
blind.

Ameto, meanwhile, has learned not only how to be a Christian but
also how to read, i.e., how to interpret the words of the nymphs and indeed the nymphs themselves, whose very physical attributes are emblematic. Unlike Ilario, who appears only briefly and represents a fixed point of
view, Ameto is changing throughout the book; he is in the process of
learning to interpret what he has heard but not fully understood. Suddenly
he sees through the allegorical possibilities of his own situation. Originally
an ignorant animal, "di carnalità costretto" (III.4) [constrained by carnal-
ity], Ameto on first seeing Lia and her companions hides in the bushes,
afraid of being noticed lest he, like Actaeon, be turned into a beast. When
he has been educated and is baptized, he takes off his animal skins and appears fully human. At that point, we find the poet, who at first had promised to teach divine love, hiding in the same bushes and afraid as Ameto
had been. The two narrators have crossed paths.

The pattern of narrative roles in this work is very similar to that in the
Filocolo. Both works begin with a fairly clear statement of Christian intent
by the narrator; then at the end of both works we are suddenly made aware
that two authors have been involved in writing this text. In the presence of
the second and Christian "author" (Ilario, Ameto), the original lover-poet
abandons all suggestions of religious understanding and becomes purely
erotic in his expressed aims. Thus we start with one narrator who combines human love with Christian meanings, but end with the narrator's
role split in two, the religious and erotic contrasted instead of combined.
In the *Filocolo* this shift does not happen until the very end; in the *Comedia
delle Ninfe*, however, the narrator's invocation in chapter II shows him already slipping into the erotic role. Perhaps the sharp juxtaposition of chap-

ters I and II is meant to alert the reader to what is going on, that is, to the artificiality of the lover's pose. For, as in the *Filocolo*, we have only one text, not two; thus the whole work, Christian elements and all, comes to us through the writing of the lover. The *Filocolo* narrator seems to be suggesting seriously that his own love for Fiammetta is real and is parallel to the good and heavenward-leading love of his protagonist. The *Comedia* narrator, however, seems to take on the role of lover purely as an allegorical means of expression—he will write as a lover, "per donna"—and to present his desires as erroneous, in opposition to the better love of his protagonist. The use of analogy, which connected the various strands of the *Filocolo* narrative, is replaced here by allegory.

The first of the seven tales, told by Mopsa or Prudence, invites us all to learn how to read allegory. In order to lure the thoughtless Afron (A-phron) from the seas where he rides in peril, she takes off her clothing. The readers who are similarly tossing in the seas of passion and fortune "con concupiscevole cuore," are thus invited to see the naked wisdom beneath the veil of fiction in this book.

The combination of erotic narrative and virtuous meaning is certainly funny. There is, for example, a humorous double entendre in the lover-poet's hope that he

> più adentro alquanto che la scorza
> possa mostrar la tua deitate [Venus],
> a che lo'ngegno s'aguzza e si sforza (II.25–27)

[may be able to show forth your divinity / somewhat deeper than the bark, / to which the intellect spurs itself on and makes effort].

Ameto too tries at first to imagine the nymphs unveiled. Mazzotta discusses, in regard to the *Decameron*, the "complicity between allegory and pornography"; both present a covered image which entices one to see "the naked truth."[7] His idea fits the *Comedia delle Ninfe* extraordinarily well.[8]

If Boccaccio is being intentionally outrageous here, it is perhaps part of his general fight to prove—to his practical father and others—that poetry, which seems to be frivolous or even immoral stuff, can also be serious if one knows how to understand it. The text with two authors is a way of declaring that literary language has multiple meanings, and that therefore accusations of frivolity merely reveal the critics' own ignorance.

Fiammetta, who reappears in this work, participates completely in the allegorical nature of the text. With its title and its use of terza rima, the *Comedia delle Ninfe* can be thought of as Boccaccio's rewriting of Dante's *Commedia*. Seung has pointed out that the seven nymphs in their final song allude to the seven virtues of Dante's pageant in the earthly paradise.[9] The whole scene is very much like Dante's Eden, the flowery field and the stream in which Ameto, like Dante, is finally baptized. Although Boccaccio's Lia seems to be associated with Matelda, however, Fiammetta is no Rachel; and the dramatic last arrival is not a Fiammetta-Beatrice but a Venus who announces herself as the triune god. Boccaccio perhaps was uncomfortable with Dante's quasi-deification of Beatrice, possibly with his own Dantesque use of Fiammetta in the *Filocolo* as well.

As Boccaccio replaces Dante's first-person narrator with a character separate from any fictive self, the shepherd Ameto, so too he replaces the single woman, despite Ameto's special love for Lia, with seven women in similar roles. Among them is Fiammetta, loved as in the *Filocolo* by someone named Caleone who is not directly identified with the narrator. We have here already the subordination of Fiammetta into a group such as will occur again in the *Decameron*. Whereas in the *Filocolo* Fiammetta was queen of the gathering, in the *Comedia* her prominence decreases; she tells the next to last and next to longest tale, followed and surpassed in length only by that of Ameto's Lia. We infer that the poet's lady is one of the nymphs, for he says that he saw her sitting with a group of gracious ladies under a laurel tree, which is where the nymphs are sitting (II.78–81 and XVII.1). However, if not for clues from the *Filocolo*—the name Fiammetta, the lover named Caleone, the date and scene of his enamorment—we would have no way of knowing which of the nymphs is the poet's own lady, for he tells us nothing specific by which to identify her, nor does she act in any way outside the narrative as in previous works.

In one sense the stories told by the seven ladies are really the same story over and over again, the seventh one (Lia's) forming a bridge between the tales and the framing tale, the story of Ameto who is their audience. In each tale a virtue wins over a lack of that virtue or an opposing vice.[10] The terms used within a particular story can usually be applied to the situation of Ameto, who listens to the tales as the student of all seven virtues in a progression from the dawning insight offered by Mopsa or Prudence through the moral to the theological virtues and ending with Lia's recitation of the Credo (XXXIX). Thus, for example, when Acrimonia tells how she changed Apaten, "Io lo rendei, di rozzo satiro, dotto giovane" (XXIX.61) [I made him from a rough satyr into a learned young man], the words apply exactly to Ameto as well as to Apaten. Ameto, identifying himself in turn with each of the lovers, is educated in the love of all seven virtues.

Boccaccio alludes through riddling clues to real historical identities for some of the ladies, but not all of them are clearly identifiable.[11] Mopsa, for example, who is an Athenian as appropriate to her significance, is thus removed from Italian events. Agapes's stemma, however, shows her to belong to the Strozzi family (XXXII.6). Acrimonia, who talks at length about her family fortunes (XXIX), gives as her family stemma that of the city of Florence under the Ghibellines (XXIX.4).[12] Branca identifies her with the "bella lombarda" of the *Amorosa Visione* (XL.66) and "Contento quasi" (46–48), but who she was remains unknown.[13] Lia informs us through a rebus that Ameto too is connected with a real family, the Nerli of Florence (XXXVIII.116), about whom very little is known.[14] The work is dedicated not to Fiammeta or any other ladylove but to the Florentine Nicolò di Bartolo del Buono (L), who presumably would have recognized the identifying clues. This kind of contemporary historical reference is common to a number of Boccaccio's works, beginning with the very early *Caccia di Diana* and continuing beyond the *Comedia delle Ninfe* to the *Amorosa Visione* and the *Decameron*.[15] Yet the tales of adultery and the cruel remarks by some of the ladies about their husbands (e.g., Agapes XXXII.13–28) could hardly have appeared flattering to any real women and their families even though the allegorical reinterpretation might protect against an absolute offense. Boccaccio may be endeavoring to give an air of reality by alluding to families without actually pointing to specific persons, as König has suggested in the case of Fiammetta.[16] It is enough for our purposes to understand that the nymphs are supposedly historical women and virtues at the same time. Here again the model of Dante's Beatrice is clear, for Dante insists on her historical existence while transforming his love for her into a power that draws him toward God.

The *Comedia delle Ninfe* provides one of the most detailed sources of information about Fiammetta. As in the *Filocolo* Fiammetta tells us that she is the illegitimate daughter of King Robert and a woman at the court of Naples, although she adds here that she cannot be absolutely sure whether her father was her mother's husband or the king.

She also fills in several parts of the story not told previously and makes some changes. First, her line of ancestry is drawn, from ancient Rome to Aquino, "di Iovenale l'oppido" [the town of Juvenal], which gave her family its name. Here is the first mention of her relation to the Aquino family.

She is not yet associated specifically with St. Thomas, as she will be in the *Amorosa Visione*, and indeed the allusion to Juvenal is a distraction, suggesting rather a literary association with the place than a religious association with the saint. The *Trattatello*, which as Billanovich has noted ascribes the same ancestors to Dante as to Fiammetta,[17] also calls the town "Aquino di Giovenale" (I.97). Fiammetta certainly first appeared as a descendant of Dante's writings—hence, perhaps, the suggested kinship.

Second, Fiammetta speaks newly about the French nationality of her mother.[18] Branca has noted that Fiammetta's parentage runs parallel to Boccaccio's own autobiographical fiction, first stated in Idalagos's account in the *Filocolo* (V.8.2).[19] Emilia, the second of the *Comedia* nymphs, repeats some details here (XXIII), telling us that the mother of her lover Ibrida was Parisian and his father from Certaldo, and that Ibrida's birth was illegitimate. As Branca has shown reason to discredit the story that Boccaccio's mother was Parisian, the reality of these details gives way to fiction and thus to figurative rather than historical interpretations.

If his mother was not in fact Parisian, why would Boccaccio repeat this item from the story of Idalagos, which in a number of other respects does seem to refer to Boccaccio's career? The name Ibrida labels the hubris of vain ambition, which is compared to that of Phaeton and the Titans. Emilia, or Justice, is requested by Venus to save Ibrida from the destruction meted out to those other examples. As the autobiography of Idalagos in the *Filocolo* may have been an attempt by Boccaccio to associate himself with the French ruling house of Naples and through it to Hector and the Trojan princes,[20] it is fitting that the story be retold in Florence as the parentage of pride and vain ambition which Justice now corrects. Indeed, Boccaccio did not afterwards repeat the claim.

Third, Fiammetta recounts the occasion of her mother's seduction by the king.[21] She is seduced unwillingly, tricked by the king. Moreover, whereas in the *Filocolo* Robert was young and not yet crowned, here the affair takes place during his reign. In sum his behavior becomes less honorable. Boccaccio has begun to refer to King Robert as "Mida" for his avarice (XXXV.32). Perhaps because of his changing attitude toward King Robert, the king's fathering of Fiammetta is now rendered uncertain and—like Boccaccio's own French origins—will hereafter not be mentioned again; in the *Amorosa Visione* Fiammetta is definitely a child of the Aquino family.

Details similar to the story of the poet's love recounted at the beginning of the *Filocolo* appear little by little through several tales. Adiona meets Dioneo in church (XXVI.77).[22] Acrimonia meets Apaten in a temple during the holiday of Venus, that is in the beginning of April or near Easter time. The identification of Venus with God in this work supports a connection between the pagan and the Christian holiday. Acrimonia's story, however, takes place in Sicily, not in Naples. With the tale of Fiammetta, all the details of the *Filocolo* scene appear at once. Caleone sees her for the first time (apart from his prophetic vision of her) in the Franciscan church of San Lorenzo in Naples, on a Saturday when the sun is in the sixteenth degree of Aries, i.e., near the beginning of April, "ascoltando io le laude in tale dì a Giove per la spogliata Dite rendute" [while I was listening to the lauds rendered to Jove on that day for the harrowing of Dis].

According to astronomers of Boccaccio's time, Aries began on March 14; the sixteenth degree, then, would be March 30, which was in fact an Easter Saturday in 1331 and 1336. But the beginning of April had also been a Roman festival to Venus (*Fasti*); thus Boccaccio is reusing a date which allows him to combine celebrations of the erotic and the holy. (He avoids, however, Venus's day, Friday, which was Petrarch's choice.) Attempts by scholars to date Boccaccio's enamorment (in this case it is actually Caleone's, not the narrator's) have resulted in various dates depending on whether one sets the beginning of Aries according to the astronomical almanacs or according to the church calendar.[23] As Boccaccio had been studying astronomy and refers to a precise number of degrees ("un grado oltre al mezzo e poco più") [one degree beyond the middle and a bit more], I am assuming that he followed the astronomers. However, any date near the beginning of April will do, for Boccaccio tells us anyway that he means it to be Easter. It is quite possible that no real year is intended. An awareness of the superimposition of Venus's and Christ's season is too common in medieval literature to need specific days and years. It fits the ambivalence of Boccaccio's allegory, in which erotic stories convey moral and Christian truths.

The hour of enamorment is the same in both works and in the *Amorosa Visione* as well. According to the *Filocolo* "la quarta ora del giorno sopra l'orientale orizonte passata" [the fourth hour of the day having passed above the eastern horizon], the fifth hour is presumably just beginning to rise. Again in the *Amorosa Visione* (Xl.31–33) Boccaccio says that the horses of the sun "saliano già sovra la quarta ora" [rose already above the fourth hour], suggesting the beginning of the fifth. In the *Comedia delle Ninfe* we read "già Febo salito era alla terza parte" [Phoebus had already climbed to the third part]. Quaglio in his notes understands this to mean one third of the day. Thus again four hours have just been completed. On a Saturday, the fifth hour brings with it the dominion of Venus. An astrologically appropriate moment, therefore, has been chosen for falling in love.[24]

In the *Comedia delle Ninfe* as in the *Filocolo*, Fiammetta is seen by her lover twice in close succession. The *Filocolo* gives no definite time between the two meetings, but in the *Comedia delle Ninfe* she appears for the second time on Easter Sunday, the very next day. She is dressed the first time in a black dress and the second time in green, which she finally adopts as her favorite color in celebration of her love affair. She explains her liking for the color "perciò che tante volte dal mio Caleone . . . avanti l'acceso amore verde fui conosciuta" [because so often before the kindled love / I was seen in green by my Caleone]. The *Filocolo* does not mention the color of her dress on either occasion. Moreover, the Fiammetta who appears there in Book IV.43 "di quel colore era vestita che il cielo ne dimostra" [she was dressed in that color which the sky demonstrates], a hint of her association with the Virgin Mary. However, Biancifiore, who wears black when imprisoned in Book II, ends up in Book V dressed in green velvet adorned with gold. The change from black to green obviously corresponds symbolically to her change of state, from prison and the threat of death to a new beginning of life. In the *Comedia delle Ninfe* this change of colors is directly associated with the Easter weekend, black while Christ is in hell and green for the Resurrection. Green is also the color symbolic of the virtue, hope, which Fiammetta represents. Through her appearance at Easter, Fiammetta figures more specifically the hope of immortality through Christ. As Caleone says of her, "niuna fatica per lei avuta sarebbe indegna a chi per quella di tale meritasse la grazia" (XXXV.97)[25] [no labor done for her sake would be unworthy of one who by that means might earn her grace].

Boccaccio was not the first to use green this way. Augustine in an exegesis on the garden of Eden had remarked: "et vitam aeternam, quae viriditate lapidis prasini significatur, propter vigorem qui non arrescit"[26] [and eternal life, which is signified by the greenness of the green stone, because of the vigor which is not staunched]. Boccaccio himself, explaining his eleventh eclogue to Fra Martino da Signa, glosses the green of the myrtle (the church) as "firmissimam spem arcam superiorem eis a Christo promissam"[27] [most firm hope in the heavenly treasure promised to them by Christ]. The green of life has become symbolic of eternal life.

However, green or black and green are colors also associated with Venus.[28] Thus Idalagos (*Filoc.* V.8.44) referred to the greenness of his tree shape as a symbol of his hope; but the tree was a pine, and his hope that of a lover. In the *Teseida*, Emilia wears green twice in sentences which compare her immediately to Venus. One occasion is her wedding:

> Quando costei apparve primamente
>
> . . .
>
> d'un drappo verde di valor suppremo
> vestita, ciaschedun generalmente
> ch'allor la vide, dal primo al postremo,
> Venere la credette. (XII.65)

[When she first appeared . . . / dressed in a green cloth of greatest value, / everyone generally / who saw her then, from the first to the last, / thought she was Venus.]

As this is the climax to a lengthy description of her beauty, it is not clear how specifically to connect the reference to Venus with the wearing of green. Venus herself never appears in green in Boccaccio's writings but usually in red ("porporeo") or white.[29] Nevertheless, on the other occasion of Emilia's wearing green, she is again linked, with almost the same phrasing, to Venus:[30]

> piacevol, bella e molto da gradire,
> ornata assai, in una verde veste,
> tal che di sé ciascuno uom facea dire
> lode meravigliose, e tal dicea
> che veramente ell'era Citerea (IV.51)

[pleasing, beautiful and very likable, / adorned in a green dress, / such that she made every man say / wonderful praises about her, and (each man) said / that truly she was Citherea].

The combination of green and black shows up as the dress of Venus in Henryson's "Testament of Cresseid."[31] This is a fifteenth-century sequel to Chaucer's "Troilus and Criseyde," which in turn is an imitation of Boccaccio's *Filostrato;* although one obviously cannot argue from Henryson's use of colors back to Boccaccio's, nonetheless the straight line of continuity connecting these writers makes Henryson's use of the colors interesting and possibly helpful. The dress of his Venus, "ane half grene, the uther half Sabill black" (l. 221), is only part of a series of contradictions in her description. She combines truth and guile, smiles and anger, laughter and weeping, sweetness and bitterness.[32] Green suggests youth, life, and springtime as opposed to old age and death.

For I traistit Venus, lufis Quene,

. . .

My faidit hart of lufe scho wald mak grene. (ll. 22–24)

Now grene as leif, now widderit and ago. (l. 238)

Love both flourishes in green youth and also renews the youth or life of the heart that it enters. It is presented as a positive color. Thus, although Harth says that in another fifteenth-century poem, "The Court of Love," green and black symbolize lust,[33] it is the combination of colors that creates the significance. For the vegetal nature of green suggests its natural mutability, the inevitable growing toward death. A Venus in green and black implies a warning that the state of love, youth, and beauty is changeable. That is, in fact, precisely Henryson's theme.[34]

For Boccaccio, however, the colors appear in the opposite order, the black giving way to green as Christ's death allows a rebirth of new life. Thus Fiammetta's green is one more ambiguous aspect of her figure. For it represents on one hand the youth and dalliance that must fade, on the other hand the new and immortal life won by Christ for all who can rise above the mutable values of the world.

Fiammetta's association with Venus is complicated by the double role of Venus in this book. Perhaps one can relate the ambiguity to Fiammetta's uncertainty as to whether she is a legitimate or illegitimate child, for Venus represents both divine love (the "legitimam Venerem") and adulterous lechery (the "illegitimam").[35]

The double aspect of love manifests itself also in the pairing of Fiammetta with Caleone. For if Venus appears toward the end of the book as the Christian God of Love, she appears more subtly through Fiammetta as the illegitimate lover of Mars. As Fiammetta represents hope, so Caleone illustrates despair. With the gesture so often portrayed in illustrations of the sin, he threatens to kill himself with an iron sword ("ferro") unless he can have her love.[36] Mars is the planet of violence and weapons, especially iron ones; thus his temple in the *Teseida* is described with frequent repetitions of "ferro" [iron] (VII.32–34, 36). Caleone first sees Fiammetta when the sun is in Aries, and enters her bed when the sun is in Scorpio. Both are the houses of Mars, and Boccaccio even points this out in the case of Aries: "tenente Titan di Gradivo la prima casa" (XXXV.104) [Titan holding the first house of Gradivus (i.e., Mars)]. The influence of Scorpio, moreover, according to Boccaccio's *Genealogia* (III.22) leads lovers to desperation and violence against themselves. Thus under the sign of Scorpio (VII, p. 787),

Fiammetta in the *Elegia di Madonna Fiammetta* also attempts suicide. The Fiammetta of the *Comedia delle Ninfe*, however, sings about the folly of such attempts, pointing to Dido and Biblis, both suicides for love who would have spared their own lives had they possessed Fiammetta's virtue, hope. Fiammetta rescues her lover from despair by offering herself, that is by offering the hope of salvation made possible by Christ's sacrifice.[37] The illegitimate love symbolized by Mars and Venus is set against the holy love of the Easter season, just as the Martian Caleone-despair is set against the Venerian Fiammetta-hope.

Lia's history of Florence, told as part of her tale, provides another important connection between Fiammetta and the love of Mars and Venus. Lia tells how Florence was named by a contest among the gods, an account obviously borrowed with elaborations from the naming of Athens. Each of the gods is challenged to bring forth something wonderful from the ground as a demonstration of his or her power. Mars, who is the winner, brings forth a "fiamma," but surrenders the right of choosing a name to his beloved Venus, who has produced a flower. Mars is commonly known as the fiery planet because of its red color, and the Greek name for it was "Pyrois,"[38] yet the "fiamma" is—in Lia's story—also the flame of his love for Venus. Florence was, in fact, dedicated to Mars, whose statue still stood in the city long after the dedication had been transferred to St. John the Baptist. Both Boccaccio and Villani report that at the hour of Florence's founding, Mars was lord of the ascendant.[39] If not for Mars's love of Venus, it seems, according to the *Comedia delle Ninfe*, that the city would have been named "Fiammetta," for "Firenze" is derived by Boccaccio from Venus's flower. A replacement of Mars by Venus in connection with Fiammetta is thus represented in two tales in a row. The association of Fiammetta with Mars seems to begin after Boccaccio's return to Florence. We will notice it again in the *Decameron*. Yet Fiammetta herself remains a Neapolitan until her appearance as a Florentine in that later work; and even there she tells a number of stories set in or near Naples. If, as discussed with regard to the *Filocolo*, Boccaccio considered Naples a region of Venus, perhaps he paired it with the Martian Florence as part of his personal mythology.[40]

In any case, the *Comedia* contains astrological connections for the other nymphs as well. Boccaccio introduces the seven virtues in the order of their arrival: Lia, Agapes and Adiona, Emilia and Fiammetta, Acrimonia and Mopsa. Comparing this order to that of the heavenly spheres from nearest to farthest, we obtain the following pairs:

Lia	Moon
Agapes	Mercury
Adiona	Venus
Emilia	Sun
Fiammetta	Mars
Acrimonia	Jupiter
Mopsa	Saturn

These relations do seem to bear some relevance to details in the text.

When Ameto first sees Lia, he is convinced that she must be a goddess; and "rimembrandosi d'Atteòn, con le mani si cercava per le corna la fronte, in sé dannando il preso ardire di volere riguardare le sante dee" [remembering Actaeon, he searched with his hands for the horns on his brow, blaming himself for his boldness in wanting to look at the holy goddesses]. He makes the comparison to Actaeon again in XXXI.8–9, realizing his own good fortune in the comparison. For Lia's effect is the opposite of Diana's; she is drawing him from animal existence to full humanity. Nonetheless, the myth points securely to a connection between Lia and Diana or the moon.

The connection between Agapes and Mercury is no less fundamental. Agapes complains in her tale (XXXI.5) that her family, once agricultural, "si dierono a seguitare di Mercurio l' astuzie" [gave themselves to follow the shrewdness of Mercury], that is, went into the banking business and, concerned only for money, made her marry a wealthy but hideous old man.[41] Her virtue, holy love, is repulsed by the cupidity of the old man reflected both in his grasping for money and in his inappropriate lust for the young wife.[42]

Venus, whom one might have expected to find linked with Agapes, is reserved for Adiona, who must temper Dioneo. Dione is one of the names of Venus, and Adiona wears a crown of myrtle in her hair. Moreover, she is third among the narrators as well as third to arrive, thus doubly linked to Venus's third heaven. Both she and Dioneo come from Cyprus, the site of Venus's temple. Dioneo, the lust born from food and drink (Cerere and Bacco), is mortal, but Adiona offers him immortality through the influence of her virtue, temperance.[43]

Emilia as the virtue of justice is paired with the sun, the central and monarchic sphere. It is very commonly the symbol of kingship not only because it outshines the planets, but also because from its central position it gives light to all the rest. She is compared to Dafne and crowned with laurel (XII), identified thus with Apollo's beloved. Ibrida, or hubris, whom she must save, compares himself to Phaeton as he drives a fiery chariot up to threaten Giove in heaven.

Se c'è forse negato che v'intriamo,
come Feton l'accese altra fiata,
e così noi la seconda l'ardiamo
con chi dentro vi sta. (XXII.40–43)

[If perhaps it be forbidden that we enter there, / as Phaeton set fire to it the other time, / so we will burn it a second time / along with whoever is in there.]

He falls like Phaeton and is nearly killed until Emilia saves him. His false splendor and foolish glory are converted by the true sun of justice.

We have already noted that Fiammetta is associated with Mars in several ways. Continuing with the remaining nymphs, one can see that Jupiter is paired suitably enough with Acrimonia, or fortitude, who is wooed by a series of kings and even admired by the priests at the temple of "sommo Giove ottimo di Campidoglio," i.e., the cardinals at Rome.[44] Mopsa, Wisdom, is paired with Saturn, the planet of contemplation and intellectual pursuits. She lives appropriately in Athens, the city of philosophers.[45] She introduces herself (XVIII) as the oldest of the nymphs, "la più antica"; Saturn is not only the oldest of the planetary gods but is also identified commonly with old age and time. It is as the oldest that she starts of the telling of tales. Boccaccio's nymphs, like Dante's seven virtues, sing (XLV.7): "Così nel ciel ciascuna appare stella"[46] [thus in heaven each of us appears a star].

In the seven stages of Ameto's education, then, there are allusions to another seven besides the number of virtues, i.e., to the seven planetary spheres through which the human soul, beginning in the "selva" of original matter, rises toward divinity and wisdom. Dante is clearly a major source but not the only one for such a journey. Bernard Silvester's *Cosmographia* (1 metr.) and Alain de Lille's *Anticlaudianus* (I.191–93) both refer to the "silva" of formless matter as prelude to a journey through the spheres to form the perfect man. For Macrobius, other Neoplatonists, and followers of the Hermetic traditions, the ascent of the soul is part of a process of purification from the stains of material existence and the passions.[47]

Ameto, understanding the allegory of virtues and vices, views Fiammetta as part of an education in the virtues, a process leading on beyond her to the faith represented by Lia and even beyond Lia to the vision of God. His originally erotic attraction to Lia develops into a better love based on the appreciation of her meaning. Thus, as in the *Filocolo*, erotic love leads to and not away from the love of God; Ameto does not have to reject Lia or fall out of love in order to become good in Christian terms. As he says himself, "E come mi poteano essi fare de' loro beni disioso sanza avermi queste [donne] mostrate?" (XV.7) [And how could they have made me desirous of their good without having shown me these ladies?] "Essi" refers here to the gods; thus simpleminded human love is part of a divine plan for our education. Lia's mission with Ameto has been not only to improve his *vision* of the true good, but to make sure that he *desires* it: "costui, seguitandomi, ho io tratto della mentale cecchità con la mia luce a conoscere le care cose; e volentoroso l'ho fatto a seguire quelle" (XXXVIII.117) [this man who is following me I have drawn from mental blindness with my light to the knowledge of dear things; and I have made him eager to follow them].

Ameto is like Dante's

> Anima semplicetta che sa nulla,
> salvo che, mossa da lieto fattore,
> volontier torna a ciò che la trastulla. (*Purg.* XVI.88–90)

Dante's child-soul is drawn by natural affection toward what pleases it; but then, with growing understanding, it must judge and select the worthy good from ephemeral or harmful pleasures. After the third nymph's tale, Ameto still imagines hugging and kissing the nymphs, his mouth watering at his fantasies: "Egli non intende cosa che vi si dica, anzi tiene l'anima con tutte le forze legata nelle dilicate braccia e ne' candidi seni delle donne" (XXVIII. 8) [He doesn't understand a thing that's being said, but keeps his mind with all his might bound in the delicate arms and white bosoms of the ladies]. After the fourth of the cardinal virtues has finished her tale, however, Ameto "caccia da sé le imaginazioni vane, alle quali gli effeti conosce impossibili, e alle vere cose entra con dolce pensiero" (XXXI.1) [dismisses vain imaginings, whose realization he recognizes is impossible, and enters into true things with sweet thought]. He begins to recognize that the material being of these nymphs is itself a fantasy; they cannot be physically embraced. Their true being resides in their significance; they are corporal images for a spiritual reality. In sum, Ameto's education consists not only in an ascent through the virtues but also in the ascent from a material to a spiritual understanding of the text in which he is involved. The lover-poet, as he presents himself in the end, fails to understand the scene's spiritual meaning. His ultimately sorrowful condition, like that of Idalagos, demonstrates that erotic love, while potentially educable, is not enough in itself. It is identified in this work with literal reading, while the better love is a reading which, developing the potential of the literal sense, passes on through it to a fuller truth.

V

Amorosa Visione

In the *Filocolo* and *Comedia delle Ninfe*, the binary terms Ovid and Dante or Priapus and Astrea were also represented as two separate "authors": the narrator and Ilario, or the narrator and Ameto. In a number of other works Boccaccio continued the use of double voices without actually making them both authors of the text. Three clear examples of this are the *Amorosa Visione*, the *Elegia di Madonna Fiammetta*, and the *Corbaccio*. In each book there are chiefly two speakers, although one may have more to say than the other. In all three, conversations between the two voices can be read as inner dialogues in which one speaker represents the rational, the other the passionate or appetitive parts of the individual soul. The three works, listed in the order they were written, show a curious decline of the status of reason and simultaneously a hardening attitude against the power of lust. These developments in turn affect Fiammetta's portrayal. They demonstrate that Boccaccio, while repeating a basic structure, was inwardly changing. Moreover, as they combine discussions of the doubleness of literature along with the doubleness of moral choices, they reveal that Boccaccio's changing attitudes have perhaps as much to do with literary as with moral matters.

The *Amorosa Visione*, written first in 1342–43 and revised fifteen to twenty years later, is an allegory and, like the *Comedia delle Ninfe*, a close imitation of Dante's *Commedia*, perhaps more obviously patterned after Dante's work than any of Boccaccio's other writings.[1] Written in fifty canti of terza rima,[2] it describes a situation much like that of the *Commedia:* it begins with the first-person narrator running lost in a wilderness and the arrival of a guide who promises to lead him on the right path. They travel, however, not through the otherworld but through a hall of painted triumphs and a garden of love. Boccaccio announces that his poem may surprise his reader "per lo nuovo stile" [by its new style], suggesting a reference to Dante's *stil nuovo*.[3] The invocation in the beginning of canto II

> O somma e graziosa intelligenza
> che muovi il terzo cielo

> [O supreme and gracious intelligence which moves the third heaven]

clearly echoes Dante's canzone from the *Convivio*, where love poetry is elaborately interpreted for hidden intellectual meanings. (Dante also repeats the line in *Par.* VIII.37.) In the first painting that Boccaccio views in his vision, Philosophy is crowning Dante, "il maestro dal qual io / tengo ogni ben" (VI.2–3) [the master from whom I have obtained everything that is good]. Both philosophers and poets stand in her triumph as teachers of wisdom. Finally, this is the only book in which Boccaccio, like Dante in the *Commedia*, names himself once, signing one of the acrostic poems "Giovanni di Boccaccio da Certaldo."

Unlike Dante, the narrator is faced at the start with a choice of roads, one leading vertically up a stairway to life and eternal repose, the other leading horizontally into a palace which contains kingdoms, dignities, great treasure, worldly glory and the joys of Love. Each road, moreover, has its champion so that, as before, the alternatives address us separately.[4] However, the game is no longer between a Dantean actor and an erring observer, for now the erotic lover-poet is himself the main actor, who is urged to repeat Ameto's ascent. He is a more reluctant pilgrim than Ameto, and does not learn his lessons so easily as his successful predecessor. The Astrean voice is taken up by another character within the narrative—a character who, however, is mysteriously able to continue existing beyond the narrator's dream into his waking state. Thus the two speakers exist, in some sense, on the same plane instead of the previous arrangement of frame and content. The lover-poet, who inclines toward the promise of worldly pleasures, must continue beyond his narrative to confront the regal, heavenly guide who persistently exhorts him to ascend toward the true good.

Who is this other speaker? Her two obvious models are Dante's Vergil and Boethius's Lady Philosophy. But the latter is one of the triumphant queens painted on the walls of the palace of worldly goods. The guide holds not a scepter and book but a scepter and orb, or golden apple. She is a heavenly queen, "tal qual nel sidereo coro / Giunon . . . ornata di corona e più che'l sole / splendida" [like Juno in the starry band, . . . adorned with a crown more splendid than the sun], and wearing a purple cloak.[5] Numerous identities have been proposed;[6] but two possibilities seem to me most in keeping with the details of the text.

One is Celestial Love, proposed by Gaspary, or Celestial Venus, as Hollander calls her;[7] the other is Reason. Hollander points to the golden apple in her hand as evidence of her Venus-like nature,[8] while her role in the narrative makes her clearly a heavenly rather than earthly Venus. Gaspary points to the invocation in canto II, addressed to the "santa dea" [holy goddess] of the third sphere. If we read the invocation carefully, however, we will notice that the goddess invoked and the guide are two different persons.

> Poi che condotto m'ha a quest'alto soglio
> costei, che sol seguir lei mi si face,
> menami tu colà dove io gir voglio. (II.13–15)

> [After she has led me to that high threshold, who makes me follow her alone, do you lead me where I want to go.]

The guide seems to be related to Venus as Vergil is to Beatrice. Moreover, the sort of Venus addressed by the narrator is not the heavenly one; for although the revised version introduces the work as a vision "ch'Amor mi fé presente" [which Love made present to me], the original version says "Cupido" instead of Amor.

To the extent that the guide has Vergil's role, her identification with reason is confirmed by Boccaccio's own commentary on *Inferno* I (alleg.150) "che Virgillo, là dove bisogna serà, nella presente opera s'intenda per la ragione a noi conceduta da Dio . . . a dirizare e a guidare ogni nostra operazione in bene: la qual cosa ella fa, mossa e ammaestrata dalla divina grazia, quante volte è da noi lasciata esser donna e imperadrice de' nostri sensi" [that Virgil, wherever it will be necessary, in the present work signifies reason granted to us by God . . . to direct and guide all our doings to the good: which she does, moved and taught by divine grace, whenever we allow her to be mistress and ruler of our senses].

The guide as Celestial Love does neatly balance the two boys in red and white who lead the narrator toward worldly goods and into the garden of love. The opposition between these figures, however, is satisfied just as well by the identification of the guide with Reason or Consiglio. Such an identification is strongly suggested by her resemblance to Lady Philosophy, whose lessons on fortune and true happiness she repeats. She even promises the narrator that she will "farti a tempo consolato" [console you in time] as if alluding to Boethius's *Philosophiae Consolatio* (L.24).[9] She urges from the start not the love of God but the temperance of desires: "Ir si convien . . . / con voler temperato" (I.82–83) [one must go . . . with tempered will]. Thus too she hopes that the beloved lady will provide a "fren" [rein] to her lover's will (XLVIII.34); "fren" is usually the image for reason in control of the passions.[10]

As she expresses her mission:

a trarti fuor d'errore e di molesti
disii discesi, e per voler mostrarti
le vere cose (III.79–81)

[to draw you out from error and troublesome desires I descended,
and because I want to show you the true things].

"Errore" becomes the narrator's literal wandering; as he sets out into the garden without her, he wonders who will guide his steps (XXXVII.76–78). She rebukes him as one who "va sanza ragion" [goes without reason] when he persists in choosing mortal pleasures (XXX.57). The conflict, in her phrase, is between his "volontà" [will] and her "consiglio vero" [true counsel] (XLVII.34–35).

Just as Ameto learned to understand rightly the images which the lover-writer of his *Comedia* took only at face value, so too in the *Amorosa Visione* the guide provides a running commentary or explication for the scenes which the lover describes but does not understand. Thus we have once again a sort of text and gloss both within the narrative. The *Visione* is also a dream, unlike the *Comedia delle Ninfe*.[11] Thus the literal sense no longer pretends to be real, and the theme of dream imagery enters the discussion of how one is to read; for the game of interpretive possibilities and ambiguities well suits the nature of dream interpretation.

Within the dream, moreover, are further illusions. The palace contains painted murals which strike the viewer with their lifelike quality.[12] Only Giotto could have painted them (IV.16–17). The figures even seem to speak. But the guide rebukes the narrator for his wonder, reminding him that the figures are not real and that the persons portrayed have all been dead for many years (VI.23–24). She repeats her point at the end of his long gazing (XXX.13ff.) where the renewed reference to death leads into the triumph of fortune and the demonstration that all these goods which seem permanently fixed by the paintings will not truly last. It is thus a warning not only against putting one's trust in worldly goods but also against believing too much in art; both mean taking illusions for reality, as did Europa, who is seen lamenting to Giove, "Omei, / ch'i'son gabbata dal falso argomento" (XVI.87–88) [Alas, I have been tricked by a false argument]. She mistook his apparent shape for truth and was deceived. "Argomento" is a specific rhetorical term referring to a possible or plausible fiction, between history and fable.[13] It is, in short, lifelike but not necessarily true. The guide warns:

> . . . Tu ti abbagli
> nel falso imaginar e credi a questi
> ch' a dritta via son pessimi seragli. (III.76–78)

> [You blind yourself in false imagining and believe in these which are very evil barriers to the right way.]

Later she repeats almost the same phrase (XXX.40–41):

> Tu t'abbagli te stesso in tanta erranza
> con falso immaginar.

> [You blind yourself in such error with false imagining.]

Both the represented goods and the enticing images of their beauty are a deceit, turning men aside from the true good. If Eucomos was a poet who intentionally led astray, the "I" of the *Amorosa Visione* is a reader easily misled. The guide's reproaches echo those of Beatrice, scolding Dante in the earthly paradise:

> e volse i passi suoi per via non vera,
> imagini di ben seguendo false (*Purg.* XXX.130–31)

> [and he turned his steps by a false way, following false images of good].

In Boccaccio's text, the given "imagini" [images] become an active "imaginar" [imagining]; the dreaming narrator is making these images himself. Like Idalagos of the *Filocolo* or Fiammetta of the *Elegia di Madonna Fiammetta*, he is deluding himself with his own art. Dante, in the *Vita Nuova*, seems to have distinguished systematically between the prophetic truth of a "vision" and the fantastical qualities of the "imagination."[14] Thus too Boccaccio can differentiate between the illusory "imaginar" of the narrator and his own *Visione* as a vehicle of truth.

Another scene lurks behind the narrator's picture-gazing in the palace.

When Aeneas, arriving at the Temple in Carthage, marvels at the pictures on it, Bernard's commentary explains that he is ignorantly marveling at the empty images of worldly good.[15] Carthage is the city of the world ruled by Dido or lust (p. 12).[16] Aeneas during his visit there is deceived by Cupid, who appears as Ascanius, lust appearing at first as honest love. Thus the heaven-sent messenger, Mercury, who will urge Aeneas's departure, becomes one more model for the guide of the *Visione*. Fulgentius's commentary on this passage in *Aeneid* I is also to the point, emphasizing as it does the naive incomprehension of Aeneas, who here represents childhood with its curiosity and lack of interpretive skills: "At vero animum pictura inani quod pascit, certum puerile studium refert, infantia enim videre novit, sentire vero quod videat nescit, sicut in picturas est visibilitas, deest sensibilitas." [But in truth the mind which feeds on an empty picture refers to the undeniable eagerness of children, for infancy knows how to see, but truly does not know how to understand what it sees, just as in pictures there is visibility but no sensibility.]

The narrator begins by accepting the guide's judgment verbally without really understanding it: "andiamo e vediam questi ben fallaci" (III.38) [let's go see these deceitful goods]. After his gazing, he has become convinced that the values depicted are good. The paintings have had a rhetorical effect:

> . . . Oh quanto vale
> avere vedute queste varie cose
> che dicevate piene di gran male!
> Or come si porria più valorose,
> che sieno queste, mai per nullo avere (XXX.7–11)

[Oh how valuable it is / to have seen these various things / which you said were full of great evil! / Now how could one ever for any price / have things worth more than these are].

The guide again reproaches him chiefly for gullibility.

> . . . Parti vedere
> quel ben che tu cercavi qui dipinto,
> che son cose fallaci e fuor di vere?

[Does it seem to you that you see / that good which you were seeking painted here, / which are misleading things and not true?]

In sum, the paintings are illusions representing illusory goods, and the whole scene of viewing them is itself part of a dream or "falso imaginar" [false imagining]. You would see the truth, says the guide, "se tu . . . con dritto occhio scoprissi" (XXX.36) [if you . . . discovered with a straight eye]; that is, to see what is really depicted requires an eye which uncovers, which pierces the veil of appearance. Here, as in Mopsa's tale in the *Comedia delle Ninfe*, is Boccaccio's advice to his own readers.

Moving from the hall of pictures into the garden removes only one of the layers of illusion. It is not a painted garden but a real one—within the dream. In the joy of loving his lady, the narrator keeps asking himself

"Sogni tu o ver sei qui, come ti pare?"
"Anzi ci son," fra me poi rispondea.
In cotal guisa spesso a disgannare
me quella donna gentile abbracciava
e con disio la mi parea basciare,
fra me dicendo ch'io pur non sognava
posto che mi pareva grande tanto
la cosa, ch'io pur di sognar dubbiava. (XLVI.35–42)

["Are you dreaming or are you really here as it seems to you?" / "Indeed I am here," I then replied within myself. / In this manner often, to undeceive myself, / it seemed that I embraced that gentle lady / and kissed her with desire, / saying within myself that truly I was not dreaming / since the matter seemed to me so great / that I suspected that I might be dreaming.]

The narrator *is* dreaming, of course, as the "mi parea" reminds us. Moreover, his fear of dreaming, caused by his exalted evaluation of love, is a fear justified by the guide's remarks. For the guide has emphasized that to value the world's goods is to be deceived by false images, i.e., to be dreaming. The narrator's dream, then, is a general state of life, the life of all who place too much value on ephemeral goods.

Boccaccio's comments on the *Commedia* enlighten his own imitation. He attributed Dante's losing his way (in *Inf.* I) to mental sleep:

nel quale, ciascuno che si diletta più di seguir l'appetito che la ragione, è veramente legato, e ismarrisce, anzi perde la via della verità. . . . Il sonno mentale, allegoricamente parlando, è quello quando l'anima, sottoposta la ragione a' carnali appetiti, vinta dalle concupiscenze temporali, s'addormenta in esse, e oziosa e negligente diventa, e del tutto dalle nostre colpe legata diviene, quanto è in potere alcuna cosa a nostra salute operare; e questo è quel sonno, dal quale ne richiama san Paolo, dicendo: "Hora est iam nos de somno surgere" (*Esposizioni* I.alleg.33)

[in which each person who delights more in following appetite than reason is truly bound, and loses himself, rather loses the way of truth. . . . The mental sleep, allegorically speaking, is that when the soul, subordinating reason to the carnal appetites, overcome by temporal concupiscences, falls asleep in them, and becomes idle and negligent and altogether bound by our sins, as much as anything has power to work for our salvation; and this is that sleep which Saint Paul refers to saying: "Now is the hour for us to rise from sleep"].

The grace of God can wake us up so that we set reason once again "si come donna e maestra della nostra vita"(34) [as lady and mistress of our life]. How does grace awaken the sleeper? Boccaccio lists several ways: sometimes it touches the mind with visions; sometimes it sends messengers, such as Mercury to Aeneas, or the loss of worldly goods which makes men recognize their instability. The *Amorosa Visione* includes all three. It is itself a "vision"; it offers us the warning words of a heavenly guide; and it demonstrates at length in the triumph of fortune (XXXI–XXXVII) the instability of worldly pleasures, wealth, and fame.

There is a further Dante echo at work as well, however, and that is Beatrice's remark in *Paradiso* I.88–91:

. . . "Tu stesso ti fai grosso
col falso imaginar, sì che non vedi
ciò che vedresti, se l'avessi scosso.
Tu non se' in terra, sì come tu credi"

[You are befuddling yourself / with false imagining, so that you do not see / what you would see if you shook it off. / You are not on earth as you believe].

This passage implies for Boccaccio's narrative that if the narrator shook off his false imaginings and looked properly, he would see not earthly things, as he takes them to be, but heavenly ones. That is, even though the guide dismisses these pictures as not worth wasting time on, Boccaccio may be suggesting that they *are* worth considering if one reads them rightly. The image of the lady who becomes the poet's love is a special example of this possibility, as we shall see later. The conclusion to be inferred from this is that the guide herself may not be entirely correct in her perceptions—unlike Dante's Beatrice in the analogous quotation.[17] While a better judge than the lover of the value of what the paintings literally represent, she seems less able than the poet to recognize their allegorical potential, i.e., to see that worldly beauty may become a lure toward higher good. The possible limitations of the guide reinforce the idea that she represents reason rather than celestial love. She too seems to be enlightened in cantos XLVII–XLVIII as she suddenly recognizes the true nature of the beloved lady. Thus in the final scene she is able to promise that the lady will be found again in heaven.

The very quality of the vision is as ambiguous as what it contains. For on one hand it is the false dream of a sleeping soul, in the sense just described. Yet on the other hand it is a means of waking the soul to truth. The lover's vision is his own delusion; but the author's *Visione* includes that lover's rude awakening and should in turn awaken its readers—who are, as lovers, equally asleep. Thus too, "lover" comes to mean not simply a lover of women but a lover of the world's goods in general.

I have suggested that the narrator and the guide are, respectively, the voices of appetite and reason. In the acrostic poem addressed to his readers, the poet describes himself as "forse da disiosi / voler troppo infiammato" [perhaps too much inflamed by desirous will], and bids the reader amend the work for him. The first acrostic poem requests the same of Maria: "per vostra cortesia / corregiate amendando il mio fallire" [correct my fault by your amendment]. This repeats earlier identifications of Maria or Fiammetta as a skillful reader who will correct the lover's faults and read *in bono* a text that may be offered partly as a seduction. Her corrective function also parallels that of the Maria within the story, who—as we shall see—is to hold the reins that restrain and direct the narrator according to the councils of reason or wisdom. In fact, she too is asked to correct the poet's work at the end:

> mirando dove cade riprensione
> mi corregiate,
>
> . . .
>
> Per vostro onore e somma reverenza
> della fé ch'io vi deggio, come a donna

di virtuosa e somma intelligenza,
   atando me la possa che s'indonna
in ciascun cuor gentil che da virtute
per accidente alcun mai non si sdonna,
   rispetto avendo ancora alla salute
che da vo' isperanza mi promette
a mitigar l'amorose ferute,
   aggio composte queste parolette (L.55–56, 61–70)[18]

[correct me where you see that blame falls, / . . . For your honor
and the highest reverence / of the faith which I owe you, as to a
lady / of virtuous and supreme intelligence, / with that power
aiding me which rules / in every gentle heart that never / by any
chance throws off the rule of virtue, / having regard also for the
salvation / which hope promises me from you / to mitigate the
amorous wounds, / I have composed these little words].

The Maria of the acrostic poem and the Maria within the text seem to be
the same. Once again she is a reader of unusual intelligence; and if the
power that rules in gentle hearts is love, it is a love which shares its rule
with virtue that cannot be shaken off. The lover's hope in her as a source of
salvation recalls the holy setting of his love in the *Filocolo* and also relates
Fiammetta to Beatrice as the lady who corrects her lover's faults and offers
him salvation. And yet the poet persists in describing himself as someone
in need of correction.

    The game is now not only between two narrators or a narrator and an
explicator but between the text and its readers, including us. The problem
of reading caused by the double voice within the work reflects the problem
in the soul, ours as well as the poet's. The reader must recognize the separate voices speaking both to and within him and attribute the proper authority to each. Thus the reader moves from sharing the passionate effu-
sions of the narrator to viewing them from a distance and appreciating the
rational control of the artist beyond him; for, as in other works, the conflict between two voices leads us to realize that the true author is not simply the character who says "I." The lessons about morality and about literature are the same. Learning to read allegory is a process of learning to
read reality in a world where fortune's goods are mere images and illusions.
It is also a process of learning to see through the images that one's own
psyche produces, to avoid the traps of self-delusion and to look with the
eyes of reason at one's own condition.

    The *Amorosa Visione* is the last work dedicated explicitly to Maria-

Fiammetta by her poet lover. Although some of the ladies from the *Comedia delle Ninfe* also reappear in the garden of the *Visione*, they no longer represent anything clearly defined.[19] The focus is once again on a single lady rather than a group. The guide uses this lady ultimately as a bait to lure the narrator upwards, just as Vergil used the promise of Beatrice to urge Dante forward through the fiery ring on Mount Purgatory. Fiammetta's role is not that of Laura, to draw the poet to virtue by her own actions, but rather that of Beatrice before Dante's absolution in the earthly paradise, the goal of his confused love toward which he is helped by a separate guide.

Although there is no prefatory letter this time, the poet names himself and the lady in two of the three poems written as an acrostic throughout the entire book.[20] The first poem, a sonnet, addresses "Madama Maria" and "Cara Fiamma," linking the names as in the *Filocolo*, but contains no reference to her relation to King Robert. Indeed, the king, rather than serving as her illustrious if adulterous father, is set among the avaricious in the wall paintings of the vision.[21] Instead, Fiammetta is connected, within the narrative, solely to the family of Thomas Aquinas (XLIII.46–54). The saint is identified as "Campagner," i.e., from Campania, the region around Naples. Thus the Neapolitan origin of Fiammetta is maintained but the family associations are gradually changed.

Aquinas speaks at length in Dante's *Paradiso* (XII) in a canto on wisdom or intellectual power. For Boccaccio too he is a man of wisdom and one who knew how to lay open veiled writings ("scritture nascoste"). Perhaps his descendant did indeed know how to read the allegorical books addressed to her. Fiammetta's connection with Wisdom will reappear two canti later.

A holy ancestor suits the heavenly aspects of Fiammetta's ambiguous nature. In the lines immediately following her relation to Aquinas, she is named as before

> . . . da quella, in cui già empresso
> stette Colui che la nostra natura
> nobilitò, . . . che poi l'eccesso
> absterse della prima creatura
> con la sua pena (XLIII.55–59)

[for her in whom He was empressed / who made our nature / noble, . . . who then cleansed / the excess of the first created woman / with its penalty].

As in the *Filocolo*, we find a reference to Mary and the sin of Eve in the middle of a garden of "amore per diletto." Christ's ennobling of human nature inserts itself after the ladies of the garden have sung in the preceding canto that love and only love has such power. As before, then, Fiammetta's nature is linked to the theme of different kinds of love.

The connections with the Virgin Mary continue beyond the name. Boccaccio's Maria is "altieramente umile" (XV.49) [exaltedly humble] or "altiera umilmente" (XLIV.37) [exalted humbly], a paradox frequently applied to the Virgin, specifically in Dante's *Paradiso* XXXIII.2. Boccaccio's use of the phrase in XV is followed soon after by another echo from the same passage of the *Commedia:* "di merzede fontana sono" (XVI.7–8) [I am a fountain of mercy] (*Par.* XXXIII.10–12). This passage of the *Paradiso*, moreover, includes the phrase from Fiammetta's naming: "che l'umana natura / nobiltasti" [you who made noble the human nature]. Yet another phrase may come from Dante's description of the Virgin. St. Bernard tells Dante: "Riguarda omai ne la faccia che a Cristo / più si somiglia" (*Par.* XXXII.85–86) [look now at the face which most resembles Christ's]. Boccaccio writes in his third acrostic poem: "ella somigli' Amor nel su' aspecto" [she resembles Love in her looks] and repeats in his description of her portrait in the triumph of love that she looks just like Love (XV.47), a line followed by "altieramente umile."[22]

Besides allusions to the Virgin Mary, the narrator includes in her description two comparisons to animals, the panther and the eagle, both of which are traditional Christian symbols:

> Io non credo ch'al mondo mai pantera
> col suo odor già anima' tirasse,
> faccendoli venir dovunque s'era
>   blandi e quieti, ch'a lei simigliasse;
> e sì parean mirabili i suoi atti
> ch'Amor pareva lì s'innamorasse.
>   Oh come nello aspetto, in detti e'n fatti,
> savia parea, con alto intendimento,
> pensando a' suo' sembianti ed a' suoi tratti!
>   Contemplando ad Amore il suo talento
> parea fermasse en la sua chiara luce:
> com'aquila a' figliuo' nel nascimento
>   con amor mostra ond'ella li produce
> a seguir sua natura, così questa
> credo che faccia a chi la si fa duce. (XV.70–84)

[I think no panther ever in the world / that with its fragrance at-
tracted the animals, / making them come mild and peaceful /
wherever she was, resembled her; / and so miraculous seemed
her actions / that Love seemed there to be in love. / Oh how wise
she appeared, in words and deeds, / with lofty understanding, /
When I think of her looks and of her features! / Contemplating
Love, her desire / seemed fixed on his clear light: / as an eagle
shows her sons at birth / with love how she produced them / to
follow her nature, so this lady / does, I believe, to whoever makes
her his leader.]

These lines conclude her portrait and take up five of the twelve terzine that
describe her. The panther is discussed by both the widely popular *Physiologus* and by Hugh of St. Victor's *De bestiis* in almost word-for-word the
same way;[23] here is the passage from Hugh:

Est animal quod dicitur panthera, vario quidem colore, sed spe-
ciosum nimis, et mansuetum valde. Physiologus dicit quod inimi-
cum est solis draconibus. Cum ergo comederit et satiaverit se de
universis venationibus, revertitur in speluncam suam, ponensque
se dormit per triduum. Surgens autem a somno, statim emittit
rugitum per altum, simulque odorem nimiae suavitatis cum
rugitu, ita ut odor hujus praecellat omnia aromata et pigmenta.
Cum ergo audierint vocem ejus omnes bestiae, quae longe vel
prope sunt, congregantes se, nimiam suavitatem ejus sequuntur.
Solus autem draco cum audierit vocem ejus, timore perterritus
abscondit se sub terrenis speluncis. Ibi autem non ferens vim
odori ejus, in semetipso contractus obstupescit et torpescit, et
manet immobilis exanimusque velut mortuus; caetera autem ani-
malia sequuntur eam quocumque vadit. Sic et Dominus noster
Jesus Christus verus panther omne genus humanum, quod a di-
abolo captum fuerat, et morti erat obnoxium, per incarnationem
suam ad se trahens eripuit, et captivam ducens captivitatem, dedit dona hominibus (*Ephes.* 4:9). Panthera enim omnis fera, quasi
omne animal odore capiens interpretatur. Sic et Deus, ut diximus, videns omne genus humanum daemonibus captum . . . ,
descendit de coelo cum nimio incarnationis suae odore, et eripuit
nos, sequimurque Dominum. . . . Et quid suavius aut dulcius
esse potest odore Domini nostri Jesu Christi? Ita enim suavis est,
ut omnes qui prope per fidem et per opera sunt, et qui adhuc
fragilitate gravati longe sunt, audiant vocem ejus.

[There is an animal called panther, of varied color, but extremely beautiful and certainly gentle. The natural philosopher says that he is the enemy only of serpents. When, therefore, he has eaten and satiated himself with all kinds of prey, he returns to his cave, and lying down sleeps for three days. Then arising from sleep, at once he emits a great roar, and at the same time a scent of extreme sweetness along with the roar, so that his scent surpasses all perfumes and ointments. Then when all the beasts have heard his voice, those which are far or near, gathering together, follow his extreme sweetness. Only the serpent when he hears his voice, terrified with fear, hides in subterranean caves. There, moreover, unable to bear the power of his scent, contracting into himself, he grows dull and sluggish and remains immobile and spiritless as if he were dead; all the other animals, however, follow the panther wherever he goes. Thus too our Lord Jesus Christ, the true panther, snatched the whole human race, which had been captured by the devil and was subject to death, drawing them to himself through his incarnation, and leading captivity captive, he gave gifts to men (Ephes. 4:9). For panther is interpreted "every beast," as if to say capturing every animal by the scent. Thus too God, as we said, seeing the whole human race captured by demons . . . , descended from heaven with the great scent of his incarnation and snatched us away, and we follow the Lord. . . . And what can be sweeter or more pleasing than the scent of our Lord Jesus Christ? For it is so sweet that all who are near through faith and through works, and those who are far until now being weighed down by frailty, hear his voice.]

The inclusion in this discussion of Christ's descent from heaven in order to draw us away from sin and make us sharers in his goodness is notably concordant with the words which Fiammetta sings from her picture, and which we will soon consider. Both bestiaries, moreover, cite the list of adjectives from Wisdom 7:22–24 as applying both to the panther and to Christ, "qui est dei sapientia" [who is the wisdom of God]. The following verses in Wisdom go on to describe wisdom as a "vapor" and "emanatio" from God, like the panther's breath. It is also a shining of God's light and an image of God's goodness, both attributes of Boccaccio's lady, who is a "graziosa . . . lucia" with shining, flaming eyes (ll. 59–63) and who will soon define herself as an image of God's beauty (see below). Solomon then declares himself a lover of wisdom's beauty, who longs to wed her; and he prays to God to send wisdom down from heaven that she may correct the path of those who are wandering in confusion, weighed down by the body and senses and by the world. (Wisdom 8:1–3; 9, esp. 10–18). These connections with wisdom will shortly be reinvoked by Boccaccio in a passage which I shall discuss below.

Meanwhile, the identifications with both Christ and wisdom are provided by the eagle image as well. As Boccaccio's lady is of "alto intendimento" and, "contemplando," has fixed her gaze and desire on the bright light of Love, so too the eagle, famous for its ability to gaze at the sun, is glossed by Rabanus in his *Allegoriae in universam sacram scripturam* as signifying the soul: "ut in Job: [24] 'Elevabitur aquila, et ponat in arduis nidum suum,' quod per contemplationem exaltatur anima, et in coelis defigit desiderium suum" [25] [as in Job: "The eagle rises aloft, and makes her nest in high places," because by contemplation the soul rises aloft, and sets her desire in heaven]. The eagle is also Christ, says Rabanus, "ut in cantico Deuteronomii: 'Aquila provocavit ad volandum pullos suos,' quod Christus discipulos suos ut de virtute in virtutem proficiant, monere non cessat" [26] [as in Deuteronomy: "The eagle urges its young to fly" because Christ never ceases to admonish his disciples to progress from virtue to virtue]. The passage in Deuteronomy indeed compares God's care of the Hebrews to the eagle's care of her young: "As an eagle stirreth up her nest, that fluttereth over her young, he spread abroad his wings, he took them, he bare them on his pinions. Jehovah alone did lead him." Hugh of St. Victor elaborates in a curious way the idea of the eagle's carrying her young:

> Aquila ab acumine oculorum vocata. . . . Nam et contra radium solis fertur obtutum non flectere, unde et pullos suos ungue suspensos, radiis solis objicit, et quos viderit immobilem tenere aciem, ut dignos genere conservat, si quos vero perspexerit reflectere obtutum, quasi degeneres abjicit. [27]

> [The eagle is named for its keenness of sight. . . . For even into the rays of the sun it can gaze without averting its sight, wherefore, carrying her young in her claws, she holds them too into the rays of the sun, and those whom she sees maintain a steady gaze she keeps as worthy of their kind, but those whom she sees turn aside their gaze she throws down as degenerate.]

Here we have the notion, as expressed by Boccaccio, that the eagle is demonstrating the *nature* of her young, which ought to be like her own. Hugh glosses the eagle as "vel subtilissimae sanctorum intelligentiae, vel incarnatus Dominus" [either the most subtle understanding of the saints, or God incarnate]. As the symbol of John the Evangelist, it stands for those who by their special understanding can look into the mysteries of God. "Similiter qui haec terrena mente deserunt, velut aquila cum Joanne per contemplationem coelestia quaerunt."[28] [Similarly those who leave behind this earthly mind, like the eagle seek out heavenly things with John through contemplation.] This is much to Boccaccio's point. The lady, who is herself contemplative and of high understanding, seeks to make others follow her and take on her ways. Thus she seeks to lead the poet from his current earthly mind to heavenly thoughts. Ultimately the panther and the eagle images are two ways of saying the same thing. Both represent the lady as Christ or an image of God or at least a lofty and contemplative understanding of God's wisdom, and as someone who leads others toward heaven, away from the bondage of the world.[29] If the sun into which this eagle is gazing is "Amor," then Boccaccio may well be suggesting that we read this Love *in bono* as an image of divine love.

The portrait, however, brings about quite mixed associations in the narrator. Indeed, whom should one expect to see in the middle of a triumph of love, next to and looking like Amor, if not Venus? The confusion of heavenly and erotic associations is clear in the narrator's immediate response, interjected into the middle of the description:

> Angiola mi pareva nel ciel nata,
> e in me più volte pensai ch'ella fosse
> quella che in Cipri già fu adorata. (XV.52–54)

[She seemed to me an angel born in heaven, and several times I thought to myself that it was she who used to be worshiped in Cyprus.]

Boccaccio even emphasized this identity by changing the laurel crown of his first version (cf. *Filocolo*) to a crown of roses (cf. *Comedia delle Ninfe*) in his later revision.[30] Whereas the laurel signifies glory and immortality, the rose can be connected either with Mary or with Venus.

Venus rules the timing of events in the garden of love.[31] The narrator enters the garden at a familiar moment: shortly past the fourth hour of a day halfway through Aries (XL.32–33). He does not say Easter Saturday, but at least the Saturday must be carried over from previous works if the fifth hour is to retain its sense, Venus's hour of dominion. Once the narrator is in the garden, twenty-four days pass before he sees his lady again and declares himself her servant (XLIV.61–85). The sun, which was rising in Aries before, is now appropriately rising in Taurus, Venus's sign. Another 135 days pass (XLVI.16–21) before the narrator's pain turns to joy; this puts the sun at the beginning of Libra, Venus's other house. Thus the garden scene reinforces Fiammetta's association with Venus in the painting.

The confusion of holy and erotic love pervades the poem, not just the image of Fiammetta. The love depicted in the painted triumph includes numerous examples of adultery and illicit love, frequently drawn from Ovid. After a series of seductions by the gods in various animal forms, the first human lovers are the tragic Pyramus and Thisbe, then the fickle Jason and Theseus and their abandoned and complaining lovers. Then follow the bestial Pasiphae, the incestuous Mirra, Narcissus, and so on. The depicted love is clearly not an ennobling spiritual condition. Yet the narrator is oblivious to the warning of the painting.

> "Con quanta gioia, credo, si conduce
> ciascun di questi ch'è pien della grazia
> di quel," incominciai, "che quivi è duce."

> ["With what joy, I believe, each of these men behaves who is full
> of the grace of him," I began, "who is here the leader."]

The lovers are "full of grace" but from the wrong god of love.

In the garden, the narrator kneels to a lady who looks as beautiful as Venus and sings so sweetly "che me di me sovente mi toglieva" (XL.81) [that it often took me from myself]. The phrase is borrowed, as Branca points out, from Dante's *Purgatorio* (VIII.15); but whereas Dante is listening to the evening hymn, here the narrator is listening to a siren song of pleasure. Another song is sung by other ladies in the garden, with a prayer to Cupid that could be applied to Christ:

> che non ci paian le ferute
> di lui noiose e grave il sofferire,
>   in cui consiste ogni dolce salute. (XLII.80–82)

> [for his wounds do not seem to us irksome or heavy to suffer, in
> whom consists every sweet salvation]

and ending:

> . . . O signor nostro,
> in te si ferma ogni nostro volere,
> tutte disposte siamo al piacer vostro (86–88)

[O our lord, may our every will be firm in you, we are all disposed to your pleasure]

a parody of "Thy will be done."

Fiammetta in her painting sings a similarly ambiguous song, here
given in full:[32]

> Io son discesa della somma altezza
> e son venuta per mostrarmi a voi.
>   Il viso mio, chi vuol somma bellezza
> veder, riguardi, là dove si vede
> accompagnata lei e gentilezza.
>   O pietà per sorella e di merzede
> fontana sono: Iddio mi v'ha mandata
> per darvi parte del ben che possiede.[33]
>   Donna più ch'altra sono innamorata
> e ma'isdegno in me non ebbe loco,
> però Amor m'ha cotanto onorata.[34]
>   Ancor risplende in me tanto il suo foco,
> che molti credon talor ch'io sia ello,
> avvegna che da lui a me sia poco.
>   Cortese e lieta son di lui vasello,
> né mai mi parran duri i suoi martiri
> pensando al dolce fin che vien da quello.
>   E ben è cieco quei che' suoi disiri
> si crede sanza affanno aver compiuti
> e sanza copia di dolci sospiri.
>   Riceva in pace dunque i dardi aguti,
> ch'alcun piacer di belli occhi saetta
> que' che attendon d'esser proveduti.
>   Tal, qual vedete, giovane angioletta
> qui accompagno Amor che mi disia:
> poi tornerò al cielo a chi m'aspetta. (XVI.2–27)

[I am descended from the supreme height / and have come to
show myself to you. / Let him who wishes to see supreme
beauty / look at my face, where it is seen / accompanied by
gentleness. / I have pity for sister and am / a fountain of mercy:
God has sent me / to give you part of the good which he possesses. / I am a lady more in love than any other / and never dis-

dain held place in me, / therefore Love has so much honored me. / His fire still shines in me so much, / that many think I am he, / since there is little difference between us. / I am his courteous and happy vessel, / nor do his torments ever seem hard to me / thinking of the sweet end that comes from them. / And he is blind indeed who thinks / that he has accomplished his desires without effort / and without an abundance of sweet sighs. / Therefore receive in peace the sharp darts, / for some pleasure of beautiful eyes shoots / those who expect to be secure. / As you see me, a young little angel, / I accompany Love who desires me: / then I shall return to heaven to one who awaits me.]

Fiammetta's song is twenty-seven lines long and divides into three groups of three terzine. The first group sounds completely holy, declaring the lady's mission from heaven. The second group describes the lady's close relation to love, Amor, and thus introduces the song's cupidinous possibilities. The third group combines both aspects as it addresses its audience. The first terzina of this last group warns that toil and effort are necessary to the accomplishment of the desired goal; this could be merely the requirement of love-service, but it also sounds like an appropriate lesson for the poet, whose attempt to fulfill his desires while avoiding the "affanno" of ascent is frustrated.[35] The second terzina bids us accept the darts of love, against which we forearm ourselves in vain. The third announces the lady's return to heaven, where the one who awaits her is presumably God that sent her. The ambiguity of the poem hinges on the identity of Amor. If the lady in some respects resembles the Virgin Mary for whom she is named, could Amor—at least in one interpretation—be Christ? Several hints suggest that this is possible. Lines 8–9 may allude to the Incarnation, since that is how Mary gave the world access to God's bliss. The idea is born out by the image of the lady as "vasello" of love. This image of Mary as container is combined with the use of "amore" for Christ in Dante's prayer to the Virgin (*Par.* XXXIII.7): "Nel ventre tuo si raccese l'amore" [In your womb love was rekindled]. Dante's line is closely followed by the image of "fontana" noted above. The term "martiri," while meaning torments in general, also means more specifically martyrdoms; Christ's martyrdom is indeed the source of "dolce fin," i.e., of man's salvation. In relation to this, the following lines take on a further meaning: just as Christ's death was necessary to bring about salvation, so people are foolish who think that they can find the true good by following the easy path of worldly pleasures;

like Christ, man must die to the world or struggle to rise above it (go up the stairs of the *Visione* dream) in order to attain complete fulfillment. The exhortation to receive the darts of love may mean, then, that we are to accept our insatiable longings as a divinely intended prod toward the ultimate Good. The "proveduti" would be, then, the worldly-wise and self-confident who are, to their own surprise, assailed by desires that cannot be satisfied here. This is a love kindled by the grace of God. God is showing us the lady's beauty in order to entice us after her to heaven.[36]

Besides the *Paradiso* echoes noted above, there are echoes also from the *Vita Nuova*. The very numbers involved in the song's structure are, of course, already one allusion to Dante's threes and nines. In *Vita Nuova* 26, Beatrice "par che sia una cosa venuta / da cielo in terra a miracol mostrare" [seems to be a thing sent from heaven to earth to show a miracle]. The second sonnet in the same chapter begins, "Vede perfettamente onne salute / chi la mia donna tra le donne vede." Together these two passages are close to the opening two terzine of Fiammetta's song. The famous canzone of chapter 19, beginning "Donne ch'avete intelletto d'amore," makes several statements similar to Fiammetta's: God has sent Beatrice into the world in order to show a human the hope of the blessed; but she will return to heaven where she is awaited with desire. Amor himself wonders at her; from her eyes come flaming spirits of love,[37] and one can see Amor painted in her face. Dante bids his poem seek out Amor, whom it will find beside his lady. Like most of Boccaccio's writings, this canzone is addressed only to those who are in love. The undercurrent of Dante's influence supports a holy reading of Fiammetta's song. Yet the ambiguities are there intentionally, one must suppose. For Mary is hardly a suitable figure for the kind of love illustrated by its victims in the painting. The image of Mary and Christ merges with that of Venus and Cupid.

In the *Comedia delle Ninfe*, the holy and erotic aspects of the scene are each understood separately by one of the two narrators, the lover and the newly baptized Ameto, or by Ameto at two different moments, before and after his enlightenment. In the *Amorosa Visione*, however, we are forced to deal simultaneously with two aspects of the narrator: as a character in his own dream he is automatically both identified with and distinguished from the waking writer of the vision.[38] If in the framing elements of acrostic sonnets and final canto the narrator acknowledges his errors and requests correction, within the dream the seemingly better perspective of the writer merges with the ignorance and "cieca mente" (XXX.59) [blind mind] of the character in the dream. If the poet has chosen to represent erotic images of holy love, the character within the dream reverses the process by speaking of *amor per diletto* erroneously in holy terms. Thus he insists to the guide that he loves Fiammetta with holy charity (XLVII.67–75):

> La qual se io sol per libidinosa
> voglia fornire amassi, in veritate
> con dover ne saresti crucciosa;
>   anzi con quella intera caritate
> che prossima persona amar si dee,
> amo.³⁹

[Whom if I loved only to furnish / my libidinous will, in truth / you would have a right to be angry about it; / but with that entire charity / with which one ought to love one's neighbor, / I love.]

Nonetheless, he is trying to ravish her when suddenly awakened from his dream.

A curious confusion enters not only the narrator's relation to Fiammetta but even the guide's. Fiammetta is in the part of the garden dedicated to *amor per diletto*, as the three-sided fountain makes clear. When the narrator first enters the garden, the guide calls after him,

> Dove tu vai, come tu hai veduto,
> è del ben transitorio e fallace:
>   del qual se tu sei bene aveduto,
> come dicevi e come'l tuo parlare
> mostrava che l'avessi entro veduto,
>   a quel non guardaresti, ma anzi andare
> il lasciaresti come cosa vana
> e intenderesti al sol me seguitare. (XXXIX.77–84)

[Where you are going, as you have seen, / is a place of the transitory and deceitful good: / which if you are aware of / as you said and as your words / showed that you had perceived when we were inside, / you would not look at that, but rather / you would let it go as a vain thing / and would be intent only to follow me.]

Yet when he returns to bring the guide to his lady, the guide greets the lady as sister, exclaiming that if she had known who the lady was, she would have hastened there much sooner (XLVIII.8–10). Landau remarks on la palese contradizione in cui cade la guida del poeta, la quale, dopo di aver messo in opera ogni sforzo per ritrarre il nostro degli allettamenti terreni, e per condurlo solo ad ammirare e desiderare le cose etterne, e la luce del sommo fattore, consente poi alla fine che tutto si consacri all'amore di una bella donna, la quale nulla ha in sè di celeste[40]

[the blatant contradiction in which the poet's guide falls, who, after having employed every effort to draw our fellow back from the worldly enticements and to lead him to admire and desire only eternal things and the light of the supreme creator, consents at the end that he dedicate himself entirely to the love of a beautiful woman, who has nothing celestial about her].

We have noted already, however, that Fiammetta is not entirely without celestial features.

Moreover, what the guide does immediately is to perform a remarkable marriage ceremony in which the poet is given as a bride to his lady (XLVIII.31–57):

> Ove poi per la destra mi prendea
> e davami a costei, poscia dicendo,
> che la sua e la mia mano in man tenea:
>   . . .
> "Io 'l ti dono tutto, io 'l ti presento:
> sempre sia tuo, né ello giammai sia ardito
> di sé partir dal tuo comandamento."
>   E poi rivolta a me mi disse: "Udito
> hai ch'io t'ho dato a questa: fa che 'n guisa
> la servi che 'l mio don le sia gradito.
>   Tiella per donna, né giammai divisa
> sia da lei l'alma tua sin che partita
> non sia, dal velo terrestre dicisa."

[Where then she took me by the right hand / and gave me to her, saying / as she held her hand and mine in her own: / . . . "I give him to you, I present him to you: / may he always be yours, and never may he be so bold / as to depart from your commandment." / And then turning to me she said: "You have heard / that I have given you to this woman: see to it / that you serve her in such a way that my gift may be pleasing to her. / Hold her as your lady, nor may your soul / ever be divided from her until she has departed, / sundered from the earthly veil."]

Fiammetta is to be the *domina* or ruler, and he the obedient servant. The guide's explanation of this marriage depends on the spiritual role of Fiammetta as husband: she is to be a "fren" [rein], ruling him with her honest speech and directing him toward that heaven from which she has descended to reveal divine beauty on earth. In his marriage not only is the narrator to serve his lady and obey her commands, as all "courtly" lovers must, but also both he and his lady are to serve and obey the guide:

Intero fa che servi suo parere,

   . . .

però ch'ella non passa il mio volere. (16−18)

[See that you serve her whole bidding . . . for she does not pass beyond my will.]

Indeed, the lady has ordered her lover to fetch his abandoned guide and to obey her. Because she is such a faithful follower of reason, the lady is to be an example for her "wife":

Costei sanza fidel consiglio mio
non ferma fatto né compon suo detto:
dunque per tal esempio il tuo disio
raffrena e segui il verace piacere. (XLVIII.11−14)

[She never does a deed or composes a speech without my faithful counsel: therefore by such an example rein in your desire and follow the true pleasure.]

We have here yet another allusion to *Vita Nuova* 2, where Dante writes of Beatrice "che nulla volta sofferse che Amore mi reggesse sanza lo fedele consiglio de la ragione" [that at no time did she suffer Love to rule me without the faithful counsel of reason]. Through this allusion Boccaccio implies that the lady should act as a Beatrice for his narrator. However, thinking that he *is* following "verace piacere," the narrator continues to pursue his "disio" and tries to make love with his lady. If the marriage were real, there might be nothing wrong with his trying to consummate it;[41] but his attempt is clearly contrary to the will of the guide, who has conveniently been left behind at that moment. It seems that the marriage is not, then, a human, flesh-and-blood relationship as the narrator misunderstands it to be. Rossi believes that the guide approves of the lovemaking, purposely leaving them alone together and subsequently comforting the lover that he will have his lady again.[42] But the lover will clearly not "have" his lady in the same way as during his dream. According to Rossi, Boccaccio's ideal expressed in this book is "il godimento ragionato e tranquillo della felicità che può dar la vita terrena"[43] [the rational and tranquil enjoyment of the happiness that earthly life can give]. That sort of felicity, however, is all subject to the wheel of fortune, whose workings have been revealed in cantos XXXI–XXXVII; according to the guide's promise, the lady will only be truly his after he has managed the ascent to eternal life.

Crescini complains of the flagrant contradiction between Fiammetta's two roles, and concludes that the *stil novo* role is merely a formal borrowing for Boccaccio into which he poured new content, the celebration of his real love for Maria.[44] I think that rather the assigned role of the lady makes evident the error of the narrator's attempt and his continual lack of understanding for the guide's teachings. He insists on treating as physical realities the images of his dream. He is, in short, not recognizing the allegorical or spiritual nature of the vision in which he is involved.

There is, furthermore, an allegorical aspect to the relation between lover and lady which has so far gone unnoticed by scholars. As the narrator declares his submission to the lady in the garden, she writes on his heart her name in letters of gold and puts on his finger a ring with a chain leading from it to her heart (XLV.10–24). On one hand, this seems merely the emblem of love: he is attached to her heart and bears her in his. On the other hand, the incident echoes lines from the proverbs of Solomon (Proverbs 7:1–4). Wisdom is speaking: "Fili mi, custodi sermones meos, et praecepta mea reconde tibi. / Fili, Serva mandata mea, et vives: et legem meam quasi pupillam oculi tui: / Liga eam in digitis tuis, scribe illam in tabulis cordis tui. / Dic sapientiae, soror mea es: et prudentiam voca amicam tuam." [My son, keep my words, and lay up my commandments with thee. Keep my commandments and live; and my law as the apple of thine eye. Bind them upon thy fingers; write them upon the tablet of thy heart. Say unto wisdom, Thou art my sister; and call understanding thy friend.] Soon after, the guide greets Fiammetta as "mia sorella" (XLVIII.7) [my sister].

The love scene is a parody of the words of Wisdom, for the narrator is entering Cupid's bondage, not binding himself to the precepts and laws of wisdom or prudence. But the possibility of an alternate meaning is there, reinforced by the greeting of the guide. Fiammetta, we recall, is the descendant of Aquinas, whose chief attribute, for Dante and for Boccaccio, is wisdom. Moreover, both she and Wisdom are associated with the Virgin Mary, and the words of Wisdom, "Ab initio et ante saecula creata sum" [from the beginning and before the ages I was created], were read regularly during the office of the Virgin. The passage quoted above from Proverbs continues with a warning against the false lures of lust. It offers, in short, the same choice between two kinds of love which Boccaccio is writing about.

Fiammetta is the object of both kinds of love. After the dreamer has awakened, the guide assures him that she will take him to his lady, who is apparently in the heaven from which she had said she descended as a harbinger of God's beauty. Nonetheless, within the dream at least, the lady is also human and even responds happily to her lover's physical attentions. Thus ultimately we are left, with the narrator, in confusion about what it is that he loves.

Part of the increased confusion since the *Comedia delle Ninfe* results from the *Visione*'s separation into two different characters of the beloved lady and the guide. In the *Comedia delle Ninfe* it is faith, in the form of the beloved Lia, who guides Ameto through his education. In the *Visione* the guide is, as I have argued, reason and is not herself an object of attraction to the narrator. Indeed for all her regal and even celestial qualities (reason is rightly the *domina* of our souls, as Boccaccio writes in his gloss on Dante's Vergil),[45] the *Visione* guide is less effective than Lia, possibly because reason is weaker than faith in effecting their common aim.

Moreover, reason here is weaker even than it has been before; for Teseo, as a champion of reason and governor of Minerva's city, successfully regains control of the passionate knights as well as victoriously quelling the rebellion of the Amazons and the cruel violence of Creon. Could it be that the *Visione* guide, royal like Teseo, is now a heavenly figure because earth seems now to Boccaccio incapable of producing such rational enlightenment and guidance? Has it become something superhuman? This would work together with the narrator's recalcitrance to declare the difficulty of the educative task. That sense of difficulty is new since the *Comedia delle Ninfe*, and is corroborated by the development of inner conflict in this later work. For if the *Comedia delle Ninfe* ends with two different views of the situation, those views are represented by two quite separate people, Ameto and the unhappy lover. In the *Visione*, however, the narrator himself both learns and unlearns. Furthermore, to the extent that the guide is his own reason, he is in conflict with himself; Ameto is not part of the *Comedia* narrator in this way. Similarly the clean separation of realms in the *Comedia*, i.e., the erotic stories and their moral or Christian meanings, has become in the *Visione* a confusion much harder to sort out—for us as well as for the narrator.

This confusion carries over, even more than in previous works, to our understanding of the narrator's situation. Does his waking at the end imply a successfully altered consciousness and final understanding? Or does the narrator in his old condition confront the guide—now *outside* his dream— in the sudden final split of viewpoints into two separate characters that we have observed in the *Filocolo* and *Comedia delle Ninfe?* The ending can be read either way; for the narrator's exclamations on awaking perfectly convey the pervasive ambiguity of the book:

> . . . e già saria finita
> la vita mia, se non che ad esso loco
>   veracemente spero che reddita
> ancor farò con essenzia perfetta,
> prendendo quella gioia ben compita
>   nella qual stetti mo', che fu imperfetta
> dormendo (XLIX.77–86)

[and already my life would be over / if not that I hope to return truly to that place / with perfect essence, / taking that joy well fulfilled / in which just now I stayed, which was imperfect / in my sleeping].

The original version continues:

> E questo l'amorosa mente
> solo disia e fermamente aspetta,
>   ove Colui, che di tutto è potente,
> me rechi e servi nella vostra grazia.

[And this alone the amorous mind / desires and firmly awaits, / where may He who is all-powerful / bring me and keep me in your grace.]

The revised version substitutes "Amor" [Love] for "Colui" [He]. The religious sense of the speech is easy to read.[46] There is the contrast between the imperfect joys of his sleeping state versus the perfect joys of his wakened understanding;[47] "essenzia perfetta" will be his after death, and his hope is for grace and joy in heaven. Yet the change to "Amor" shows Boccaccio's insistence on the double nature of love. God is Love, but Amor or Cupid too "vincit omnia." The "gioia ben compita" in this sense means real physical love as opposed to the dream of it. The prayer is to Cupid to put him in his lady's grace, so that she will accept his desires. When the narrator asks toward the end of the final canto (L.79–81) that his lady extinguish the flame in his heart by her mercy, we can think both of common prayers to the Virgin Mary to defend the sinner from lust and of the merciful yielding that a carnal lover begs for.[48] The final line of the first version, "io v'aco-mando al Sir di tutta pace" [I commend you to the Lord of all peace] is changed completely in Boccaccio's revision to a statement of his firm love for the lady. As the author of the poem and acrostics is closely identified with the character who says "I" within the dream, not only by his love for Maria but also by his admission of error and need for correction, it is pos-sibly both author and narrator—i.e., possibly Boccaccio himself—who ac-knowledges his persistent erotic attraction to the woman who ought to be his Beatrice.

Fiammetta's triple appearance may be based on the Neoplatonic tri-plicity which Ambrose formulated as "Umbra in lege, imago in evangelio, veritas in caelestibus"[49] [a shadow in the law, an image in the gospel, truth in heaven]. First, Fiammetta appears in a painting, a reflection or *umbra* of reality. Second, she appears physically in the garden. This is a layer closer to her true essence, but she is still only an image of the heavenly idea which she represents. The physical presence as mere image is reinforced by the narrator's dreaming. Third, she will be found truly and lastingly in heaven. As for Ambrose, this third realism is still a promise to be fulfilled at some time in the future: "Prima igitur umbra praecessit, secuta est imago, erit veritas. . . . Ascende ergo, homo, in coelum, et videbis illa quarum umbra hic erat vel imago. Videbis non ex parte, non in aenigmate, sed in consum-matione" (1052). [First preceded the shadow, the image followed, the truth will be. . . . Rise therefore, man, into heaven, and you will see that of which the shadow or image was here. You will see not in part, not in enigma, but in consummation.] Perhaps the narrator's attempted consum-mation in the flesh is a parody of that other consummation, and is inter-rupted to demonstrate that it cannot be complete in the present world.

Fiammetta embodies the narrator's confusion. She exists both within the dream and beyond it. On one hand, she herself suggests one under-standing of her role—of her beauty as an object of love—in her speech in canto XVI: God has sent her as a sign of His beauty; one is to love her with *caritas*, the sort of love that leads through her to God. On the other hand, she speaks from the center of a triumph of Cupid and sits in a garden of *amor per diletto*. Though from the start the *Visione* offers a choice of ways, she is to be found at the end of either path. Most simply she is the object of the narrator's desires, and her image keeps shifting to fit the different views of what is desirable. She is the projection of the poet's dreaming and waking mind, the ultimate image of his "imaginar," for him—and us—to define.

VI

Elegia di Madonna Fiammetta

Written soon after the *Amorosa Visione*, the *Elegia* again presents two main speakers: a passionate lover and rational counselor.[1] The lover this time is a woman, but it is still the lover from whose point of view the book is written. The femaleness of the narrator emphasizes the distinction between narrator and author; yet, as in the *Visione*, the councils of reason are transmitted only by the passionate narrator who rejects those councils. Consciously and willfully she chooses to follow the "furore" of love, kneeling to a Venus who becomes identified with the fury Tesiphone. Her declaration "seguitai l'appetito" [I followed appetite] clearly associates Fiammetta with those who turn from Astrea to serve Priapus. Acknowledging that her old nurse speaks truth in criticizing passionate obsession, Fiammetta nonetheless rejects her advice. This outright rejection goes beyond the wavering "erranza" of the *Amorosa Visione* lover. Furthermore, the illusions of the *Visione* dreamer become in the *Elegia* the illusions of the wideawake Fiammetta; thus there can be here no final waking into a possibly better understanding.

In the *Elegia*, the representative of reason is no longer an awe-inspiring queen from heaven but rather an old gray-haired servant who can counsel her mistress but must ultimately obey Fiammetta's will. When the narrator of the *Amorosa Visione* wanders heedless of his guide's warning into the garden of love, the guide simply stays behind for a while. But the nurse of the *Elegia*, seeing that all remonstrances are useless, actively helps Fiammetta arrange her adulterous affair. Here we are presented allegorically with the subservience of reason to the appetite. Reason may protest but is impotent to redirect the will or to counteract the attractive power of lust. The irrationality of lust leads Fiammetta into total insanity.

If the *Amorosa Visione* lover is a slow learner and has failed by the end of the book to make the ascent toward heaven, at least there is still hope that he will finally follow his persistent guide if only to see again the promised lady. His wavering course is a series of advances and backwards slippings as he learns new lessons and then quickly forgets them. In the *Elegia di Madonna Fiammetta*, however, the narrator descends dramatically straight toward hell. Fiammetta is another Francesca, telling her story as if she were a victim; but her deterioration involves a descent farther and farther into hell. She turns against herself both violence and fraud, attempting suicide and, despite her knowledge of the truth, obsessively fixing herself on the illusion that Panfilo may still return. The book ends with its lover-writer in a state of desperate damnation, with all the immovable pride of Satan. Thus, along with the increased helplessness of reason, Boccaccio also darkens his portrayal of those who cast aside its guidance. The consequences are no longer amusing; they are hell itself, including within the concept of hell the state of the soul while it is still on earth. This understanding of hell is part of Boccaccio's legacy from Dante,[2] and Fiammetta in her madness is described with phrases from Dante's minotaur.[3] In sum, the *Elegia* can be seen not only as an Ovidian *Heroides*, to which it has been compared, but also as an *Inferno* rewritten by Boccaccio—an inferno from which, however, there seems to be no way out for the narrator.[4]

Again Ovid merges with Dante, providing an elegiac model for a Christian theme.[5] But whereas the *Filocolo* made important reference to the *Ars amatoria*, Boccaccio here is using the *Heroides*, the complaints of women betrayed by love. That is, Boccaccio is moving to safer ground among the texts of Ovid, for the darkening image of passion cannot allow any more the lighthearted mockery of the *Ars* or *Amores* or the risk of suggesting to the foolish that passion can be good. With the *Corbaccio* we will move from the laments of the *Heroides* to the cure of the *Remedia amoris*.

The Fiammetta in the *Elegia di Madonna Fiammetta* is almost totally unlike the Fiammettas to whom those earlier works, discussed so far, were addressed. For the *Elegia* as for Boccaccio's other works, one need not know anything about Fiammetta's previous roles in order to appreciate the new text. In this case, however, previous knowledge does add some enjoyment. A reader acquainted with the *Filocolo*, *Teseida*, or *Amorosa Visione* would be startled by the new Fiammetta. First of all, she is now the narrator of the entire book. Secondly, she is telling a story of her own betrayal by her lover and by love. Thirdly, she is associated not with Mary any longer but with Eve.

Because she takes over what was previously the position of the male narrator, and because Panfilo's departure enticingly resembles Boccaccio's own move from Naples to his father's house in Florence, the critics who were looking at Boccaccio's fictions as autobiography suggested either that Boccaccio is putting into Fiammetta's mouth his own sorrow at having to leave her, perhaps as a kind of apology, or else that in bitterness at having been betrayed by her, he is writing a story in which their situation is reversed.[6] Yet making Fiammetta the narrator was not only an imitation of the *Heroides*, as scholars have noticed,[7] but also a brilliant stroke which enabled Boccaccio to have her fulfill two roles at once. She is on one hand a female version of the usual narrator-lover or poet-seducer, who hopes that her enterprise of writing will win the reward of love returned, or at least of compassion from the beloved. Like many of the poet-lovers, she is ignored and frustrated by the object of her attentions. Like them, she provides through her frustration and folly a lesson of what to avoid, quite the opposite lesson from the one she hopes to teach her beloved, for whom the writing is meant as a lure. But besides being the would-be seducer, she is also the victim of seduction and an explicit warning to other women addressed by seductive flatterers such as the narrators of the *Filostrato* and *Teseida*. Thus there are two different audiences each addressed by one of her roles: Panfilo she hopes to seduce; other women she hopes to warn away from enslavement to passion. Earlier narrators similarly addressed other lovers as well as their own beloved but, unlike Fiammetta, did not consciously intend two such opposite readings. Here the double audience replaces the double author as a means of pointing out two quite diverse intentions or meanings of the text. Scholars who view Fiammetta in this work as a noble victim are responding the way she hopes Panfilo will. But other readers are intended to be horrified and repelled by what she has made of herself.

Fiammetta remains in part the glorified woman of love poetry. The young man who meets her in church whispers holy words of adoration. Yet he is so soon unfaithful that the reader must wonder whether the whole religion of love is not being scoffed at here.[8] Because Panfilo's resemblance to Boccaccio reminds the reader of the narrator's pose in his earlier fictions, the *Elegia* suggests that the poet-lover and others of his ilk would, if they managed to seduce their angel-ladies, leave them in a while for someone else. Fiammetta's very effort through art to hang on to that love and eternalize it only serves to construct an elaborate monument to its very fleet-ingness and loss.

Similarities between the *Elegia* and the *Filostrato* support the idea that the *Elegia* is, in a way, Fiammetta's answer to the earlier poet-lover fictions, especially as one work is almost the mirror of the other. Panfilo, like Criseida, is forced unwillingly to leave town and join his father but quickly forgets the old love for a new one. As Troiolo, abandoned by the fickle Criseida, falls into despair and rushes to his death, so too Fiammetta grows desperate and attempts suicide; for both Boccaccio uses the same lines from Dante's description of the minotaur. The title in both cases refers to the name of the narrator and suggests a tragic mode, the "Elegia" and the victim beaten by love. Instead of telling his own tale of woe, Filo-strato has found a classical tale which mirrors his case. Fiammetta similarly searches through classical mythology for an example comparable to her own, but she can find none sufficiently tragic to match her own condition. Both books are addressed to lovers in hopes that such readers will pity the narrator's sorrows. Both books hope on the one hand to win back the fickle lover and on the other hand to warn other young men and ladies about the sufferings caused by love.

Sapegno points to the *Elegia* to support his thesis of Boccaccio's de-veloping realism that would reach its height in the *Decameron*.[9] But al-though the *Elegia* resembles a seventeenth- or eighteenth-century novel of psychological analysis, such as for example the *Princesse de Clèves*, or even later novels, Boccaccio is not interested in psychology per se. He does not want us to empathize with Fiammetta; he wants us to see in her steadily worsening condition a demonstration of the effects of sin.

Fiammetta shows herself damned from the start. She announces the topic as love and its torments "le quali a me, che altro non cerco, di dolore perpetuo fieno cagione" [which will be to me, who seek for nothing else, cause of perpetual pain]. She recognizes that "dolore perpetuo" is hell itself and urges her female readers to think how unstable their own condition is, and by comparing her past happiness with her present condition ("da quella felicità allo stato presente argomento prendendo"), to acknowledge her the most unhappy of women. Here again is an echo from the infernal Francesca (and also, by now, from the *Teseida*'s lover-poet). Yet intent on creating and nourishing her own hell, she wants to arouse the pity of others not in order to console herself but in order to increase her grief, to justify her own self-pity.

At the beginning of her narrative, Fiammetta tells us that already as a child she began to glory in her own beauty. Later she delighted in luring men to adore her as their only god.[10] One of the elements that the *Elegia* repeats from earlier works is the first meeting of the lovers in church, during a "solenne oficio" [solemn office] in spring, which we may assume from other works is the Easter service. But whereas in the *Filocolo* Fiammetta's qualities seem consonant with the meanings of the holy day, in the *Elegia* she intentionally sets herself in conflict with the Christian religion, delighting in the extent to which her beauty distracts both men and women from their worship and glorying in herself as a goddess. One can see here that Fiammetta has switched from a Mary to an Eve, the original proud woman who sought to become like God and who lured Adam to follow her instead of God's law.

There is further evidence to support this radically new identification. Early in chapter I Fiammetta has a premonitory dream. She is gathering flowers "quale Proserpina allora che Pluto la rapì alla madre" [like Proserpina when Pluto abducted her from her mother]. Suddenly she is bitten by a serpent just as Euridice was. Both these classical women are about to go to Hades, or in Christian terms to hell. Fiammetta recognizes this in the case of Proserpina, leaving Euridice without comment. Both allusions, partly thanks to Dante (*Purg.* XXVIII.49–51), might remind a Christian reader of the fall from Eden; there is the lovely garden, then the serpent. The gloss to the *Elegia* says more specifically "uno serpente il quale la morse nel calcagno" [a serpent which bit her in the heel] and calls the underworld "inferno." The serpent wounding the heel is a parallel to the prophecy in Genesis. There God says to the serpent: "I will put enmity between thee and the woman, and between thy seed and her seed; he shall bruise thy head, and thou shalt bruise his heel" (3 : 15). The wounded heel was generally taken as a reference to the fall of man through Eve, the wounded head as a reference to the redemption through Mary's bearing of Christ. Fiammetta here is on the Eve side of the Eve-Mary pair in the prophecy, opposite the Fiammetta of the *Filocolo*. Like Eve, Fiammetta is undone by her decision to follow appetite instead of reason: "ma ogni considerazione all'ultimo posposta, seguitai l'appetito, e subitamente atta divenni a potere essere presa" (p. 709) [but setting aside every consideration at last, I followed appetite, and suddenly I became disposed to be able to be taken]. Just as in the *Filocolo* the Mary-Eve contrast is related to the contrast between the worship of Astrea and Priapus, so Fiammetta as an Eve is also a worshipper of Priapus or appetite.[11] Boccaccio tells the story of Euridice in *Genealogia* V.12, and glosses it as follows. Euridice is the natural concupiscence which every mortal has. The fields in which she walks represent temporal desires. Aristeo or virtue loves her and wants to lead her to proper desires, but she in fleeing virtue is bitten by the serpent of fraud which hides in temporal things. Thus those who think that temporal goods will lead them to beatitude find that they lead instead to eternal death.

We know that Fiammetta is not the real name of the lady in the *Elegia* but a name made up for her by Panfilo. We never learn her "real" name, but if it is Maria, as in the other works, then she is acting out a role opposite to her name, the role of Eve who, following her appetite, fell from felicity. However, of this entire scriptural and moral frame of reference Fiammetta seems totally unaware. She thinks of her fall only in terms of fortune and the loss of worldly joys. Yet Boccaccio is reminding his readers of the more serious fall from grace and of the human responsibility involved in that transgression.

Although already married, Fiammetta suddenly falls in love with a handsome youth and "di libera donna, divenni miserissima serva" (p. 710) [from a free mistress I became a wretched servant]. She is not, however, merely a helpless victim, for her falling in love is a kind of justice: while she was trying to capture others with her beauty, she was captured herself (p. 708). Moreover, her nurse later reproaches her:

> Amore, ancora che potentissimo signore sia, e incomparabili le sue forze, non però, te invita, ti poteva il giovine pignere nella mente: il tuo senno e gli oziosi pensieri di questo amore ti furono principio; al quale se tu vigorosamente ti fossi opposta, tutto questo non avvenia, ma libera, lui e ogni altro averesti potuto schernire. . . . Amore, come io di sopra ti dissi, niuna ingiuria ti fa o t'ha fatto, più che tu t'abbi voluto pigliare. (pp. 800–801)

> [Love, although he is a very powerful lord, and his forces incomparable, could not, however, paint the young man in your mind against your will; your judgment and your idle thoughts were the beginning of this love, to which if you had vigorously opposed yourself, all this would not have happened, but free, you would be able to scorn him and every other man. . . . Love, as I said above, does and has done you no injury more than you wanted to take on yourself.]

Alone in her room after church, she is in that dangerous state of idleness which breeds an obsessive love.[12] In his gloss on the temple of unholy love in the *Teseida* (VII.50), Boccaccio had written:

Il quale amore volere mostrare come per le sopradette cose si generi in noi, quantunque alla presente opera forse si converrebbe di dichiarare, non è mio intendimento di farlo, perciò che troppa sarebbe lunga la storia: chi desidera di vederlo, legga la canzone di Guido Cavalcanti *Donna mi prega*, etc., e le chiose che sopra vi fece Maestro Dino del Garbo.

[to show how this love through the above-mentioned things is born in us, although it would perhaps suit the present work to declare, it is not my intention to do so, because the story would be too long: whoever wants to see it, let him read the canzone by Guido Cavalcanti *Donna mi prega*, etc., and the glosses on it which Master Dino del Garbo made.]

Here in the *Elegia* Boccaccio undertakes to fill in that story of the beginnings and progress of love, and his account still agrees closely with Dino del Garbo's.[13] Dino, a medical doctor, explains how Cavalcanti's poem demonstrates that love is a passion, like anger, which in excess "turns man away from the good of his natural disposition so that he tends toward melancholy, as the writers on medicine say." "Although love can make the appetite its slave because of the strength of its impression, nevertheless, at the start man is free to choose it or not."[14] The passion of love is found most in noble men as they are the least distracted by work, for distraction is the best cure of love. Moreover, nobles are encouraged by hope more than the poor because wealth and power make success seem more likely. But "Guido advises well in saying that no one should allow himself to adhere to this passion, since there is neither utility nor solace nor wisdom and virtue in it."

Fiammetta's nurse says chiefly the same things: that love is a kind of illness which attacks the idle and the well-to-do; that it quickly takes over, as does a disease, but that an early act of will can stop it before it gets out of hand. The nurse, who, like the guide in the *Amorosa Visione*, is a mouthpiece of reason, emphasizes critically the irrationality of passion.[15] Fiammetta herself introduces it in the beginning of chapter I as "il furioso amore" (p. 706). In her monitory dream, it is a serpent's poison which distorts her body (p. 707).[16] The nurse uses the same words of madness and unhealth, calling it "furore," "pazzia," "veleno," and "pestilenza" [fury, madness, poison, plague].

But just as the lover in the *Roman de la Rose* banishes reason from his proceedings, so too Fiammetta, while acknowledging the truth of her

nurse's words, consciously takes up the side of "furore" against that of reason. "O cara nutrice, assai conosco vere le cose che narri; ma il furore mi
costrigne a seguitare le peggiori, e l'animo consapevole, e ne' suoi disiderii
strabochevole, indarno li sani consigli appetisce; e quello che la ragione
vuole è vinto del regnante furore." (p. 715) [O dear nurse, well enough I
know that what you say is true; but the fury constrains me to follow the
worse, and the mind although knowing, and excessive in its desires, in vain
seeks healthy counsels; and what reason wants is overcome by the reigning
madness.] The god of love, she claims, compels her to obey his dictates;
therefore she is not free to choose what she knows is the better course.

This is a familiar argument of lovers. Francesca too pleads helplessness
before the power of love; yet she is in hell for her adultery. Fiammetta's
claim and later Venus's reaffirmation of it include an echo of Vergil's *Georgics*
III (242–44):

> Omne adeo genus in terris hominumque ferarumque
>
> . . .
>
> in furias ignemque ruunt: amor omnibus idem.

> [Every kind of man and beast on earth . . . rushes into furies and
> fire: love is the same for all.]

There too the sexual drive is a kind of madness, and the poem ends with a
horrifying plague that burns up the victim from within.[17] Nonetheless, as
Fiammetta's nurse emphasizes the existence of free will and moral choice,
Fiammetta is forced to admit that she is deliberately and perversely choosing to ignore her own better judgment as articulated by the nurse. Indeed,
their dialogue could easily be an argument within Fiammetta herself; for
she is thinking over the nurse's words and ready to accept them when Venus
appears. The nurse turns out to have been right when she warned Fiammetta against the deceitfulness of love: "i falsi diletti promessi della sozza
speranza" (p. 715) [the false pleasures promised by foolish hope]. The
Venus apparition does in fact lie to Fiammetta, promising to her Panfilo's
eternal love.

Venus is not meant to be a pagan goddess with any real power; rather
she is Fiammetta's own creation. The nurse rebukes Fiammetta and women
like her who make a god of their own inner passions:

> Voi, turba di vaghe giovini, di focosa libidine accese sospingen-
> dovi questa, vi avete trovato Amore essere iddio al quale piuttosto
> giusto titolo sarebbe furore; e lui di Venere chiamate figliuolo,

dicendo che egli dal terzo cielo piglia le forze sue, quasi vogliate alla vostra follia porre necessità per iscusa. O ingannate, e veramente di conoscimento in tutto fuori! (p. 715)

[You, throng of desirous young ladies, kindled with fiery lust, impelled by this (lust), have contrived that Love is a god, for whom a juster title would be madness; and you call him the son of Venus, saying that he takes his power from the third heaven, as if you wanted to make necessity an excuse for your folly. O deceived ones, and truly far from knowledge!]

This overturns any reading which suggests that Fiammetta is truly a victim of forces she cannot help.[18]

To reify the power of sexual desire is the pagan error ("O ingannate . . . !"); the Christian reading of "Venus" and "Cupid" must understand these words as poetic fictions representing moral truths about our own desires, which we ought ourselves to judge and govern. These ideas are repeated later in the *Corbaccio*, where the guide explains that the image of Cupid is meant to teach a lesson and yet "il chiamate iddio e . . . gli fate sacrificio delle vostre menti" (p. 57) [you call him god and . . . sacrifice to him your minds], and in the commentary on *Inferno* V (litt.162): "questo amor per diletto chiamano i poeti Cupido e dicono che egli fu figliuolo di Marte e di Venere . . . dico che questo Cupidine, o Amore che noi vogliam dire, è una passione di mente" [this love-for-pleasure the poets call Cupid and say that he is the son of Mars and Venus . . . I say that this Cupid, or Love as we like to say, is a passion of the mind]. *Genealogia* IX.4, using almost the same phrases but in Latin, refers to Seneca's Octavia and Hippolitus as sources for the ideas (1) that love is nourished by leisure and comfort, and (2) that the wicked call love a god in order to excuse their own furor. The nurse in the *Elegia* keeps emphasizing Fiammetta's free will to choose her own actions; but Fiammetta chooses to worship the goddess as a real external power rather than to recognize it as a projection of her own inner desires.

Her "seguitai l'appetito" [I followed appetite] is ritualized as she kneels to Venus saying, "sia come ti piace" (p. 720) [thy will be done]. Although Fiammetta seems innocent of any liturgical echoes, Boccaccio certainly meant these words to jolt the reader as they are applied to the pagan deification of lust. Two things at least prevent one from taking her words as the declaration of a revolutionary stance on the part of Boccaccio. One is the tragic consequence of Fiammetta's choice; the other is the way the definition of that choice repeats the old Priapus-Astrea, Eve-Mary, pagan-Christian, furor-reason polarities, in which Fiammetta is clearly on the wrong side.

The word "Elegia" in the title becomes more and more relevant as the intensity of Fiammetta's fall increases.[19] Of the nine chapters, the fifth or central one is a real turning point.[20]

> Lievi sono state infino a qui le mie lagrime, o pietose donne, e i miei sospiri piacevoli a rispetto di quelli, i quali la dolente penna . . . s'apparecchia di dimostrarvi. E certo, se bene si considera, le pene infino a qui trapassate, più di lasciva giovane che di tormentata quasi si possono dire; ma le seguenti vi parranno d'un' altra mano. (p. 751)

> [Light have been my tears so far, o pitiful ladies, and pleasant my sighs with respect to those which the grieving pen . . . prepares to show you. And certainly, if one will consider rightly, the pains passed up to now can almost be called those of a lustful rather than of a tormented young woman; but the ones that follow will seem to you of another sort.]

Fiammetta's monitory dream of chapter I has its parallel in chapter V; she dreams of the golden age before the birth of Cupid, when men lived simply and without sin. This is the innocent paradise from which she, like Eve, has fallen, a state of mind or soul rather than a historical moment. She describes the corruption of the innocent world through the entrance of avarice, pride, and "il duca e facitore di tutti i mali, e artefice de' peccati, il dissoluto amore" (p. 781) [the leader and maker of all evils, and the artificer of sins, dissolute love]. The statement is similar to Fiammetta's in the *Filocolo*, but it is now spoken from experience by a sadder Fiammetta. She exclaims in clear recognition of her guilt with phrases from Ovid's "Phaedra Hippolyto": "O felice il mondo, se Giove mai non avesse cacciato Saturno, e ancora l'età aurea durasse sotto caste leggi! Però che tutti alli primi simili viveremmo. Ohime! che chiunque è colui li primi riti servante, non è nella mente infiammato dal cieco furore della non sana Venere, come io sono" (p. 780) [O happy world if Jove had never chased out Saturn and the golden age still lasted under chaste laws. For we would all live like our ancestors. Ah me! for whoever it is that keeps the orginal rites is not inflamed in the mind by the blind madness of the unhealthy Venus, as I am]. By chapter VI she is summoning the furies with horrid curses and proclaiming her damnation in a state of total frenzy and insanity.

As her sorrows destroy her beauty, now recognized as a fleeting thing in which no wise man ought to trust, she no longer cares to dress up for church, explaining hypocritically to her neighbors that God is pleased by virtue alone and not by fancy apparel aimed at winning human approbation. Yet within herself she winces as she speaks. Calling herself a sinner ("peccatrice") and grieving for her dishonest love, she tells herself that if she could do it without danger, she would speak out the truth of her condition and undeceive all those who are taken in by her pretended virtue. But of course that is not possible. The torments of love merge into torments of guilt.

It is hard to understand how one could say, "Assente è nell'*Elegia di Madonna Fiammetta* il sentimento della colpa, l'angosciosa conscienza del peccato, ogni preoccupazione escatologica, il senso di Dio e dell'aldilà."[21] [Absent from the *Elegia di Madonna Fiammetta* is the sentiment of guilt, the anguished consciousness of sin, any escatalogical anxiety, the sense of God and of the after life.] "O crudelissime spelunche abitate dalle rabbiose fiere" [O cruel caves inhabited by the raging wild beasts], exclaims Fiammetta in chapter VI, thinking of her unsuspecting husband's love and anxiety:

> o inferno, o etterna prigione decretata alla nocente turba, o qualunque altro essilio maggiore più giù si nasconde, prendetemi, e me a' meritati suplicii date nocente. O sommo Giove, contro a me giustamente adirato, tuona e con tostissima mano in me le tue saette discendi; o sacra Giunone, le cui santissime leggi io sceleratissima giovane ho corrotte, véndicati. (p. 793)

> [O hell, o eternal prison decreed for the harmful throng, or whatever other greater exile is hidden farther down, take me and give to pernicious me the merited torments. O supreme Jove, justly angered against me, thunder and with swiftest hand let your arrows descend upon me; O holy Juno, whose holiest laws I, most wicked young woman, have corrupted, avenge yourself.]

Love has led her into "ira" and "corruccio" (p. 804) [rage]. Using the words which Dante had used to describe the minotaur, symbol of bestial wrath (*Inf.* XII.22–24), Fiammetta describes herself on the verge of suicide: "impetuosamente su mi levai, e, quale il forte toro ricevuto il mortal colpo furioso in qua e in là saltella, sé percotendo, cotale dinanzi agli occhi miei errando Tesifone, . . . dietro alla furia correndo . . ." (p. 807) [impetuously I arose and, as the strong bull having received the mortal blow leaps furious here and there, striking himself, so with Tesiphone wandering before my eyes, . . . I, running after the fury].

Boccaccio's gloss on Dante's minotaur discusses precisely the progressive degeneration from natural to unnatural vices and from lust to violence (*Esposiz.* XII.lit.17–18, alleg.2–12). Pasiphae, says Boccaccio, represents the human soul wedded to reason, or Minos, but infected by the poison of Venus, who symbolizes both appetites, the concupiscible and the irascible. (We have already seen how the *Elegia* uses the notion of love as a poisonous infection.) Abandoning reason, the soul falls first into the indulgence of natural appetites, then into unnatural ones, thus producing the bestial minotaur, i.e., the soul's own inwardly growing bestiality. This minotaur especially signifies bestial fury or madness, including the unnatural turning of violence against oneself. Dante writes that the minotaur bites itself "Sì come quei, cui l'ira dentro fiacca" [like those whom wrath breaks up within]; Boccaccio glosses "fiacca" as "cioè rompe e divide dalla ragione" [that is, breaks and divides from reason]. The whole myth for Boccaccio symbolizes the soul's choice between following reason and following appetite. Fiammetta's "seguitai l'appetito" declares her resemblance to Pasiphae, and she proceeds to give birth to her own self-destructive furor. Dante refers to Pasiphae again in *Purgatorio* XXVI (41–42, 82–87), as an example of lust which is natural in the sense of being heterosexual but bestial in following animal appetite rather than human reason. Dante's lines here are likely to be a main source for Boccaccio's gloss on *Inferno* XII.[22] The emphasis of this gloss is not simply that the wrong choice was made once, but that this choice is the first step in a progressively worsening condition as slight or natural ills produce more dire evils. Venus's turning into Tesifone is a parallel symbol for lust's generation of madness that leads Fiammetta on into her crazy violence.

The nurse tries to draw her away from her deep despair, which is itself a sin, a denial of God's power of mercy. She tries to persuade Fiammetta that there remains always open the possibility of regaining health, sanity, and salvation:

> tu, più volonterosa che savia, lasciando li miei consigli, seguisti li tuoi piaceri, onde al fine debito a cotali falli con dolente viso ti veggo venuta. Ma però che sempre, solo che altri voglia, mentre si vive si può ciascuno da malvagio camino dipartire e al buono ritornare, mi sarebbe caro che tu omai gli occhi alla tua mente dalle tenebre di questo iniquo tiranno occupati svelassi, e loro

della verità rendessi la luce chiara. . . . quel fine che da amore si
può disiare, prendesti; e, come già è detto, brieve diletto essere il
conoscesti. . . . metti la ragione innanzi alla volontà, e te
medesima saviamente cava de' pericoli dell'angoscie, nelle quali
mattamente ti se' lasciata trascorrere. . . . Adunque lascia li do-
lori li quali volontaria hai eletti, e vivi lieta negl'iddii sperando, e
opera bene (pp. 795, 802)

[you, more willful than wise, leaving my counsels, followed your
pleasures, whence with sad face I see you arrived at the end
proper to such errors. But because always, if only one wants to,
while he is alive, any person can depart from the evil road and
return to the good one, it would be dear to me if you would now
unveil the eyes of your mind which have been occupied by the
darkness of this unjust tyrant, and return them to the clear light
of truth. . . . the end which one can desire from love, you took;
and, as has been said already, you recognized that it is a brief
pleasure. . . . put reason ahead of your will, and wisely rescue
yourself from the dangers and from the anguish into which you
have madly let yourself run. . . . Leave then the sorrows which
you have willingly chosen, and live happy hoping in the gods,
and do well].

Fiammetta hears the words and once again acknowledges their truth
(p. 796); but she has become obsessed with her own degeneration. She has
ceased to be Eve-like and has become satanic. Everyone can use the benefit
of his liberty as it suits him, says the nurse (p. 800). Fiammetta, with a
twist of her pride, chooses to become the most wretched woman in history. Nothing will console her, she resolves, except this role. Like Milton's
Satan, she prefers to rule hell than to be second best in heaven, and compares the fiery pains of her love to the lesser pains of famous sinners in
Hades: Tityus, Tantalus, Ixion (pp. 798–99). Furthermore, comparing her
own losses and pains to those of other lovers in various myths, she proves
in each case that her grief exceeds all others': "il che a non piccola gloria mi
reco" (p. 822) [which brings me no little glory].

Her prayer at the end of chapter VIII to "Iddio" [God] for "salutevole
acqua" [health-bringing water] to quell the fires of her passion evokes the
possibility of grace and renewal only to reject it. What she wants is death or
the return of Panfilo. She makes a similar prayer to God at the end of chapter V. The prayer sounds orthodox until we hear what she is asking for. She

argues that sinners ought to be dearer to God alive and able to repent than dead without hope of redemption, but she has no intention of giving up her sin. "Vengano le mie voci nel tuo cospetto . . . sì che impetrandomi grazia, *prima quaggiù lietamente*, e poi nella fine de' miei giorni costassù con voi io possa vivere." [May my words come before your face . . . so that begging grace for me, I may live *first happily here below* and then at the end of my days up there with you.]

She is true to Panfilo throughout her *Elegia* not because she really cares about him any more but because she wants constantly to exacerbate her own misery. She is true to her own despair, having made that her glory, and prays for Panfilo's return knowing that he will not come. Her final static situation is the low point after her dramatic fall.[23]

Sapegno is right about the increasing realism in Boccaccio's writing if what he means is that Boccaccio turned from the allegorical figures of the *Comedia delle Ninfe* and *Amorosa Visione* to a human—although somewhat exaggerated—example in order to demonstrate his moral philosophy. In this regard, the *Elegia* could almost take its place as a tragic example in the *De Mulieribus Claris* although, being a fiction and not a true history, the narrative is classified by Fiammetta herself as "argomento" (Prologo, p. 703).[24] But if Sapegno means, as Hauvette seems to have meant, that Boccaccio has lost interest in the virtues and vices and has turned his attention to real life for its own sake, he is obviously wrong.[25] Fiammetta finally addresses her book, bidding it serve as an example to those who are happy, so that they may set some measure to their goods and avoid becoming like her (p. 834).

Fiammetta's shift from allegorical figure to moral example is worth noting, nonetheless, as a parallel to Boccaccio's increasingly severe treatment of erotic love. The nurse's long harangues and Fiammetta's self-accusations add a considerable weight of moralizing to the narrative, which—unlike the *Filocolo*, *Comedia delle Ninfe*, or *Amorosa Visione*—no longer tries to suggest that erotic passion can lead toward or signify virtue in any even comical way. Boccaccio, it seems, while progressively losing confidence in the powers of reason, felt the need not only to condemn lust[26] more vigorously but also to write in a more direct manner lest his readers prove as foolish to their harm as the naive readers in his books. Fiammetta is an example not only of lustful obsession but also of naive reading, and her misuse or misunderstanding of rhetoric is one of the issues of the book.

The Fiammetta of the *Elegia* is modeled on the women of the *Heroides* and the heroines of Seneca's tragedies rather than on Beatrice or Laura.[27] Renier has described the *Elegia* as set "nel bel mezzo della paganità"[28] [right in the middle of paganism], and as for the references to the Christian God "non si sa come regga li entro" [one doesn't know how they can hold up in there]. Even Segalla, despite his interest in Boccaccio's religion, calls the *Elegia* "ben pagana per quello spirito di sensualismo che anima tutta la narrazione e ch'è l'ideale dell'autore"[29] [certainly pagan for that spirit of sensuality which animates the whole narrative and which is the author's ideal]. Fiammetta presents herself as a pagan woman inhabiting "Partenope," and yet, as has been often noted, she is just as clearly a Neapolitan contemporary of Boccaccio and his audience. We are thus introduced into a double world.[30] While Fiammetta invokes the classical deities, she and her nurse speak of "Dio" and divine mercy, and even the pagan names usually veil Christian meanings, "Giove" for God and "Giuno" for marriage. In the *Mythologia Allegorica* of 1339 and the *Comedia delle Ninfe* of 1341–42, Boccaccio had already played with phrasing biblical events and Christian doctrine in a pagan vocabulary. However, Fiammetta's constant comparisons between her contemporaries and the famous names of antiquity manifest a felt distance in time between the two periods. This very sense of distance allows Boccaccio to make a cultural *translatio* dear to the humanists and, while talking about his own society in ancient terms, to revivify the ancient language with modern meanings. But is the rhetoric of the *Elegia* Boccaccio's or Fiammetta's? Is she aware of the double meanings of her words? And what, finally, is the function of all this elaborate rhetoric and mythological reference in terms of the character of Fiammetta?

One of Boccaccio's frequent uses of classical allusion is to introduce a distance between the author and the narrator by evoking associations of which Fiammetta seems naively or even willfully ignorant. This starts in chapter I and continues through the book, and it is a useful means for working into the text moral warnings beyond those uttered openly by Fiammetta or her nurse.

Describing her dream in chapter I, for example, Fiammetta remarks that the day darkened as it did for the Greeks at the sin of Atreus; the sin was a horrible revenge by Atreus for Thyestes' adultery with his wife. The issue of adultery is raised openly at the very beginning of chapter I as Fiammetta describes her happy initial state (p. 76): "Io era unico bene e felicità singulare del giovine sposo, e così egli da me era igualmente amato, come egli mi amava. Oh quanto più che altra mi potrei io dire felice, se sempre in me fosse durato cotale amore!"[31] [I was the sole good and unique happiness of my young husband, and he was equally beloved by me, as much as he loved me. O how much happier than any other woman I could call myself, if such love had lasted within me always.]

Reference to her sin of adultery is slipped in again through classical allusion as Fiammetta, adorning herself for the temple, considers herself similar to the goddesses seen by Paris in the valley of Ida (p. 707). The men and women in the temple gaze at her beauty as if she were Venus or Minerva (p. 708). One goddess has been omitted without Fiammetta's seeming to notice: Juno, the goddess of marriage.[32] Later on Fiammetta will call out to her in despair (p. 793):

O sacra Giunone, le cui santissime leggi io scelleratissima giovine ho corrotte, véndicati. . . . Niuna pietà, niuna misericordia in me sia usata, poiché la fede debita al santo letto posposi all'amore di strano giovine. . . . Dove abbandonasti tu la pietà debita alle sante leggi del matrimonio? Dove la castità, sommo onore delle donne, cacciasti allora che per Panfilo il tuo marito abandonasti?

[O holy Juno, whose holiest laws I, most wicked young woman, have corrupted, avenge yourself. . . . Show me no pity, no mercy, since I set the faith owed to the holy bed below the love of a young stranger. . . . Where did you leave the piety owed to the holy laws of marriage? Where did you drive chastity, the highest honor of women, when you abandoned your husband for Panfilo?]

Venus's own speech is a mine of classical allusions with a hidden edge.[33] Even the gods are subject to love, argues Venus, taking as her first example Apollo. To strengthen her point she adds that he was subject to love not only once but many times: "ora per Danne, ora per Climenes e quando per Leucotoe, e per altre molte" [now for Daphne, now for Climenes, and at some time for Leucothoe, and for many others]. This ought to warn Fiammetta about what fidelity she can expect from Panfilo. The human examples which Venus cites are not more comforting: Hercules carding wool for Iole is perhaps the least destructive one; Paris, Helen, Clytemnestra, Aegisthus, and Dido follow, among others. Treachery, murder, and suicide are the immediate associations with their names. Also listed is Ariadne, deserted by her lover, and Scylla, turned into a monster. "Santo è questo fuoco" [holy is this fire] is hardly the proper conclusion to such a list.

Venus counters the possible objection, "Io ho marito, e le sante leggi e la promessa fede mi vietano queste cose" [I have a husband, and the holy laws and promised faith forbid me such things], by pointing to the examples of Pasiphae and Phaedra, Jason, Theseus, and finally Ulysses. The two women do not seem like inviting examples, and Ulysses, placed rhetorically at the end, suggests Penelope as a counterexample disproving Venus's thesis that no one keeps the marriage vow.

A similar and humorous use of examples occurs in chapter V, where Fiammetta, looking about at the women in her city, describes their elegance: "quella per alterezza, dicendo, Semiramìs simigliare; quell'altra, agli ornamenti guardando, Cleopatràs si crederebbe; l'altra, considerata la sua vaghezza, sarebbe creduta Elena; e alcuna, gli atti suoi bene mirando, in niente si direbbe dissimigliare a Didone" (p. 775) [saying that one for dignity is like Semiramis; that other, looking at her adornments, one would take for Cleopatra; and the other, considering her charm, one would take for Helen; and another, looking well at her gestures, one would say is not at all unlike Dido]. The qualities by which these women are compared with their classical counterparts neglect the most salient associations with those names. In case a reader should miss the point, the gloss hammers it home. Semiramis is the "lussuriosissima" or very lustful queen who wanted to lie with her son. Cleopatra is another "lussuriosissima." Dante's *Inferno* V.52–66 lists precisely these three names in the same order as examples of sinful lust. Once again, however, Fiammetta, looking only at the most superficial aspects, fails to hear the critical note introduced by such examples.

Fiammetta kneels to Venus but wonders afterwards whether it had not been Tesifone the fury to whom she kneeled. The warning explicit in this confusion of love and madness contains an implicit foreshadowing as well; as Ovid wrote in the *Heroides*, when Dido recalls her reunion with Aeneas in the cave (11. 95–96):

audieram voces; nymphas ululasse putavi—
Eumenides fatis signa dedere meis!

[I heard voices; I thought nymphs were howling—the Furies gave the sign to my fates.]

The letter of Phyllis to Demophoon uses the same idea and names the specific fury: "pronuba Tisiphone thalamis ululavit in illis"[34] (l. 117) [Tesiphone, presiding over the wedding, howled in the bed chambers]. Both women, like Fiammetta, have been abandoned as they write.

Fiammetta's final catalogue of classical examples does at last take notice of their tragic endings. Even here, however, when the same names that we have seen before recur with their stories' conclusions unveiled, Fiammetta refuses to learn from them. Rather she uses them to bolster her pride in her own tragic pose. She turns to rhetoric and fiction not to teach and move herself to change but instead to fix her situation as a stubborn monument to her own failing. Battaglia describes it well: "È un ribadire con diversi accenti la stessa condizione: e ogni pagina l'arricchisce di toni e di motivi, ma anche la conferma in una fissità immobile . . . alterna vicenda di ricordi delusi e di risorgente illusione."[35] [It is a reaffirming, with various accents, of the same condition: and every page enriches it with tones and motifs, but also confirms it in an immobile fixity . . . alternating between disillusioned memories and resurging illusions.] Battaglia does not go on from this observation to infer that Fiammetta is at fault. Yet all along rhetoric is for her the means to deceive herself. Her careless readings lead her astray, and her art of persuasion is put to use to justify her own behavior to herself. The proper use of rhetoric is to teach and move toward moral truth, not self-delusion. This proper rhetoric is the rhetoric of Boccaccio, who has Fiammetta write her own history as a warning example to other women to avoid her fate. For Fiammetta the warning is merely part of her pride; she wants no rivals in misery. But for the author the book is an example of the destructive workings of passion and rationalization.

A reading in which Fiammetta is only part of a whole person, the appetitive or passionate part, suits the constant fiery furor and excess both of feeling and of language. Fiammetta's limited control of her own rhetoric and her wrong use of it are closely related to her lack of rational judgment in love. She has a classical model for both in the *Heroides*. Phyllis or Phaedra, from whose laments come many passages of the *Elegia*, each tells her own story as a monument of self-justification. Phyllis's sculpted epitaph will fix her plight forever, as the static ending of the *Elegia* will do for Fiammetta. Yet Phyllis and Phaedra are fooling themselves and, unless the reader knows their histories from other sources, might fool their audience as well. Ovid, however, could trust that his readers did already know these tales. Here too, then, the reader is aware of more than the narrator seems to be, and the result—while not a moral lesson from Ovid—is certainly a distancing of our sympathies from the speakers, a recognition that they are offering only a limited view of the truth. Just as for Fiammetta, the elaborate rhetorical ploys of Ovid's women are ultimately monumental rather than persuasive. Even Dido, whose Aeneas is still at Carthage and could still receive her letter, has no hope to move him; all her words are finally "in tumuli marmore carmen" [a verse on a marble tomb].

It is interesting to see how within the sixteenth century readings of the *Elegia* changed from an interpretation close to the one suggested above into a more romantic one.[36] Bernardo di Giunta began his edition of 1517 with a dedicatory letter to Cosimo Rucellai in which he wrote:

> Voi leggendo il presente trattato troverrete una donna ne' lacci d'Amore involta, e in essi miserissima quanto alcuna altra non fu giamai. Le cui sospiri, le cui lagrime, le cui dolente rammaricationi, e a voi, e a qualunque altro che quinci leggierà per aventura potranno essere utilissimo exemplo di non mettersi incautamente negli amorosi pericoli.

> [You who read the present treatise will find a woman tangled in the snares of love, and more wretched in them than any other woman ever was. Whose sighs, tears, sorrowing complaints, both to you and to whoever else by chance will read them, may be a most useful example against putting oneself incautiously into the perils of love.]

Tizzone's edition of 1524 shows more sympathy for Fiammetta in its dedicatory letter to Dorothea di Gonzaga (perhaps because the edition is addressed to a woman): the reader will find

> la forza infinita d'Amore, i modi bellissimi e dolcissimi di parlare, la vera osservanza de l'utilissima nostra commune lingua, gli argutissimi andamenti in un perfetto amare adoperati, gli affetti amorosi, et non infinti da una donna adoperati, uno infelicissimo fine d'amore nato da felicissimo principio fra duo amanti accaduto, un continuo dolere et con pianto amarissimo, et con lamento assai degno di compassione, et in brieve quanta forza ha sopra i mortali la non pieghevole fortuna

> [the infinite power of Love, the most beautiful and sweetest ways of speaking, the true observance of our most useful common tongue, the most clever proceedings adopted by a perfect lover, the amorous affections, and not pretended ones, used by a lady, a most unhappy ending of love born from a most happy beginning that happened to two lovers, a continual grieving with a most bitter plaint, and with a lament quite worthy of compassion, and in brief how much power unbending fortune has over mortals].

Although a moral lesson remains, it has much less to do with Fiammetta's own responsibility for her downfall. This reading accedes to Fiammetta's claim that she is the victim of fortune and not suffering justly from the consequences of her own choices. Even farther along this line are the sentiments of Filippo Giunti expressed in his dedicatory letter to Iacopo di Francesco Nerli in the edition of 1594: "questa sua opera da lui intitolato Fiammetta, nella quale, sotto nome di Panfilo, egli descrive un amor di sua gioventù, e amor veramente da gloriarsene" [this work entitled by him Fiammetta, in which under the name of Panfilo he describes a love affair of his own youth, and a love truly to take glory in]. He sends the book to Nerli as one who is a descendant of Boccaccio's family, "e giovane, e forse non men che so foss'egli in quel tempo, ora acconcio ad amare" [and a young man, and perhaps no less than he was at the time, now suited for love]. In this last letter, the lesson has been completely turned around. Fiammetta has become a glorious model for lovers to follow, and the fiction has been attributed to Boccaccio's own experience. We are at the beginning of the critical tradition that read everything he wrote as fragments of a sentimental autobiography. Indeed, the sixteenth-century Sansovino is the first biographer of Boccaccio to write about his love for Fiammetta, taking all his information from the fictional texts.

The autobiographical critics had to deal with the question of why Boccaccio was writing so cruelly about the woman he had been pursuing through all those earlier works. Their answer was generally that she had betrayed him. But the true answer is that we need to distinguish between the narrators' seductive and educative aims, and to recognize the allegorical as well as erotic aspects of previous Fiammettas. The *Elegia* records from a literal or physical Fiammetta's point of view the consequences of the lover's successful seduction. The book is a warning, then, to Boccaccio's readers about how to read his earlier works: a warning against the seductive powers of literature as well as against the poetry of seduction.[37]

VII

Corbaccio

The *Corbaccio* was written at a time when Boccaccio was revising the *Amorosa Visione* (c. 1355).[1] Like the *Amorosa Visione* it tells about a dream vision in which the narrator sees himself running lost in the wilderness. Again a guide approaches, and again it turns out that the narrator has lost his way by wandering into the garden of love. The garden that looked so promising at first has turned by degrees into the dark and thorny wasteland where lovers have, like Circe's, become howling beasts. The transformation of the love garden from a paradise into a hell is a reworking of Fiammetta's elegiac fall.

Once again the problem is a conflict between reason and appetite. The *Corbaccio* narrator has reversed the hierarchic order of his soul. He complains that he has managed "nelle mani d'una femmina dare legata la mia libertà e sottoposta la mia ragione; e l'anima, che, con queste accompagnata, solea essere donna, senza esse divenuta vilissima serva" (p. 65) [into the hands of a woman to give my liberty, bound, and to subordinate to her my reason; the soul, which accompanied with these used to be mistress, without them has become a lowly servant]. The words are similar to Fiammetta's in the *Elegia;* she too has become "miserissima serva" [most wretched servant] instead of "libera donna" [free mistress] because of her rejection of the government of reason and her enslavement to passion.

This time, however, the lover is ready to learn from his guide or counselor, for the pleasures of love have turned bitter. Before falling asleep and dreaming his vision, the narrator, addressed already internally by his reason, seeks out a friend for conversation. First they discuss the slippery turnings of fortune and the folly of trusting in fickle goods. From the topic of fortune, the friends move on to nature and its perpetual order; from there they go on to talk about God. The narrator has already cured his grief when he falls asleep. As the process of contemplation ascends from topic to topic, moving from the fickle to the stable and from the material to the spiritual, it imitates Boethius's *Consolation* along with the *Amorosa Visione*.

The narrator's conversation first with his own reason and then with a friend is repeated one more time in his dreamed conversation with the ghost of his lady's husband. The husband's soul, like Vergil's, has been sent at the bidding of the Virgin Mary to put the narrator back on the right road and help him escape from the perilous situation into which he has literally run. The relation of husband and wife often represents the relation between the governing reason and the appetite to which it has been wed. That appetite is amply embodied in the wife, now widow; but the husband has failed at his task. He is suffering the pains of purgatory precisely for not having governed his wife as he ought. As a figure of reason, therefore, he has notably failed to control lust. Indeed, lust is alive and triumphant, while reason is in the grave. Thus the image of reason has sunk to a new low. Neither regal as in the *Teseida* and *Amorosa Visione*, nor even subservient to passion as in the *Elegia*, the figure of reason here is dead and buried. It can only cry its warning in a ghostly voice to those who have rushed after the lure of lust.

At the same time, the image of lust is even harsher and grimmer than before. Fiammetta in the *Elegia* was a beautiful young woman for whom we had, at least in the first half of the book, some sympathy or compassion. The widow of the *Corbaccio* is a hideous old hag replete with every vice. Her widow's weeds become the appropriate demonstration of her black nature, while her epithet "old crow" is set in contrast to the white swan and the Virgin Mary. If the *Filocolo, Teseida*, or *Ninfale Fiesolano* celebrated human love in marriage, the *Corbaccio* does not even consider this option. The clean polarities of this book leave out the ambiguous middle realm in which we all exist. The condition of love is hell, a dark and fearsome valley of bellowing, miserable lovers, whereas the escape from love's bondage allows the narrator to climb, Dante-like, to a paradise on earth. In sum the contrast between extremes has become greater, and the realm of appetite more thoroughly hideous, while reason has grown weaker than before. It is only the mercy of the Virgin and the grace of God that can turn the lover around and set him in the right direction.

When Petrarch drew from the *Amorosa Visione* for his own *Trionfi*, he insistently clarified the morality of the love relation within the narrative. The series of triumphs leads from Cupid all the way to Eternity, developing explicitly the heavenly goal which Boccaccio leaves as a suggestion at the end of his work. Laura, the object of the poet's affection, is the champion of Chastity who vanquishes Cupid and frees the poet from his bonds. After the triumph of Death, she descends from heaven to inform her lover of her mission to draw him toward heaven; Fiammetta had said similar things in the *Visione* but from the middle of Cupid's triumph and while still alive. Petrarch clearly associated the lady of the *Amorosa Visione* with his own Laura, but he carefully avoided the ambiguities of her appearance in the triumph of love or the love-garden scenes.

Perhaps Boccaccio too was troubled by his own poem, afraid that readers would, like Europa, be misled by the "argomento." If the two faces of love, worldly and heavenly, seemed incongruously paired in the *Comedia delle Ninfe*, in the *Amorosa Visione* they were perilously confused. Once again, then, Boccaccio separated the two, this time setting them not as an allegory one for the other but as irreconcilable opposites. The lady who had been both Mary-like and Venus-like is split into two opposing characters. There is no more hanging on to a human love-object with all the confusion that entails; the choice of ways is made so clear that the narrator falls out of love. Indeed, love becomes no longer even a temptation. The scales are so heavily weighted to one side that there is no longer a problem of choosing.

Although the narrator once again praises Maria, this time it is the Virgin Mary herself. Having sued as a lover for the grace of Maria-Fiammetta in previous books, the narrator here has been helped by the Virgin's grace: "una spezial grazia: non per mio merito, ma per sola benignità di Colei che, impetrandola da Colui che vuole quello che Ella medesima, nuovamente mi fu conceduta. La qual cosa faccendo . . . sanza niun dubbio potrò a molti lettori di quella fare utilità" (pp. 39–40) [a special grace: recently granted to me not for my own merit but only through the kindness of Her who begged it for me from Him whose will is the same as Her own. By doing which (writing this book) . . . I will be able without doubt to be of use to many of its readers]. Boccaccio's moral instructor tells him, in an imitation of Vergil's words to Dante:

> Egli è vero che, per quello ch'io sentissi nell'ora che questa commessione di venire qui a te mi fu fatta, non da umana voce, ma da

angelica, la quale non si dee credere che menta già mai, che tu sempre, qual che stata si sia la tua vita, hai in ispeziale reverenza e devozione avuta Colei nel cui ventre si racchiuse la nostra salute e che è viva fontana di misericordia e madre di grazia e di pietà; e in lei, siccome in termine fisso, avesti sempre intera speranza. (p. 56)

[It is true that, by what I heard in the hour that this commission to come here to you was given to me, not by a human voice but by an angelic one which one must not believe ever lies, that you always, whatever your life was like, have had a special reverence and devotion to her in whose womb was enclosed our salvation and who is a living fountain of mercy and mother of grace and of pity; and in her, as in a fixed goal, you had always complete hope.]

It is she who, seeing the lover so lost and impeded that he was no longer mindful of himself, has besought grace for his salvation. He proclaims himself her very faithful servant and hopes to join her in eternal life.

We cannot help recalling the end of the *Amorosa Visione*, where the "I" is beginning to ascend the stairway to eternal life in hopes of finding his beloved lady at the top. Boccaccio's declaration of a lifelong special devotion and his phrases identifying Mary echo lines about his Maria in previous works, lending support to the notion that the Maria there is a figure associated in part with the heavenly Mary.[2] Now, however, Maria can be only the Virgin herself, with no erotic aspect. Just as in the *Comedia delle Ninfe* the arrival of Beatrice into the earthly paradise among the seven virtues is replaced by the arrival of God (in the guise of Venus), so too in the *Corbaccio* Beatrice's bidding to Vergil to go help the lost poet is replaced by that of the Virgin Mary. Recurrently, then, Boccaccio shies away from the confusion of human and divine, just as he recurrently creates that very confusion. According to the *Corbaccio*, the Virgin is the only woman deserving of love and praise; the exaltation of any other woman is simply misplaced, a mistake. One is reminded of Petrarch's final canzone to the Virgin Mary as "vera beatrice." Like Petrarch, Boccaccio's narrator finally directs his love to the Virgin Mary, addressing her with lines like those which he had erroneously addressed to a human: "e prima spero si troveranno de' cigni neri o de' corbi bianchi, che a' nostri successori d'onorarne alcuna altra bisogni d'entrare in fatica; per ciò che l'orme di coloro che la reina degli agnoli seguitarono sono ricoperte" (p. 84)[3] [and I hope sooner that one will find black swans or white crows than that our descendants will need to undertake the labor of honoring any other woman; because the tracks of those who followed the queen of the angels have been covered over].

As Boccaccio had opposed Eve and Mary in earlier works, so now he opposes the Virgin not to Eve but to the widow, an old bawd as in the *Roman de la Rose*. Like Eve, she is the representative of *cupiditas* opposed to *caritas*. She is the very figure of carnal love. If the Fiammetta of the *Amorosa Visione* is associated with wisdom, here the widow's definition of "savia" is to have as many lovers as her appetite desires; those who do otherwise are merely fools.[4] The instructor, who is the ghost of her husband, in purgatory for not having disciplined her better, ascribes to her lust, wrath, pride, gluttony, and other sins. On the other hand, he says:

> "dove questa di costoro il concupiscibile appetito a disonesto desiderio commuove e desta, così quella della reina del cielo ogni villano pensiero, ogni disonesta volontà di coloro cacciava che la miravano; e d'un focoso e caritevole ardore di bene e virtuosamente operare sì maravigliosamente li accendeva, che laudando divotamente Colui che creata l'avea, a mettere in opera il bene acceso desiderio si disponeano. E di questo in lei non vanagloria, non superbia veniva, ma in tanto la sua umiltà ne cresceva" (pp. 82–83)

> [where this woman moves and arouses their concupiscible appetite to dishonest desires, so that queen of heaven chased away every base thought, every dishonest will from them that looked upon her; and she kindled them so marvelously with a fiery and charitable zeal to do good and virtuous works that, praising devotedly Him who had created her, they disposed themselves to put into effect the well-kindled desire. And from this there did not come to her vainglory, nor pride, but all the while her humility increased].

Like the Fiammetta of the *Elegia*, the widow goes to church in order to pick up new admirers. She is the idol of an anti-religion based on unholy love. This widow, then, is not necessarily some new amour of Boccaccio's but, in fact, the object of that earlier narrator's love. She sits in church waiting for some fool to fall in love with her and to make her the idol of his erotic worship.

The Virgin and the widow are, of course, the swan and crow in the lines cited above. The title *Corbaccio* alludes at least in part to the widow in her black dress and through her to the lust she represents. According to one of the lessons of the bestiaries, the crow which eats corpses, pecking first the eyes and then the brain, is a sign for the kind of love which blinds and maddens men.[5] We find in the text of the *Corbaccio:* "Vedere adunque dovevi amore essere una passione accecatrice dell'animo, disviatrice dello'ngegno, . . . genitrice de' vizi e abitatrice de' vacui petti . . . vizio delle menti non sane e sommergitrice della umana libertà." (p. 70) [You should have seen then that love is a passion which blinds the mind, misleads the understanding . . . a mother of vices and inhabitant of empty breasts . . . a vice of the unhealthy mind and a submerger of human liberty.] These words do not represent a new and embittered attitude on the part of Boccaccio, for we have heard the same kind of statement from Fiammetta in the *Filocolo* and we have seen it in action in the *Elegia di Madonna Fiammetta*. Even in the *Decameron* we can find comments of this sort, notably in VIII.7, where the widow remarks how her student-lover has lost his wits.

The problem of seeing aright, or of appearance versus truth, was a dominant theme in the allegories of the *Comedia delle Ninfe* and *Amorosa Visione*. The *Corbaccio* guide also speaks to the issue. The narrator cannot have loved the widow for her virtues because such love is contrary to wicked desire. What he loved, therefore, were her appearance and the recognition of her vices, which gave him hope for success in the affair. As the love of virtues seeks out the unchanging good, so lust seeks out the deceitfully mutable on which to practice its own deceits. The result is self-delusion. The *Corbaccio* narrator has followed the path of lust from the apparently pleasant fields of its beginning through the transformation of that landscape into a dark desert full of howling beasts. The soul through *cupiditas* creates its own hell, deceiving itself with the false images of the good: "il falso piacere delle caduche cose . . . m'ebbe menato" (p. 49)[6] [the false pleasure of fallible things . . . led me here]. But enlightened by *caritas* the soul can escape from the desert "inferno" uphill to a lovely fertile scene where the sun of truth shines brightly. The similarity of these two gardens, the false one below and the true one above, to the garden and paradise of the *Amorosa Visione* is obvious. The *Roman de la Rose* is also, no doubt, a model, with its double rose bringing in as well the reference to Maria versus erotic love.

Boccaccio's commentary on Dante interprets the inferno through which Dante travels as "gli atti degli uomini terreni, li quali, a rispetto de' corpi celestiali, ci possiam reputare di essere in inferno" (*Inf.* I.alleg.157) [the actions of men on earth who, with respect to the heavenly bodies, we can consider to be in hell]. Hell is the miseries of the present life which poets say is in the hearts of men. Cerberus, or the insatiability of desires, keeps men from leaving; and Acheron is the slippery and fluid condition of the things desired (*Esposiz.* Accessus.46–49). Clearly Levi was wrong to say that despite the many echoes of Dante's *Commedia* "non v'e nel *Corbaccio*, quanto a contenuto, orma di pensiero dantesco"[7] [as to content, there is in the *Corbaccio* no trace of Dantesque thought]. Moreover, this hell of human desires, which Boccaccio thought of as Dante's, does not appear here for the first time. The parody of Dante in the *Filostrato*, the emblematic quality of the imprisoned knights in the *Teseida*, and the despair of Fiammetta in the *Elegia* all illustrate the hell on earth described in Boccaccio's commentary. The *Corbaccio* makes emphatic that the choice between eternal good and worldly good is a choice between heaven and hell.

The lover has blinded himself and his eyes must be opened, like the eyes of Ameto or the lover in the *Amorosa Visione*. But whereas Ameto's eyes were opened to the beauty of the virtues, the *Corbaccio* narrator must have his eyes opened to the ugliness of the vices he has pursued. Thus the praises of women are replaced by harsh criticism, not necessarily because Boccaccio had been mocked by a real widow and wanted revenge, but because the woman this time is the essential object and embodiment of lust.[8] The point is not that this particular woman was the wrong one or that the fault is hers but that the problem lies in the narrator's own condition. This is the lesson begun by the narrator's reason: "Tu, non ella, ti se' della tua noia cagione" (p. 41) [You, not she, are the cause of your harm], and continued by the dream guide. The guide wants to cure the lover not of love for one woman but of the wrong kind of love for any woman. Critics who claim that Boccaccio is writing to take revenge on a widow all neglect this point, which Boccaccio establishes clearly near the beginning of his work. His comment is like Petrarch's own unvengeful complaint about love: "altri che me non ho di ch'i'mi lagne" (Canz. 311) [I have no one but myself to complain against].

The vilification of the beloved is a technique advocated by Ovid in his *Remedia amoris* to cure men from obsessive love:[9]

Saepe refer tecum sceleratae facta puellae
et pone ante oculos omnia damna tuos: (299–300)

[Often remind yourself of the deeds of the wicked girl and set before your eyes all the damages (she has caused)]

Profuit adsidue vitiis insistere amicae,
Idque mihi factum saepe salubre fuit. (315–16)

[It helped me to harp persistently on the vices of my girlfriend,
that was often good for my health.]

The *Corbaccio* guide explains that he must use harsh medicine to cure
the grievous sickness of the "I": "con vocaboli, con argomenti, con demo-
strazioni puzzolenti purgare e guarire si voglia" (p. 109) [with words, with
arguments, with stinking demonstrations one needs to be purged and
cured]. Again this is an echo from Ovid's *Remedia:*

Dura aliquis praecepta vocet mea: dura fatemur
Esse, sed ut valeas, multa dolenda feres.
Saepe bibi sucos, quamvis invitus, amaros
Aeger. (225–28)

[Some may call my precepts harsh: I confess they are harsh, / but
you bear many painful things in order to become well. / When I
was sick, I often drank bitter potions, as much as I disliked
them.]

One of the *Corbaccio* manuscripts even appears with the subtitle, "libro del
rimedio dello amore."

The narrator is sick and must be cured. The cure, as before, comes
through reason. The narrator's own reason begins the curative process;
within the dream which follows, the voice of reason, a guiding figure as in
the *Amorosa Visione*, is embodied in the soul of the widow's husband. In
one sense he is literally a dead man whose spirit is tormented in purgatory
for having tolerated his wife's vices instead of governing her properly. In
another sense, just as she is the figure of lust itself, so he is the figure of
reason which has failed in its role: "io tentai alquanto di voler porre freno a
questo indomito animale; ma perduta era ogni fatica" (p. 90) [I tried a
little to put a rein on this untamed animal; but all my effort was lost], complains the husband. Reason must "porre freno" on the passions, just as the
narrator of the *Amorosa Visione* must be bridled by his spouse in that curiously reversed marriage.

Levi, considering the book a work of real vendetta, is led to conclude
that the notion of a cure is merely an unsatisfactory excuse for pouring out
foul language.[10] Baricelli and Cassell think the book is critical of the narrator's revulsion as well as of the widow, for the narrator merely swings

irrationally from excessive love to excessive hatred.[11] The narrator's revulsion, however, is not simply from a woman but rather from the deformity of vice and is the result of reason's gaining control in the soul. Boccaccio in his *Esposizioni* on *Inferno* VII (alleg.144) criticizes both "ira" and "accidia . . . il qual dove bisogna non s'adira" [sloth . . . which does not get angry where it should]. It is the very "tiepidezza" [tepidness] of the husband which has earned him his fiery robe in purgatory. He should have been angry, and now he is suffering by divine will from the "sdegnosa fiamma nella mia mente accesa contra di lei per li modi suoi" [angry flame kindled in my mind against her on account of her ways], which are deservedly to be blamed (p. 116). Scorn and hatred are purgative for him as well as for the narrator. The light and fertile scene where the narrator emerges at last shows clearly that the cure has worked. The freed lover's attitude will no longer be such a passionate hatred but rather the laughter of detachment. The ghost of the husband, describing the widow's treachery, says to the lover: "riso te ne' avresti . . . il che forse testè teco medesimo fai; e fai saviamente, se'l fai" (p. 125)[12] [you would have laughed . . . and perhaps just now you are laughing to yourself; and you do wisely if you are doing so].

The disillusioned pursuit of love is particularly embarrassing to the narrator, "avendo riguardo che io la maggior parte della mia vita abbia spesa in dovere qualche cosa sapere, e poi, quando il bisogno viene, trovarmi non sapere nulla" (p. 65) [considering that I have spent most of my life in being supposed to know something, and then, when the need arises, to find that I know nothing]. His instructor continues the remonstrance: "Gli studi adunque alla sacra filosofia pertinenti infino dalla tua puerizia . . . ti piacquero, e massimamente in quella parte che a poesia appartiene. . . . Questa, non menoma tra l'altre scienzie, ti doveva parimente mostrare che è amore e che cosa le femmine sono, e chi tu medesimo sii e quel che a te s'appartiene." (p. 70) [Then the studies pertinent to sacred philosophy since your childhood . . . pleased you, and especially that part which belongs to poetry . . . This, not least among the other sciences, ought equally to have shown you what love is and what women are, and who you yourself are and what is suitable to you.]

Here Boccaccio expresses the notion that literature teaches philosophy and reasserts the moral value of his earlier studies and writings as well as of the present work. Yet at the same time he seems to be suggesting that the study of literature does not really do much good, that a foolish audience—even himself—will either not truly understand or not apply its lessons to themselves. Therefore the author must make his point more plainly and emphatically and stop dallying with the images of worldly delight. Unlike the narrator of the *Amorosa Visione*, then, the *Corbaccio* narrator speaks from the perspective of a completed conversion. Thus the ambiguities of the lover's final prayer in the *Amorosa Visione*[13] yield to the direct religious invocation of the newly out-of-love narrator. Boccaccio prays to God for aid with his writing, in order that it may work effectively for the good of its readers.

The topic of good and bad uses of writing takes its place beside the topic of reason and lust. Thus the old bawd who caused the narrator so much grief is contrasted not only to the Virgin Mary, the source of true "salute," but also to the muses, whose celestial beauty "non t'inciterà al disonesto fuoco, anzi il caccerà via e i lor costumi ti fieno inreprobabil dottrina alle virtuose opere" (p. 88) [will not incite you to dishonest flame, but rather will chase it away, and their manners will be to you an irreproachable lesson in virtuous doings]. While the bawd, who had been described to the narrator as eloquent, knows only how to chatter idly or to lie, the muses teach natural and moral sciences: the causes of the changing seasons, the labors of the sun and moon, what hidden virtue nourishes the plants, etc. The moral teachings are those of Boccaccio's own writings such as the *Amorosa Visione*: "per quali scale ad essa [la divina bontà] si salga, e per quali balzi si trarupi alla parte contraria; e teco, poiché i versi d'Omero, di Virgilio e degli altri antichi valorosi avranno cantati, i tuoi medesimi, se tu vorrai, canteranno" (p. 88) [by which stairs one ascends to it (divine goodness) and by which leaps one crosses over to the opposite shore, and with you, after they have sung the verses of Homer, Vergil, and other worthy ancestors, they will sing, if you like, your own songs].

The opposition between the old bawd and the muses' follows Boethius's *Consolatio* where Philosophy drives away the "whores" and "sirens" who "kill the fruitful harvest of reason with the sterile thorns of the passions" (the *Corbaccio* landscape) and replaces those muses with her own curative poetry. Like the *Corbaccio* narrator, Boethius is rebuked particularly because a man of his learning should have known better than to fall for such "sweet poison." This prose section (I.i) is immediately followed by verses contrasting Boethius's former study of "the causes of things," the nature of the heavens, planets, plants, etc., and his present bondage, "the light of his mind gone out." The echoes of Philosophy's words in the mouth of the *Corbaccio* husband strengthen his identification with reason.

The crow of the title may refer to the theme of good and bad writing as well as to the theme of lust. The raven (*corvus*) according to Ovid's *Fasti*

(II.243–66) is a liar, a fraudulent servant to none other than Apollo, god of poets. Athena sets the crow in opposition to the owl: on one side, the bird of wisdom; on the other side, the idle chatterer.[14] According to Pliny and others, crows never perch on the Temple of Athena because she has banished them from her sanctuary.[15] The *Fasti* (II.89) mentions in passing that Orpheus's power is so great that even owls and crows sit together in peace. The opposition between Athena's owl and the chattering crow can be compared to the contest between the muses and the daughters of Pierus (*Metamorphoses* V.250–678), vain and ignorant chatterers who were turned into magpies. Boccaccio glosses the tale in his *Genealogia* (XI.2): "et cum multa dicere ignaris videantur, nec aliquid tamen dicant rationi consonum, nec sese loquentes intelligant" [and although they seem to the ignorant to say many things, yet neither do they say anything consonant with reason nor do they understand their own speeches].

They are like poets who write without the guidance of reason texts which they themselves do not understand, i.e., like the first-person narrators of some of Boccaccio's earlier works. Dioneo in the *Decameron* (IX.10) declares himself to be a crow rather than a swan, both alluding to the nature of his tales and contrasting his "foolishness" to the virtues of the ladies. The old *Corbaccio* widow, who had been praised for her eloquence, turns out to be a fraud, a fool, and a liar.

She not only tells lies in order to allure the poet's desire, but she also reads in order to arouse her own concupiscence. This sort of reading is opposed to prayer, the use of language which connects men with God:

> le sue orazioni e paternostri sono i romanzi franceschi e le canzoni latine, . . . ella tutta si tritola, quando legge Lancelotto, o Tristano o alcuno altro con le loro donne nelle camere segretamente e soli raunirsi, sì come colei, alla qual pare veder ciò che fanno, e che volentieri, come di loro immagina, così farebbe, avvegna chè ella faccia sì che di ciò corta voglia sostiene (p. 120)

> [her prayers and paternosters are French romances and Latin songs . . . she gets all worked up when she reads that Lancelot, Tristan, or someone else secretly reunite themselves with their women in their bedrooms: and as she seems to see what they are doing and what willingly she would do too just as she imagines them doing, it happens that she acts so that she need only briefly sustain her desire for it].

As in previous works, Boccaccio is referring to the Francesca scene of *Inferno* V and is condemning not so much the literature itself as the use the reader makes of it. The widow is just the sort of reader that the lover-narrator of those earlier works was hoping for: one who would be aroused to desire by tales of love.

The recurring references to Paolo and Francesca's reading scene throughout Boccaccio's works reveal a decline in Boccaccio's trust of readers. Florio and Biancifiore fall in love over that most dangerous of books, Ovid's *Ars amatoria;* yet they remain entirely innocent. At the time they are too naive to proceed beyond a kiss, and later they interrupt their embraces to perform a marriage ceremony before finally making love. Thus although Ovid's work opens their eyes to their own feelings, they are easily able to contain those feelings within the bounds of "honesty" and social correctness. Their purity is all the more striking as it is in notable opposition to the sin of Dante's lovers. The narrator of the *Teseida* is in a more slippery condition, for he quotes Francesca's words while he offers his book to Fiammetta in order to kindle her love. He admits that he is barely able to restrain himself from breaking all rules of social honesty under the force of his passion. Fiammetta, however, seems to be the same kind of reader as Florio and Biancifiore, for her response to the book is a reference to marriage. The *Teseida* thus includes one reader *in malo* and one *in bono* for its own narrative romance, one imperiled and one innocent member of the couple. In the *Corbaccio* there is only the fallen reader, who not only succumbs to the excitement of romances but even seeks them out in order to arouse herself. In sum, the use of ambiguous or dangerous reading material steadily declines from honest to dishonest as appetite more and more prevails over reason in the persons handling the text. That is, the declining power of the representatives of reason and the increased blackening of the figures of lust run parallel to the growing misuse of texts in the imitations of Dante's famous reading scene.

The crow is contrasted to the swan in the *Corbaccio* in reference also to the harsh tone of Boccaccio's book.[16] In the *Metamorphoses* of Ovid (II.534–636) the crow and raven are both punished for gossiping about unfaithful women:

lingua fuit damno: lingua faciente loquaci
qui color albus erat, nunc est contrarius albo. (539–40)

[his tongue was his undoing: because of his chattering tongue his color which used to be white is now the opposite of white.]

The hoarse voice of the crow brought Apollo tidings that he did not want to hear, reporting the infidelity of the woman he loved. Similarly the ghost in the *Corbaccio* tells a lover the harsh truth about his woman. The title of the book may be in part a warning to lover-readers that they will not be pleased by what they hear.[17]

The harshness of tone in this diatribe against women and lust goes along with Boccaccio's pushing apart of the polar terms with which he had worked all along. The reason for this emphatic drive toward extremes is perhaps not only Boccaccio's changing feelings about love but also, perhaps even more so, his growing uneasiness with fiction. The "velo" of the earlier works obscured the truth within. If their purpose was to lead the lover-reader to reason and a better kind of love, they could have spoken more urgently and more directly. The *Corbaccio* presents its case twice: once through the speech of reason while the narrator is awake, and a second time through the dream which is set off by those waking thoughts. If one recognizes in the husband the voice of reason, then the second part is an image of the first, a transformation of reason's direct speech by the "virtù fantastica." The writing remains direct; the waking and the dream are both true seeing.[18] There is no room for an erotic vision and a lusty narrator who misunderstands his own text. Apparently the reader is no longer trusted to mend the narrator's faults on his own, as Boccaccio asked us to do in the *Amorosa Visione*. Instead the narrator, like Ameto, learns successfully to undo his own former delusions.

"Favellare" becomes a term of dispraise; it is the language of falsehood, opposed perhaps to "ragionare." For those who have opened their ears ("apri gli orecchi"), speakers who "favellano" about "fallace amore" [misleading love] produce the howlings and bellowings of beasts. The narrator is surprised to discover that these fearful sounds have been coming from his own mouth (pp. 57–58).[19] Here is certainly a lovesick narrator who has not heard his own words with a clear mind, i.e., the sort of narrator found in earlier works. But now that his ears are opened, he identifies and rejects the animal voice of appetite.

The false love letter written as a joke by the widow's more successful lover is also "per più largo spazio aver di favellare" (p. 66) [to have more room for false chattering]. The husband must translate this false reply, defining what it really means by "cortesia," "savia," "gentilezza," etc. (pp. 102ff.). As Fiammetta had argued in the *Filocolo*, the language of false love is a false language intended to deceive. If the widow likes "i grandi favellatori," it is because she herself excels in telling lies: "della sua onestà, della sua divozione, della sua santità e di quelli di casa sua favellare . . . le favole e le bugie sue" (pp. 107–8) [lying about her honesty, her devotion, her holiness and that of the members of her household . . . her fables and lies].

The narrator is urged as an act of penance to do everything in reverse: to hate what he had loved, to love the widow's soul with *caritas*, and to replace the "favellare" of lovers with the true speaking of a rational man. "Dove l'averla glorificata tu avresti mentito per la gola . . . e tesi lacciuoli alle menti di molti . . . dirai il vero, sgannerai altrui, e lei raumilierai" (pp. 136–37) [where to glorify her you would have lied in your throat . . . and set snares for the minds of many . . . you will speak the truth, undeceive others, and rehumiliate her]. This book then is to be composed contrary to the writings of a lover. Rather than praise and exalt his lady, he is to criticize and humiliate her. Rather than long to see her again, he regrets ever seeing her at all. Rather than wish that the book may come into his lady's gentle hands, he hopes it will avoid her rough treatment. And rather than hoping to inspire love in his reader, he hopes to teach the reader to fall out of love and to shun its traps in the future.[20] The human language of reason undertakes to undo love's illusions and to warn us against the lies of its seeming eloquence.

The idea for this reversal undoubtedly comes from Ovid. He wrote in the *Ars amatoria* (II.657–58, 660–61):

Nominibus mollire licet mala: "fusca" vocetur,
    Nigrior Illyrica cui pice sanguis erit;
            . . .
Sit "gracilis" macie quae male viva sua est;
Dic "habilem," quaecumque brevis, quae turgida, "plenam."

[Let the defects be softened by their names: let her be called "tan" / whose blood is blacker than Illyrian pitch; / . . . let her be "slender" who looks scarcely alive for her thinness; / say "just right" if she's short, "full-bodied" if she's fat.]

In the *Remedia*, he turns around his advice (325–28):

Qua potes, in peius dotes deflecte puellae
    Iudiciumque brevi limite falle tuum.
Turgida, si plena est, si fusca est, nigra vocetur;
    In gracili macies crimen habere potest.

[Insofar as you can, turn the girl's gifts to the worse / and deliberately falsify your judgment by a slight distinction. / Let her be called fat if she is full-bodied, black if she is tan; / In a slender girl thinness may be a fault.]

Boccaccio's imitation of Ovid implies that at least some of the books preceding the *Corbaccio* were a kind of *Ars amatoria;* and indeed, there was often a lover-narrator trying to win his lady-reader's love. The *Corbaccio* now comes as a remedy to any reader who regrets having fallen into the trap. Not only does it reverse the previous advice, however; it demonstrates—unlike Ovid's *Remedia*—that that advice was foolish and false, and that those who pursue the path of love will inevitably be sorry in the end. Ovid announces at the beginning of the *Remedia* that he himself is in love just as before; he is writing only for those lovers who are in despair in order to help them to happier affairs. Boccaccio makes his own lover-narrator one of those desperate cases, who, seeing the error of his past ways, removes himself from love altogether. Thus Ovid's *Remedia* is remedied in turn by its transposition among Christian concepts of love: the widow's lust, the Virgin's charity. The narrator's escape from love becomes a Dantean journey from hell to paradise.

Scholars tend to consider the *Corbaccio* "a sudden and substantial reversal of attitude" on the part of Boccaccio, "the work which announces the author's personal moral and intellectual crisis and the consequently dramatic change in his way of thinking and writing": [21] "il libro costituisce la prova d'un orientamento culturale, morale e religioso radicalmente diverso da quello che aveva ispirato tutte le opere volgari precedenti del poeta" [22] [the book constitutes the proof of a cultural, moral and religious orientation radically different from that which inspired all the preceding vernacular works of the poet].

We must be careful, nonetheless, about what precisely has changed. For Cottino-Jones: "What had been in the *Decameron* and in Boccaccio's earlier works a whole-hearted admiration for natural love and spontaneous physical attraction becomes in the *Corbaccio* a stern condemnation of love." [23] Spontaneous physical attraction was not always wholeheartedly endorsed in the previous works, as we have seen. Nor does the *Corbaccio* condemn all love; it is attacking specifically the abdication of reason to lust. But so did the earlier works. In this sense even the *Decameron* is not so radically different. It too, after all, is introduced as a *remedia amoris.* Thanks to the equally Ovidian ironies of Boccaccio's earlier writings, the *Corbaccio* is not so different from the earlier works. That is, the means are different, but the purpose, and the view of the purpose of literature in general, remains the same. The books are all teachers of reason and faith, attempts to persuade lover-readers to see the limitations as well as the pleasures of mortal things: "ingegnera'ti d' essere utile a coloro, e massimamente a' giovani, li quali con gli occhi chiusi, per li non sicuri luoghi, troppo di sè fidandosi, sanza guida si mettono; e del beneficio da me ricevuto dalla Genetrice della nostra salute, sarai testimonio" (p. 143) [You will endeavor to be useful to them, and especially to youths, who go with closed eyes through dangerous places, overconfident in themselves, without a guide; and you will bear witness to the benefit received by me from the mother of our salvation]. The "closed eyes" describe the *Amorosa Visione* dreamer just as well as the *Corbaccio* dreamer. Both dream visions were written to wake us up.

What has changed radically, however, is that the two polar terms, the two kinds of love, the heavenly and worldly aims, have been pushed to extremes. They can no longer be made to overlap or represent each other. The tolerance for ambiguities is lost. The feeling of conflict intensifies, and the possibilities of mediation are denied. We encounter the choice of ways not at the fork where both roads meet but, instead, farther on where one cannot even see the old connection. Indeed, the choice between heaven and earth of the *Amorosa Visione* has here been rewritten as a choice between heaven and hell. As the split widens, the object of human love, that once seemed a possible bridge to or sign of the divine, slips from Mary's mediating role to the role of fallen Eve and on to the unrepentant devilry of the old bawd.

VIII

Decameron

Having traced certain patterns of development in Boccaccio's "minor" writings through to the *Corbaccio*, I must come back at this point to pose the question: how does the *Decameron* fit into these patterns? What is its relation to Boccaccio's other writings in regard to his growing distrust of the power of reason and concomitantly to the quality of readership represented within the work? And what has happened to Fiammetta in all of this?

i. Reason

Reason is certainly one of the key words of the *Decameron*. The author in his preface states that his love-misery was alleviated only by the "piacevoli ragionamenti . . . e laudevoli consolazioni" [pleasant conversations / reasonings . . . and praiseworthy consolations] of an unnamed friend. One can think both back to the "consolation" offered by the Philosophy-like guide of the *Amorosa Visione* and forward to the narrator's conversations in the *Corbaccio* first with his own reason and then with a friend. It is just such helpful "ragionamenti" that Boccaccio wishes to pass along for the aid of other melancholy lovers through the brigata's activity of "ragionare." "Ragionare" is the speech of rational creatures, as the word implies; it is not the utterance of animals that we have encountered in both the *Caccia* and *Corbaccio*. The author presents himself in a new light here relative to his earlier works, though not to the *Corbaccio:* he is no longer someone in need of the corrective responses of his lady or other readers but rather someone who has successfully learned a lesson and wants to teach it in turn. Most notably, he is no longer himself under the influence of love but instead has passed through love and out the other side of it so that he both understands it and is free of its illusions, thankful for his new rational freedom from love's self-induced miseries. He was suffering, he says, not from the lady's cruelty but from his own "poco regolato appetito" (ill-regulated appetite). He presents his *Decameron*, then, as a *remedia amoris* for others in his previous condition: "se per quegli [pensieri] alcuna malinconia, mosso da focoso disio, sopraviene nelle lor menti, in quelle conviene che con grave noia si dimori, se da nuovi ragionamenti non è rimossa" (Proemio 11) [if because of those thoughts any melancholy, moved by fiery desire, takes possession of their minds, they must remain in it with grave distress unless it is removed by new speeches/reasonings].

Women, says Boccaccio, are most in need of help; most of the time they stay shut up within the small circuit of their rooms and, sitting idle, immerse themselves in dangerous thoughts. They cannot participate in the activities of hunting, business, and travel with which men are free to distract themselves from their passions. Ovid's *Remedia amoris* listed these various occupations, advising men to drive away Cupid by keeping busy. Thus, just as in the *Corbaccio*, Boccaccio has set himself the task of writing another *Remedia amoris*, aiming it at an audience hitherto neglected. Ovid's work was addressed primarily to men; Boccaccio speaks to women, reversing the relationship of reader and writer from his previous works: the male writer is correcting or helping amorous and erring female readers instead of being himself the one in love and in need of the lady's and reader's corrections.

> Adunque, acciò che in parte per me s'amendi il peccato della fortuna, la quale dove meno era di forza, sì come noi nelle dilicate donne veggiamo, quivi più avara fu di sostegno, in soccorso e rifugio di quelle che amano, per ciò che all'altre è assai l'ago e'l fuso e l'arcolaio, intendo di raccontare cento novelle. (13)[1]

> [Then, so that through me may be amended in part the crime of fortune who was more stingy of support where there was less strength, as we see in delicate women, for the succour and refuge of women who love, because for others the needle and distaff and skein-winder are enough, I intend to tell one hundred stories.]

The *Corbaccio* begins with its lover in exactly the same initial condition as the *Decameron* readers: "ritrovandomi solo nella mia camera, . . .

m'avvenne ch'io fortissimamente sopra gli accidenti del carnale amore cominciai a pensare" [finding myself alone in my room, . . . it happened that I began to think very hard about the mishaps of carnal love].

Those thoughts led the narrator to despair and to desire death until divine grace allowed him a more consoling line of thought. Conversations with friends also helped. Both writers now want to pass on the help to other lovers. Boccaccio wants us to know before we start reading the tales of the *Decameron* that he is now "libero," free from love, because as in the *Corbaccio* he is himself an example for the reader.

The author's escape from the bondage of love to rational freedom finds a parallel in the ascent of the narrators from the hell of physical and moral corruption in Florence to the paradise of fertile and rational order in the garden on the hill.[2] Following "natural ragione" [natural reason] and "fuggendo come la morte i disonesti essempli degli altri" [fleeing like death the dishonest examples of others], they decide to go "onestamente" [honestly] to a place in the country. There they will live with what pleasure they can "senza trapassare in alcuno atto il segno della ragione" [without overstepping in any act the bounds of reason]. Moderation and "onestà" are repeatedly associated with reason. Moderation was the common advice of physicians for preserving one's health during the plague; Boccaccio considers together both the physical and spiritual aspects of "salute." The avoidance of death becomes the avoidance of spiritual death as well. The ten friends will leave behind in Florence those who act "senza fare distinzione alcuna dalle cose oneste a quelle che oneste non sono, solo che l'appetito le cheggia" [without making any distinction between things which are honest and those which are not honest, only as their appetite demands], or as Panfilo describes them later (IX.concl.) "che al ventre solamente, a guisa che le bestie fanno, . . . serve"[3] [who serve only their bellies, as do the animals]. The degeneracy of behavior in Florence is animal-like in that only immediate gratification of the appetite counts, and all rational judgment or forethought is forgotten. With the assembling of the ladies, reason begins to reassert its dominance. The ascent, both physical and moral, from the animal or appetite-driven to the human or rationally governed is similar to the ascent, accomplished or in progress, that one can see in the *Comedia delle Ninfe* and *Amorosa Visione*, as well as in the *Corbaccio*.

The process contains also, of course, an echo of Dante's ascent in the *Commedia*. Boccaccio's brigata, ascending a hill to an earthly paradise, make only part of Dante's journey. Their emphasis on reason suits the limit of their ascent, and their crowning in Book IX may be a parallel to Dante's crowning at the top of Mount Purgatory, for like him they can govern themselves and freely stay within the bounds of reason. Similarly the *Comedia delle Ninfe*, despite its obvious Christian concerns, climaxes with an imitation of the end of the *Purgatorio* and does not continue into heaven.[4] The return of the *Decameron* narrators to Florence at the end—in contrast to Dante's ending with a vision of God—suggests that Boccaccio's interest is not in transcending the world but in living properly within it, and not in the heavenly state of the blessed but in the process of escaping from the bondage of sin to the autonomy of rational judgment.

Outside the city, says Pampinea, they will be able to see the heavens, which "ancora che crucciato ne sia, non per ciò le sue bellezze eterne ne nega" [although they are still frowning, do not for all that deny us their eternal beauties]; outside the city they can wait to see what end heaven reserves for these events. Branca has pointed out that "le sue bellezze eterne" is an echo from Dante;[5] and it is interesting to see the two contexts where Dante uses the phrase. One is in *Purgatorio* XIV.149:

Chiamavi 'l cielo e 'ntorno vi si gira,
mostrandovi le sue bellezze etterne,
e l'occhio vostro pur a terra mira;
onde vi batte chi tutto discerne.

[the heaven calls you, and turns around you, / showing you its eternal beauties, / and your eye looks only at the earth, / wherefore he who sees all things beats you.]

This fits Pampinea's speech and its context quite well. While most of the survivors in town have their eyes only "a terra," Pampinea wants to regain the view of heaven. Dante uses the phrase again in *Paradiso* VII.66, where he discusses man's fall from the eternal beauty of divinity. Those "etterne bellezze" attract men back to God, whose love has allowed the possibility of redemption. We see in Florence the lowest state to which men can fall; they have relapsed to the state of animals, surviving from moment to moment without any kind of civilization. But the beauties of nature described in this passage—and of more than nature, for nature's beauties are never "etterne"—beckon Pampinea toward a more dignified and healthier manner of life. She recalls her friends' attention to the other, the heavenly or rational, aspect of human nature. The same phrases are used again in the *Corbaccio;* there the narrator remarks that God loves us more than we do ourselves: "li quali colle nostre malvage opere continuamente ci andiamo sommergendo, dov'egli colla sua caritativa pietà sempre ne va sollevando, e le sue etterne bellezze mostrandoci, a quelle, come benignissimo padre, ne va chiamando" (p. 55) [who with our evil deeds continually lower ourselves, whereas he with his charitable piety always keeps raising us up again and, showing us his eternal beauties, like a kind father, goes on calling us to them].

Those eternal or divine beauties had, in the *Filocolo*, *Comedia delle Ninfe*, and *Amorosa Visione*, been represented by a lady. Not so in the *Decameron*, although Boccaccio may be referring to his past use of the lady when he writes in his Proemio (3):

> dalla mia prima giovanezza infino a questo tempo oltre modo essendo acceso stato d'altissimo e nobile amore, forse più assai che alla mia bassa condizione non parrebbe, narrandolo, si richiedesse, quantunque appo coloro che discreti erano e alla cui notizia pervenne io ne fossi lodato e da molto più reputato

> [since my earliest youth up to this time I was burning beyond measure with a most high and noble love, perhaps much more than might seem suitable to one of my lowly condition in the telling, although among those who were perceptive and who noticed it, I was praised for it and thought much more of].

The "discreti" in this case might be wiser readers who understood the point that he was making in his narratives ("narrandolo"). His declaration that he is now out of love, although the memories of it remain pleasant to him, could signify not only a new role for the author but also a rethinking of the figure of the lady, a shift away from his previous use of the correspondences between erotic and heaven-directed love. This would imply as well a shift away from the kind of allegory he had written in the past.

What has happened, then, to the idea of writing for a woman now that the woman has become plural and is no longer of special personal interest to the author? Several ways have been suggested of understanding this definition of the audience.

For one, Boccaccio may really be turning to a new sector of the reading public.[6] The new public, however, was not necessarily female. Boccaccio wrote to Maghinardo dei Cavalcanti: "Sane, quod inclitas mulieres tuas domesticas nugas meas legere permiseris non laudo, quin imo queso per fidem tuam ne feceris." [Indeed, that you permit the renowned women of your household to read my trifles I do not approve, but rather beseech you by your faith not to do so.] Neither Padoan nor Branca takes this letter seriously as a recantation of the *Decameron*. For Padoan it manifests "una certa posa letteraria, resa più evidente dal fatto che il Boccaccio aveva da poco nuovamente trascritto amorevolmente e con cura il suo capolavoro"[7] [a certain literary pose, rendered more evident by the fact that Boccaccio had recently recopied, lovingly and carefully, his masterpiece]. Nonetheless, readers of the *Decameron*—at least in Florence—were likely more frequently to be men than women.[8]

According to some scholars, the notion of "donne" may be understood not literally but as meaning a popular audience in general. Dante in his *De Vulgare Eloquentia* considers women the proper audience for vernacular writings in the low style and dealing with love; and Dante's Epistle XIII.10 repeats the idea: "remissus est modus et humilis, quia locutio vulgaris in qua et muliercule communicant" [the style is low and humble, because it is the common speech in which even women communicate]. The address to women, therefore, could be a way of declaring that the work will be of this style.[9] There is some support for this from Fiammetta's comment in X.6 that disputations ought to be avoided because the audience comprises women and not scholars. Boccaccio's conclusion repeats the point: the tales were told neither among students nor among philosophers but among young ladies in a garden. This declaration of a non-scholarly audience identified as women also suits one of Boccaccio's comments in the *Teseida*; the gloss to VII.30 ends: "a me basta, scrivendo questo ad istanzia di donne, averne detto quello che qui appare" [for me it is sufficient, writing this at the request of women, to have said what appears here]. There too scholarly discussion is cut short on behalf of a more popular tone. The praise of women as effective muses is no doubt a way of exalting the vernacular, "istilo umilissimo"[10] [lowest style].

Quite a different interpretation is put forth by Mazzotta.[11] "Writing for the ladies, however coy a claim it can be, is concomitantly an admission of estheticism and futility." By addressing idle women Boccaccio makes "the ironic claim that literature is of no serious use and that the text occupies the interstices of active life. . . . The eroticism of literature is necessarily connected with its failure to function in its vital historicity upon the world: pornographic literature, in other words, is that literature which is an intransitive esthetic experience, which has been reified, preserved and *used to be enjoyed*."[12] The garden becomes a symbol of the privacy of the reader and book "shutting out the world."

The garden, however, is a place not of private reading but of social telling, the location of a group of people who have restored the possibility of interacting with one another. Indeed, one of the dire results of the plague has been the breakdown of social bonds; and the members of the brigata, who have been living in fearful isolation because of the plague, consciously desire to restore social interaction.[13] The group needs some kind of rational order to function for any length of time, just as does the soul. Caleone, in love in the *Filocolo*, was helped to his own recovery by the task of creating social cohesion among men who had been living like animals scattered in the forest. So too the very sociability of the *Decameron* narrators provides a corrective to the isolated brooding of the lovers to whom Boccaccio's book is addressed. Rather than simulating the reader's privacy, the garden full of narrators attempts to bring the reader from dangerous and melancholy isolation into a fictive society, that is precisely to draw the reader out of him or herself back into the social world. The ladies of the brigata are avoiding the perils of "ozio" by their tale-telling, and the written book is meant to perform the same service for the idle readers in their rooms.

The audience is not merely women but women in love. Boccaccio even explicitly excludes other women: "in soccorso e rifugio di quelle che amano, per ciò che all'altre è assai l'ago e'l fuso e l'arcolaio, intendo di raccontare cento novelle" [for the succour and refuge of women who love, because for others the needle and distaff and skein-winder are enough, I intend to tell one hundred stories]. The introduction to the fourth day repeats this definition of the audience: "Per certo chi non v'ama e da voi non disidera d'essere amato, sì come persona che i piaceri nè la virtù della naturale affezzione nè sente nè conosce, così mi ripiglia: e io poco me ne curo." [Certainly he who does not love you and does not desire to be loved by you reprimands me as he is a person who neither feels nor knows the pleasures or the virtue of natural affection, and I care little about him.] One may note that the audience this time is masculine—those who love women—as well as feminine ("vi" addresses "donne"). The important factor is that the readers defined by Boccaccio in both the preface and the introduction to Book IV are persons in love.

The rejection of those who cannot love "naturalmente" is nothing new. The *Comedia delle Ninfe* similarly addressed "chi ama . . . ; degli altri non curo" [whoever loves . . . ; I don't care about the rest]. The purpose of this selection in both cases is twofold, I think. For one thing, lovers are in need of helpful distraction and cannot be further endangered by material treating of love. For another, the ability to love proves that the reader is educable. The *Comedia delle Ninfe* had promised to lead the reader "per donna" to the celestial beauty which women resemble. So too in the *De-*

cameron Boccaccio reminds his readers that God made him suited to love women; and though he remarks that at his age he still feels the impulse to love, he includes Dante as someone like himself. Boccaccio's "natural affezzione," then, can possibly be associated with Dante's natural turning of the "anima semplicetta," the essential energy or motion of the soul which can be trained by rational judgment to pursue true rather than deceitful happiness. The audience rejected by Boccaccio consists of those who either cannot be warmed by love at all or who incline instead to unnatural appetites. Such persons are unteachable.[14]

Possibly, then, "women" means anyone under the power of passion or ruled by appetite rather than reason. Boccaccio certainly uses in other writings the traditional notion that passion is a feminine aspect of the soul. In the *Genealogia* IX.3, Boccaccio writes about Mars and Venus and lovers in general: "Verum dum in contrarium, fervor inordinate concupiscentie fertur, fit ut occultis vinculis, id est cogitationibus atque delectationibus lascivis artius alligetur insipiens, quibus *effeminatus* solvi non possit." (my emphasis) [On the other side, in truth, while a passion of inordinate concupiscence is borne, it happens that, unwitting, he is bound tightly by hidden chains, that is by lascivious thoughts and pleasures, which he, rendered *effeminate*, cannot loose.] In the *De Mulieribus Claris* ("Pentesilea") he remarks again that idleness and *voluptas* make men feminine. His *Accessus* (55–56) to the *Esposizioni* interprets the daughters of Danaus, who are condemned to fetch water in sieves, as men who with effeminate folly ("la efeminata sciocchezza") continually spend themselves in sex, in a vain attempt to satisfy lust. The patricide which brought this penalty is glossed as the overthrow of rational guidance. In his fifteenth eclogue, Phylostropos accuses Typhlus of being a slave to the world and to his passions, and a "femina." Petrarch, represented by Phylostropos, comments similarly in his own *Trionfi* (*Trionfo d'Amore* IV.105) that love "ogni maschio pensier de l'alma tolle" [takes every masculine thought from the soul]; and his *De Vita Solitaria* II.7 describes Ovid as "lascivi et lubrici et prorsus mulierosi animi"[15] [of a wanton and slippery and utterly feminine mind].

The female lovers to whom the *Decameron* is addressed are, in this light, analogous to those Florentines who follow their appetites blindly. Thus not only sexual passion is addressed but the loss of rational government in general. The passionate and melancholy readers have lost their psychological balance. Following these traditional notions, the brigata women desire the presence of men as "guides" and bringers of "order" who "know how to regulate" matters with "providence" (I.intro.74–76). The author's concern for its restoration within the individual runs parallel to the concern of the brigata for the reestablishment of rational government within their society.

Pampinea's first sentence in the opening speech in Santa Maria Novella says: "niuna persona fa ingiuria che onestamente usa la sua ragione" [no one does wrong who uses his reason honestly]. The desire to defend one's life from the plague or any other threat is "natural ragione," she continues. Thus reason is introduced as a natural faculty which can offer "remedii" of many kinds, to preserve both physical life and mental happiness. If "ragione" also means a right, as in the right to defend one's life, the word implies that such rights are rationally, not arbitrarily, derived; for reason is the commonly defining characteristic of human nature. Speech or "ragionare," as the activity of rational beings, is the means by which it works. Because the ideals of the *Decameron* are often social ones, the satisfactory marriage, the satisfactory friendship, the satisfactory relation of child and parent, servant and master, governed and governing, language becomes important as the means to these interactions, and the problem of deceitful language is a problem of deceitful relationships. One whole day and many tales besides are devoted to the witty use of language to correct improper social behavior: the lust of a king for his subject, the avarice of a host toward his guest, the impudence of a young lady to an old man. These tales within tales form a bridge across social boundaries: the subject can speak to his king, the merchant to his noble client, etc., through clever indirection. Even Boccaccio, comparing his writing, in its most humble style, to the very dust on the road, presents his stories with the same intent: to restore society through an indirect address. His concern for the possibilities of language, in sum, does not divert from but rather coalesces with his concern for social arrangements.[16]

On the one hand, the dangers of passion are frequently warned against in the *Decameron*, largely because of their antisocial nature. Thus, for example, the very topic of love tales with happy endings begins with the brutal violence of Cimone, whose love—despite the pseudo-ennobling qualities described at the start—turns him from a harmless idiot into a destructive monster, while Boccaccio furthermore allies him, through Lisimaco, with the corruption of government office for personal, passionate ends.[17] The ultimate irrational event, of course, is the plague, a phenomenon which challenges human reason to make sense of it, and which is associated, as we have seen, with the rule of appetites. On the other hand, the victorious self-crowning of the brigata near the end of their sojourn—with oak, the tree of Jove, who signifies benevolent rationality and temperate balance—suggests that their activity of "ragionare" has indeed worked to save them from the mortal or at least the moral threats by which they are surrounded and imperiled. Here, in sum, reason appears as peculiarly human, not celestial, and yet also as remarkably effective, at least for a few people of the right sort—this in a work chronologically between the *Elegia* and *Corbaccio*, in which reason takes its most dramatic plunges from success. The *Decameron*, then, seems like a cheerful moment of respite from Boccaccio's declining view of reason's power; not, certainly, that the world of the *Decameron* is free from the irrational but that a precarious balance in the soul seems at least temporarily possible. Perhaps it is the very irrationality of the plague that called forth this idyllic vision of a possible or at least hoped-for rational government of the self and society.

ii. Fiammetta and Dioneo

Although she is now submerged within the group, Fiammetta is once again crucial to the expression of this view. Boccaccio had used a brigata of narrators before, in the *Filocolo* and in the *Comedia delle Ninfe*.[18] As the brigata increases in importance from a mere episode in the *Filocolo*, to a major part of the work in the *Comedia delle Ninfe*, to the total structure of the *Decameron*, the prominence of Fiammetta within the group diminishes. In the *Filocolo* Fiammetta is queen of the young society and is elevated above the rest of the group by special associations with the divine. In the *Comedia delle Ninfe* she is no longer above the others; nonetheless, she is placed last except for Ameto's Lia and is given a story much longer than the preceding ones. Her story, with its echoes from the *Filocolo*, suggests that she is still the narrator's own beloved. In the *Decameron* she has faded even further. Nothing but the name Fiammetta associates her now with the "author" who speaks outside the brigata; nor is she exalted in any obvious way above the other members of the group.

She is a middle-class Florentine now, not a noble Neapolitan, although a number of her stories refer to Naples and its ruling family.[19] She names no relatives, and even her own first name Maria is no longer mentioned.[20] With it vanishes her association with the divine. She is neither a messenger from heaven nor an allegorical figure of hope. Although Boccaccio does say that all the narrators have been given fictional names within the book, the effect is not to link Fiammetta in any way with Mary, but rather to make her seem more than ever human and historical, in need of a covering name to protect her real person from embarrassment.

Some of her attributes from earlier books are now distributed among other members of the group. For example, the words which Fiammetta spoke in *Amorosa Visione* XVI about her beauty as a sign of God's goodness are now repeated fairly closely in Lauretta's song. Boccaccio seems to be acknowledging here the mastery of Petrarch in treating that kind of love relation and to be declaring his present deviation from that model. Fiammetta is no longer sent to urge men's thoughts toward heaven. For another example, whereas Fiammetta had been leader of the group in the *Filocolo*, it is now Pampinea who leads the young men and ladies from Florence and takes charge of their new arrangements at the villa. Otherwise each of the narrators is equally king or queen for one day. Nonetheless, Fiammetta is placed strategically in a way which requires some discussion of the overall organization of the *Decameron*.

A number of critics in the last several decades have begun to pay attention to the ways in which Boccaccio is structuring his hundred tales.[21] The subject has been discussed at some length in a paper of mine which I will repeat more briefly here.[22] Boccaccio used at least two organizing schemes, both of which he probably borrowed from Dante: one is symmetry and the other a nine-plus-one pattern.

Symmetry or centering shows up in many of Boccaccio's works. In the *Filocolo* the men and women in the garden are symmetrically distributed, and the central question is emphasized both by a break in the narrative and by the identification of the questioner as the man in love with Fiammetta.

Fiammetta

```
        M 13       1 M
    M 12               2 M
    F 11               3 F
    M 10               4 M
    M 9              5 M
        F 8       6 F
```

Caleone

Victoria Kirkham has pointed out a symmetry to the whole romance as well, for the three books about the love, separation, and reunion of the lovers are preceded by a book on the conversion and pilgrimage of Biancifiore's parents and followed by a book on Florio's own conversion and pilgrimage with Biancifiore.[23] In the *Amorosa Visione* the choice of Hercules that is described in the center of the book presents a parallel to the narrator's situation.[24] The *Elegia di Madonna Fiammetta* has an explicit turning point in the fifth of nine books.[25]

The chart below outlines the symmetrical arrangement of elements in the *Decameron*. One may notice that these are chiefly elements from the framing narrative; that is, the cornice provides a balanced structure to contain the hundred tales.

The plague; the city left behind
  I. Free topic
   II. Topic linked to III
   Friday and Saturday
       III. New location; Fiammetta and Dioneo sing together.
       IV. Interruption by half-tale; Filostrato is king and also sings.
       V. Fiammetta is queen; Dioneo sings.
       VI. Interruption by servants' quarrel; Elissa is queen and also sings.
       VII. New location; Fiammetta and Dioneo sing together.
   Friday and Saturday
   VIII. Topic linked to VII
  IX. Free topic
X. Fiammetta sings; return to the city

The *Decameron* begins with a description of the plague-ridden city which the narrators decide to leave and ends with their resolve to return to the city. The stories they tell in between are divided into ten days of ten tales each, with a topic assigned for each day; but the first and ninth days are proclaimed free in regard to choice of topic. This suggests the establishment of a center on the fifth day. It is not surprising to find that Fiammetta is ruler on this central day. Moreover, Dioneo, who stands out by telling the last tale every day (except the first day), sings when Fiammetta is queen. Thus special emphasis is given to the fifth day.

Only twice does the ruler of the day also sing that day's song: on the fourth and sixth days, surrounding Fiammetta's reign. At the beginning of the fourth day we find the half-tale inserted by the author in his own voice. It tells about a young man who, despite his monastic upbringing, was distracted by women as soon as he saw them for the first time. The sixth day also begins with an interruption, this time a quarrel among the servants about whether some particular woman was chaste or not at her marriage. The woman servant is outraged not that Tindaro should cast doubt on the woman's chastity, but, on the contrary, that he should suspect her of being so foolish as not to have used her time well or to have been at all cowed by her family's restrictions. The two interruptions form a matched pair in which for men and for women sex is proclaimed the uncontrollable natural instinct. Parental precautions come to naught.[26]

The topic of the fourth day is love which comes to a tragic end. In the song that ends the day, Filostrato complains of betrayal by love. What had begun by seeming sweet has become torment and sorrow. He prays for death to release him from the "furore" that possesses him.

> La fede mia, la speranza e l'ardore
> va bestemmiando l'anima che more
>
> [my dying soul goes cursing my faith, hope and love]

sings Filostrato. Faith, hope, and charity are what his soul requires for its salvation. But he knows where his salvation lies. He crowns Fiammetta to rule the next day "come a colei la quale meglio, dell'aspra giornata d'oggi, che alcuna altra, con quella di domane queste nostre compagne raconsolar saprai" [as she who will know better than any other how to console these companions of ours for the harsh day today with that of tomorrow]. Hers is the fifth day, the marriage number.[27] Although the stated topic for the fifth day is simply how lovers come to a happy end, in every tale (except Dioneo's) that happy end is a marriage which renders the lovers' desires concordant with social order.

For many decades critics, looking at Boccaccio's introduction to the fourth day apart from its context given by the symmetrical structure, have seen in it Boccaccio's declaration of rebellion against the social restrictions of his day.[28] However, the half-tale has been placed so that it matches the words of the servant class—whose names derive from the satires and satirical comedies of Juvenal and Plautus[29]—and the humorous judgment of Dioneo in the beginning of the sixth day. The fifth day, placed between these interruptions, shows lovers' tribulations and fears caused by their attempts to circumvent the social order—to elope or unite without marriage—and their final happy reconciliation with society. In the half-tale a father, overreacting to the death of his wife, tries to withdraw from society altogether and to ignore the natural desires of his son. The foolish father is akin to Tancredi, whose attempt to deny and suppress his daughter's desires leads to the tragic results in IV.1. Boccaccio's solution is neither monkishness nor licentiousness but marriage,[30] a solution celebrated in earlier works as well.

The fifth day is explicitly presented as a correction to what has come before. The tale that most directly counters the trend of the fourth day is, significantly, the fourth tale, told by Filostrato as a recantation for his cruel topic. In his new tale, the father, finding the desires of nature unrestrainable in his daughter, marries rather than punishes the young couple, giving to their love a regulated social form as Teseo had done in the *Teseida*. Thus Filostrato under the reign of Fiammetta provides the alternative response to that chosen by the father in Fiammetta's tale (Tancredi) under the reign of Filostrato. Cruel revenge is converted into marriage again in the sixth and seventh tales. Even Dioneo's tale offers a perverse example of a husband's revenge yielding to a happier solution of social harmony.[31]

At the end of the sixth day the women narrators discover the Valle delle Donne, where the tales of day VII are told. According to our scheme of symmetry, we look at day III and find that there too the narrators are telling their stories in a new location. Not only do the gardens appear in a carefully balanced order, but they are themselves the image of that balance and order within which life flourishes at its best. They are arrayed evenly around a central point, the fountain or pond, a visual representation of the garden of tales (as Dioneo refers to them in V, Emilia at the end of VIII, and the author in his concluding remarks).

Although Boccaccio seems to be making a distinction between the fountain and planned pathways of the garden on one hand, and the uncut rocks and pathless valley on the other, nonetheless, the marvel of the valley is that nature looks so much like art. The circle of the meadow seems to have been marked off with a compass, writes Boccaccio. Moreover, the slopes are terraced like a theater, "come ne' teatri veggiamo i gradi infino all'infimo venire successivamente ordinate"[32] [as we see in theaters the steps ordered successively all the way down]. No one is present, yet each hill is crowned with a villa. This is no wild and tangled valley but an orderly, gardenlike place. Its circularity is only one way of expressing its perfection. Just as the fifth day reconciled natural desires and social order, so the garden and valley both demonstrate a perfect harmony between the works of man and nature.[33] It is in these most serene and regular surroundings that the bawdiest tales are told, while the honesty of the narrators' own behavior is reasserted by Dioneo himself, who has proposed the topic of the seventh day.[34] It is also on the third and seventh days and only then that Dioneo and Fiammetta sing together, the rebel advocate of pleasure and the ruler of the marriage day in harmony with each other.

Describing the two "worlds" of the *Decameron*, the noble, romantic, idealized world and the lower-class, realistic, or farcical one, Padoan contends that the two never meet; they are not only different but even "forse non raffrontabili"[35] [perhaps not confrontable]. However, Boccaccio's point on the third and seventh days especially (and in the *Decameron* as a whole) seems to me to be that the two worlds or points of view can and ought to merge; that natural impulse and rational order, or realism and idealism, present together a more fruitful option than either side alone.

The third and seventh days are surrounded by the Fridays and Saturdays on which storytelling is replaced by religious observance in remembrance of "quello . . . che in così fatti giorni per la salute delle nostre anime addivenne" (VII.concl.17) [that which happened on such days for the salvation of our souls]. Although days II and VIII are not directly paired, the topic of II, the power of fortune, is answered by the topic of III, the power of the human will; and the topic of VII, women's tricks on men, by VIII, the tricks that both men and women play on each other. Lauretta, the ruler of VIII, says she was tempted to make the topic men's tricks on women but decided to avoid a petty revenge for VII.

The villa to which the narrators come on the very first day is also a part of the general symmetry. If it is only sparsely described relative to the later sites, it offers nonetheless a complete change of mood from the plague, catering to life and pleasantness as the plague catered to death and horror. This first escape from death balances the briefly mentioned forest where the narrators walk at the beginning of the ninth day. There they crown themselves with oak leaves, the sign of their inner strength and victory over the threat of death: "e chi scontrati gli avesse, niuna altra cosa avrebbe potuto dire se non: 'O costor non saranno dalla morte vinti o ella gli ucciderà lieti'"[36] [and whoever had met them would not have been able to say other than: "O these will either not be vanquished by death or else they will die happy"].

The songs that end each day also bear out a significant pattern of symmetry. In the first song Emilia contemplates beauty in herself; in the ninth Neifile contemplates the beauty of her lover in that of the flowers. Silber has pointed out that both songs echo phrases from Dante's *Purgatorio*, cantos XXVII–XXVIII. Neifile gathering flowers resembles Matelda, while Emilia's self-contemplation picks up the reference to Rachel:[37]

Ma mia suora Rachel mai non si smaga
dal suo miraglio, e siede tutto giorno.
Ell' è d'i suoi belli occhi veder vaga. (XXVII.104–6)

[But my sister never moves from her mirror, and sits all day. She is desirous to see her beautiful eyes.]

Songs II and VIII are joyful songs by the oldest lady and man, Pampinea and Panfilo, who both declare the good that comes from love.

Songs III and VII are songs of longing for a love once happy. Lauretta sings of her present jealous husband on earth and her longing for the former love now in heaven. Her beauty, which was created in heaven as a sign of God's beauty, is on earth "mal conosciuta" [ill-known] and "dispregiata" [unappreciated]. Filomena also desires to return to her distant lover, who seems, however, to be a human one. The shift toward discontent increases as one approaches the center. Songs IV and VI are unhappy. Filostrato (IV) sings how assurance has led to his fall, how love has deceived him. Desperate, he prays to love for hope. Elissa (VI) also complains of being deceived by love and, caught between torturing hope and despair, begs love to set her free. In the center comes Dioneo's bawdy offering and its replacement. The final song is Fiammetta's, happy in love except for her jealous fear of rivals.

The pattern of symmetry that I have been outlining considers the first nine days apart from the tenth. This is justified, I believe, for several reasons. The tenth day is really different from the others in that it presents models of magnanimity that rise above the more familiar level of the first nine days. It is introduced explicitly as a correction for all nine preceding days. Thus symmetry combines with progress as the ninth day not only echoes the first but also prepares for the tenth. Moreover, Fiammetta as queen on V and singer on X and Dioneo as singer on V and teller of the hundredth tale, provide links between the final day and the center of the symmetrical grouping. Both V and X are the same day of the week.

Boccaccio uses the nine-plus-one pattern with special attention to Dioneo. When Dioneo ends each day by telling a story that is allowed to break the day's topic and that is likely to parody the established themes of the day, Dioneo's tenth twists the nine preceding tales toward the perverse. However, Dioneo is involved with two other occurrences of the pattern: after offering a series of nine bawdy songs on the fifth day, he sings a tenth which is acceptable to the brigata; and after telling a series of nine bawdy tales on the first nine days, he follows it with a tenth which is the most extreme example of control over one's feelings and desires. This tale tops not only his own nine previous tales but also the nine other tales of the final day. For whereas their emphasis has been on the magnificence of kings and sultans, Dioneo's example of true spiritual magnificence is a pigherd's daughter while the behavior of the noble Gualtieri is "bestiale." In these cases the tenth rises above the previous nine. These two occasions of reversal from Dioneo's usual role of comic foil[38] take place on the fifth and tenth or central and final days, adding to the rhetorical emphasis of their positions.

Finally, I think these patterns are not fortuitous because they help one understand the meaning of the *Decameron*. By emphasizing the fifth and tenth days in a number of ways, Boccaccio sets up those two days as special points of reference among the other tales.[39] The topics for those two days are both presented explicitly as corrections for what has come before. Just as the fifth day offers a happy concord for lovers and their families through the social form of marriage, so the tenth day offers other forms of ideal social harmony with its examples of the ideal relationship between friends, ruler and subject, and so on. Good will and a cheerful reasonableness seem to be the main qualities required, while "furore" such as obsessive passion, jealousy, or anger and the equal blindness of stupid vanity are rejected as destructive to the "concordia" and "fraternal dimestichezza" [fraternal familiarity] for which the brigata is praised at the end.

The patterns of organization just outlined have the effect of selecting Fiammetta and Dioneo from the rest of the group and giving special emphasis to the moments when they are paired, just as Fiammetta and Caleone were singled out by their placement in the *Filocolo* garden.[40] Numerous endeavors have been made to distinguish among the *Decameron* narrators on the basis of the way they are described, the songs they sing, the topics they choose, or the tales they tell.[41] Attempting to solve Boccaccio's hints and identify the couples in love among the narrators, scholars have generally agreed in pairing Dioneo and Fiammetta.[42] Whether or not these two are in love with each other, they represent two quite different attitudes which Boccaccio makes balance each other, just as he balances the structure of the book. In a sense, they represent Padoan's two worlds, although Dioneo is "gentile" like the other narrators.

In the *Comedia delle Ninfe* Dioneo, whose name means "Venerean," had been matched with Adione or temperance. Meanwhile, in the *Comedia delle Ninfe* and also in the *Filocolo* Fiammetta had been paired with a passionate lover, Caleone. Caleone, in the *Filocolo*, becomes the founder of Certaldo; Dioneo in the *Decameron* tells the one tale set in Certaldo. Thus allusions to the town link both men to Boccaccio himself. But whereas Caleone, restored from passion to reason, is an unheeded model for the lover-narrator of the *Filocolo*, the *Decameron* author, announcing in his preface that he has been freed from passion, creates in Dioneo a laughing advocate for the pleasures of the flesh. While Dioneo replaces the devoted lover with a generalized enjoyment of sex, Fiammetta, ruler of the day of marriages, takes over Adione's tempering role. In their combination, license and marriage or energy and order are bound together. Fiammetta's position is thus much the same as in the *Filocolo* or *Teseida*, but Dioneo is in control of his own ironies as the early lovers and lover-poets were not.[43] It is the very self-consciousness of his role which allows him to remain within the group, a laughing rebel who never seriously disturbs their order.

Fiammetta's concern with marriage as the proper solution for sexual desires is not only established during her reign on day V but is also reflected in many of her tales. Dioneo's tale, the first bawdy story of the book, is followed immediately by Fiammetta's story, in which a married woman politely repulses the amorous advances of a king and teaches him a lesson about the foolishness of his attempt.[44] Similarly Giovanna in V.9 pays no attention to Federico until after her husband has died; then she marries him instead of becoming his lover. The king in X.5, who has lusted after two young girls, gives them good husbands instead of ravishing them. The kings of I and X, who learn the folly of their illegitimate desires, find a comic parallel in Calandrino (IX.5), whose hope for an adulterous affair brings down on him the mockery of his friends and a sound beating from his wife. The tragedy of IV.1 is caused by a father's refusal to let his young daughter remarry. He is like a jealous old husband in regard to his daughter's lover. Two other tales discuss the problem of jealousy, one (III.6) in the wife, and the other (VII.5) in the husband. In both cases jealousy leads precisely to the feared result, and the narrator's comments in the latter tale warn married people against this folly.

Dioneo's tale under the rule of Fiammetta offers a parody of marriage: a contented arrangement among three people. Fiammetta offers a similar parody herself in VIII.8, with a happy arrangement between two couples; but its very humorousness implies that it is not a serious model for imitation. The tale concerns not Florentines but Sienese, whom Dioneo (VII.10) has already pronounced famous for stupidity ("besaggine"). It is told, moreover, as a comic correction for the cruel vengeance of VIII.7:

> Piacevoli donne, per ciò che mi pare che alquanto trafitte v'abbia
> la severità dell'offeso scolare, estimo che convenevole sia con al-
> cuna cosa più dilettevole rammorbidare gl'innacerbiti spiriti; e
> per ciò intendo di dirvi una novelletta d'un giovane, il quale con

più mansueto animo una ingiuria ricevette e quella con più mo-
derata operazion vendicò.

[Pleasant ladies, because it seems to me that you were somewhat
pierced by the severity of the offended scholar, I think it fitting to
soften your embittered spirits with something more delightful;
and therefore I intend to tell you a story about a young man who
received an injury with milder spirit, and avenged it with a more
moderate procedure.]

Here too she is tempering the sentiments of the speaker she follows,
though in this case it is not Dioneo but Pampinea.

Together Dioneo and Fiammetta sing two songs apart from the songs
that end each day. On day III, a day full of illicit sexual adventures, they
sing "La dama del Vergiù" the story of an adultery with tragic consequences, which leads from III into the tragic topic of IV.[45] (Fiammetta suggests typically that Filostrato chose the tragic topic of the fourth day to
temper the merriness of the previous days.) On day VII they sing "Arcita
and Palemone." Segre has noted that the theme of the song imitates that of
the tale (Dioneo's) which it follows: two men love the same woman; one of
them dies and leaves her to the other.[46] The difference, however, is that the
story of Arcita and Palemone concludes with a marriage, while VII.10
deals with two adulteries. Thus the two songs are one more balanced pair,
dealing with passion which leads in one case to tragedy and in the other
case to marriage.

As Fiammetta follows Dioneo's tale with her own on day I, so she
follows his tale with her song on day X, and again her words are related to
the story just told. The final test of Griselda is the threat of her replacement
by another, younger wife. This theme leads to Fiammetta's prayer that
other women may not take away her beloved. Thus when Dioneo has reversed his usual pose to tell a tale of extreme fidelity withstanding the most
outrageous tests, Fiammetta also changes her position and confesses that
jealousy and uncertainty necessarily accompany human love. Petrarch, imitating the Griselda tale in Latin, wrote that it deals not with human marriage but rather with the relation of the soul to God. If this allegorical interpretation is possible for Dioneo's story as well as for Petrarch's version
of it, then Fiammetta is bringing the topic back to a purely human relationship. In any case, the Griselda story is a kind of saint's life, whereas
Fiammetta is singing about a more common and realistic relationship. The
solution she seeks, unlike the celestial aspirations of Lauretta's song, is a

solution for normal human life on earth. The doubts which she expresses even in the midst of happy love create a transition from the idealism of Griselda and the narrators' paradisical garden to the realities of Florence, whither the group is about to return. By this kind of transition, this area of hope and doubt combined, Boccaccio seems to be intentionally bridging his usual dichotomy between extreme polar terms and acknowledging the complexity of their application to life.

In a sense the Fiammetta-Dioneo pair is one more version of Astrea-Priapus, but Dioneo through his own self-conscious humor and control becomes acceptable among the group of "onestissimi" young people. At the same time Fiammetta no longer preaches against love as in the *Filocolo* nor declares herself a means toward the love of God, but rather seeks out social channels for feelings described as both human and natural. Reason and desire, in conflict throughout previous works, now seem to be able to get along, at least within the ideal society of the narrators. Yet the brevity of their sojourn in a garden which Boccaccio compares to the earthly paradise may suggest the precariousness of the harmony they have achieved.

As days V and X, when Fiammetta rules and sings, are both Tuesday, *martedì* or Mars's day, she and Dioneo, like Fiammetta and Caleone in the *Comedia delle Ninfe*, suggest through their names a Mars and Venus couple. This is, of course, a much less rational aspect of their pairing. Their joint songs on days III and VII set the planetary combination which signifies adultery and fornication to mark the two days of bawdiest tale-telling. Moreover, the prevalence of themes of anger and violence, seemingly incongruous with the topic of happy loves, is appropriate to their combined importance on day V. For Mars and Venus represent the two passions, the irascible and amorous, both disruptive forces threatening individual and social happiness. V.6 is a clear example of their combination. It begins as a Hero and Leander story in which Gianni da Procida swims at night between Ischia and a nearby island in order to see his beloved. It is not a watery death which is prepared for him, however, but a death by fire; for the Hero and Leander situation is only a prelude to the tale. Gianni's girl is carried off by pirates who offer her to Federigo of Aragon in Palermo. Gianni finds her and manages to enter the room where she is being kept. The two young lovers, caught in bed, are tied to a stake and sentenced to be burned when an admiral recognizes Gianni as the nephew of the famous Gianni da Procida who helped Federigo to his throne. The girl Restituta is similarly the daughter of one of Federigo's key supporters. Therefore, revising his hasty judgment, the king releases them and marries them to each other with generous gifts.

Pampinea introduces the tale with comments on the power of love: "Grandissime forze, piacevoli donne, son quelle d'amore, e a gran fatiche e istrabocchevoli e non pensati pericoli gli amanti dispongono, come assai per cose raccontate e oggi e altre volte comprender si può." [Very great are the powers of love, gracious ladies, and they dispose lovers to great travails and to extreme and unimagined dangers, as one can learn from many stories told both today and at other times.] The tales of "altre volte" may well include not only the previous *Decameron* days but also Vergil's *Georgics* III.258–63, which recounts the story of Leander to demonstrate precisely Pampinea's point: "quid iuvenis, magnum cui versat in ossibus ignem / durus amor? nempe abruptis turbata procellis / nocte natat caeca serus freta" [what of the young man in whose bones harsh love poured a great fire? forsooth, late in the blind night he swims the strait churning with rough waves]. Vergil blackens the power of love into a kind of madness which drives the youth into the raging sea, itself emblematic of his dark and tumultuous passions. The night is "blind" as love is; Boccaccio himself glossed Cupid's blindfold as a sign that lovers have lost their judgment (*Gen.* II.4). The danger to Gianni of death by fire, which Boccaccio introduces as a variation on the watery death, takes on a symbolic quality such as Vergil had given to Leander's sea. Water and fire are another Venus and Mars pair,[47] which become for Boccaccio the underlying symbols of concupiscence and wrath, as Gianni blames his imminent death jointly on his love and the king's anger, "Amore, e l'ira del re."

It is the latter, however, which especially merits a warning in this tale; Federigo learns not to let himself be driven to indiscretion by the force of sudden wrath. His blind and hasty anger nearly costs him his kingdom, given that the youngsters are close kin of his leading supporters, "per l'opera del quale tu se' re e signor di questa isola" and "la cui potenza fa oggi che la tua signoria non sia cacciata d'Ischia" [thanks to whom you are king and lord of this island, (and) whose power keeps your rule from being driven out of Ischia]. Thus personal upset expands into the possibility of political upheaval. When the king honors them with a wedding, he assures not only their peace of mind[48] but also the peace of his kingdom. Boccaccio's concern about the destructive power of the passions and social efforts to channel them into less destructive forms is the same here as in the *Teseida*, where marriage is both the socialized form for love and also the symbol for a Platonic harmony within the soul. The introduction to day V suggests the theme of social and political order as Fiammetta, "non dimenticato il preso ordine" [not forgetting the established order] presides "pro tribunali" over the songs, dances, and tales.[49]

Another example of the combination of both passions and the expansion of individual to social concerns is the famous story of Cimone (V.1). Marcus has noted that the model for the second half of this story is the gruesome battle of Centaurs and Lapiths in Ovid's *Metamorphoses*.[50] To Marcus's excellent analysis of this tale, I would like to add only some further observations. The bloody struggle of Centaurs and Lapiths takes the place of the Trojan War within Ovid's narrative,[51] and thus connects with the names of Boccaccio's two unfortunate brides, Efigenia and Cassandra, whose tragedies frame the history of the war. Cassandra, we recall, was taken away from her slain fiance by the Greeks, and Iphigenia too found her promised wedding turned into bloodshed.[52] The Trojan War is, of course, the notable example of how lust and wrath destroy a whole civilization.[53]

Panfilo's story ends with the happiness of Cimone and Pasimunda, who "lieti della loro rapina goderono" [happily enjoyed their plunder]; but the last we hear of the two brides is their screams and tears as they are carried away. As this is one of the very few tales set in ancient times, it is perhaps to be compared with X.8, also set in ancient Greece, in which one young man freely gives his beloved lady to a friend. Although Cimone and Pasimunda are ultimately readmitted to their societies, this kind of "accommodation" is not possible as a general rule without the utter breakdown of society. The plague has ended social cohesion in Florence by exacerbating the concern of every man for himself: "l'un fratello l'altro abbandonava, e il zio il nipote e la sorella il fratello e spesse volte la donna il suo marito; e, che maggior cosa è e quasi non credibile, li padri e le madri i figliuoli, quasi loro non fossero, di visitare e di servire schifavano" [one brother abandoned the other, and the uncle his nephew, and the sister her brother, and often the wife her husband; and what is more and almost unbelievable, fathers and mothers avoided seeing and taking care of their children as if they were not their own]. It is this situation which the *Decameron* takes as its ground, and on which it tries to reconstruct a new society, without delusions about human nature. But humans are capable of a wide range of behaviors, and the socialization of individual appetites is only one kind of solution.

If Lisimaco—whose name ironically means "ending strife"—claims in V.1 that the way to overcome fortune is to take up arms, X.1 offers a different idea. There when Ruggiero, given the choice between a chest filled with the royal crown, scepter, and many jewels and a chest filled with dirt, picks the worthless one, the king opposes fortune ("m'opponga alle sue forze") by freely giving Ruggiero the other. For the tenth day in general, "virtù" consists not in the power to take what one wants but in the strength to overcome one's own desires and give everything away. Thus, for example, X.5 celebrates a young man who converts his "concupiscibile amore" into "onesta carità" [concupiscent love . . . honest charity]. Such renunciation of love, claims Lauretta in X.4.4, surpasses the magnificence of previous tales with their gifts of wealth and even life, for "i tesori si donino, le inimicizie si dimentichino e pongasi la propria vita, l'onore e la fama, ch'è molto più, in mille pericoli per potere la cosa amata possedere" [one gives away treasures, forgets enmities, and puts one's very life, honor, and reputation, which is much more, into a thousand perils in order to possess the beloved object]. The lover's gift of the lady back to her husband who had thought her dead is again an opposition to fortune which has brought the lady to him ("egli per la sua buona fortuna aveva riccolto"). Not only does Messer Gentile temper his love ("temperò onestamente il suo fuoco")—a love which, not content to suffer any limitation ("sì come noi veggiamo l'appetito degl'uomini a niun termine star contento"), had led him so far as to fondle a corpse—but he even suggests that his love was caused by God as a means of saving the lady's life, i.e., that within the providential scheme even cupidity can be used for a charitable end: "io ti giuro per quello Iddio che forse già di lei innamorar mi fece acciò che il mio amore fosse, sì come stato è, cagion della sua salute." Thus the tenth day returns to themes of the first, where Ciappelletto's wickedness or the corruption at the papal court turn out to confirm the faith of others.

If Messer Gentile makes a big show of his own generosity in returning the lady to her husband, it is his celebration of his own power to behave nobly despite his original desires. The extreme example of this power is Griselda, whose seeming total passivity is actually an incredible demonstration of will, the will to live out her pact with Gualtieri despite all the events that, as for Messer Gentile, might easily justify a loss of concern for the husband. These are cases of generosity beyond the call of duty, out of a sheer pleasure in self-control. This inversion of the desire for power into a sense of power over the self rather than over others is the solution suggested by the tenth day for allowing a society to exist among persons of strong individual will.[54]

The attitude of the author in his preface is somewhere between the possible extremes presented in his tales, for he is no longer in love and yet he has also not conquered his passion but simply in time grown out of it. He is thus in a position to recognize the limitations of love while not taking on the heroic posture of Messer Gentile. By this very position he can

imply to his amorous readers that even if they fall short of the final magnifi-
cent examples, they will discover in time that passion is not truly as ever-
lasting as it feels and thus perhaps less valuable than they currently assume.
The brigata members too occupy a middle ground, for they are in love—
the three men have been wooing three of the ladies—and yet, as Panfilo
remarks at the end,

> "quantunque liete novelle e forse attrattive a concupiscenzia dette
> ci sieno e del continuo mangiato e bevuto bene, e sonato e can-
> tato (cose tutte da incitare le deboli menti a cose meno oneste),
> niuno atto, niuna parola, niuna cosa nè dalla vostra parte nè dalla
> nostra ci ho conosciuta da biasimare: continua onestà, continua
> concordia, continua fraternal dimestichezza mi ci è paruta vedere
> e sentire" (X.conclus.)

> [even though we have been telling many merry tales and ones
> perhaps enticing to concupiscence, and have continually eaten
> and drunk well, and played music and sung, all of which might
> arouse weak minds to less honest things, I have known of no act,
> no word, nothing that can be blamed either on your part or on
> ours: continual honesty, continual harmony, continual fraternal
> familiarity is what I have seen and heard].

The brigata, I have suggested, are or at least aspire to an ideal society, a
plural form of the individual psyche. They are not exempt from the feelings
and desires that cause so much violence and fraud in their tales, yet they are
able to control their behavior sufficiently to maintain social concord,
"senza trapassare in alcun atto il segno della ragione" [without overstepping in any action the bounds of reason].

If the detached author with his offer of helpful advice and his audience of melancholy lovers plays a more complicated variation on the old
theme of dialogue between a rational counselor and erring lover, so too the
brigata is divided into two groups, defined by Dioneo:

> "Leggiadre donne, infra molte bianche colombe agiugne più di
> bellezza un nero corvo che non farebbe un candido cigno; e così
> tra molti savi alcuna volta un men savio è non solamente ac-
> crescere splendore e bellezza alla loro maturità, ma ancora diletto
> e sollazzo. Per la qual cosa, essendo voi tutte discretissime e mod-
> erate, io, il quale sento anzi dello scemo che no, faccendo la
> vostra virtù più lucente col mio difetto, più vi debbo esser caro

che se con più valore quella facessi divenire più oscura; e per consequente più largo arbitrio debbo avere in dimostrarvi tal qual io sono." (IX.10.3–4)

[Lovely ladies, among many white doves a black crow adds more beauty than a white swan would; and so among many wise persons sometimes one less wise not only augments the splendor and beauty of their maturity but also is a delight and amusement. Therefore, as you are all most discreet and moderate, I, who am more of a fool than not, making your virtue brighter by my defect, ought to be dearer to you than if with more worthiness I made it more obscure; and consequently I ought to have more freedom in showing you what I am.]

Here Dioneo is consciously playing the clown as a foil to the others, perversely proving their values by his very opposition. As he is the one member who tells a tale set in Boccaccio's hometown, he might be identified with Boccaccio, his posture considered analogous to the role of lover donned intentionally by the narrator of the *Comedia delle Ninfe* and played off against the contrasting figure of Ameto. But Boccaccio in the *Decameron* carefully distinguishes himself from the brigata, claiming that he heard their stories from one of the ladies involved.[55]

Dioneo's opposition to the rest of the group and to the author's prefatory claims operates in several ways. Boccaccio states in the preface, whether seriously or not, that his tales are meant to be "utile" [useful] and to teach "quello che sia da fuggire e che sia similmente da seguitare" [what is to be shunned and what similarly is to be followed]. Other narrators within the brigata repeat the claim of usefulness for their tales. At the end of the first day Filomena remarks that tomorrow "al novellar torneremo, nel quale mi par grandissima parte di piacere e d'utilità similmente consistere" [We will return to storytelling, in which it seems to me that a great deal of pleasure and usefulness similarly exist together]. Again in the middle of the book, Elissa proposes the topic for the sixth day "per ciò che la materia è bella e può essere utile" [because the material is pretty and may be useful]. At the start of the first tale on the tenth day, Neifile announces, "Dironne adunque una novelletta assai leggiadra, al mio parere, la quale rammemorarsi per certo non potrà esser se non utile" [I will tell, then, a little tale, rather charming to my mind, which certainly cannot be other than useful to remember]. Panfilo, Pampinea, and Filostrato also remark on the usefulness of their tales to teach by positive and negative example. It is the Priapan Dioneo who insists over and over that his stories are intended only to cause delight and amusement. He introduces his first story (I.4)— the first bawdy tale of the book—with a defense: as we are here with the duty only to give ourselves pleasure by telling stories, each person ought to be permitted to tell whatever tale he believes will most delight: "noi siamo qui per dovere a noi medesimi novellando piacere; e per ciò, solamente che contro a questo non si faccia, estimo a ciascuno dovere esser licito (e così ne disse la nostra reina, poco avanti, che fosse) quella novella dire che più crede che possa dilettare." When king, he chooses his topic because it will be pleasurable to talk of "piacevole a ragionarne" and his own tale that day "ancora che in sè abbia assai di quello che creder non si dee, nondimeno sarà in parte piacevole a ascoltare" (VII.10) [although it contains a certain amount of what one ought not to believe, nonetheless it will be partly pleasing to hear]. He clearly does not mean his tales as examples to be imitated; in defending his topic against the complaints of the ladies, he argues that such stories will not lead honest listeners to bad actions:

> "se alquanto s'allarga la vostra onestà nel favellare, non per dovere con l'opere mai alcuna cosa sconcia seguire ma per dar diletto a voi e a altrui, non veggio con che argomento da concedere vi possa nello avvenire riprendere alcuno. Oltre a questo la nostra brigata, dal primo dì infino a questa ora stata onestissima, per cosa che detta ci sia non mi pare che in atto alcuno si sia maculata nè si maculerà con l'aiuto di Dio"

> [if you somewhat widen your honesty in storytelling, not that anything shameful should ever follow in your actions, but to delight yourselves and others, I don't see with what unanswerable argument anyone could possibly blame you for it in the future. Besides, as our brigata has been most honest from the first day until this hour, it doesn't seem to me that it could be stained nor will be stained, with the help of God, by anything which is said here].

To preserve his right to the topic, he is ready to divorce the tales from any effect on reality, and to refer to them as "favellare," i.e., as lies "che creder non si dee."

Dioneo intends his stories to be laughed at, and points out that laughter distances the material from those who laugh. It is human habit "il rider più tosto delle cattive cose che delle buone opere, e spezialmente quando quelle cotali a noi non pertengono" (V.10) [to laugh rather at naughty things than at good deeds, especially when those (naughty things) don't pertain to us], he says in the story that follows Fiammetta's. And later (VI.concl.) he adds that if the ladies were to cease telling jokes of this sort, one would have reason to suspect that they were feeling guilty and therefore did not want to talk any more about sex.

For Dioneo tale-telling "a niuno altro fine riguarda se non a dovervi torre malinconia e riso e allegrezza porgervi" (V.10) [56] [looks to no other end than to take away melancholy and replace it with laughter and joy]. The announced goal of the *Decameron* is to drive out the melancholy of women in love. Thus the very nature of Dioneo's tales, comic bawdry, may be a cure for obsessive love. The lightness of the tales suits an audience whose passionate melancholy needs alleviating, for laughter requires and creates detachment. It is important in this regard that the treatment of sex be comic. Boccaccio himself in his conclusion declares that he is not "grave" [heavy, serious] but "lieve" [light] because he is writing to chase away the melancholy of women.

Dioneo jokes also by taking phrases literally in a ridiculous way. After V.9, for example, has ended in Giovanna's choice of "uomo che abbia bisogno di richezza" [a man in need of riches] over "ricchezza che abbia bisogno d'uomo" [riches in need of manhood], Dioneo's following story twists her statement by applying it to a wife who complains that her husband supports her in financial comfort but is a homosexual. "Uomo" here has dwindled from signifying nobility of character to meaning merely the male animal. Dioneo plays this trick again on the ninth day. Emilia in IX.9 recounts Solomon's advice to a man to treat his unruly wife as a mule, that is, to beat her into submission. Whereupon Dioneo follows this with the story of a peddler who literally wants to turn his wife into a horse in order to increase his profits. The peddler is duped by a cleverer man who carries out his wish metaphorically instead of literally. Dioneo's comic literal-mindedness is appropriate to his role as advocate for the flesh; for literal reading, like purely carnal love, has left out the "spirit" of man or text. Nonetheless, unlike the earlier lover-poets who failed to penetrate the surface of their own texts, Dioneo clearly knows what he is doing and is not so simple as he pretends.

His literality playfully extends to his comments on his own final tale. Griselda is a Job figure and as such appropriately placed to prepare the brigata for their return to Florence. (The figure of Job, for obvious reasons, became popular in painting around the time of the plague.) As

Gualtieri cruelly tests her patience, she replies that all she has is from him ("ignuda m'aveste") and therefore he may take it all away again if he wishes; Chaucer and Petrarch openly cite Job at this point.[57] The theme of man's persistent faith in an apparently unjust God connects the final story to Panfilo's introductory speech in I.1 on the need to preserve one's faith despite the plague because the strength to bear the "angoscia" and "fatica" of the transitory world comes from God in his liberality. Dioneo's comment at the end of the Griselda story is twofold. First he concludes "che anche nelle povere case piovono dal cielo de'divini spiriti" [divine spirits rain from heaven into poor houses too], suggesting like Panfilo that it is divine grace which has enabled Griselda to be so patient. Secondly he notes that Gualtieri deserves a woman who "quando, fuor di casa, l'avesse fuori in camiscia cacciata, s'avesse sì ad un altro fatto scuotere il pilliccione, che riuscito ne fosse una bella roba" [when he had chased her out of the house in a shift, would have so shaken another man's skin that she got a pretty dress from it]. The remark makes sense only on the human level of the tale. Gualtieri is one of those many insufferable husbands who deserve to be cuckolded. If, however, Gualtieri's "antiveduto fine" is any analogy to divine providence, and if Griselda's relation to her "signore" does indeed represent the relation of the soul to God, the soul having nothing to offer into the bargain but faith and faithfulness, then Dioneo's comment is an ironic literalization of the tale, which goes along with his previous literalizing jokes.[58] The joking suggests that literal readings are not in fact useful as the author and other narrators have promised their tales to be, but that a deeper reading is required to extract more than entertainment from these tales.

iii. Allegory

That notion is reexpressed in a number of ways. In the first tale, as in others, there are at least two audiences: the gullible who admire the facts they are hearing and the more knowledgeable who admire the rhetorical skill involved in the lie. Beyond them are the brigata members who hear, as the hosts do not, Panfilo's moralizing context and are thus invited to read the tale as an example of how God can use even extreme evil (e.g., the plague) for his own good ends.[59] Beyond them we find the author and his amorous ladies; and beyond them in turn Boccaccio and us. Possibly the meanings of the tales extend even beyond the brigata's understanding,[60] although Boccaccio describes them in the end as a perfect audience for these stories. The nesting of narrators and readers (or hearers) is like the multi-plication of authors and audiences in Boccaccio's earlier writings and works to the same purpose to imply the existence of different levels of reading.[61]

Day VI, which has been considered Boccaccio's *ars narrandi*,[62] has much indeed to contribute to our understanding of Boccaccio's method in this regard; it teaches us how to read. Two tales on that day have drawn repeated critical commentary and have been almost the sole focus of inves-tigations into Boccaccio's narrative art. One is the first tale, which critics like because it emphasizes the aesthetics of narration and disregards the content. In fact, we never find out what the story is about that the knight is botching so terribly. All we know is that the story "in itself was a very good one"—whatever that means—but that the teller, by repeating himself, mixing up names, forgetting details and having to backtrack, makes his sensitive audience almost physically ill. This story, then, seems to suppport the view of Boccaccio as the great aesthetician and sly rebel against the moral exemplary functions of narrative. The other tale from the sixth day which attracts attention is the tenth, the story of fra Cipolla. When prank-sters replace with lumps of coal the feather which fra Cipolla had adver-tised as one of the angel Gabriel's, Cipolla cleverly sidetracks his audience from their initial expectation and leads up to a miraculous presentation of coal from St. Lawrence's martyrdom. His elaborate impromptu speech wins the admiration of the pranksters. Again the reason for critical interest is that this story seems to demonstrate that literature is a lie, that its content is irrelevant, and that Boccaccio's focus is on the art of presentation, the skill with language. One should note, however, that the teller of this tale is Dioneo, the one member of the brigata who consistently claims that stories ought only to please. Furthermore, if the sixth day really is Boccac-cio's *ars narrandi*, one should consider other stories on that day, some of which take up the very problems of meaning that these two tales seem to avoid.

The fifth tale recounts how Giotto and an important lawyer and states-man, Forese da Rabatta, were traveling home to Florence after the holi-days. Both men were ugly, we are told, and were riding ugly old broken-down rented nags. Caught in a storm, they took shelter with a peasant whom they knew and borrowed from him some hideous old cloaks and worn-out hats in which to continue their trip. On top of all this they were soon thoroughly splattered with mud splashed up by the horses' hooves. Forese remarked, "Giotto, a che ora venendo di qua allo 'ncontro di noi un forestiere che mai veduto non t'avesse, credi tu che egli credesse che tu fossi il migliore dipintore del mondo, come tu se'?" ["Giotto, if some stranger who had never seen you now came toward us, do you think he would believe you were the best painter in the world, as you are?"] And Giotto replied, "Messere, credo che egli il crederebbe allora che, guardando voi, egli crederebbe che voi sapeste l'abbiccì" ["Sir, I think he would believe it as soon as, looking at you, he would believe that you know the ABCs"]. Now this is a story about the unobvious relation between surface appearances and contents, and the theme is elaborated in a number of ways. (1) There is the pile-up of layers of deceitful appearance: Giotto's own ugly body, his clothing, the mud. (2) There is the narrator's introduction to the tale:

> Carissime donne, egli avviene spesso che, sì come la fortuna sotto vili arti alcuna volta grandissimi tesori di virtù nasconde, come poco avanti per Pampinea fu mostrato, così ancora sotto turpissime forme d'uomini si truovano maravigliosi ingegni dalla natura essere stati riposti.

> [Dearest ladies, it often happens that, just as fortune sometimes hides under lowly occupations great treasures of *virtù*, as Pampinea recently demonstrated, so too one finds that under the most shameful forms of men nature has placed marvelous intellects.]

Panfilo's remark connects his tale to previous tales and especially to Pampinea's very similar introduction to VI.2. Both these introductions identify terms of humility with hiding, explicitly hiding something of value from envy or scorn. What Panfilo from his position in the text cannot allude to, but what we the readers can relate to his comment, is Boccaccio's own description of his whole book at the beginning of day IV:

> non solamente pe' piani, ma ancora per le profondissime valli [tacito e nascoso][63] mi sono ingegnato d'andare; il che assai manifesto può apparire a chi le presenti novellette riguarda, le quali non solamente in fiorentin volgare e in prosa scritte per me sono e senza titolo, ma ancora in istilo umilissimo e rimesso quanto il più si possono

> [I have tried to go not only through the plains but even through the deepest valleys (quiet and hidden); which may appear quite manifestly to whoever looks at these little tales, that I wrote not only in the Florentine vernacular and in prose and without a dedication but also in the most humble and low style possible].

(3) Like Boccaccio, Giotto is described as extraordinarily humble:

> meritamente una delle luci della fiorentina gloria dir si puote; e tanto più, quanto con maggiora umiltà, maestro degli altri in ciò, vivendo quella acquistò, sempre rifiutando d'esser chiamato maestro. Il quale titolo rifiutato da lui tanto più in lui risplendeva, quanto con maggior disidero da quegli che men sapevano di lui o da' suoi discepoli era cupidamente usurpato

> [he can deservedly be called one of the lights of Florentine glory, and all the more as he acquired this during his lifetime with the greatest humility such that, although he was the master of all others, he always refused to be called master. The rejected title shone all the more in him because others who knew less or were his students with great desire eagerly usurped it].

This humility of character becomes analogous to the humility of his attire in contrast to the brilliance it tries to cover. The scene of Giotto inside the peasant's hut can be viewed either as an image of humility, like Aeneas's stooping into the humble hut of Evander, or as one more layer of deceiving appearance. (4) Boccaccio's description of Giotto's art further develops the theme of the tale about the artist: "avendo egli quell'arte ritornata in luce, che molti secoli sotto gli error d'alcuni, che più a dilettar gli occhi degl'ignoranti che a compiacere allo'ntelletto de savi dipignendo, era stata sepulta" [he returned that art to the light which for many centuries had been buried under the errors of some, who painted more to delight the eyes of the ignorant than to please the understanding of the wise]. The eyes in opposition to the understanding are one more analogy to Panfilo's terms of lowly occupation versus great treasures of *virtù* or ugly appearance versus brilliant intellect. The stranger who encounters Giotto or Giotto's art must use not his eyes but his mind to perceive correctly what is before him by an almost literal discovering.

Now the phrase about pleasing the eye versus pleasing the understanding was used before by Boccaccio in his *Comedia delle Ninfe Fiorentine*. Near the end of this obviously Christian allegory, Ameto, who has been fantasizing about touching the beautiful nymphs, realizes the allegorical nature of their tales and indeed of the nymphs themselves; and Boccaccio writes: "vede che sieno le ninfe, le quali più all'occhio che allo 'ntelletto erano piaciute, e ora allo 'ntelletto piacciano più che all'occhio . . . e non poco in sé si vergogna de' concupiscevoli pensieri avuti" (XLVI.3) [he sees what the nymphs are, which had pleased his eye more than his understanding, and now please his understanding more than his eye . . . and he is not a little ashamed of his earlier concupiscent thoughts]. The same phrase, then, which recurs ten years later in the *Decameron*, has signified for Boccaccio the distance between vehicle and tenor in an allegory. Ameto learns how to read his own story. Are we readers of the *Decameron* being similarly admonished to look beyond the surfaces of its art? And if so, how might that work?

The *Decameron* has long been celebrated as a work of great realism.[64] Di Pino noted quite accurately Boccaccio's shift, for example, from fictional to documented historical characters such as Giotto and Forese, and his use of a historical setting for both tales and frame. Boccaccio is here even more than in the *Elegia* attempting to link his text closely to real time and space and real or realistic people.[65] In this light the *Decameron* is already part of Boccaccio's slow shift from fable or romance or dream vision to history.[66] Yet, on the other hand, the author of the *Decameron* had up until then written almost nothing but allegories and moral *exempla*—precisely the sort of literature that he is supposed to be rebelling against.[67] If there is allegory in the *Decameron*, it is certainly not as self-evident as in previous works.

Let us consider a few examples of what I might call submerged allegory in these tales. II.5 is the story of Andreuccio who goes to Naples to buy horses and is duped by a prostitute posing as his half-sister. She invites him to dine and sleep in what looks like an elegant house, but then lets him fall through a loose board in the bathroom floor into the sewer while she pockets all his money. The whole second day is devoted to the topic of fortune, and Joan Ferrante has noticed that, at least on that day, women often appear as the agent or "arm of fortune."[68] The prostitute who cons Andreuccio is one of the female agents of fortune cited by Ferrante; but one can carry the point further, for the scene at her house resembles the description of the House of Fortune in the *Roman de la Rose* (ll. 6079ff.). Andreuccio has reason to mistake her for a noble lady, for not only is she well dressed and adorned, but her dwelling too looks most elegant when he enters. It is perfumed with roses and orange blossoms, and furnished richly with beautiful things. She has servants at hand and can offer Andreuccio a splendid dinner. But having come in at the front door, he is dropped rudely and abruptly out the rear. His fall is caused by a loose board that gives way; and as he has taken off his clothes to go to bed, he is dumped naked and penniless into the sewer. Now fortune and her house are described at length by Reason in the *Roman de la Rose*. Part of the house shines with silver and gold and fine workmanship; but the other part is made of poor materials, weak and gaping with cracks so that it shakes. When fortune wants to be honored, she moves into the beautiful part of her house and dresses like a queen, with rich apparel and perfumes. But then she roams into the other part of her house, where she stumbles and falls; and there she becomes stripped of her clothing and wealth and goes to live in a whorehouse. She pays no heed to merit but dumps the good into the mud and steals from them. The house is on a mountain slope, at the bottom of which winds a dark, stinking, and filthy river (ll. 6023ff.), undoubtedly the inspiration for the sewer into which Andreuccio falls. Boccaccio's interest in this passage is supported by the two barrels of good and bad fortune, mentioned slightly later in Reason's speech, which reappear in X.1 of the *Decameron*, another tale explicitly about fortune. Moreover, by naming the prostitute's neighborhood Malpertugio, Boccaccio equates the deceits of fortune with the foxy trickster from the *Roman de Renard*, whose den is named Maupertuis. The name, of course, which means "bad hole," also equates this tricksterism with prostitution and with Andreuccio's unsavory fall. In sum, we can read the episode as a submerged allegory in which Andreuccio is deceived both by a specific woman and by fortune herself, equally sly and nasty tricksters.

Another example of a tale whose images can be seen through is V.3. Pietro, forbidden by his parents to marry Agnolella, tries to elope with her. Elissa, whose name evokes a tragic love relation unconsecrated by marriage, introduces the two lovers as "due giovanetti poco discreti" [two youngsters of little discretion]. As their lack of discretion leads them to suffer "una malvagia notte" [a bad night] in which they wander lost in the woods in darkness, one may infer that their subsequent "lieti giorni" [happy days] are contrastingly civilized and enlightened; for their plight is a result of their attempted escape from society. Significantly they lose their way when Pietro chooses the wrong—the left—road at a fork. It is a realization of the metaphorical choice of roads presented to the young Hercules; [69] and Pietro's ignorance of his route matches Elissa's description of his poor discretion.

Separated by misfortune, the lovers undergo two similar and two different perils. Pietro is assailed by brigands who wish to seize his possessions; but Pietro himself is acting as a brigand, taking what others have refused to give him, in contravention of social law. The antisocial nature of his action is expanded twice, first through the factionalism which induces his attackers to try to kill him once they realize what family he belongs to, and then through the surprise attack of a second group against the first. Thus, having left the city of Rome, a focal point of civilization, Pietro rapidly finds the world around him turn into a free-for-all among unequal forces. In short, the trip from Rome into the forest is a reversal of the conversion from forest to city in the *Filocolo* V.48–49.[70] Meanwhile Agnolella, "non sappiendo dove andarsi, se non come il suo ronzino stesso dove più gli pareva ne la portava, si mise tanto fralla selva, che ella non poteva vedere il luogo donde in quella entrata era" [not knowing which way to go except as her horse wished to take her, she got so far into the woods that she could not see the place from which she had entered it]. The horse, of course, is an old and common symbol for the passions, especially lust. Thus by letting her horse choose the way, she has gotten herself into a predicament which echoes the opening of Dante's *Commedia:* Dante too, having in error left the right road, is so lost in the woods that he cannot tell where he entered it ("io non so ben ridir com'i' v'entrai").[71] Hiding in a haystack from another band of brigands, Agnolella is nearly pierced in the left breast by the lance which one of them unwittingly throws her way; the location of the lance near her heart threatens the very part which has gotten her into danger. Both lovers later lose their horses, Pietro to wolves, Agnolella to brigands, and this loss symbolically prepares the youngsters for their restoration to society. The wolf which devours Pietro's horse has at least two significant associations. As the mascot of Rome, the city which Pietro has left, it may represent society's revenge on those who choose to break her laws for the satisfaction of personal desires. At the same time, it is the wolf of Mars, on whose day this tale is told, and whose violent powers are unleashed by love as in the story of Cimone at the start of that day.[72] Indeed the bonding of Venus and Mars, representing the almost ineluctable involvement of passion with violence, is one of Boccaccio's favorite themes. The mutual friend at whose home the two lost lovers are by chance reunited first scolds Pietro soundly, then sees to their marriage and reconciles their parents to the fact. Their happy long life together demonstrates the validity of this solution, where desires and social order meet. The error was partly the parents' for allowing social snobbery to obstruct a love defined by the friend as "onesto"; but the youngsters' response to the situation is not condoned.

In a more speculative vein, I wonder whether the names Pietro and Agnolella, combined with the setting in Rome, do not suggest something about the relation between the church or papacy and the Christian flock. Dante's bitter criticism of the simonist popes in *Inferno* XIX singles out one of the Orsini as its butt. Is it in response to this that Boccaccio makes one of the Orsini, a "bonissima e santa donna" [very good and holy woman], the friend who reunites Peter with his lamb and reconciles them to the society from which they had fled? If so, why is Boccaccio interested in restoring the Orsini's reputation? Is Pietro's excursion from Rome into the wilderness a reference to the papal sojourn in France? If so, the story ends with a wishful thought, for Boccaccio never lived to see the pope's return to Rome. Or is the choice of the road to the left a veiled criticism, much like Dante's, of the church's interest in goods of this world? And are we to see, in the spear that nearly pierces Agnolella's side, an indication of the death of Christ—nearly killed anew by the erring leadership of the church? Dante blames the church for leading their flock astray as Pietro has done, but he usually names Peter as the original good example of a pope. In *Inferno* XIX Peter is named to shame the sinful Orsini; but in Boccaccio's tale it is an Orsini who shames the erring Peter. I do not know how far to push the allegorization of this story, but the elements are certainly suggestive.

My final example cuts across several tales and songs; it starts back on day VI, that day of stories about the use of language. VI.8 is a brief anecdote about Cesca who snobbishly complains how unpleasant everyone is. Her uncle tells her that if she wishes to avoid unpleasant people, she must never look in a mirror.

> Ma ella, più che una canna vana e cui di senno pareva pareggiar Salamone, non altramenti che un montone avrebbe fatto intese il vero motto di Fresco, anzi disse che ella si voleva specchiar come l' altre; e così nella sua grossezza si rimase e ancor vi si sta.

> [But she, more empty than a reed and thinking herself the equal of Solomon in wisdom, hearing Fresco's true saying, understood it no better than a sheep would have done; rather she replied that she wanted to look in mirrors like anyone else; and so she remained in her thickheadedness and is still that way.]

Cesca has failed to understand both verbal language and an image. She gazes at the mirror with her eye but not with her understanding, to pick up terms from the shortly preceding Giotto story. Moreover, the figure of a woman gazing into a mirror is the very symbol of wisdom and contemplation; and the reference to Solomon underlines the presence of this meaning. It is an image with further supporting resonances in other parts of the book. Emilia, who tells this story, sings the song on day I in which she describes herself as gazing contentedly at herself in a mirror. Silber has noted that Boccaccio's phrases echo Dante's description in *Purgatorio* XXVII of Rachel, identified with the contemplative life.[73] Emilia sees in her mirror a good unassailable by fortune, thus obviously not her physical beauty. It is a good, she says, which pleases the understanding but lies beyond the full comprehension of most mortal minds.

> Io veggio in quella, ognora ch'io mi specchio,
> quel ben che fa contento lo 'ntelletto:
>   . . .
>
> dir nol poria né prendere intenzione
> d'alcun mortal già mai
> che non ardesse di cotal vaghezza.

> [I see in it (my beauty), whenever I look at myself in the mirror, / that good which makes content the understanding. / . . . no mortal could ever / express or understand it / who did not burn with similar desire.]

The beauty that she sees there and the joy that she feels because of it are a promise which gives her hope for what is to come:

> gustando già di ciò ch'el m'ha promesso:
> e maggior gioia spero più dappresso
> sì fatta, che già mai
> simil non si sentì qui da vaghezza

> [tasting already what he has promised me: / and greater joy I hope for later / such that no like desire was ever felt here].

The allegorical qualities of this song have long ago been noticed. Emilia seems to maintain her contemplative associations when telling the story of Cesca. For when she is called upon to speak, she rouses herself with a sigh, "non altrimenti che se da dormir si levasse" [as if waking from sleep] and remarks that "un lungo pensiero molto di qui m'ha tenuta gran pezza lontano" [a long thought has been holding me far from here for a great while]. She can be considered the fulfillment of the sign of which Cesca is the empty image.

In the immediately following tale, Cavalcanti too is found "speculando" by a bunch of good-timers who challenge his philosophizing. Cavalcanti answers them with a remark which leaves them baffled. He is on

the opposite side from Cesca, as if the very mirror image led to this re
sal; for he speaks and is not understood, where she was spoken to and did
not understand. Thus Cesca's mirror-gazing of the eye is followed by a
speculation of the intellect. Durling has suggested that the interpretation
of Cavalcanti's cryptic remark by Messer Betto within the tale is by no
means a complete explication; for Boccaccio's message to us through this
story, with its obvious reference to Dante's *Inferno* X, surpasses Messer
Betto's understanding.[74] Cavalcanti's importunate friends believe that his
"speculazioni eran solo in cercare se trovar si potesse che Iddio non fosse"
[speculations were only in search of a proof that God does not exist], a
charge which Cavalcanti seems to deny by leaping over and escaping from
entrapment against the tomb which holds his heretical father in hell. This
meaning is reinforced by Emilia's song; because whereas Cavalcanti's
fellow-citizens hold philosophy in suspicion as contrary to faith, Emilia's
speculation or contemplation leads her toward God. The allusion to
Rachel in Emilia's song is reflected in the meaning of these later tales. Thus
Boccaccio defends the intellectual life, opposing it to the horrid stupidity
and ignorance of Cesca and others.

In conclusion, it seems not so farfetched to view the *Decameron* as a
work which is making good use of a long allegorical tradition in order to
convey certain moral points. The increasing realism of the vehicle does not
negate the persistence of a submerged tenor, so that the text must be not
simply seen but seen through. Just as Fiammetta, while maintaining her
associations with Astrea and Mars and her participation in a Venus-Mars
pair, has nonetheless become much less obviously an allegorical figure,
being presented not as a nymph or virtue nor even as an example of life
ruled by passion but as a historical woman whose identity must be protected, so too Boccaccio's whole manner of writing allegory has changed.
Allegory has not disappeared but rather has become submerged under a
more historical surface whose elements do not obviously require interpretation. This is far from his mode of writing in the *Comedia delle Ninfe*
and has gone even beyond the *Amorosa Visione*, where already some of the
allegory is less openly displayed. The implication of this submergence is
that subtler readers are needed than before. Therefore, the whole issue of
readers recurs repeatedly in this text.

If the *Decameron* has many possible readings, then it is up to the
reader to handle the text in any way that will benefit and not harm him.
Boccaccio seems unsure of the reader's widom, however, for he remarks
several times explicitly on the reader's responsibility, especially in his con-

clusion to the book: the tales "e nuocere e giovar possono, sì come tutte l'altre cose, avendo riguardo all'ascoltatore" [they can hurt and help, just like all other things, depending on the reader]. Even the Sacred Scriptures have led to perdition those who misunderstood or misapplied the text. His final adieu to the lady readers expresses the hope that "forse alcuna cosa *giova* l'averle lette" (my emphasis) [perhaps it may help somehow to have read them]. And although he defines the readers as "semplici giovinette" [simple young ladies], he also bids them read "con ragionevole occhio da intendente person" and "sanamente" [with the rational eye of an understanding person . . . healthily], with a mind "ben disposta" that cannot be corrupted by any "terrene brutture" in the book [well disposed . . . earthly dirtiness].[75] The brigata members, "mature e non pieghevoli per novelle" [mature and not pliable by stories], are exemplary readers in this respect.[76]

The answer to critics at the beginning of day IV implies that a number of Boccaccio's readers have been less than ideal. To the objection that he should be attending to the muses and not still trying at his age to please women, Boccaccio replies that women have been his muses and thus "queste cose tessendo, nè dal monte Parnaso nè dalle Muse non mi allontano quanto molti per avventura s'avisano" [in weaving these things, I am not going so far either from Mount Parnasus or from the muses as many happen to think]. This coupled with the name of Dante as a lover of women implies that "many" are not reading beyond a superficial level. Boccaccio may have actually been getting some comments from readers of the first thirty tales,[77] but we can find his concern about readers even earlier in the book: the very subtitle "Galeotto" works hand in hand with the remarks in the conclusion as a warning about the reader's responsibility for his use of the text. It refers to Francesca's seduction by literature into sin; but at the same time it refers to Dante's poem whose expressed purpose is to lead men from sin and misery to grace. Thus Mazzotta is right to say that it shows Boccaccio "aware of literature as an erotic snare," but not if he means that literature can only be this way. For Boccaccio is once again offering a choice of readings.[78] The group's continual honesty, harmony, and brotherly familiarity which Panfilo notes with approval despite the incitements of leisure, comfort, and lusty tales is a form of *amore onesto* which specifically contrasts with Paolo and Francesca's concupiscence. Indeed, Fiammetta's story on the final day provides a corrective to Francesca's fault. The story is not obviously about reading. It tells of King Carlo's infatuation with two girls and his ultimate victory over his own lust, following the advice of a counselor appropriately named Guido. But the two girls' names are equally significant: they are Ginevra la bella and Isotta la bionda, names of the famous heroines of two romantic tragedies. Ginevra is none other than Francesca's model, by following whose example Francesca was led to her own unhappy end. King Carlo, admiring the beauty of these girls, gives them each a dowry and a noble husband. The substitution of marriage for illegitimate lust harks back to the day of Fiammetta's reign while the king's difficult but successful victory over his own illicit impulse presents a nobler alternative to Francesca's response.

When Boccaccio asserts in his preface that his tales are meant to teach us to recognize what to shun and what to follow, perhaps, unlike Pabst, we should take him seriously. According to Mazzotta, the *Genealogia* represents a major change in Boccaccio's attitude; there he rejects "useless" literature and seeks to demonstrate its hidden teachings, turning away from the dangers of the aesthetic imagination.[79] But those dangers had been warned against already. In his earlier writings, such as the *Comedia delle Ninfe*, *Amorosa Visione*, and *Elegia di Madonna Fiammetta*, the dangers of fiction are classed with the dangers of illusion altogether, including the psychological delusions of erotic fantasy. The analyses by which Boccaccio "saves" pagan myths are not very different from the way in which he "saves" the stories of the *Comedia delle Ninfe*. In both cases he assumes that the tales were meant from the beginning to be saved in just this way.

Later in life Boccaccio stopped writing fiction and turned to making historical compilations or to explaining what fictions say (Dante's as well as the ancient myths). But this turning does not necessarily imply that Boccaccio now rejected his earlier works as "useless" or wrong. On the contrary, he continued to copy, correct, and diffuse them. His anxiety was that readers might not understand them properly.

> Possent tamen obicere hoc ad oportuna, non ad supervacanea fore concessum, fabulas autem supervacaneas esse. Quod negari non posset, si poeta simplicem composuisse fabellam intellexisset. Sed iam diu premonstratum est longe aliud, quam sonet cortex, a fabulis palliatum. Et hinc sic non nulli consuevere fabulam diffinire: Fabula est exemplaris seu demonstrativa sub figmento locutio, cuius amoto cortice, patet intentio fabulantis. (*Gen.* XIV.9)

> [But, they may object, nature meant this gift (speech) for a useful purpose, not for idle nonsense; and fiction is just that—idle nonsense. True enough, if the poet had intended to compose a mere

tale. But I have time and time again proved that the meaning of fiction is far from superficial. Wherefore, some writers have framed this definition of fiction (*fabula*): Fiction is a form of discourse, which, under guise of invention, illustrates or proves an idea; and, as its superficial aspect is removed, the meaning of the author is clear.] (trans. Osgood)

Perhaps he hoped that these remarks in the *Genealogia* would make some readers think again about his earlier works.

IX

The *Rime* and Late Writings

From the narrator's response at his first sight of Fiammetta in church, Boccaccio's readers have been prepared to look for the Beatrice nature of the newly introduced Fiammetta. At least until the *Elegia* Dante is obviously a major source both of descriptive phrases and of the lady's role in general. Slowly Petrarch's influence enters the picture as well; but the date of the beginning of Petrarch's influence on Boccaccio is a subject for debate. Billanovich calls Fiammetta "minore sorella di Laura, benchè pure parente di Beatrice" [younger sister of Laura, although also related to Beatrice] and suggests the influence of Petrarch already in the *Filocolo*.[1] König too, quoting Billanovich, concludes that Fiammetta is modeled on Laura.[2] But if Boccaccio wrote the *Filocolo* in 1336, as Branca indicates, his knowledge of Petrarch's writings must have been slight at best. In 1338 Petrarch's friend Dionigi di Borgo San Sepolcro went to Naples and met Boccaccio; the first copies in Boccaccio's *zibaldone* of anything by Petrarch are from this time (a letter from Petrarch to Dionigi).[3] It is possible that Sennuccio del Bene had already introduced Boccaccio to a few Petrarch poems. Wilkins has tried to argue that the *Filostrato* makes use of a sonnet sent by Petrarch to Sennuccio.[4] Silber, however, has cast serious doubts on the matter;[5] and although he assumes from Hauvette that the date of the *Filostrato* is 1338, Ricci and Branca have suggested that it was written even earlier than the *Filocolo*, in 1335,[6] making the influence even less likely. Between the completion of the *Filocolo* in 1336 and the writing of the *Teseida* and *Comedia delle Ninfe* in 1340–41 and 1341–42, Petrarch had circulated his first collection of poems, including twenty-two sonnets and a canzone of his own plus two sonnets by other friends.[7] The canzone was half of what was to become poem 23 in the *Canzoniere*. It and a number of the sonnets were developing the theme of love for a laurel-lady connected closely with poetic inspiration and Petrarch's desire for the poet's crown. According to Wilkins, "About a hundred of the extant Italian lyrics were presumably written before September 1340."[8] Calcaterra and later Bernardo, who follows Wilkins's chronology of the poems, have found that the earliest poems treat chiefly a Laura of literary fame, and that the Christianizing of the image is a later development.[9] Thus Boccaccio had some reason to write in his biography of Petrarch, shortly after Petrarch's coronation in 1341, "Laurettam illam allegorice pro laurea corona . . . accipiendam existimo"[10] [I think that Laura is to be taken allegorically for the laurel crown]. And Petrarch in a letter of December 1336 (*Fam.* II.9) replied to Bishop Giacomo Colonna's suggestion that Laura was a fiction representing the much-desired crown for poetry.[11] Similar literary uses of the *donna* appear in later *Rime* of Boccaccio, but the Fiammetta of the *Filocolo* seems not to participate in this aspect of Laura.

According to Branca, there is no sure evidence that Boccaccio knew Petrarch's poems before 1351, and the similarities between Boccaccio and Petrarch may be the result of the influence of earlier poets on both of them.[12] This observation would support my contention that the Fiammetta of Boccaccio's earlier works is derived much more from Dante's poetry than from Petrarch's, despite Fiammetta's obvious differences from Beatrice.

However, Boccaccio's use of Lauretta in the *Decameron* surely indicates a knowledge of Petrarch's poetry prior to 1351. Moreover, the *Comedia delle Ninfe*, for all its obvious imitation of Dante's *Commedia*, contains perhaps the first signs of a Laura-like Fiammetta. Her green dress, besides identifying her with hope and with Venus, may also allude in part to Petrarch's "verde lauro." In chapter XVII, the seven nymphs, of whom Fiammetta is one, sit in the shade of a "bello alloro" [beautiful laurel], and the poet alludes to this scene in his introduction, saying that he has seen his lady among others resting under the shade of a laurel tree. The laurel leads him immediately to talk of "bel parlare" and his hope to write in a worthy style. The same verses refer to Apollo's enamorment, a dominant theme in Petrarch's earliest poems.[13] Boccaccio appeals to his lady for literary aid:

dunque l'aiuto grazioso e pieno
di te in me discenda . . .

   . . .

acciò che io possa parlando piacere (II.63–64, 66)

[then may your full and gracious aid / descend to me . . . so that
I may be able to please with my speaking].

In the very last chapter Boccaccio returns to the laurel and his poetic aspirations: "le meritate ghirlande coronino la bella donna, della faticata penna
movente cagione" [may the deserved garlands crown the beautiful lady
who causes my laboring pen to move]. She is his inspiration for writing, as
Laura is for Petrarch, and her unreality is suggested by the ease with which
Boccaccio turns to dedicate the book to a male Florentine, not to his lady
as on previous occasions.

Boccaccio's *Rime*, written over a long period of time, reveal clearly the
influence of Petrarch as well as that of Dante. Boccaccio did not gather his
Rime into an ordered collection like Dante's *Vita Nuova* or Petrarch's *Canzoniere*. They were distributed variously by their author and the manuscripts all contain different poems or sets of poems. Clearly then, as Branca
has deduced, Boccaccio intended the poems to be read separately, except
for a few paired poems, and not as pieces of a larger composition.[14] Branca
notes in his edition of the *Rime* the strong influence of Dante and other
stilnovisti on Boccaccio's earlier *Rime* and the development of Petrarchan
imitations in the later ones.[15] But the chronological order of composition is
difficult to guess in many cases. Although some of the poems seem to echo
scenes or phrases from other, longer writings,[16] one cannot know for certain whether such poems were written contemporaneously with the longer
works, or earlier as ideas reused subsequently in a larger context, or later as
lyric extractions from previous books.

As only a few of the poems actually name Fiammetta, it is not obvious
whether other poems are about her or someone else. Moreover, the image
of the woman varies as in other works. Fiammetta is named in XCVII in a
vision of her death and ascension clearly modeled after Dante's *Vita Nuova*
23. The flame which appears on her crowned head becomes a cloud, and
we are witness to the exodus of Fiammetta from this world to the other.[17]
Poems C and CI, which refer to this death, once again oppose the errors of
the "mondo bugiardo" [lying world] with its "pensier fallace" [deceiving
thought] to the "sommo e vero bene" [supreme and true good], inviting
the lover to follow Fiammetta to the kingdom of God. CII addresses
Dante, who followed Beatrice "per cambiar fallace vita a vera" [to change
from false to true life]. Fiammetta too urges her lover to see the true good
and to abandon the lies of his present existence.

The appearance of the lady as an invitation to higher things occurs
frequently in lyrics dealing with literary rather than religious aims, thus

coming closer to Petrarch's poetry than to Dante's. Poem XC, for example, is spoken by an unnamed female who offers her lover-poet a glorious end contrasted to the repose of the nonintellectual world. Whereas in other poems the poet hoped his poetry would help him win the rewards of Amor, here it is Amor who urges him on toward the goals of poetic ambition. In one sense, this Amor is undoubtedly a love of poetry; but in another sense, perhaps it is the very subject matter of his other poems, the theme which has inspired so many pages. Indeed in CVIII the syntax becomes ambiguous:

> Il vivo fonte di Parnaso, e quelle
> frondi, che furn'ad Apollo più care,
> m'ha fatto lungo tempo Amor cercare.

> [The living fountain of Parnasus and those leaves that were dearest to Apollo has Love made me seek for a long time.]

Love has made him pursue poetry, but certainly poetry has also made him seek out love, given the long-established poetic tradition of the lover pose. In XCI he follows a nymph who sings "Infra l'eccelso coro d'Elicona" [among the lofty band of Helicon] and finds himself entering the "amorosa festa"[18] [amorous festivity]. Hence too the playful confusion in the *Decameron* between *muse* and *donne;* to stay with one is not to be far from the other.

The theme of lover translates perfectly into that of poet. He aspires to an object higher than himself; he must suffer pains and yet the beauty of lady or poetry calls forth his further efforts; he is afraid he has wasted his time, yet he can blame only himself. Unlike the lady, however, whom he can at least briefly possess (LIX), poetic glory is never securely his.

Boccaccio's poems about literature tend to refer to nymphs or angelic creatures rather than directly to Fiammetta, and the poems about Fiammetta which have been placed toward the end of what editors call the "Vita" section are usually not about poetic aspiration but rather about erotic and religious love. Nonetheless, Fiammetta and the literary muse do merge at times, under the clear influence of Petrarch. Thus Fiammetta in LXXX inspires his "penne" [plumes] to a lofty flight. In CI the poet, called toward the kingdom of God, wonders "come qui impennarmi / possa, a volar al suo beato regno" [how I can plume myself to fly to his blessed kingdom]. The pun on "impennarmi" is reused in CV, specifically for writing religious verse. As Homer failed to describe Helen's beauty, so Boccaccio does not know how to write about the glorious good of paradise; he needs divine aid: "di sacra virtu s'impenni l'ale" [may my wing be plumed with sacred virtue (or power)]. Thus the question "how can I ascend to heaven?" becomes the question "how can I write about such a high subject?"

One of the answers to this latter question is, as in the *Comedia delle Ninfe*, "per donna." In XXII, a poem in terza rima, Boccaccio writes:

> Amor, che con sua forza e virtù regna,
> nel summo cielo ardendo sempre vive
> e l'anima gentil di lui fa degna,
>
> regge mia vita e quel che la man scrive,
> dimostra el cuor divoto a sua deitade
> e del suo regno el fa ministro e cive.
>
> Amor vol fede e con lui son legate
> speranza con timor e gelosia,
> e sempre con leanza umanitade.
>
> Unde sovente per Rachele a Lia
> fa star suggetta l'anima servendo
> con dolce voglia e con la mente pia.

[Love, who reigns with its power and virtue, / lives always burning in the highest heaven / and makes the gentle soul worthy of him, / rules my life and what my hand writes, / shows my heart devoted to his divinity / and makes it a minister and citizen of his kingdom. / Love wants faith and with him are connected / hope with fear and jealousy, / and always compassion with loyalty. / Wherefore often he makes the soul be subject / to Lia on behalf of Rachel, / serving with sweet will and pious mind.]

Here, as in the *Comedia delle Ninfe*, the Amor seems to be a heavenly one ("nel summo ciel"), which the poet because of timidity about his limited powers addresses through a *schermo* or screen as did Dante. The phrase about Rachel and Lia may also echo the end of Petrarch's *Canzoniere* CCVI: "Per Rachel ho servito, e non per Lia." [19] [I have served for Rachel and not for Lia.] The poem of Boccaccio's which follows in this collection remarks on the same theme:

> Nè posso, a mio guidicio, dir con vero
> che per cosa terrena esser felice
> io cerchi, ma d'effige alta e divina. (XXIII)

[Nor can I, to my judgment, say truly that I seek to be happy through something earthly, but for a high and divine image.]

Many of Boccaccio's poems are neither allegorical nor about religious love; the frequent echoes of Ovid make evident that Dante and Petrarch are not his only models.[20] Ferreri in his study on the *Rime* emphasizes Fiammetta's unmystical qualities. "Fiammetta—perduta ogni prerogativa trascendentale ed emblematica—è decisamente una donne terrena."[21] [Fiammetta—having lost every transcendental and emblematic prerogative—is decidedly an earthly woman.] This is undeniably true of many of the poems, especially those set in real locations near Naples, or those in which the lady speaks in the same passionate terms as the male (e.g. XXVI, where, however, the lady is unnamed). Confronting Boccaccio's poems with Petrarch's, Ferreri argues further that even Boccaccio's more transcendental poems remain basically worldly, his narrative mode opposed to the symbolic mode of Petrarch.[22] One must keep in mind, however, that a significant number of poems are attributed to both Boccaccio and Petrarch according to different manuscripts, and it is still not absolutely certain in many cases which attribution is correct.[23]

It is also clear that the conversion of erotic love into holy love is not something Boccaccio turned to only in his later years, after Fiammetta, in proper poetic tradition, had died. The lines in CIV declaring that his lady's "viso angelico" has returned to heaven

. . . dond'era a noi venuto
per farne fede dell'altrui bellezza

[when she had come to us to give us faith in the beauty of another]

are merely one more repetition of an idea which had occurred in earlier works. The *Amorosa Visione* XVI.1ff. is perhaps the most obvious example besides the *Comedia delle Ninfe*. A more startling example of this idea, in almost the same phrases as the *Amorosa Visione*, is Lauretta's song in the *Decameron* III, coming at the end of a day of particularly lusty tales. There as in the *Amorosa Visione*, *cupiditas* and *caritas* are confronted, and the lady becomes a pivot from one to the other.

For Branca the "rivolgersi a Dio" [turning to God] of the later poems —and one might include with these the later eclogues—is a "testimonianza dell'itinerario spirituale del poeta da una visione galantemente raffinata e superficialmente mondana della vita a quella intima e pensosa dei valori umani commisurati agli universali ed eterni"[24] [evidence of the poet's spiritual itinerary from a gallantly refined and superficially worldly view of life to one intimate and thoughtful about human values measured against universal and eternal (values)]. And yet the measuring stick of eternal values was present since the *Filocolo* and in other early writings. What is new for Boccaccio is not the introduction of eternal values or religious thoughts but the abandonment of worldly love, no doubt made easier at last by the poet's age. Fiammetta, once an ambiguous combination of the human and divine, the real and the symbolic, now ceases to be human at all and, dying, reascends to the pure heavenly realm from which she previously claimed to have been sent. Thus the link between heaven and earth is lost.

Her flight to heaven marks also Boccaccio's humanistic idealization of the poetic enterprise. Poem XCVI prays for divine help toward both "salute" and the laurel crown, and CXII seeks in the same line "fama perenne ed etterna salute" [perennial fame and eternal salvation]. The "virtù" which is necessary for attaining this double goal is both moral virtue and literary prowess. Petrarch's influence is obvious in this combination of themes. Fiammetta is now, for the first time, explicitly placed beside Beatrice and Laura; thus Boccaccio expresses his hope to take his own place near Dante and Petrarch, and also his fear of failure if left to his own *virtù* or *ingegno*.

The *Rime* offer many Ovidian attempts, through praise or complaint, to win the lady's regard. Boccaccio also puts his poetry into the mouths of women, who strive in a similar fashion to win the hearts of men. But as in his fictions, the role of seducer-poet is often undercut by the singer's own text. For example, in the pair of *Rime* IV–V, the poet follows a sound of wonderful singing only to find himself inflamed with love. The lady's song, says *Rime* V, surpasses that of Mercury, who put to sleep all the eyes of Argus. Mercury played a song of seduction which lulled to sleep Io's watchful guard. This song, then, runs counter to those which urge the lover to open his eyes and see clearly, e.g., the *Comedia delle Ninfe* and the *Amorosa Visione*. Boccaccio's own attempts to win his lady by his verses suffer the same comparison in LVI:

> Se quel serpente che guarda il tesoro,
> del qual m'ha fatto Amor tanto bramoso,
> ponesse pur un poco el capo gioso,
> io crederei con un sottil lavoro
> trovar al pianto mio alcun ristoro:
> nè in ciò sarebbe il mio cor temoroso,
> come che pria, in punto assai dubbioso,
> già mi negasse il promess'adiutoro.

Ma pria Mercurio chiuderà que' d'Argo
cantando di Siringa, che'n que' due
io possa metter sonno col mio verso

[If that serpent which guards the treasure, / for which Love has
made me so desirous, / would put his head down just a little, / I
believe I would with subtle work / find some remedy for my
complaint: / nor in that would my heart be fearful, / as it was before when, at a very dangerous moment, / it denied me the
promised help. / But sooner will Mercury close the eyes of
Argus / by singing about Syrinx than I will be able / to put sleep
in those two eyes by my verse].

The meaning of the myth is clear. The poetry is a seduction.[25]

The lady's song in V is compared secondly to the song by which Amphion built Thebes. Thebes is generally for Boccaccio a city symbolic of
the passions.[26] The song which builds Thebes is thus a song arousing passion. Amphion, moreover, according to mythology received his lyre from
Mercury, the seducer-poet.

Thirdly, the lady's song is compared explicitly to that of the sirens
"quando si scosse / invano Ulisse provvido al fuggire" [when Ulysses
vainly shook himself, provident against his own escape]. The poet here is
not so "provvido."

These songs of seduction, however, often contain hints of their own
undoing. Just as in V Ulysses' providence in escaping the siren's song is an
object of praise which contrasts with the poet's folly, so too LVI, cited
above, is partly a celebration of the lady's honesty against which the poet's
seductive attempts will not work. Furthermore, one can read the first eight
lines in another, more phallic way which suggests that the poet is even
critical of his own erotic impulse, or complaining of the independence of
the flesh from his control.

The call of the sirens is associated with the sea, and in *Rime* VI and
VII Fiammetta and other ladies sing from boats in the sea near Naples.
Again their song is a lure:

Chi non crederà assai agevolmente,
s'al canto d'Arion venne il delfino
facendo sé al suo legno vicino,
al suo comando presto ed ubbidiente,
che, solcando costei il mar sovente

in breve barca, nel tempo più fino,
alla voce del suo canto divino
molti ne venghin desiosamente?

[Who will not believe quite easily, / if to Arion's song the dol-
phin came, / drawing near to his boat, / ready and obedient to
his command, / that as she cuts through the sea often / in a little
boat, in the finest season, / many men come with desire / to the
sound of her heavenly song?]

The poet, describing the effects of the lady's song, is hoping to have the
same effect on her, that is, to attract her desire. Thus the two songs, male
and female, mirror each other playfully. The relation between male and female becomes a competition in seductive wit.

If the *Rime* are self-confessed endeavors to seduce, just like some of
the longer works sent by their hopeful author to his lady, so too Fiammetta
is allowed to answer her lover in the *Rime*. As in the *Filocolo* the lover gets a
cold reply (XLV):

O iniquo uomo, o servo disleale,
di che ti duol? di che vai lagrimando?
di che Amor e me vai biasimando
quasi cagion del tuo noioso male?
Qual arco apersi io mai, o quale strale
ti saettai? quai prieghi, o dove, o quando
ti fur fatti per me, che, me amando,
mi dessi il cor, di cui sí or ti cale?

[O wicked man, o disloyal servant, / what are you complaining
about, what are you crying about? / Why do you go blaming
Love and me / as if we were the cause of your grievous ill? /
What bow did I ever pull, or what arrow / did I ever shoot at
you? What prayers or where or when / did I ever make to you
that you, loving me, / should give me your heart, which you are
now so worried about?]

The final blow is "del mio onore / mi cal più troppo che del tuo affanno" [I
care much more about my honor than about your troubles]. The lady's
undermining reply to her seducer's verses is reminiscent of those Provençal
tenzoni in which the male poet makes himself look foolish in debate with
his desired woman. As in the *Filocolo*, Fiammetta, named in this poem, un-

does the whole fiction of love and directs attention to its dishonorable goal. This is the opposite of singing to seduce; it is singing to disenchant. Thus the *Rime* play with both roles of eloquence as do the longer works.

Boccaccio also seems to have rewritten certain poems, turning them from human to divine objects of love. For example, the blazon to Fiammetta in X

> Se bionde treccie, chioma crespa e d'oro,
> occhi ridenti splendidi e soavi,
> atti piacevoli e costumi gravi,
> sentito motteggiare, onesto e soro
> parlar in donna, com'in suo tesoro,
> pose natura mai o finser savi:
> tutt'è'n costei, Amor, in cui le chiavi
> della mia pena désti e del ristoro.
>   . . .
> Questa li mia pensier urge ed avanza
> con gli occhi suoi a sì alto desiro

[If blond locks, curly golden hair, / laughing eyes, splendid and mild, / pleasing gestures and grave manners, / wit, honest and youthful speech, / in a woman, as if in her treasure, / nature ever put or wise men ever feigned: / all these things are in her, Love, to whom you gave the keys / of my pain and of my restoration. / . . . This one urges and drives forward my thought / with her eyes to such a high-reaching desire]

is countered by a probably much later poem, CXVII, which seems to be a purposeful reworking of the earlier one and of other similar poems: [27]

> Non treccia d'oro, non d'occhi vaghezza,
> non costume real, non leggiadria,
> non giovanett'età, non melodia,
> non angelico aspetto né bellezza
> poté tirar dalla sovrana altezza
> il Re del cielo in questa vita ria
> ad incarnar in te, dolce Maria,
> Madre di grazia e specchio d'allegrezza;
>   ma l'umiltà tua, . . .
>   . . .

Quella ne presta adunque, Madre santa,
si che possiamo al tuo beato regno,
seguendo lei devoti, ancor salire.

[Not golden locks, not charming eyes, / not regal manners, not mirth / nor youth nor melody / nor angelic aspect nor beauty / could draw from lofty heights / the King of heaven into this wicked life / to incarnate himself in you, sweet Mary, / Mother of grace and mirror of joy; / but your humility . . . / Lend that to us then, holy Mother, / so that we may be able, following you with devotion, / to ascend still to your blessed kingdom].

Although Boccaccio's late poems to Mary may have been influenced by Petrarch's final canzone to the Virgin, Boccaccio could also have drawn from his own early associations between Fiammetta and Maria or from his later opposition between the old widow and the Virgin.

For another such example of redirected themes, Fiammetta is introduced in the famous "Contento quasi" (LXIX) as "il tuo sole" (40); and XCVIII further associates her with the sun, emphatically using "sole" as a rhyme word four times. The lover sees in the sun his own "fiamma" [flame] with her "capei d'oro" [golden hair]. Yet CXV, "O Sol, ch'allumi l'un e l'altra vita" [O Sun which illumines this and the other life] is addressed not to Fiammetta but to God. This poem, like the one to Mary, sets the two loves against each other:

Io ho, seguendo gli terren diletti,
e i tuo'commandamenti non curando,
offeso spesso la tua maiestade:
. . .
però, di grazia, addomando pietade.

[Following worldly delights / and not caring about your commandments, / I have often offended your majesty . . . / therefore, by your grace, I beg for mercy.]

One love is strictly erotic desire, the other appeals directly to God or Mary for "pietà" and "salute."

To the extent that Boccaccio is consciously using the same key words and images from one poem to another in order to oppose the religion of Amor and the religion of the other "Signore" who is Love, he is converting the poetry of seduction into religious verse.[28] However, unlike the *Filocolo* or *Comedia delle Ninfe* which manage to preserve Ovidian delight in the midst of a conversion to Christian meanings, these late *Rime* seem to reject the Ovidian mode altogether. As in the *Corbaccio*, the two kinds of love and of poetry are irreconcilably opposed.

One can witness the abandonment of Ovid more explicitly in Boccaccio's writings about literature. One of the new themes of both the later poems (CVII, CVIII, CXIII) and some of the later letters, such as the letter to Iacopo Pizzinga, is that of literary discouragement: Boccaccio's beloved masters have after all done everything too well for him to follow, and he wonders whether he has not wasted his time—not by writing about love but by writing altogether. Hence his gesture of burning the poems because Petrarch's are better. Hence too, perhaps, his vulnerability to the accusation of Pietro Petroni, a vulnerability not shared by Petrarch. The counterimpulse was an insistent defense of poetry and the life devoted to poetry, in the *Genealogia* (XI.2; XIV and XV),[29] the life of Dante, the commentary on Dante's *Commedia* (lez. III), the *De Casibus* (III.16), and several letters (besides the one to Pizzinga, also one to Pietro di Monteforte, 1373). The need to legitimize his own activity of writing led Boccaccio finally to restrict the realm proper to his defense. Using Boethius's image of Philosophy's muses throwing out the sirens, and using even Ovid's own contest of the muses versus the daughters of Pierus, he rejected some kinds of poetry in order to save the rest. Ovid's love poetry, which Boccaccio had imitated in his own *Rime* and *Elegia*, Ovid's "dulciloquos versus" [sweet-speaking verses] and "reverenda actoritas" [reverend authority] which the letter "Sacre famis" had admired along with the writings of Vergil, Lucan, Statius, Salust, and Livy, become a chief example of the sort of poetry to be abandoned (*Gen.* XIV.15).

Boccaccio's distrust is rather of readers than of poets. The conclusion to the *Decameron* had argued that "quelle (parole), che tanto oneste non sono, la ben disposta non posson contaminare, se non come il loto i solari raggi o le terrene brutture le bellezze del cielo" [Those (words) which are not so honest cannot contaminate the well-disposed, any more than the mud (contaminates) the rays of the sun, or worldly ugliness the beauties of heaven]. But the *Esposizioni* support Plato's banishment of lascivious comedians: "per ciò ché spesso vi si facevano intorno agli adultèri, che i comedi recitavano, di disoneste cose, si movevano gli appetiti degli uomini e delle femine, riguardanti, a simili cose disiderare e adoperare; *di che i buon costumi e le menti sane si corrompevano* e ad ogni disonestà discorrevano" (I.litt.87, my emph.) [because the comedians often did dishonest things about the adulteries which they were performing, they used to move the appetites of the watching men and women to desire and to do similar things; whence good manners and healthy minds were corrupted, and they ran to every dishonesty].

Whereas Dioneo in the *Decameron* trusts his lady readers to do as in a garden, "distesa la dilicata mano, cogliete le rose e lasciate le spine stare" (V.10), in Book XIV.22, of the *Genealogia* it is the church which "like the wise maiden . . . gathered flowers among the thorns without tearing her fingers, simply by leaving the thorns untouched" ("more solertis virginis, quae inter spineta flores illesis colligit digitis, et spinarum aculeos sinit separati vilescere"). The allusion is no longer to the reader's judicious use of literature but to the church's selection of texts fit to be read. Therefore, when Boccaccio goes on to advise, "aequa lance poetarum dicta librate, et quae minus sancte scripta sunt, sinite" [weigh the words of the poets in a true balance, and put away the unholy part], this putting away involves whole works, not merely less moral meanings; it is a process of selecting "the poets we revere" from "the disreputable sort." "Sit satis vobis in illecebres comicos irruere, in hos iras evomere" (*Gen.* XIV.22) [Let the lewd comic writers feel the stream of your wrath].

Dioneo's comment about the roses and thorns prefaced a "lewd comic" tale, but comedy is no longer trusted to distance the effects of the material. Ovid's poems, like Dioneo's tales, work a self-mockery through humor; in this regard, Boccaccio's lover-narrators are more Ovidian than Dantean or Petrarchan. But now the whole pose is called into question, for it has given poetry a bad name among less subtle readers. Describing in the *Genealogia* XI.1 how ignorant people believed at face value the stories about Jupiter's adulteries and, what is worse, transferred their ideas about Jupiter to the true God ("ad verum Deum, vere deorum dominum"), Boccaccio concludes: "ego non laudo per illecebres fictiones divinam designare potentiam" [I do not praise the signifying of divine power through seductive fictions]. This is certainly a change from his own earlier practice.

The "semplici" will never interpret such fictions properly even when they are explained. In *Rime* CXXII–CXXV Boccaccio blames himself for expounding Dante's poem to the crowd:

> che li concetti del suo alto ingegno
> aperti sien stati al vulgo indegno (CXXIII)

> [that the conceits of his lofty intellect were opened to the unworthy mob].

217

Trying to teach the crowds was a mistake because such an audience can never really understand great poetry but can only be deluded into false vanity:

> Io ho messo in galea senza biscotto
> l'ingrato vulgo, e senza alcun piloto
> lasciato l'ho in mar a lui non noto,
> ben che sen creda esser maestro e dotto (CXXV)

[I have set the ungrateful mob in the galley / without a biscuit, and I have left them without any pilot / in the sea unknown to them, / although they think they have mastery and learning].

The use of the vernacular was perhaps similarly deceitful, allowing unskilled readers to think they understand. Writing in Latin was one way of ensuring a more intellectual audience.[30] The eclogue "Saphos" (XII) discusses the abandonment of vernacular and popular writing for loftier Latin verse. "Non ego te vidi pridem vulgare canentem / in triviis carmen, misero plaudente popolo?" [Didn't I see you earlier singing a vulgar song at the crossroads, to the applause of the wretched crowd?] asks the muse Caliope. And Aristeus confesses that she did; "ast nunc altior est etas, alios que monstrat amores" (48–53) [but now my age is older, and the loves which it shows me are different]. The best of poetry is not intended to please the many but rather "to set forth with lofty intelligence" and "in exquisite style and diction" the noblest thoughts of man (*Gen.* XIV.6). Caliope, repeating the terms and arguments of the *Genealogia* XIV and XV, complains that poetry has been attacked as immoral and false (lying) and that the muses have been called sirens. The abuses of poetry have stained its honor, "sic sanctum nimio contemnitur usu" (133) [thus the sacred is scorned through too much use], and therefore Saphos has hidden herself from the common mob in a cave high on a mountain (126).

> Anne putas, vulgus stolidum seu garrula turba
> auritos tondens asinos permitteret ista? (119–20)

[Or do you think that the foolish mob or babbling crowd, shearing its long-eared donkeys, would permit those things?]

The phrase "auritos asinos" probably came to Boccaccio from Ovid's *Amores* II.7. There Ovid complains that his mistress is unjustly accusing him of having an affair with her maidservant; the following poem to the servant proves the accusation true. Boccaccio is similarly confronted with the reproach that he has pursued the lower of two audiences; thus here as elsewhere, he equates making love with writing poetry. The influence of Ovid's love verses persists even into the rejection of Ovidian writing. There may also be here a reference to Midas, whose barber saw the ass's ears that Midas had grown when preferring Pan's music to Apollo's. The implication is that common readers will stupidly prefer the wrong kinds of writing, or the wrong readings of an ambiguous text, the passionate rather than the contemplative. Boccaccio's discouragement about his own ability to write may have been connected with a failure on the part of many readers to understand what he was doing.[31]

Boccaccio's growing distrust of his audience goes hand in hand with his increasing acceptance of the humanists', i.e., of Petrarch's, ideas about literature. It is Petrarch who, in "Saphos," can guide Boccaccio to his literary goal, and it is Petrarch who, in "Phylostropos," persuades Boccaccio to leave the pursuits of this world for those of heaven. Boccaccio's theory of poetry as set forth in the *Genealogia* is much influenced by Petrarch's *Familiares* X.4, also a defense of poetry in relation to theology and Scripture.[32] Poetry, claims Boccaccio, is inspired by God; at least good poetry is. But the *Genealogia* XIV.6 condemns "Poetae, si tales Poetae dicendi sunt, qui seu ratione quaestus, seu ad gratiam populi promerendam, sic eo exquirente seculo, et illecebri suadente lascivia" [poets, if such deserve the name, who, either to get money or popularity, study contemporary fashions, pander to a licentious taste]. In Eclogue XV Phylostropos, or Petrarch, condemns Typhlus's attraction to Crisis and Dyones, whose names suggest "money" and "licentious taste." Dyones in particular undoubtedly alludes to Dioneo, the figure of intemperance in the *Comedia delle Ninfe* and the priapic narrator of the *Decameron*. Crisis, in turn, is derived from the Greek word for gold.[33]

As the crowd is always more inclined to applaud the appetites than to attend to difficult and educative writing, writing for a popular audience becomes equivalent to writing about dishonest loves. "Fu adunque Virgilio poeta, e *non fu popolare poeta*, ma solennissimo, e le sue opere e la sua fama chiaro il dimostrano *agl'intendenti*" (I.litt.112, my emph.) [Vergil, then, was a poet, and *not a popular poet* but a most solemn one, and his works and fame clearly demonstrate it *to those who understand*]. Boccaccio's own *Rime* might well be included in his attack in the *Esposizioni* on modern songs; for when Vergil refers to his own activity as "cantai," Boccaccio comments:

E non erano li lor canti di cose vane, come il più delle canzoni odierne sono, anzi erano versi poetici, ne'quali d'altissime materie o di laudevoli operazioni da valenti uomini adoperate [si trattava], sì come noi possiam vedere nella fine del primo dello *Eneida* di Virgilio, dove, dopo la notabile cena di Didone fatta ad Enea, Iopa, sonando la cetera, canta gli errori del sole e della luna, e la prima generazione degli uomini e degli altri animali, e donde fosse l'origine delle piove e del fuoco e altre simili cose.

[Their songs were not about vain things, like most of the songs of today, rather they were poetic verses in which were treated the loftiest matters or praiseworthy actions done by worthy men, as we can see at the end of Book I of the *Aeneid* of Vergil, where, after the famous dinner made by Dido for Aeneas, Iopa, playing the zither, sings about the wanderings of the sun and the moon, the first generation of men and of the other animals, and whence the origin of the rain and fire and other such things.]

"Saphos" too separates the bad poets who sing of love affairs (138–47) from the true poets who write holy verses about the seats of the gods, the causes of lightning, etc. (162–64).

The "elegiaci passionati" are thrown out along with the "comici disonesti" by Lady Philosophy, according to Boccaccio's reading of Boethius (*Esposiz.* I.litt.III). In the letter "Sacre famis," Boccaccio had remarked that his only consolation for his misfortunes lay in reading about the griefs of others, according to the proverb "Misery loves company" ("Solatium est miseris sotios habere penarum"). But the *Esposizioni* blast this attitude: Boethius

non attendeva colla considerazione a trovare i rimedi oportuni a dover cacciar via le noie che danno gl'infortuni della presente vita; anzi cercava di comporre cose, le quali non liberasson lui, ma il mostrassero afflitto molto, e per conseguente mettessero compassion di lui in altrui. E questa gli pareva sì soave operazione che, senza guardare che egli in ciò faceva ingiuria alla filosofica verità, la cui opera è di sanare, non di lusingare il passionato, che esso, con la dolcezza delle lusinghe del potersi dolere insino alla sua estrema confusione avrebbe in tale impresa proceduto (I.litt.108) [did not set his attention to finding opportune remedies which should drive away the griefs which the misfortunes of the present life offer; rather he sought to compose things which would not free him but would show him much afflicted and consequently arouse compassion for him in others. And this seemed to him such a sweet activity that, without considering that he was thereby doing injury to the philosophical truth, whose work is to cure and not to flatter the passionate, in the sweetness of the blandishments of being able to lament for himself he would have proceeded in this enterprise unto his own ultimate confusion].

Boccaccio identifies this kind of writing with that of the dishonest comedians, both aiming to "lusingare e di compiacere alle inferme menti" [to flatter and please sick minds].

But how different really is Boccaccio's attitude from what it was before? The narrators of the *Filostrato*, *Teseida*, *Amorosa Visione*, and *Elegia* as well as of most of the *Rime* are exactly like the sick Boethius and writing with the same stated intent. Yet Boccaccio's laughing criticism of their pose is part of the meaning of the works which their complaints frame. The narrators' laments are set against the wisdom of a second speaker or reader or against the meaning of the tale. The pose of the early lover-poet signifies a consciousness of the limitations of understanding, an attitude to which Boccaccio returned with increasing humility. But the expression of this attitude in "Sacre famis" (1339) sounds as much like the early *Filocolo* as like the later eclogues:

Proinde sicut anxius eger, sue conditionis ignarus, valitudinem animus persepe suspirat, quam in desiderio summi boni, etiam per nebulas interiores, licet vix adhuc perspicio . . . veniat zeffirus ille celestis, . . . tenebras meas dissipet, et diluat disipatas, quo perspicacius gradum amandorum distinguam: et distinguens afficiar ordinate, ac ordinatis affectibus pre concordia carnis et spiritus, non levia gravia sentiam, non bonum malum et malum bonum paralogizatus a fallacia mundi oppiner: sed que levia sunt et iocunda, iocunde recipiam, et vere pestifera, non minus quam puer ad anguis aspectum, formidando pallescam.

[Consequently just as a sick man (does), ignorant of his condition, so my soul often sighs for health, which in my desire for the supreme good, even through internal clouds, I have so far with difficulty been allowed to glimpse . . . may that heavenly breeze come . . . may it disperse my shadows, and dissolve them when they are dispersed, so that I may distinguish more clearly the degrees of things to be loved: and distinguishing I may order my affections, and having ordered my affections to a harmony of flesh and spirit, I may not feel light things as heavy nor, mistaking good for evil and evil for good, believe in the deceits of the world: but that I may receive as pleasant the things which are light and pleasant, and that I may grow pale in terror at the truly evil, no less than a boy at the sight of a snake.]

The *Corbaccio* and some of the later *Rime* could simply be regarded as more directly stated attempts to "sanare" instead of "lusingare." Thus the *Esposizioni* to Dante's work could serve as a commentary on Boccaccio's own, explaining the nature of the narrator's pose. The change would be not so much a recantation of his earlier writings as a growing distrust of his readers and a felt need to make manifest to them that poetry is indeed a moral teacher.

Conclusion

Boccaccio undoubtedly fell in and out of love with a woman at least once during his life. He also fell in love, quite early, with literature and especially the poetry of Dante. Boccaccio's first writings as a lover to his lady—not yet named Fiammetta—manifest an important element of parody of Dante's works, while the humor of his texts undermines both Dante's spiritual intensity and any autobiographical seriousness. For the mocking relationship between author and narrator, Boccaccio drew from his other great master, Ovid. The ancient poet of erotic love and the Christian poet of religious love cross paths over and over in Boccaccio's texts, most strikingly in the *Filocolo* and *Comedia delle Ninfe Fiorentine* where two "authors" are named for each text: one narrator a holy hermit or newly baptized Christian, the other a lover with erotic goals.

Fiammetta participates in this doubling of viewpoints. She is not a constant and well-defined character; rather her role shifts from work to work. She is introduced in the *Filocolo* as a moral teacher, associated in various ways with the Virgin Mary and opposed to the appetites of Eve. Her lover within the narrative learns to govern his passion with reason, while the narrator suggests that, as with Dante, his love for her may be a way toward faith. In the *Amorosa Visione* Fiammetta becomes the object of an ambiguous love. She should be the Beatrice-like lure toward God, but the narrator falls back continually into the Ovidian mode, confusing his own sexual desires with *caritas*. Fiammetta's role is reversed in the *Elegia di Madonna Fiammetta*, where she becomes an Eve-like figure of the passions which have made reason their servant instead of their master. As an example of the destructive results of such a condition, she demonstrates what would happen if the lover-poet of earlier writings obtained his desire. At the same time, paradoxically, she takes over the role of seducer-narrator, thus continuing the double perspective of the earlier texts. Fiammetta's reversed role as the appetitive Eve is carried over into the *Corbaccio* where the nameless widow is opposed explicitly to the Virgin Mary as a figure of lust and vanity. The narrator falls out of love.

Is this reversal of the woman's role a sign of Boccaccio's own sudden reevaluation of love? Had experience made him bitter? Two points argue against such a conclusion. First, the *Ninfale Fiesolano* with its idyllization of love and the *Decameron* with its "onestissima" Fiammetta come chronologically between the *Elegia* and *Corbaccio*. Second and more important, the lessons about love in the early works are essentially the same as those in the later ones.

One possible explanation for the shift in the woman's role is a literary rather than a psychological one: just as Boccaccio repeatedly reversed elements from one tale to another within the *Decameron*, so too he developed ideas for new writings by reversing elements from one book to another, trying out the range of possibilities within a given plot or form. This variation in terms of literary form is explicit in the *Corbaccio* with the ghost's suggestion that Boccaccio write an opposite kind of book from his previous ones. It is evident also in the shift of Fiammetta from reader to narrator in the *Elegia*. Boccaccio's tendency to work with polar terms, Eve and Mary, Astrea and Priapus, etc., makes tempting just such reversals from one term to the other.

There are also more personal reasons for the direction of change in the role of the beloved woman. Having tried to find a place for Ovidian love poetry within a Christian framework, Boccaccio later felt unable to trust his readers to handle properly Ovid's seductive verses. The sense of conflict between two kinds of love which had earlier allowed Boccaccio to achieve the dramatic tour de force of a reconciliation that could include even the *Ars amatoria* intensified to the point that any reconciliation became impossible. It used to be fashionable to speak of a moment of crisis and conversion in Boccaccio's life, when the dying monk Pietro Petroni sent a warning to both Petrarch and Boccaccio that their secular literary pursuits would lead them and others to perdition. The effect of Petroni's warning on Boccaccio's life has been much downplayed by Branca.[1] It has also become clear in recent years that many of Boccaccio's earlier works, once thought of purely as expressions of passionate love, are moral—even moralizing—works with considerable reference to Christian faith. Thus the radical break or crisis seems to be denied. Nonetheless, those previous scholars were not simply foolish, for their hypothesis attempted to explain a real phenomenon, a perceptible change in Boccaccio's manner of writing. We can no longer define the shift as one from passionate immorality or amorality to a moralizing Christianity. And yet the moralizing elements are certainly more *apparent* in the *Corbaccio* and in the *Esposizioni* on Dante than in the *Filocolo* or *Teseida*. The explicit and protracted lecturing and lesson-giving of those later works is certainly a new emphasis. Moreover, the distance between allegorical vehicle and tenor, which was vast in the *Filocolo*, *Teseida*, and *Comedia delle Ninfe*, has shrunk to near identity in the *Corbaccio* as the characters speak directly to the moral point. They are not simultaneously acting out some other story.

Boccaccio's early works, the *Filocolo* and *Comedia delle Ninfe*, both attempt to combine erotic narratives with Christian meanings. A prime example of this is Mopsa's undressing in front of her thoughtless lover in order to teach him how to read; for as the nymph of prudence, she reveals to Afron, or nonthinker, the naked truth beneath her fictive veil. Boccaccio here suggests that literature is a kind of seduction, but a seduction of the pleasure-loving reader toward some moral truth. The forced conjunction of erotic and moral extremes in which one is claimed to mean the other is certainly a virtuoso exercise in allegory; and although critics have long complained about the inappropriateness of vehicle to tenor in this work, that is clearly just what Boccaccio intended, perhaps in an effort to demonstrate that one cannot judge fiction by its surface, or perhaps in sheer delight at the linking of opposites. His point, moreover, is also that human love can be educated into the love of God. Similarly it is Boccaccio who, in the *Filocolo*, added Books I and V—about Christ's redemption of man and an interrupted pilgrimage completed by Florio and Biancifiore along with the conversion of many people—to the preexisting romance of two lovers, thereby suggesting that Florio's pilgrimage of love may have its Christian meanings too.

The *Teseida* also makes demands on the allegorizing imagination of its readers as its allegories are not obvious; and in the *Amorosa Visione* the guide tells the narrator insistently not to be deluded by appearances, by "falso argomento" or "falso imaginar," but to discover their meanings ("scoprissi"), a process akin to Mopsa's unveiling. The *Visione* presents erotic love as a distraction from the true good rather than a symbol of its pursuit. Nonetheless, there remains the suggestion in the end that if the narrator would only adhere to his guiding reason, he would be able to make human love a lure toward heaven, just as Dante's love for Beatrice drew him up to paradise. While remaining ambivalent himself about whether he wants his good in the flesh or in the spirit, the narrator requests the reader to amend the text for him in case he may be making a mistake. The *Decameron*, too, repeatedly emphasizes the reader's responsibility in handling the text and suggests occasionally that a naive reading is not the correct one.

By the time he wrote the *Decameron*, however, Boccaccio was already unsure of how far he could trust his readers' abilities. The inserted reply to critics and the author's preface and conclusion all show this uneasiness and try to make explicit both his own intentions and his readers' responsibility for taking things *in bono*. Written just several years before the *Decameron*, the *Elegia di Madonna Fiammetta* demonstrates a similar concern. Not only is erotic love treated more severely in this work, and not only do the nurse's harangues and Fiammetta's own self-accusations add a considerable moralizing weight, but also Boccaccio's manner of writing is now more direct. Unlike her namesake in the *Comedia delle Ninfe*, this Fiammetta is less an allegorical figure and more an illustrative example for the author's lesson on the dangers of rejecting rational government within the soul. The story is basically an exemplum. It is no longer trying to suggest that erotic passion can signify virtue in any even comical way. The *Decameron*, while more tolerant and laughter-provoking, is similarly exemplary rather than allegorical for the most part.

If the *Amorosa Visione* presented a narrator in the process of deluding himself and wandering into error, and if the *Elegia* then pursued the consequences of such passionate self-delusion, the *Corbaccio* goes even further. Its narrator pushes on far enough to see the garden of love turn into a wasteland. Thus when a guide again appears and offers a long harsh criticism of erotic blindness and folly, the narrator is ready, even eager, to agree. There is no room here for the reader to choose sides or meanings. Moreover, the very word "favellare" becomes here a term of dispraise as the language of falsehood. The narrator, who describes himself as someone devoted to literature, is urged to abandon "favellare" and to speak the truth. The *Corbaccio* is, in fact, Boccaccio's last work of fiction.

His later productions are instead almost all explanations of what fictions mean when they are read correctly. The *Genealogia* and *Esposizioni* are both works not of invention but of interpretation to help others read. So too the dictionary of names of mountains, rivers, etc., was intended as an aid to readers. All these careful explanations of how to interpret are a long way from the farfetched and unglossed allegories of the earlier writings.

The increasingly open moralizing of Boccaccio's writings, the turn toward a select audience, and the volumes of literary explication later in his life reveal a growing distrust of his readers' abilities to understand ironies and allegories more than a drastic change in his own moral and religious attitudes. Partly there was a change in the audience itself as Boccaccio moved from the court of Naples to the bourgeoisie of Florence; but no neat line can be drawn to demarcate one attitude or style from the other. Rather there seems to have been a gradual disillusionment with readers, perhaps aggravated by the move to Florence but not necessarily explained by that. The ambivalence of literature's powers of seduction seems to have become more problematic for Boccaccio. It is a theme perfectly illustrated by Paolo and Francesca, and theirs is a problem which Boccaccio is persistently anxious to avoid. For Dante, clearly, the reader remains responsible for his or her use of the text; but attacks against the immoral influences of literature were too common for Boccaccio to ignore. "Certissima cosa è che come gli ingegni degli uomini sono diversi, così esser convengono le maniere del dare la dottrina."[2] [It is most certain that as the intellects of men are diverse, so too ought to be the manner of teaching them.] If readers are naive, the sophisticated author cannot totally disclaim responsibility for their confusion. Thus the image of the reader created within the fictions must bear a close relation to the manner in which the book is written. As we have seen, allusions to Paolo and Francesca's reading scene recur throughout Boccaccio's works in an increasingly negative manner, from the innocent counterexample of Biancifiore and Florio, through the slippery condition of the *Teseida* narrator and the warning subtitle of the *Decameron*, both paired with the wise readings of Fiammetta or the honest brigata, to the purely pornographic readings of the *Corbaccio* widow.

Furthermore, we have seen that this decline accompanies a similar decline in power of the figures representing reason within Boccaccio's texts, from the royal Teseo and *Amorosa Visione* guide, through the unheeded servant in the *Elegia*, to the ghost of the dead *Corbaccio* husband, who is suffering in purgatory for his failure to be effective in life. If Boccaccio's expectations concerning the power of reason in humans was declining in this way, it is not surprising that the *Corbaccio* abandons "favellare" on behalf of explicit moralizing, nor that Boccaccio subsequently stopped writing fiction and turned to explicating it. At the end of his life, depressingly, he despaired of accomplishing even this and, having interrupted because of illness his public lectures on Dante's *Commedia*, regretted the whole undertaking. Eclogue XII discusses his abandonment of popular audiences on behalf of a more selective group of readers. His explication of pagan myths, the *Genealogia deorum*, he addressed explicitly to educated readers, and indeed wrote it in Latin to assure himself of such an audience. His disappointing experiences with readers, it seems, prepared him to follow Petrarch's humanistic exhortations to reject popular audiences and write for the fit though few.

Editions of Boccaccio's works used for this book:

Amorosa Visione, ed. Vittore Branca, *Tutte le Opere* III (Verona: Mondadori, 1974).

Boccaccio on Poetry, trans. Charles Osgood (New York: Bobbs-Merrill Company, Inc., 1956). This is a translation of the preface and Books XIV and XV of the *Genealogia deorum gentilium*.

Caccia di Diana, ed. Vittore Branca, *Tutte le Opere* I (Verona: Mondadori, 1967).

Comedia delle Ninfe Fiorentine, ed. Antonio Enzo Quaglio, *Tutte le Opere* II (Verona: Mondadori, 1964).

Corbaccio, ed. Tauno Nurmela, *Suomalainen Tiedeakatemia Toimituksia* (Helsinki) 146 (1968).

Decameron, ed. Vittore Branca, *Tutte le Opere* IV (Verona: Mondadori, 1976).

De Mulieribus Claris, ed. Vittorio Zaccaria, *Tutte le Opere* X (Verona: Mondadori, 1970).

Elegia di Madonna Fiammetta, ed. Cesare Segre in *Opere di Giovanni Boccaccio* (Milan: Mursia, 1963). For the text of the gloss, which may or may not be by Boccaccio, see the edition by Vincenzo Pernicone (Bari: Scrittori d'Italia, 1939).

Esposizioni sopra la Comedia di Dante, ed. Giorgio Padoan, *Tutte le Opere* VI (Verona: Mondadori, 1965).

Filocolo, ed. Antonio Enzo Quaglio, *Tutte le Opere* I.

Filostrato, ed. Vittore Branca, *Tutte le Opere* II.

Genealogie deorum gentilium libri, ed. Vincenzo Romano (Bari: Scrittori d'Italia, 1957).

Lettere Edite e Inedite, ed. Francesco Corazzini (Florence, 1877).

Ninfale Fiesolano, ed. Armando Balduino, *Tutte le Opere* III.

Opere Latine Minori, ed. Aldo Francesco Massèra (Bari: Scrittori d'Italia, 1928).

Rime, ed. Vittore Branca (Padua, 1958).

Teseida delle Nozze d'Emilia, ed. Alberto Limentani, *Tutte le Opere* II.

Trattatello in laude di Dante, ed. Pier Giorgio Ricci, *Tutte le Opere* III.

All translations are my own unless otherwise noted. I have used Osgood's translations of the *Genealogia* where possible (Books XIV and XV), but not for the epigraph.

NOTES

Introduction

1. Robert Hollander, *Boccaccio's Two Venuses* (New York, 1977), pp. 97–98 and indirectly throughout the book.

2. For the dates of Boccaccio's writings I am following Vittore Branca's outline; see his "Profilo biografico," in Boccaccio, *Tutte le Opere*, I.

3. Boccaccio, *Esposizioni* II.litt.83; cf. *Trattatello* I.30–32 or II.26–27.

4. Boccaccio, "De vita et moribus domini Francisci Petracchi de Florentia," *Opere Latine Minori*, p. 243.

5. Critics who treat Boccaccio's works as autobiography include: Giovanni Batista Baldelli, *Vita di Giovanni Boccaccio* (Florence, 1806). Rudolfo Renier, *La Vita Nuova e la Fiammetta* (Turin, 1879). Marcus Landau, *Giovanni Boccaccio sein Leben und seine Werke* (Stuttgart, 1877). Gustav Koerting, *Boccaccios Leben und Werke* (Leipzig, 1880). Camillo Antona-Traversi, "Della Realtà e della vera natura dell'amore di messer Giovanni Boccaccio per madonna Fiammetta," *Rivista Europea* (1883) and *Propugnatore* 17 (1884). Vincenzo Crescini, *Contributo agli studi sul Boccaccio* (Turin, 1887). Eugenio Rossi, *Dalla mente e dal cuore di Giovanni Boccaccio* (Bologna, 1900). Henri Hauvette, "Une confession de Boccace," *Bulletin italien* I (1901). Arnaldo della Torre, *La giovinezza di Giovanni Boccaccio* (Città di Castello, 1905). Ernest Hatch Wilkins, *Boccaccio Studies* (Baltimore, 1909). Edward Hutton, *Giovanni Boccaccio: A Biographical Study* (London, 1910). Aldo Francesco Massèra, "Studi boccacceschi," *Z. für rom. Phil.* 36 (1912), 192–220. Francesco Torraca, *Per la biografia di Giovanni Boccaccio* (Milan, 1912). Giuseppe Gigli, "Per l'interpretazione della *Fiammetta*," *Misc. stor. della Valdelsa* 21 (1913), 68–71. Henri Hauvette, *Boccace: Etude biographique et littéraire* (Paris, 1914). Francesco Torraca, *Giovanni Boccaccio a Napoli* (Naples, 1915). Giuseppe Lipparini, *La vita e le opere di Giovanni Boccaccio* (Florence, 1927). Nicola Bruscoli, *Giovanni Boccaccio: L'Ameto, Lettere, Il Corbaccio* (Bari, 1940). Carl Grabher, *Giovanni Boccaccio: Leben und Werke* (Hamburg, 1946). Attilio

Momigliano, *Storia della letteratura italiana* (Milan, 1958). Natalino Sapegno, *Storia letteraria d'Italia: il Trecento* (Milan, 1966). Salvatore Battaglia, ed., *Elegia di Madonna Fiammetta*, with intro. (Milan, n.d.); and *Giovanni Boccaccio e la riforma della narrativa* (Naples, 1969). Battaglia, although critical in *Giovanni Boccaccio e la riforma della narrativa* of autobiography-seekers who ignore the transformations of experience into art, nonetheless accepts the reality of Boccaccio's love for Maria d'Aquino, illegitimate daughter of King Robert.

Even recent writers who should know better still carry on the old ideas: e.g., Daniel Donno in the introduction to his translation of *The Nymph of Fiesole* (New York, 1960); Howard Schless, "Transformations: Chaucer's Use of Italian," in *Geoffrey Chaucer*, ed. Derek Brewer (London, 1974), p. 208; and Patricia Gathercole, *Tension in Boccaccio: Boccaccio and the Fine Arts* (University, Miss., 1975), esp. pp. 18 and 21.

Critics who argue for the fictionality of Fiammetta include: Girolamo Tiraboschi, *Storia della letteratura italiana* (Milan, 1822–26), vol. 5, pp. 836– 39. John Addington Symonds, *Giovanni Boccaccio as Man and Author* (London, 1895). Giuseppe Billanovich, *Restauri boccacceschi* (Rome, 1947). Vittore Branca, *Boccaccio medievale* (Florence, 1956) and "Profilo biografico." Bernhard König, *Die Begegnung im Tempel* (Hamburg, 1960). Hollander, *Boccaccio's Two Venuses*, esp. pp. 94–96. Mario Marti, "Alle origini dell' umanesimo del Boccaccio," *L'albero* 16, 47 (1971), esp. p. 4.

6. One of the questions argued about was the timing of the affair. Della Torre, for example, concluded from sonnet 86,

> Se io potessi creder che in cinqu' anni
> ch'egli è che vostro fui, tanto caluto
> di me vi fosse, che aver saputo
> il mio nome voleste,

> [If I could believe that in the five years / that I have been yours, you cared enough / about me to want to know / my name]

that Boccaccio loved Fiammetta for five years before she learned of his love; but Torraca objected because in the *Filocolo* Boccaccio wrote at her request soon after having seen her for the first time (*Per la biografia*, p. 23). Vincenzo Pernicone argued that the *Filostrato* showed Boccaccio already intimate with his lady ("Il *Filostrato* di Giovanni Boccaccio," *Studi di filologia italiana* 2 [1929], 82), opposing Crescini, who considered the work to predate such intimacy (*Contributo*, pp. 164–65).

While the timing of the affair depended on clues from various texts, at the same time the dating of the texts was partly based on the sequence of events in the affair. Thus, for example, Hortis and Torraca attributed to the *Filostrato* a date much later than is now accepted because in the preface the lover-poet has already been abandoned by his lady. (Attilio Hortis, *Studi sulle Opere Latine del Boccaccio* [Trieste, 1879], pp. 265–66; Torraca, *Giovanni Boccaccio a Napoli*, pp. 173–77; Pier Giorgio Ricci, "Per la dedica e la datazione del *Filostrato*," *Studi sul Boccaccio* 1 [1963], 347; Branca, *Boccaccio medievale*, p. 198.) The fact that the poem is not addressed to Fiammetta at all but rather to Filomena seemed irrelevant; for both men assumed—and many others as well—that whatever the fictional name, the affair described was Boccaccio's own. Thus too Crescini suggested that the *Filocolo* was finished many years after it was begun, i.e., again a date much later than now supposed; for whereas in the beginning of the work the narrator is just starting his labor of love and Fiammetta is showing her first signs of sympathy, later in the work Caleone, who loves the Fiammetta within the narrative, has already lost her favor (*Contributo*, p. 79). Moreover, Idalagos, whose autobiographical account within the fiction bears some resemblance to Boccaccio's life, has also lost his lady. The assumption again was that the fictions of various lovers all refer to Boccaccio's own story.

Another issue of debate was the exact progress of the affair: did Fiammetta become Boccaccio's lover and did she then betray him? Torraca tried to defend Fiammetta from the accusations of infidelity leveled against her by della Torre (Torraca, *Per la biografia*, pp. 70ff.; della Torre, *Giovinezza di Giovanni Boccaccio*, pp. 289–318), and Crescini noted a critical debate over whether Fiammetta ever yielded to Boccaccio or not (*Contributo*, pp. 164–65).

The real question in all these investigations was which of the many and contradictory fictions represented Boccaccio's real life and in how much detail? Crescini, reporting on the debate over Fiammetta's intimacy with Boccaccio, remarked: "O qua o là il Boccaccio deve avere mentito" (ibid., p. 164) [Either here or there Boccaccio must have lied]. Hauvette too commented: "A vouloir additioner tous les détails épars dans le *Filocolo*, l'*Ameto*, la *Fiammetta*, et l'*Amorosa Visione* sur le compte de Maria d'Aquino, on aboutirait à tisser une trame hautement fantaisiste." [If one wanted to add up all the details scattered in the *Filocolo*, the *Ameto*, the *Fiammetta*, and the *Amorosa Visione* about Maria d'Aquino, one would end up weaving a highly fantastical story.] Nonetheless he believed that the fictions do give at least some accurate information about the real affair (*Boccace*, p. 48): "il y a lieu de retenir les quelques détails essentiels . . . qui ne contiennent évidemment pas d'intentions allégoriques; telles sont par examples les données chronologiques, dont on n'apercevrait pas le sens si elles n'étaient pas rigoureusement exactes" [there is reason to hold on to some essential details . . . which evidently do not contain allegorical intentions; such for example are the chronological data, which would make no sense unless they were rigorously exact]. The realism of the dates given by Boccaccio, however, must strike one as suspect when the falling in love takes place, of all days, on Easter weekend and when, as Billanovich has pointed out, the good events all happen in spring, the misfortunes in autumn and winter (*Restauri*, p. 96). Torraca joined the criticism against accepting every detail as historical (*Per la biografia*, p. 56): "la tendenza a vedere Giovanni e Maria dovunque appariscano insieme un uomo e una donna, ricorda un po' troppo la smania di quei mitografi o mitologi, che . . . scoprivano un mito solare ogni volta che vedevano un gatto rincorrere un topo" [the tendency to see Giovanni and Maria wherever a man and a woman appear together resembles a bit too much the mania of those mythographers or mythologers who . . . used to discover a solar myth every time they saw a cat run after a mouse]. Yet he too felt that he could tell which details to trust and which not, and that the love between Boccaccio and Fiammetta was basically a true story.

7. Girolamo Tiraboschi, *Storia della letteratura italiana* 2 (Milan, 1833), 447–48. In the *Filocolo*, he noted, King Robert made love to Fiammetta's mother before his coronation; in the *Comedia delle Ninfe* afterwards. In the former book Fiammetta's mother is married after her affair with the king; in the latter she is already married before it. Finally the *Elegia* completely reverses the situation described by earlier prefaces, showing Fiammetta abandoned by her lover instead of the other way around.

8. Renier, *Vita Nuova e Fiammetta,* p. 218, simply remarks: "non è senza meraviglia che osserviamo il Tiraboschi, illuso da certe contraddizioni fittizie, e non mai tali, anche se vere, da far forza alla storia, trovare in esse *evidente argomento* per conchiudere che il Boccaccio, 'benchè forse sia vero che in Napoli s'innamorasse di una giovane di alto affare, in ciò nondimeno che ci racconta dell'oggetto e del frutto de' suoi amori, abbia favellato non da storico ma da poeta'" [it is not without astonishment that we note that Tiraboschi, deluded by certain fictitious contradictions and which, even if true, are not such as to do violence to the history, finds in them *clear evidence* for concluding that Boccaccio "although it may be true that he fell in love in Naples with a young lady of high standing, nonetheless in what he narrates about the object and fruit of his love writes fiction, not as a historian but as a poet"].

Baldelli, *Vita*, pp. 364–67, similarly denies the existence of contradictions, and reinterprets a few passages in order to circumvent the problems.

9. Hauvette, *Boccace*, p. 45. See also Hutton, *Giovanni Boccaccio*, pp. 131–32.

10. Symonds, *Giovanni Boccaccio*, p. 52.

11. Billanovich, *Restauri*, p. 85n.

12. Salvatore Battaglia, "Elementi autobiografici nell'arte del Boccaccio," *La cultura* 9 (1930), 241–54.

13. Vittore Branca, "Tradizione letteraria e cultura medievale nell' autobiografia romanzesca del Boccaccio," *Formen der Selbstdarstellung: Festgabe für Fritz Neubert* (Berlin, 1956), p. 13; Ricci, "Per la dedica."

14. Branca, *Neubert,* p. 21; Mario Serafini, "Le tragedie di Seneca nella Fiammetta di Giovanni Boccaccio," *Giornale storico della letteratura italiana* 126 (1948), 95–105.

15. Branca, "Profilo biografico," p. 27.

16. König, *Begegnung.*

17. Giovanni Boccaccio, *Fiammetta*, with intro. and commentary by Giovanni Parazzoli (Milan, 1944), is a collection of such excerpts.

18. Guido Almansi, *The Writer as Liar: Narrative Technique in the Decameron* (Boston, 1975), p. 16.

19. Aldo Scaglione, *Nature and Love in the Late Middle Ages* (Berkeley, 1963), pp. 45 and 67 especially.

20. Robert Kilburn Root, *The Book of Troilus and Criseyde* (Princeton, 1926), p. xlix.

21. Sanford Meech, *Design in Chaucer's Troilus* (Syracuse, 1959), pp. viii, 4–6, 368, 431.

22. Paul Ruggiers, *Companion to Chaucer*, ed. Beryl Rowland (New York, 1968), p. 152.

23. Hollander, *Boccaccio's Two Venuses*, is the notable exception among critics in this regard.

I. Before Fiammetta

1. Branca, "Profilo biografico," p. 41.

2. See Ernst Robert Curtius, *European Literature and the Latin Middle Ages,* trans. Willard R. Trask (New York, 1963), p. 505, on uses in literature of the number thirty-three. For the notion of Beatrice as a representative of Christ, see Charles Singleton, *An Essay on the Vita Nuova* (Cambridge, Mass., 1949).

3. Victoria Kirkham, "Numerology and Allegory in Boccaccio's *Caccia di Diana,*" *Traditio* 34 (1978), 303–29; Hollander, *Boccaccio's Two Venuses*, pp. 16–20.

4. See Hollander, *Boccaccio's Two Venuses*, p. 38, and *Filocolo* IV.134.2.

5. In conversation with Victoria Kirkham.

6. The nymphs of the *Comedia delle Ninfe* hunt like nymphs of Diana, but their worship of Venus in the end is not seen as a break from their former activities. As Venus in this case represents God, her worship does not require a revolt against Diana's injunction to sacrifice to Giove. On the other hand, it is possible that in the *Caccia* Diana means her injunction as an exhortation to monastic celibacy, an extreme then rejected by Boccaccio.

7. See Branca's notes to the *Caccia* and also his "Nuove note sulla *Caccia di Diana,*" in *Tradizione delle opere del Boccaccio* (Rome, 1958), pp. 145–98.

8. Yet do not the literal tales told by the nymphs in the *Comedia delle Ninfe* similarly insult the families to which these "nymphs" belong?

9. Branca's notes to the *Caccia*, p. 691, n. 6; see, for example, Boccaccio's own *Amorosa Visione* XXXIX.19.

10. Branca's introduction to the *Caccia*, pp. 10–11.

11. Billanovich, *Restauri*, pp. 87–88.

12. By "parody" I do not mean to suggest only a negative, mocking, or critical imitation, but rather any composition consciously based on a previous one while diverging from it for its own purposes. Thus hymns have been written as parodies of popular songs. Boccaccio's parodying of Dante's writings in no way contradicts his admiration for Dante, nor is the divergence necessarily a way of saying that Dante was wrong in certain ways. It may reflect simply the need for Boccaccio to do something different enough to be his own.

13. Ricci, "Per la dedica," p. 347; Branca's introduction to the *Caccia*, pp. 3–5.

14. Cf. *Filocolo* III.28.5: "i dolci canti della dolente Filomena." Branca suggests that "Filomena" is a past participle meaning "beloved" (notes to *Filostrato*, p. 846). Adolfo Albertazzi, "I novellatori e le novellatrici del *Decameron*," in *Parvenze e sembianze* (Bologna, 1892), p. 174n., with reference to the Filomena of the *Decameron*, interprets the name "lover of song," making the word a compound like "Filostrato." Both these suggestions seem to me outweighed by the obvious classical allusion.

15. Ricci assigns the work an early date *because* it addresses a woman other than Fiammetta-Maria.

16. Branca, introduction to *Filostrato* p. 3: "nel *Filostrato* non appare affatto—né direttamente né indirettamente, né sotto proprio nome né attraverso emblema o *senhal*—la figura di Fiammetta" [in the *Filostrato* there does not appear at all—neither directly nor indirectly, neither under her own name nor through an emblem or *senhal*—the figure of Fiammetta]. Baldelli, Corazzini, Landau, Koerting, Hutton, Hauvette, Crescini, della Torre, Torraca, and Pernicone all assumed that the dedication was to Fiammetta; Francesco Corazzini, ed., *Le Lettere Edite e Inedite di Messer Giovanni Boccaccio* (Florence, 1877). Even Donno in the introduction to his translation of the *Nymph of Fiesole* (1960) still assumes it. See Ricci, "Per la dedica."

17. Andreas Capellanus, *The Art of Courtly Love*, trans. John Jay Parry (New York, 1957), Bk. I, chap. 1. Branca points out in his notes that Troiolo's behavior as a lover also follows Capellanus's "rules": he does not eat or sleep, he pales in his lady's presence, etc.

18. See *Filocolo* IV.46; also Janet Smarr, "Boccaccio and the Choice of Hercules," *MLN* 92 (1977), 146–52.

19. Henry Ansgar Kelly in *Love and Marriage in the Age of Chaucer* (Ithaca, 1975), pp. 50 and 51, confesses: "When discussing the first-person narratives of these [Chaucer and Boccaccio] and other authors, I have found it cumbersome and not very helpful to distinguish between the author and an assumed persona." This failure to distinguish vitiates his reading of the works, and leads him to such statements as: "The fact that extramarital love is defended in the *Filostrato* . . ." For a better understanding of the problem, see L. Spitzer, "Note on the Poetic and Empirical 'I' in Medieval Authors," *Traditio* 4 (1946), 414–22.

20. This text was later copied and edited by Philip de Vitry, Petrarch's friend. The allegorization by Chrétien Legouais de Saint More is printed as appendix III to *Philomena*, ed. C. de Boer (Paris, 1909). Boccaccio's *Genealogia* (IX.8, and XII.74–75) does not follow this interpretation but rather one offered by Barlaam.

21. In the "Phylostropos," Boccaccio's Eclogue XV (with a title sounding reminiscent of the *Filostrato*), the wise Phylostropos reproaches Typhlus ("blind") for running after girls named Crisis (Crisidis, gen.) and Dyones. In this case, where Dyones clearly refers to Venerian lusts, Crisis is a reference to money (cf. Eclogue XIII, "Laurea"), but this object of love seems hardly applicable to Troiolo. See B. Zumbini, "Le ecloghe del Boccaccio," *Giornale storico della letteratura italiana* 7 (1886) 142. Nevertheless, Crisis is an object of the kind of fortune-dominated love which Typhlus is urged to renounce. In any case, this much later allusion to the name is critical and not sympathetic; the speaker who loves her is named for his mental blindness. "Typhlus pro me ipso intelligi volo et pro quocunque alio caligine rerum mortalium offuscato, cum 'typhlus' grece, latine dicatur 'orbus.'" (Letter to Fra Martino da Signa) [Typhlus I mean to be understood as myself and or as whoever else is blinded by the darkness of mortal things, since "typhlus" in Greek is called in Latin "orbus" ("blind").]

22. Most of the parallels are pointed out in Branca's notes; a few, marked with an asterisk in n. 29, are my own observation. All quotations from Dante's *Commedia* come from the edition by Charles Hall Grandgent and Charles Singleton (Cambridge, Mass., 1972).

23. Cf. Beatrice's connection to Mary in *Vita Nuova* 28: "lo segnoro de la

giustizia chiamoe questa gentilissima a gloriare sotto la insegna di quella regina benedetta virgo Maria, lo cui nome fu in grandissima reverenzia ne le parole di questa Beatrice beata" [the lord of justice called this most gentle lady to triumph under the sign of that blessed virgin queen Maria, whose name was in great reverence in the words of this blessed Beatrice].

24. See also Hollander, *Boccaccio's Two Venuses*, pp. 175–76.

25. Cf. Propertius, *Elegies* II.1.

26. Peter Dronke, "L'Amor che move il sole e l'altre stelle," *Studi medievali* ser. 3, 6 (1965), 417. For further argument against Dronke's interpretation of this prayer, see Hollander, *Boccaccio's Two Venuses*, p. 178. See also Branca's *Filostrato*, n. 61, p. 856.

27. Dante's eagle, furthermore, is associated with the Roman world government, during which Christ's incarnation took place. Troiolo, however, is compared not to an eagle but a falcon in a passage immediately following the account of his hunting with eagles and falcons. This kind of hunting was traditionally linked to amorous pursuits, and the line following the comparison emphasizes the connection: "Era d'amor tutto il suo ragionare." [All his talk was of love.] In sum, we have here one more example of Boccaccio's purposeful divergence from meanings of divine justice and Christian faith to amatory meanings and from the Christian heaven to an erotic one.

28. Cf. Chaucer's addition of Troilus's ascent to heaven and new perspective upon his former life's desires.

29. I am indebted to Hollander for suggesting that the *Caccia* also uses this same pattern. The references in the *Caccia* and *Filostrato* are as follows:

Caccia di Diana

I.53–55 cf.	*Vita Nuova* XLII
II.17	*Purg.* XIX.1
IV.12	*Purg.* XXVII.96
IV.18–21	*Purg.* IX.19
VIII.10	*Inf.* IV.118.
VIII.31–32	*Purg.* VIII.103–8
IX.1	*Purg.* XXIII.1–2 (and cf. 3–6 for contrasting contexts)
X.19	*Purg.* XX.147
XIII.42	*Inf.* XII.76
XVII.3	*Purg.* XXXI.65 or *Par.* X.80
XVII.57	*Purg.* XXVIII.40–41
XVIII.29–30	*Vita Nuova* XLX
XVIII.52	*Vita Nuova* XLII

Filostrato

* Proemio.25	cf. *Vita Nuova* XXXI
" .12–13	" " XXVIII or XXX
I.2	*Inf.* XV.55–56
II.64,137	*Inf.* II.103,106–7
II.80	*Inf.* II.127-

II.135	*Purg.* III.78
III.1	*Par.* I.13-
* III.2	*Par.* I.28
* III.74	*Par.* XXXIII.124
* III.87	*Inf.* V.23–24
* III.91	*Par.* XIX.34-
IV.27	*Inf.* XII.22-
VII.69	*Par.* XV.35–6 and XVIII.16–21
VIII.17ff.	*Purg.* VI.118–120
IX.8	*Vita Nuova* XII

30. Branca in his notes includes also one reference from XVII.29 to either *Inferno* XXVI.38–39, or *Vita Nuova* 23; but the connection is merely one word, not a definitely allusive phrase.

II. *Filocolo*

1. Indeed, Vergil himself even moved from Rome to Naples, which Boccaccio refers to in the "Mavortis miles" letter as "virgiliana . . . Neapolis."

2. Cf. the surprising transformation of the narrator at the end of the *Caccia*.

3. See Charles Singleton's commentary on *Paradiso* XXVII.82–83, "il varco folle d'Ulisse" (Princeton, 1975).

4. The exhortation to "seguir virtute e canoscenza" recurs in the advice of Florio's dying father toward the end of the book (V.92): follow the virtues, flee the vices, and "sempre davanti agli occhi porta la tua fine" [always carry your end before your eyes]; thus one will learn from mortality to beware of avarice and the gifts of fortune and to love God, justice, and charity. In short, Boccaccio seems to be using the phrase *in bono* without the negative connotations of its original context. However, the Ulysses reference may imply also a warning about the powers of rhetoric to persuade us to our harm and thus an admonition to the reader to think carefully about what the book is actually counseling. Cf. the discussion below on Idalagos.

5. The sea of Ulysses' journey comes to represent the deceitful allures of the world. Thus Dante writes: "tratto m'hanno del mar d'amor torto, / e del diritto m'han posto alla riva" (*Par.* XXVI.62–63) [they have drawn me from the sea of crooked love and set me on the shore of straight love], and Beatrice exclaims:

O cupidigia, che i mortali affonde
sì sotto te, che nessuno ha potere
di trarre gli occhi fuor delle tue onde! (*Par.* XXVII.121–23)

[O cupidity, who so drowns mortals beneath you that no one has the power of drawing his eyes out from under your waves.]

The presence of the siren, who claims (*Purg.* XIX.19–23) to have successfully turned Ulysses from his way, adds to this understanding of the sea as "mar dell'amor torto." (See Singleton's commentary on *Par.* XXVI.62–63; and Robert

Hollander, *Allegory in Dante's Commedia* [Princeton, 1969], chap. 4) The *Commentum quod dicitur Bernardi Silvestris super sex libros Eneidos Virgilii*, ed. Julian Ward Jones and Elizabeth Frances Jones (Lincoln, Nebr., 1977), similarly glosses the sea as "mundi vel carnis" [world or flesh] or "libidini carnis et commotioni temporalium" (pp. 49 and 32) [the lust of the flesh and the agitation of worldly things]. Boccaccio uses the image more specifically as the realm of erotic ventures.

6. "[L]e vie son molte, ma tra tutte non è che una che a porto di salute ne meni, e quella è esso Idio, il quale di sé dice nell'Evangelio: 'Ego sum via, veritas et vita.'" [The ways are many, but among them all there is only one which leads to the port of salvation, and that one is God, who says about himself in the Evangel: "I am the way, the truth and the life."] Boccaccio, *Esposizioni, Inf.* I.alleg.47.

7. And the "ardito gusto" of the "prima madre" is in turn an echo of the naming of Fiammetta-Maria in I.1. Cf. also I.3.2: Pluto, i.e., Satan, is relegated to "etterno essilio" in hell.

8. The latter occurrence is in part a correction to the former; for the first refers to Caiaphas and the rest of the council that suggested killing Christ, "del concilio / che fu per li Giudei mala sementa" (122–23). The second time "concilio" and "Virgilio" are rhyme words as before, but here the reference is to the blessed council of heaven:

. . . Nel beato concilio
ti ponga in pace la verace corte,
che mi rilega nell'eterno esilio.

[In the blessed council in peace may the true court set you, which binds me in eternal exile.]

Vergil, sadly conscious of his own eternal exile from heaven, acknowledges here the possibility of salvation for others. Both Statius and Caiaphas appear in the image of Christ: Caiaphas lies crucified in hell, whereas Statius is compared to the resurrected Christ who appeared to two disciples on the road. The change is from death to new life, both Christ's and ours.

9. The narrator first sees Fiammetta in the church of San Lorenzo (I.1). The life of this saint in the *Legenda Aurea* includes a long discussion of the laurel: "Haec autem arbor est victoriae . . . Beatus igitur Laurentius dicitur a lauro, quia victoriam obtinuit in sui passione." [Moreover this is the tree of victory . . . therefore the blessed Laurence has his name from the laurel, because he obtained victory in his passion.] Boccaccio did use the *Legenda Aurea* for other parts of the *Filocolo*. And see below, n. 35.

10. Meiss notes the emphasis on humility as a chief quality of Mary in the works of fourteenth-century poets, such as Petrarch and Jacopone da Todi. The word for "earth" in Latin is *humus*, whence the significance of her pose, seated on the ground. A follower of Simone Martini painted a Madonna of Humility for the tomb of Giovanna Aquinas in Naples. Meiss suggests that Simone Martini painted a Madonna of Humility during his stay in Naples in the early fourteenth century, and that his painting became the model for a number of imitations. Millard Meiss, *Painting in Florence and Siena after the Black Death* (New York, 1964),

pp. 132ff., 140, 152; and "The Madonna of Humility," *Art Bulletin* 18, no. 4 (1936), 435–64.

11. The centrality of Caleone's position is further emphasized by the symmetrical seating arrangement of the male and female members of the group.

12. "[E]ssendo già Titan ricevuto nelle braccia di Castore e di Polluce" (IV.12); cf. the Pentecost birthday of Florio and Biancifiore "essendo Febo nelle braccia di Castore e di Polluce insieme" (I.39). Fiammetta is also related to Biancifiore through the reference to Tulio, who, though born of a servant, was raised by the queen as her own son and ultimately crowned. Again the story of the lovers is linked implicitly to the story of Christ, another person of lowly birth who became king. On the sources of this episode in Boccaccio, see Quaglio's notes to *Filocolo*, pp. 794–95.

13. Cf. also *Convivio* III.viii.16: Dante, explicating his own poem, writes: "E però dice che la biltade di quella *piove fiammelle di foco*, cioè ardore d'amore e di caritate; *animate d'un spirito gentile*, cioè diritto appetito, per lo quale e del quale nasce origine di buono pensiero." (The emphases are Dante's and refer to lines from the canzone.) Notice in our context that the "gentile" quality of the lady may refer not only to her being the daughter of a "prencipe" but also to her being properly turned toward the correct object of desire, that is, toward the divine.

14. Aristotle, *Ethics* VIII.2–4.

15. Bernard Silvester, *Commentum super sex libros Eneidos*. Alain de Lille also describes two Venuses, one of cosmic harmony and reproduction within marriage, the other of illicit lust, in his *De planctu Naturae*, especially meter l and prose 4.

16. The phenomenon of the lover chasing away reason had been illustrated perfectly in the *Roman de la Rose*.

17. The wise nurse in Book I of the *Elegia di Madonna Fiammetta* says very similar things. And cf., of course, the definition of love by Andreas Capellanus.

18. Hollander, *Boccaccio's Two Venuses*, p. 156, suggests that Boccaccio may be confused in his reference to Vergil.

19. Bernard's *Commentum super sex libros Eneidos* p. 16, glosses "Huius civitatis [Troy] incendium est prime etatis fervor naturalis."

20. Hollander, *Boccaccio's Two Venuses*, pp. 37–38, 156, discusses the marriage ceremony and corrects Nicolas Perella's neglect of this important event in "The World of Boccaccio's *Filocolo*," *PMLA* 76 (1961), 330–39.

21. See Vincenzo Crescini, *Il cantare di Florio e Biancifiore*, 2 vols. (Bologna, 1889 and 1899). *Flore et Blanchefleur*, trans. into modern French and edited by H. Williams and M. Guillet-Rydell (University, Miss., 1973).

22. The incident with the poisoned peacock may be an allusion to the king's distaste for their marriage, as the peacock is Juno's bird.

23. *The Hours of the Divine Office in English and Latin*, a bilingual ed. of the Roman Breviary text (Collegeville, Minn., 1964), vol. 2, p. 1391.

24. Perhaps Boccaccio associated Biancifiore's name with the white rose of Dante's paradise? Cf. the identification of Florio's loss of Biancifiore with the "eternal exile" caused by the Fall.

25. Petrarch decided to write the *Africa* in 1338, according to Ernest Hatch Wilkins, *The Making of the Canzoniere* (Rome, 1951), p. 31.

26. Georg Rabuse, "Dantes Jenseitsvision und das Somnium Scipionis," in *Dante Alighieri: Aufsätze zur Divina Commedia*, ed. Hugo Friedrich, Wege der Forschung 159 (Darmstadt, 1968), p. 506.

27. Curiously there is no reference to her illegitimacy in Book IV. König, *Begegnung*, proposes that this fiction was a device allowing Boccaccio to follow the topos of writing at the request of a higher authority (p. 59) by addressing a lady of the highest nobility while concealing her identity through the story of illegitimacy lest readers discover too quickly her nonexistence (p. 28). It is a trick, then, on the part of Boccaccio to set up a screen name for her, because the real name is also a fiction.

28. Cf. the naming of the other quasi-celestial Fiammetta-Maria in IV.16.

29. Ernest Hatch Wilkins, "The Enamorment of Boccaccio," *Studies on Petrarch and Boccaccio*, ed. Aldo S. Bernardo, Studi sul Petrarca 6 (Padua, 1978), p. 322, suggests that Boccaccio "may well have learned" of Petrarch's Good Friday enamorment in church from poem 3 of the present *Canzoniere*.

30. Sources of information on the celebration of this holiday include: *Breviarium ad usum isignis ecclesiae Sarum*, iuxta editionem maxima Paris 1531 (Cambridge, 1882), vol. l, dccxcviii and ff. *Corpus Ambrosiano Liturgicum: Das Sacramentarium Triplex*, ed. Odilo Heiming (Aschendorff, 1968). Adrian Fortescue and J. B. O'Connell, *The Ceremonies of the Roman Rite Described*, new ed. (Westminister, Md., 1958). P. Henry, *The Liturgical Year* (Milwaukee, 1940), pp. 101–18.

31. Honorius of Autun in his *Speculum Ecclesiae*, PL 172.964, writes: "Hebraeus quoque populus de Aegyptica servitute in paschali nocte per paschalem agnum liberatus ac per mare Rubrum translatus, ad montem Synai quinquagesimae die pervenit, quem fumus et ignis replevit, atque de medio ignis Dominus ei legem timoris in tabulis scriptam dedit: sic Christianus populus, de diabolica oppressione in paschali nocte et per paschalem agnum Christum ereptus, per baptismum quasi per mare Rubrum transvectus, quinquagesimo die, scilicet hodie, *igne legem amoris accepit*, quam eum in corde Dominus scribere praecepit, ut videlicet post facerent sponte Dei amore quod prius fecerant coacti timore." (my emphasis) [The Hebrew people, freed from Egyptian slavery on Easter night by the Easter lamb and brought through the Red Sea, came on the fiftieth day to Mount Sinai, which smoke and fire filled, and from the middle of the fire God gave them the law of fear written on tablets; thus the Christian people, snatched away from the devil's oppression on Easter night by the Easter lamb Christ, brought through baptism as if through the Red Sea, on the fiftieth day, that is today, *received in fire the law of love*, which God instructed them to write in their hearts, that afterwards they might do freely for the love of God what previously they had done coerced by fear.]

32. *Il Saltero della B. V. Maria*, compilato da San Bonaventura, Scelta di curiosità letteraria 126 (Bologna, 1872).

33. Branca, "Profilo biografico," p. 17.

34. Antonio Casetti, "Il Boccaccio a Napoli," *Nuova antologia* 28 (1875), 569–70.

35. Torraca, *Giovanni Boccaccio a Napoli*, p. 102n.: "Molto probabile mi pare che da Paolo egli avesse avuto la *Legenda Aurea* di I. da Varaggio, della quale, per il discorso del prete Ilario, tolse i segni maravigliosi, che annunziarono al mondo la nascita di Cristo." [It seems very probable to me that from Paolo he had obtained

the *Legenda Aurea* of I. da Varaggio, from which he took, for the discourse of the priest Ilario, the marvelous signs that announced to the world the birth of Christ.] And see Quaglio's notes to V.54.

36. "Quinque ignes exteriores quodammodo habuit, quos tamen superavit fortiter et exstinxit. Primus fuit ignis Gehennae, secundus ignis materialis flammae, tertius carnalis concupiscentiae, quartus ardentis avaritiae, quintus furentis insaniae . . . et tres ignes in corde portavit, per quos omnem ignem exteriorem et refrigerio mitigavit et majori ardoris incendio superavit. Primum namque refrigerium fuit desiderium regni coelestis, secundum meditatio divinae legis, tertium puritas conscientiae. [Five external fires he had in a certain way, which yet he overcame bravely and extinguished. First was the fire of Hell, second the fire of material flame, third of carnal concupiscence, fourth of burning avarice, fifth of raging madness . . . and three fires he carried in his heart, by means of which he assuaged with coolness every external fire and overcame it with the heat of greater ardor. For the first refreshment was the desire for the kingdom of heaven, the second was meditation on the divine law, the third was purity of conscience.]

Similarly, Alain de Lille in his *Distinctiones*, PL 210.793, glosses "Flamma" as the gift of the Holy Spirit, the heat of carnal desire, and the burning of charity.

37. Enrico Burich, "Boccaccio und Dante" in *Deutsches Dante-jahrbuch* 23 (1941), 38, maintains that despite Boccaccio's endeavors to connect his own expressions of love to Dante's in the *Vita Nuova*, Boccaccio's love is purely earthly and sensual and thus the parallel between Beatrice and the faithless Fiammetta "hat kein fundamentum in re." Elisabetta Cavallari, *La Fortuna di Dante nel Trecento* (Florence, 1921), p. 415, had previously said the same thing: the *Filocolo* imitates the *Vita Nuova* only to result in "il contrasto che nasce dall'accordo cercato ma non trovato fra sentimenti così diversi" [the contrast which arises from an accord sought but not found between sentiments so diverse].

38. Cf., for example, Venus's torch in the *Roman de la Rose*.

39. See Ernst Guldan, *Eva und Maria: Eine Antithese als Bildmotiv* (Cologne, 1966), pp. 103–4, about images of Mary with the moon beneath her feet; interpreted as Mary's dominion over fortune or the mutable world, they nonetheless allowed the use of Diana images as a model. Diana's chastity of course reinforced the connection. In his *Ovidius moralizatus* cap. 1: "De formis figurisque deorum," Petrus Berchorius identifies Diana *in bono* with the Virgin Mary and her nymphs with other holy virgins. Jean Seznec, *The Survival of the Pagan Gods* (Princeton, 1972), p. 266, notes a Renaissance cult of Diana as a representative of the Virgin Mary. Guldan comments also on the association of Venus with Eve as seductive temptresses.

40. Vittore Branca, "Giovanni Boccaccio, rinnovatore dei generi letterari," in *Atti del Convegno di Nimega sul Boccaccio*, 28–30 ottobre 1975, Istituto di lingua e di letteratura italiana dell'Università Cattolica di Nimega, ed. Carlo Ballerini (Bologna, 1976), p. 18, suggests that Boccaccio's address to lovers and women is a polemic stance "a favore del romanzo e del suo pubblico caratteristico" [in favor of the romance and its typical public]; Boccaccio is mediating between literary and extra-literary or popular traditions (pp. 24–25), writing literature for a new, expanded audience.

41. He is, in fact, repeating the wisdom of Fiammetta's remarks on love in IV.46.

42. E.g., Bernard Silvester's commentary on the *Aeneid* III includes a long comparison of the city to the human body and soul. The government palace is the head "in quo sapientia sedem habet."

43. Cf. *Teseida* XII.34.

44. See *Filocolo* IV.13.2 and Billanovich, *Restauri*, p. 91.

45. See Rosario Ferreri, "Ovidio e le Rime di Giovanni Boccaccio," *Forum italicum* 8 (1974), 46–55; V. Ussani "Alcune imitazioni ovidiane del Boccaccio," *Maia* 1 (1948), 284–306.

46. See Antonio Enzo Quaglio, "Parole del Boccaccio," *Lingua nostra* 20 (1959), 37–38.

47. Boccaccio does not worry about the chronological difficulties of having Caleone found in V.48–49 the town in which, forty chapters earlier, Idalagos says his father was born.

48. See especially Crescini, *Contributo*, pp. 44–70.

49. Actually there is an Airam apart from the Alleiram whom Idalagos loves; in this episode, the figure of the proud and cruel beloved lady is fragmented into four such women.

50. Crescini, *Contributo*, p. 16.

51. Cf. Ameto's life in the forest at the beginning of the *Comedia delle Ninfe*.

52. William Allan Neilson, *The Origins and Sources of the Court of Love* (New York, 1967), p. 36.

53. See Quaglio's notes to V.6, on the phrases borrowed from Dante.

54. Cf. *Corbaccio*, p. 88; the muses teach "le cagioni de'variamenti de' tempi e delle fatiche del sole e di quelle della luna," etc.; or *Gen*. XIV.4 (p. 25, trans. Osgood): "the poets have chosen a science or pursuit of knowledge which by constant meditation draws them away into the region of stars, among the divinely adorned dwellings of the gods and their heavenly splendors." The *Esposizioni* contrast modern frivolous songs to those of the bard in the *Aeneid* who sang of "altissime materie . . . gli errori del sole e della luna, e la prima generazione degli uomini" (I.litt.114). Besides the *Aeneid*, Boccaccio undoubtedly drew from the *Georgics* II.475ff. in which poetry is described as teaching "caelique vias et sidera . . . / defectus solis varios lunaeque labores; / unde tremor terris," etc. Antonio Enzo Quaglio, *Scienza e Mito nel Boccaccio* (Padua, 1967), pp. 59–80, has persuasively identified Calmeta as Andalo da Negro, Boccaccio's real astronomy and astrology teacher. What interests me here, however, is the way in which Boccaccio is using this character within his fiction.

55. *Filocolo*, p. 925, n. 101.

56. Victoria Kirkham, "Reckoning with Boccaccio's *Questioni d'amore*," *MLN* 89 (1974), 47–59.

57. "Caleone è il Boccaccio," Giosue Carducci, *Petrarca e Boccaccio*, Edizione Nazionale delle Opere 11 (Bologna, 1962), p. 319. "Caleone, cioè il Boccaccio stesso . . ." Luigi Russo, *Letture critiche del Decameron* (Bari, 1967), p. 23 ["Caleone is Boccaccio," "Caleone, that is Boccaccio himself"].

58. Cf. the envoy of Statius's *Thebaid* 12.816–17: "nec tu divinam Aeneida

tempta, / sed longe sequere et vestigia semper adora" [nor attempt the divine *Aeneid* but follow it at a distance and always adore its footsteps] and of Alain de Lille's *Anticlaudianus* IX.412–14: "nec antiques temptes sequare poetas, / Sed pocius veterum vestigia semper adorans / Subsequere" [and do not try to equal the ancient poets, but rather follow the steps of the ancients always with adoration].

59. In the final chapter or envoy to the book, the narrator does appear much more erotic and much less religious than in the beginning, as he fantasizes hopefully that his lady will hold his volume and maybe even kiss it. But this new emphasis is made possible by the introduction of Ilario into the picture. The role of narrator is now split into two, the lover and religious writer separated into two distinct characters. In this way the double aspect of the text (love romance and religious history) and all the other polarities (Priapus and Astrea, Eve and Mary, etc.) find their final reflection in the two narrators, whose roles match the acknowledged double model of Ovid and Dante.

60. Hollander, *Boccaccio's Two Venuses*, p. 116, remarks wisely on the combination of "identification and distance" characterizing Boccaccio's sense of Ovid. In a different vein, Angelo Monteverdi ("Un libro d'Ovidio e un passo del *Filocolo*," in *Studia philologica et letteraria in honorem L. Spitzer* [Bern, 1958]), takes literally and without irony Boccaccio's use of "santi versi" and "santo libro" for Ovid's *Ars amatoria*. Boccaccio, he claims, "sa quale è su quel libro l'opinione dei ben pensanti, e vi oppone, quasi a sfida, la sua. Crede nella santità della vita (della vita di questa terra); e perciò nella santità dell'amore (di tutto l'amore, che è anche, e non può non essere, anche, senso). E se trova un poeta che ne sia fatto aperto esaltatore, quale Ovidio, ripara sotto la sua autorità" (p. 339) [he knows what the opinion of the thoughtful is about that book, and he opposes, almost as a defiance, his own. He believes in the sanctity of life (the life of this earth); and therefore in the sanctity of love (of all love, which includes, and cannot exclude, the sensual). And if he finds a poet who has made himself the open exalter of it, such as Ovid, he takes shelter under his authority]. Monteverdi ignores the issue of married versus unmarried love and also the place of the Ovid-Scripture pair within the set of polarities established by the book.

61. Augustine, *Confessions*, trans. R. S. Pine-Coffin (London, 1970), I.13: "I was obliged to memorize the wanderings of a hero named Aeneas, while in the meantime I failed to remember my own erratic ways. I learned to lament the death of Dido, who killed herself for love, while all the time, in the midst of these things, I was dying, separated from you, my God and my Life, and I shed no tears for my own plight." I.15: "you . . . forgave me the sins that I committed by taking pleasure in such worthless things. It is true that these studies taught me many useful words, but the same words can be learnt by studying something that matters, and this is the safe course for a boy to follow."

62 Salvatore Battaglia, *Mitografia del personaggio* (Milan, 1968), pp. 513–17. Also excerpted in *Questioni di Critica Dantesca*, ed. Giorgio Petrocchi and Pompeo Giannantonio (Naples, 1962), pp. 280–84.

63. Of course Dante too uses Ovid within a Christian scheme; but Vergil is much more central for Dante, and Ovid for Boccaccio.

64. See the discussion on the narrator's position vis-à-vis his audience in Dennis Howard Green, *Irony in the Medieval Romance* (Cambridge, 1979), pp. 359–64.

III. *Teseida*

1. See Victoria Kirkham, "Chiuso parlare in Boccaccio's *Teseida*," in *Dante, Petrarch, Boccaccio. Studies in the Italian Trecento in Honor of Charles Singleton* (Binghamton, N.Y., 1983), 305–52; Janet Smarr, "Boccaccio and the Stars: Astrology in the *Teseida*," *Traditio* 35 (1979), 303–32.

2. See Hollander, *Boccaccio's Two Venuses*, pp. 101–2.

3. Cf. the discussion on whether men should love women of higher or lower rank, *Filocolo* IV.47–50.

4. *Rhetorica ad Herennium* II.31.50; Cicero, *De inventione* I.iv.106.

5. It echoes also, of course, the beginning of Aeneas's narration to Dido about the fall of Troy; however, as the *Teseida* narrator is recalling the story of his own love, he more closely resembles Francesca than Aeneas.

6. Billanovich, *Restauri*, pp. 81–82: the indications about Maria are "contrastanti frammenti di complesse e lontane situazioni romanzesche, quasi tutte retoriche eredità di strascicate tradizioni e spesso coll'anemia di un congenito scolasticismo" [contradictory fragments of complex and faraway romance situations, almost all rhetorical inheritances from drawn-out traditions and often with the anemia of a congenital scholasticism]. Cf. pp. 49–78.

7. G. Padoan, "Il mito di Teseo e il cristianesimo di Stazio," *Lettere italiane* 11 (1959), 439.

8. Bernard Silvester, *Commentum super sex libros Eneidos*, pp. 56 and 88.

9. For example, Filomena's comment in I.intro.74; Elissa's soon after, 76; Emilia's introductory remark to IX.9.3–5. When one realizes that marriages in fourteenth-century Florence were frequently between a man in his late twenties or older and a girl in the beginning of her teens, this view of the relationship appears somewhat more justified than modern readers might at first appreciate.

10. Similarly Boccaccio followed Bernard Silvester in interpreting Euridice as natural concupiscence and Orpheus as an eloquent man of wisdom (*Gen.* V.12; Bernard's *Commentum super sex libros Eneidos*, p. 54).

11. See below, Chap. VII.

12. Guido di Pino, "Lettura del *Teseida*," *Italianistica: Rivista di letteratura italiana* 8 (1979), 27, recognizes the Amazons' return to femininity as the recovery of natural order; however, ignoring allegorical possibilities in this, he sees little connection between the first book and the subsequent tale.

13. Alberto Limentani suggests that the phrases applied to Creon echo Dante's description of Farinata; see his notes to *Teseida* II.63 and his introduction, p. 238.

14. Thebes is commonly the locus of discord: its first citizens were the fratricidal warriors sprung from the teeth of a dragon sacred to Mars; Atreus and Thyestes, Polynices and Etiocles continued the tradition of fraternal conflict. In the *Anticlaudianus* II.212–21, it is the first example of discord; in Boccaccio's *Esposizioni* VII.

alleg.123, the two pairs of Theban brothers are examples of irrational anger which destroys both self and kin. The *Filocolo* II.32 links the destructive pride of Thebes with the fall of Troy, I think as representations of the irascible and concupiscible passions.

15. See Robert Hollander, "The Validity of Boccaccio's Self-Exegesis in His *Teseida*," *Medievalia et Humanistica* n.s. 8 (1977) 163–83, on the importance of these glosses.

16. Boethius, *Philosophiae consolatio*, ed. R del Re (Rome, 1968), IV.pr.3; *The Consolation of Philosophy*, trans. by Richard Green, Library of Liberal Arts (New York, 1962). Bernard's *Commentum super sex libros Eneidos* (p. 34–35) also cites this passage. Cf. also Boccaccio's *Esposizioni* I.alleg.106–7: "e qual porco crederem noi che uccidesse Adone, altro che il soperchio coito con Venere?" [and what boar should we think killed Adonis other than excessive coitus with Venus]

17. E.g., *Anticlaudianus* IV and V, where Reason is charioteer and the five senses are his horses.

18. Bernard Silvester, *Commentum super sex libros Eneidos*, p. 51.

19. For similar locations of the passions within the architecture of the body, cf. Petrarch, *Seniles* IV.5 on the cave of the winds in the *Aeneid*: "E che altro son esse le cupe grotte, entro le quali i venti si rintanano, se non le ascose e le recondite cavità de' nostri petti ove, secondo la dottrina platonica, han loro albergo le passioni? La mole sovraimposta indica il capo, che Platone stesso assegnò come sede alla ragione." *Lettere senili di Francesco Petrarca*, trans. G. Fracassetti (Florence, 1869), vol. 1, p. 244. [And what else are the dark grottos within which the winds have their lair, than the hidden and enclosed cavities of our chests where, according to Platonic doctrine, the passions are lodged? The heap placed over them indicates the head, which Plato himself assigned as the seat of reason.] Here again an epic is being read as moral allegory about the passions and reason.

20. See Hollander's discussion of the temples and glosses in *Boccaccio's Two Venuses*, pp. 53ff. and 185.

21. In his *Esposizioni* in *Inferno* VII.alleg.144, Boccaccio criticizes both "ira" [wrath] and "accidia . . . il qual dove besogna non s'adira" [sloth . . . which does not get angry when it should]. Cf. Bernard's *Commentum super sex libros Eneidos*, p. 112: "ARMA mistice diximus animi potentias, PIA vero arma dicuntur dum eis hostes ceduntur id est vicia extirpantur, et sui defenduntur, id est virtutes conservantur. Hoc autem fit dum irascibilitas vitia impugnat, concupiscentia sibi virtutes vendicat, animositas vicia vertit et virtutes deffendit. IMPIA vero hec arma dicimus dum horum usus habetur contrarius, quod fit dum irascibilitas contra virtutes se accendit, concupiscentia vicia querit, animositas bona impugnat et mala conservat." [ARMS we said means figuratively the powers of the soul. Truly the arms are called PIOUS when enemies are killed by them, i.e., vices are wiped out, and when one's own people are defended, i.e., the virtues are saved. This is also done when wrath fights against the vices and concupiscence defends virtue, courage averts the vices and defends the virtues. Truly the arms are called IMPIOUS when their use is the opposite, as when wrath kindles itself against the virtues, concupiscence seeks out the vices, courage fights against the good and protects the bad.] And cf. Boccaccio's letter "Mavortis miles" in which Mars can make one either quarrelsome or

"preliabilis contra vitia que pernecant" [ready to fight against the vices which destroy].

22. Limentani notes that the last line echoes Ovid's *Metamorphoses* II.846–47, where Jove puts off his majesty and turns into a bull in order to carry off Europa; it is "signoria" and "amore" which cannot exist together, and the divine is laid off in favor of the bestial. *Teseida* V.13.

23. Both knights suffer loss because of horses. Palemon loses the tournament when Deiphobus's horse bites him and refuses to let go. Arcita loses Emilia despite his victory because of the fall from his horse. The horse is commonly equated with lust. Bernard, for example, writes in his *Commentum super sex libros Eneidos*, p. 102: "Significat etiam equus luxuriam. . . . Equus ideo hanc figuram quia in hoc animali plurimum luxuria viget. Dicit enim Plinius in libro de naturali historia equas tam impacientes libidinis esse . . ." [The horse also signifies lust . . . . Indeed the horse has this aspect because in this animal lust is very vigorous. For Pliny says in the book on natural history that mares are so impatient in lust that . . .]. Cf. D. W. Robertson's analysis of the "Knight's Tale," in *A Preface to Chaucer* (Princeton, 1970), pp. 105–10, 260–66.

24. The idea of presenting the passions through two major characters may very well come from the *Aeneid*. In Fulgentius's commentary, Dido and Turnus, Aeneas's two greatest challenges, represent lust and rage. The parallel is supported both by Arcita's identification with Turnus and by Teseo's with Aeneas (above, p. oo). Palemon's association with Aeneas in the final battle possibly prepares for his reconciliation with Teseo.

25. In the *Summa theologiae*, Q.81, art.2, Aquinas observes that concupiscence leads to the irascible appetite as its means, and that the irascible thus terminates in the satisfaction of the original desire. Arcita (his lust having lead him into rage) is similarly terminated at the achievement of his goal.

26. Macrobius, *Commentarii in Somnium Scipionis*, ed. I. Willis (Leipzig, 1970), I.10.6; G. Rabuse, *Der kosmische Aufbau der Jenseitsreiche Dantes* (Graz, 1958), pp. 67–68. For further reference on the tradition of these ideas, see Pierre Courcelle, "Tradition platonicienne et traditions chretiennes du corps-prison" *Revue des études latines* 43 (1965), 406–43.

27. Hollander discusses these temples at length, in *Boccaccio's Two Venuses*, pp. 55ff., and clearly I agree with his analysis. I am partly repeating the discussion here as useful to my own reading, and partly adding further details.

28. Cf. the *Filocolo*'s close association between Paris's venery and the resulting destruction.

29. Cf. *Elegia*: "O Venere . . . per quello venerabile e intrinseco amore che tu portasti ad Adone, mitiga i miei mali." (V, p. 74) [O Venus . . . by that venerable and intimate love which you bore for Adonis, mitigate my pains.]

30. Tereo is the son of Mars, a fact interpreted astrologically in the *Genealogia* IX.8. Cf. Arcita's devotion to Mars.

31. Raffaello Ramat is wrong to see in the *Teseida* a victory of Venus over Diana, which he compares to the victory of the Athenians over the Amazons or "il trionfo cioè della razionalità e della civiltà sulla irrazionale barbarie dell'antinatura" (*Scritti su Giovanni Boccaccio* [Florence, 1964], p. 11)[the triumph of rationality and

civilization over the irrational barbarism of the antinatural]. This last phrase is true enough, but it is to be equated with the rational and civil marriage of Venus and Diana, not the triumph of one goddess over the other.

The *Ninfale Fiesolano*, using the same verse form as the *Teseida*, offers similarly a warning about the dangers of Venus and Diana in isolation and a celebration of their combined qualities in marriage.

Once again the narrator presents himself in a situation similar to that of the protagonist of his tale. He loves a woman whom he describes as "fera" [cruel], and wishes she were more "pietosa." His book is not addressed to her, and we know almost nothing about her, not even her name. The framing tale is reduced to a minimum.

The first line of the poem, "Amor mi fa parlar" [love makes me speak], is an echo from the words of Beatrice in *Inferno* II (72); the repetitions of "Amor" at the beginning of every other line in stanza two echo the speech of Francesca in *Inferno* V (100–108). Thus, right away two kinds of love are introduced: the *caritas* of Beatrice who wishes to help Dante toward his salvation, and the *cupiditas* of Paolo and Francesca. The tale of the *Ninfale*, however, concerns a third kind of love: one that leads to marriage and family life. Africo's first thought when he sees Mensola is:

> . . . Qual saria
> di me più grazioso e più felice,
> se tal fanciulla io avessi per mia
> isposa? (27)

[Who would be more thankful and happier than I, if I had such a girl for my wife?]

Throughout the book details of family life are warmly described: Girafone covering his sleeping son, Alimena telling her husband not to disturb the boy and preparing a bath with herbs to heal Africo's complaints, Mensola playing with her baby, the baby smiling at his grandfather. (Massèra in his introduction to *Il Ninfale Fiesolano* (Turin, 1926), p. xvi, also notes the domestic details.)

What thwarts the domestic happiness of everyone is Diana's law, strict chastity. When Africo proposes to Mensola, she answers as if she were a nun:

> I'non mi misi a seguitar Diana
> per al mondo tornar per niuna cosa;
> ché, s'i'avessi voluto filar lana
> con la mia madre, e divenire sposa,
> di qui sarei ben tre miglia lontana
> col padre mio. (291)

[I did not set out to follow Diana in order ever to return to the world for any reason; for if I had wanted to spin wool with my mother and become a wife, I would be a good three miles away from here with my father.]

She considers even married love a sin:

> . . . ch'io teco ne venga
> a casa tua, per voler palesare

il mio peccato, ed ancor mi convenga
in questo si gran mal perseverare (290)

[that I come with you to your house, in order to lay open my sin, and that
I be obliged still to persevere in such a great evil].

Venus too is little concerned with marriage. Counseling Africo to use fraud
and "Non temer di sforzarla" (203) [Don't be afraid to force her], she ceases to help
him once he has possessed Mensola. Alone in his room, crying and in love, Africo
resembles the readers to whom the *Decameron* is addressed. He remains alone without a friend to speak to him or draw him from his isolated melancholy. Meanwhile
Venus's fires drive him to desperate suicide as they did Fiammetta in the *Elegia*.
Diana similarly causes the death of Mensola.

The happy resolution comes in the next generation. Pruneo's marriage and the
proliferation of his children and descendants go hand in hand with the establishment of Fiesole. The characters' names identify them with rivers and bushes of the
landscape, as if their fortune signified the fortune of the region. Guido di Pino, *La
Polemica del Boccaccio* (Florence, 1953), p. 182, calls the "paesaggio, uno dei protago-
nisti dell'opera" [landscape one of the protagonists of the work,] and Massèra, in
his introduction to the *Ninfale*, p. vii, writes: "il soggetto vero prestabilitosi del
poeta è la celebrazione delle origini mitiche di Fiesole" [the true subject which the
poet has set for himself is the celebration of the mythic origins of Fiesole]. Town
and family are established together. The wooded hill becomes a town, and the
people who had lived scattered in the woods become its citizens.

The situation is similar to Caleone's founding of Certaldo in the *Filocolo* where
inhabitants scattered in the woods are gathered into a society which represents human reason and civilization overcoming their former animallike existence. (Francesco Maggini points to the establishment of Certaldo in the *Filocolo* as a parallel to
the founding of Fiesole in this book, without elaborating the comparison. "Ancora
a proposito del *Ninfale Fiesolano*," *Giornale storico della letteratura italiana* 61 [1913],
39.) The meaning is changed in the *Ninfale* from what it was in the *Filocolo;* the
goal is not a cure for love, as in Caleone's case, but rather the celebration of a fruitful married life. Diana is in effect chased away from her former lands; the nymphs
of Diana either marry or disperse. Meanwhile the Venus who appeared with Cupid
also vanishes from the narrative. What is left is a flourishing society and a married
couple with many children.

The narrator addresses only lovers, bidding those who cannot love to stay
away. We know very little about his personal intentions; but his book celebrates the
socialization of love, the bonds both of family and of citizenship.

32. See also Aly, whom Boccaccio cites; Aly Aben Ragel, *El libro conplido en los
iudizios de las estrellas*, trans. for Alfonso the Wise, ed. Gerald Hilty (Madrid, 1954),
V.5, p. 266. Julius Firmicus Maternus, *Matheseos Libri VIII*, ed. W. Kroll and F.
Skutsch (Stuttgart, 1968), V.2.8–12. Ptolemy, *Tetrabiblos*, ed. and trans. F. E. Rob-
bins, Loeb Classical Library (Cambridge, Mass., 1971), III.13. Chauncey Wood,
Chaucer and the Country of the Stars (Princeton, 1970), pp. 118–19. Walter Curry,
Chaucer and the Medieval Sciences (New York, 1960), p. 103. For further discussion of
astrological meanings at work in the *Teseida*, see Smarr, "Boccaccio and the Stars."

33. Boethius, *Consolation of Philosophy* III.m.10.

34. Thus Dante refers to "il temperar di Giove" (*Par.* XXII.145), and Boccaccio's teacher Andalò calls it the planet of "rationem et sapientiam" [reason and wisdom]. See Quaglio, *Scienza e mito nel Boccaccio*, p. 93n. and the *Genealogia* II.2.

35. Cf. Boethius, *Consolation of Philosophy* III.m.9, which begins: "O qui perpetua mundum ratione gubernas, / terrarum caelique sator," and ends with a prayer to help the soul rise from its earthly weight toward the light of heaven.

36. Crescini, *Contributo*, p. 215, has proposed that the poet is Arcita because both men lose their ladies. Limentani, in his introduction to the *Teseida*, p. 243, chooses Arcita because of his greater lyrical effusion. Torraca, *Giovanni Boccaccio a Napoli*, pp. 174–75, suggests Arcita because he flirts secretly with his lady as did Boccaccio—i.e., as did Panfilo in the *Elegia*. John Humphries Whitfield, "Boccaccio and Fiammetta in the *Teseida*," *Modern Language Review* 33 (1938), 22–30, argues for Palemon as the knight closer to Boccaccio's physical appearance and the one who, like the narrator, is subject especially to Venus.

37. Cf. *Roman de la Rose* ll. 7081–198 where Reason mocks the use of religious language for carnal desires as hypocrisy and fraud.

38. See Kirkham's "Chiuso parlare in the *Teseida*" on Emilia's identification with Diana via the number seven. Curiously, even in the *Decameron* Emilia is queen on a Monday or moon day.

39. Hollander, *Boccaccio's Two Venuses*, p. 63.

40. This moral and social rather than religious emphasis is true also of the *Ninfale Fiesolano*, where, as in the *Teseida*, both positive and negative endings are given alternately for the parallel stories of four generations.

41. Torraca, *Giovanni Boccaccio a Napoli*, pp. 169–70.

42. Branca, *Neubert*, pp. 14–15.

43. Mario Marti, introduction to Boccaccio, *Opere Minori in Volgare* (Milan, 1969), cited within a review by Cesare de Michelis, *Studi sul Boccaccio* 6 (1971), 267.

IV. *Comedia delle Ninfe Fiorentine*

1. Quaglio remarks in the introduction to his edition: "Ciò permette al Boccaccio . . . di tenere l'operetta su un doppio registro, che pure non raggiunge sovente gli accordi dell'armonia." (p. 669) [This permits Boccaccio . . . to keep the work on a double register, which however does not often attain the accords of harmony.] Hauvette, *Boccace*, pp. 133–34: "La disparité absolue, paradoxale entre le signe employé et la chose signifiée atteint ici les confins du grotesque; il faudrait peu de chose pour que le récit versat dans une indécente bouffonerie." [The absolute and paradoxical disparity between the sign employed and the thing signified reaches here the limits of the grotesque; it would take little to turn the narrative into an indecent joke.]

2. I disagree with Battaglia when he writes (*Boccaccio e la riforma della narrativa*, p. 146) that in the *Comedia delle Ninfe* "il Boccaccio ha chiarificato la sua posizione estetica, come contemplativa valutazione di pura bellezza terrena, goduta per se stessa, senza veli metaforici e senza preoccupazioni etiche. In questa am-

bizione esclusivamente d'arte, per cui l'estetica ritrova in se stessa la sua morale e i suoi fini, il Boccaccio ha individuato forse per primo la sensibilità umanistica." [Boccaccio has clarified his esthetic position, as a contemplative appreciation of pure worldly beauty, enjoyed for itself, without metaphorical veils and without ethical preoccupations. In this ambition exclusively of art, through which esthetics finds in itself its own morality and its own ends, Boccaccio has singled out perhaps for the first time the humanistic sensibility.] This seems to me a strange view of humanism as well as of the *Comedia delle Ninfe.*

3. On the topos of authorial humility, see Curtius, *European Literature*, pp. 407–13.

4. Cf. Boccaccio, *Amorosa Visione* XVI.8–9.

5. Obviously I disagree with Robert Hastings, *Nature and Reason in the Decameron* (Manchester, 1975), p. 64: "Certainly none of the earlier works in the vernacular (including the *Decameron*) is imbued with the active presence of the Christian faith. Clearly, he is still not greatly concerned with religion." All religious elements, such as the credos recited by Ilario (V.56) and Lia (XXXIX) are for him "lip service to the traditional morality" contradicted by "the blatantly mundane and sensual interests of the author."

6. Boccaccio may have derived this idea from another pastoral source: Dante's second eclogue to Giovanni del Virgilio ends by revealing that Iollas has all along been hiding and listening to the conversation of Tityrus and Alphesibeus. It is Iollas who then reports the scene, which at first we thought we were witnessing directly.

7. Giuseppe Mazzotta, "The *Decameron:* The Literal and the Allegorical," *Italian Quarterly* 18 (1975), 62–63.

8. In a way, it is an old idea. Richard de Bury wrote in his thirteenth-century *Philobiblon:* "Idcirco prudentia veterum adinvenit remedium, quo lascivium humanum caperetur ingenium quodammodo pio dolo, dum sub voluptatis iconio delicata Minerva delitesceret in occulto." (cap. 13) [Therefore the prudence of the ancients came up with a remedy by which the lascivious mind of humans might be caught as by a pious deceit, while under the image of pleasure dainty Minerva might secretly conceal herself.]

9. T. K. Seung, *Cultural Thematics: The Formation of the Faustian Ethos* (New Haven, 1976), p. 169. See also Hollander, *Boccaccio's Two Venuses*, p. 76.

10. The negative prefix *a*- shows up sometimes in the name of the virtue and sometimes in the name of the lover. Thus Mopsa or Prudence lures A-fron, but A-diona lures Dioneo.

11. See Branca's notes.

12. Cf. *Paradiso* XVI.151–54.

13. Branca, n. 11, p. 942.

14. Cf. *Paradiso* XV.115. Perhaps Dante's praise of the Nerli, "contenti alla pelle scoperta," seemed appropriate to Boccaccio's pastoral hero.

15. Billanovich traces some of these allusions in his *Restauri.*

16. König, *Begegnung*, pp. 60–61.

17. Giuseppe Billanovich, "La leggenda dantesca del Boccaccio," *Studi danteschi* 28 (1949), 103.

18. In "Fiammetta" (*Restauri*, pp. 93–94), Billanovich comments: "è final-mente indispensabile che la donna abbia un cognome e una famiglia; così che possa, come le altre sei realissime narratrici, adombrare nel suo racconto, se pur finta, l'esatezza di una genealogia. Le è assegnata l'origine dai d'Aquino . . . mitologicamente risalendo, attraverso i Romani, al sangue degli uomini di Enea, bene se affianchi a chi colla madre parigina pure si nobilita per gli esuli Troiani" [it is finally indispensable that the lady have a last name and a family; so that she may, like the other six very real narrators, hint in her story, even if it is fiction, at the exactness of a genealogy. She is assigned an origin from the d'Aquino family . . . mythologically traced back through the Romans to the blood of Aeneas's men, it matches well with one whose Parisian mother is ennobled through the Trojan exiles].

19. Branca, "Profilo biografico," p. 27. Branca comments in regard to the *Filo-colo* that the autobiographical fiction there matches the tale: "È la sempre suggestiva favola dell'oscuro bastardo riconosciuto e reintegrato nel grado che gli spetta da un amore principesco: la bella favola, cioè, di Florio e Biancifiore." [It is the always suggestive fable of the unknown bastard recognized and reintegrated in the rank that belongs to him by the love of a prince or princess: the pretty fable, that is, of Florio and Biancifiore.]

20. Ibid., pp. 26–27.

21. The king first saw Fiammetta's mother at a big festival when the sun was in Gemini. In the *Filocolo* the festival at that season is Pentecost, the time of birth of Florio and Biancifiore. There is too little evidence to be sure that Pentecost is meant again in the *Comedia*, but it is possible that Boccaccio is once more linking Easter and Pentecost, the beginning and end of the Easter season.

22. But see König, *Begegnung*, on the long tradition of this motif.

23. For attempts to date Boccaccio's enamorment, see Baldelli, *Vita*, pp. 364, 372–73. Landau, *Giovanni Boccaccio*, pp. 28–32. Della Torre, *Giovinezza*, pp. 31–101. Hauvette, *Boccace*, pp. 24–26. Casetti, "Boccaccio a Napoli," pp. 561–62. Torraca, *Giovanni Boccaccio a Napoli*, pp. 11–12, and *Per la biografia*, pp. 11–34. For argu-ments against such dating efforts, see Renier, *Vita Nuova e Fiammetta*, pp. 244–45. Branca, *Boccaccio medievale*, chap. 7, "Schemi letterari e schemi autobiografici," pp. 193–204. Billanovich, *Restauri*, pp. 82–100.

24. For an explanation of planetary dominion of the hours, see *Genealogia* I.34, and above, p. 53.

25. Cf. Boccaccio's *Esposizioni* I.alleg.III: "La stagione del tempo similmente gli diè buona speranza, conoscendo che in quella stagione era cominciato il tempo della grazia e aperta la via alla nostra salute." [The season of the year likewise gave him good hope, as he knew that in that season had begun the time of grace and the way been opened to our salvation.] The Easter season produces good hope, i.e. Fiammetta, in Boccaccio's *Comedia* too.

26. Augustine, *De Genesi contra Manicheos*, PL 34.203–4.

27. Boccaccio, *Opere Latine Minori*, ed. Massèra, pp. 218–19; and *Lettere edite e inedite*, ed. Corazzini, p. 271. Note that the church is represented by Venus's tree.

28. See Charles Dahlberg's notes to his translation of the *Romance of the Rose*

(Princeton, 1971), ll.557, 595–6; John Fleming, *The Roman de la Rose: A Study in Allegory and Iconography* (Princeton, 1969), pp. 174–75. Oiseuse is dressed in green, along with other Venerian attributes.

29. See Hollander, *Boccaccio's Two Venuses*, pp. 44, 186–87, 206.

30. In the case of the *Teseida* the allusions to Venus balance Emilia's association with Diana in order to bring about the final marriage which is the climax of the epic. Similarly Biancifiore must reconcile in herself Venus and Diana in order to marry Florio. In the *Comedia delle Ninfe* Fiammetta seems to be connected only to Venus, while the Diana references are attached to Lia (e.g., seeing her for the first time, Ameto is afraid of being turned into a stag like Actaeon).

31. Robert Henryson, "The Testament of Cresseid," *The Poems and Fables of Robert Henryson*, ed. H. Harvey Wood (London, 1958).

32. Sidney Harth, "Henryson Reinterpreted," *Essays in Criticism* 11 (1961), 475, comments that "writers like Guillaume de Machaut, Martial d'Auvergne, and others regularly use green to stand for disloyalty and changeableness, and black to stand for sorrow. . . . Henryson obviously had some such unpleasant significance in mind." However, it seems clear that green is meant to be an opposite of black, both for Henryson and for Boccaccio. See also Douglas Duncan, "Henryson's 'Testament of Cresseid,'" *Essays in Criticism* 11 (1961), 128–35.

33. Harth, "Henryson," p. 475.

34. On green as a symbol of inconstancy associated with the succession of seasons, see André Ott, *Etudes sur les couleurs en vieux francais* (Paris, 1899), pp. 136ff.

35. See above p. 40; Alain de Lille also in the *De planctu Naturae* prose 5. 195ff. contrasts the married love of the good Venus with the adultery of the licentious Venus.

36. The gesture is applied to both anger and despair, equally governed by Mars. For examples see Emile Màle, *The Gothic Image*, trans. Dora Nussey (New York, 1972), pp. 100, 104, 113, 115.

37. Thus the woman's erotic offering of her body becomes, as an act of saving love, a parody of Christ's offering his body to death.

38. See e.g., Apuleius, *De mundo* II.293, p. 123, or Cicero, *De natura deorum* II.52–54.

39. Boccaccio, *Esposizioni*, Inferno XIII. litt. 98; Giovanni Villani, *Cronica* (Florence, 1823) III.1 and I.38.

40. Thus the Venerian hope and Martian despair carry over from Caleone's story to the narrator's gloomy return from Naples to Florence. The pairing of Florence and Naples with Mars and Venus may have been intended also by Dante, who recounts the history of the kingdom of Naples in the Venus sphere of Paradiso (canto VIII), and offers as an example of suicide an anonymous Florentine who, Spitzer suggests, represents Florence herself, destroyed by internal wars through the influence of her old patron Mars. See Leo Spitzer, "Speech and Language in Inferno XIII," in *Dante: A Collection of Critical Essays*, ed. John Freccero (Englewood Cliffs, N.J., 1965), p. 98, and Rabuse, *Kosmische Aufbau*, esp. pp. 53–56.

41. See Quaglio's n. 6 to the *Comedia*.

42. Cf. the miserly old father in chap. XLIX.

43. Dioneo's parents can be compared to the presence of Ceres and Bacchus in the temple of Venus in the *Teseida* VII.50ff., and contrasted to Ceres and Bacchus who represent the sacrament in the *Comedia delle Ninfe* XXXIX.64–66.

44. *Comedia delle Ninfe* XXIX.36, and Quaglio's n. 51, p. 944.

45. Dante, *Convivio* III.xiv: "Per le quali tre virtudi [theological], si sale a filosofare a quelle Atene celestiali, dove li Stoici e Peripetetici e Epicurii, per la luce de la veritade etterna, in uno volere concordevolmente concorrono." [By which three virtues one rises to love wisdom in those celestial Athens where the Stoics and Peripatetics and Epicureans, by the light of eternal truth, all agree in one harmonious will.]

46. This is line seven of a forty-nine-line song sung by the seven nymphs together.

The threes, sevens, and tens which dominate Dante's poem play a significant role in Boccaccio's *Comedia* too. During the main part of the narrative, the nymphs each sing one song, Venus sings two, and the nymphs all together sing one more; in sum, ten songs by the celestial ladies, a number symbolic of perfection. The very last song of the book, the poet's final verses, is exactly one hundred lines, the only song with so conspicuous a number. It occurs in chapter XLIX, which is connected to the sevens of the nymphs. The nymphs' final song is forty-nine lines, the square of their own sevens. Between the nymphs' song and the poet's comes the last song of Ameto, seventy lines. As seven times ten, it mediates between the seven times seven of the nymphs and the ten times ten of the poet, just as Ameto himself mediates between them; for the poet has been watching Ameto, who learns directly from the nymphs. Ameto has three songs altogether; they are the third, sixth, and eighteenth songs in the book. Two are sung before the storytelling, the third after his baptism. These threes associate him with the triune goddess who descends to give him grace. His threes also complement the sevens of the virtues to add up to the final and perfect tens.

The book has fifty chapters, and this too is significant. Augustine discusses this number in his commentary on Psalm CL (*PL* 37.1960–61): "Septies quippe septem quadraginta novem faciunt; quibus unum additur, ut fiant quinquaginta. Qui numerus quinquegenarius usque adeo magnae significationis est, ut ex Domini resurressione tot diebus completis, ipso quinquegenario die venerit super eos qui in Christo fuerant congreganti, Spiritus Sanctus (Act. II:1–4). Qui spiritus sanctus in Scripturis septenario praecipue numero commendatur, sive apud Isaiam, sive in Apocalypsi (Apoc. I:10); ubi apertissime septem Spiritus Dei perhibentur, propter operationem septenariam unius ejusdem Spiritus." [For seven times seven make forty-nine; to which one is added that they may make fifty. This the number fifty is so far of great significance, as from the resurrection of the Lord that many days were completed and on the fiftieth day the Holy Spirit came upon them who were gathered in Christ (Act. II:1–4). This holy spirit in the Scriptures is especially associated with the number seven, whether according to Isaiah, or in the Apocalypse (Apoc. I:10); where openly seven Spirits of God are mentioned, on account of the sevenfold working of that one Spirit.]

Fifty is the epiphany of the Holy Spirit after his sevenfold workings (through the seven nymphs). (See also Vincent Foster Hopper, *Medieval Number Symbolism*

[New York, 1938], pp. 25, 71, 81.) Here, perhaps, is one more allusion to Pentecost, which plays an important role in the *Filocolo*.

47. On Dante's use of Macrobius's *Somnium Scipionis*, see Rabuse, "Dantes Jenseitsvision und das Somnium Scipionis," pp. 499–522.

Studies of the Hermetic texts were renewed wherever Platonic studies flourished, e.g., in the twelfth century with Hugh of St. Victor as well as in the fifteenth century with Ficino. See Frances Yates, *Giordano Bruno and the Hermetic Tradition*, p. 13. Apuleius, whom Boccaccio calls "platonico," was thought to be the translator of the Hermetic *Asclepius*, to which Boccaccio refers in his *Genealogia* III.20 and VIII.1. Apuleius's own *Metamorphosis* shows a conversion from animal to human through a vision of the goddess Isis much like Ameto's conversion from a creature romping with his dogs in the forest to a divinely imaged man through the vision of Venus or God.

If one agrees with the nymph-planet pairing discussed above, then one is left to face the question: how and why did Boccaccio change the order of the nymphs during their tale-telling? The order of narrators is: (1) Mopsa, (2) Emilia, (3) Adiona, (4) Acrimonia, (5) Agapes, (6) Fiammetta, and (7) Lia.

The order of speakers to some extent follows the order of virtues in the earthly paradise of Dante. Of the four cardinal virtues, prudence comes first. The sequence love-hope-faith is the same as Dante's, who gives no order to the cardinal virtues other than placing prudence in the lead. The rationale for the ordering goes beyond a mere imitation of Dante, for reason leads man to the first four virtues, and love—both ascending human love and descending divine love—leads man to the other three.

Lia, who arrived first, speaks seventh; Mopsa, who came seventh, speaks first. The moon, first when one counts from the earth, is seventh when one counts toward the earth; and vice versa for Saturn. Seven is the "virgin" number associated both with Diana or the moon and with Minerva, i.e., both with Lia and with Mopsa, who serves Minerva. (See Macrobius, *Somnium Scipionis* I.6.11; also William Stahl, Richard Johnson and E. L. Burge, *Martianus Capella and the Seven Liberal Arts* [New York, 1971], p. 152.) The pair of nymphs represent rational understanding and faith, one the human starting point, the other the divine revelation rewarded at the end. Yet, in a circular manner, faith is required as the starting point for the whole educative process which will lead Ameto through the virtues and back to faith again.

Fourth or central is Acrimonia, the only one of the nymphs who must be wooed by her man instead of wooing him. She is surrounded by Adione and Agapes, who arrived together in chapter IX and form nearly a pair of opposites: A-dione must temper the love of Dioneo, the Venerian, while Agapes must arouse the love of her indifferent A-piros. They are in turn surrounded by Emilia and Fiammetta, again a pair that arrived together (XII) and the two narrators most closely connected to Boccaccio's own mythical autobiography: Emilia, whose lover's parents come from Paris and Certaldo, Fiammetta, whose lover has long been interpreted as Boccaccio himself. There seems, then, to be a conscious pattern once again. The highly artificial nature of the whole *Comedia* makes this complexity of patternings plausible.

V. *Amorosa Visione*

1. Crescini, *Contributo*, pp. 154ff., compares the *Amorosa Visione* with Dante's *Commedia*.

2. Cf. the *Comedia delle Ninfe*'s fifty chapters and use of terza rima. Hollander, *Boccaccio's Two Venuses*, p. 205, suggests that the fifty here may be an expression of modesty with regard to Dante's hundred; but it also fits with Boccaccio's previously demonstrated interest in Pentecost. In this work, too, Maria is a "fiamma" descended from heaven.

3. Crescini, *Contributo*, p. 134: "Il Boccaccio si propose di esaltare Fiammetta, e ne trovò il modo nella tradizione de' poeti dello *stil novo*. Qui infatti la donna sua ha niente meno che l'ufficio altissimo di condurlo sulla via che guida al cielo. Fiammetta si ricollega in tal guisa a Beatrice." [Boccaccio proposed to exalt Fiammetta, and he found the way in the tradition of the *stil novo* poets. Here indeed his lady has no less than the lofty office of guiding him on the way which leads to heaven. Fiammetta is in this way connected to Beatrice.]

4. See Smarr, "Boccaccio and the Choice of Hercules." For the stairway cf. *Purgatorio* XXVI.145–46, where Arnaut addresses Dante "per aquella valor / que vos guida al som de l'escalina" [by that worthiness which guides you to the top of the stair].

5. Cf. the *Teseida*, where reason is represented by the repeatedly victorious king Teseo.

6. Crescini, *Contributo*, pp. 114–15, suggested first that she is Reason, then changed his mind and offered Fortitude, to me a much less convincing suggestion. Baldelli, *Vita*, p. 61, proposed "Celestiale Intelligenza" [Celestial Intelligence]. Koerting, *Boccaccios Leben und Werke*, p. 544, offered several possibilities: virtue or truth or faith. Marco Antonio Parenti, "Chi sia la guida dell'*Amorosa Visione*," in *Saggi di studi sul Boccaccio* (Florence, 1915), suggests the Virgin Mary; Cavallari, *Fortuna di Dante*, p. 436, argues against this suggestion: "troppo poco efficace è il suo aiuto al poeta, che si mostra financo annoiato di essere in sua compagnia, irreverenza eccessiva se egli fosse stato alla presenza della Vergine" [too little efficacious is her aid to the poet, who even shows himself bored with her company, an excessive irreverence were he in the presence of the Virgin]. She prefers the identification with reason. Branca, in his introduction to the poem, p. 16, and his note to I.34–42 on p. 560, proposed "l'aspirazione alla virtù" [aspiration toward virtue], but warned at the same time that the figure remains vague and cannot be too closely defined.

7. Adolfo Gaspary, review of Koerting's *Boccaccios Leben und Werke* in *Litereraturblatt für germanische und romanische Philologie* (1881), no. 1; Hollander, *Boccaccio's Two Venuses*, pp. 80–81.

8. Hollander cites XXVII.12–15, where Paris gives her the "pomo d'oro." But note also VI.60, where Gloria too holds a "pomo d'or." The attribute, it seems, is not necessarily Venerian.

9. Cf. also *Inferno* II.67–69.

10. Cf. the discussion in regard to the *Teseida*, pp. 69–70.

11. And clearly modeled on the *Roman de la Rose*.

12. Boccaccio's use of an acrostic in the *Amorosa Visione* may be an elaboration of Dante's use of an acrostic to accompany his description of the pictured walls in purgatory (*Purg.* 25–69). But lifelike paintings of men's customs can also be found on the walls of Nature's palace in the *Anticlaudianus* I, esp. 119ff.

13. Cicero defines the three types in *De Inventione* I.19.27, and similar definitions appear in the *Rhetorica ad Herennium* I.8.3. See also Curtius, *European Literature*, pp. 452–55, on repetitions of these definitions by Isidore et al.

14. See Singleton, *Essay on the Vita Nuova*, pp. 14–15; and Robert Hollander, "*Vita Nuova*: Dante's Perceptions of Beatrice," *Dante Studies* 92 (1974), 1–18. Macrobius, *Somn. Scip.* I.3, discusses five kinds of dream, from the true *visio* to the false phantasms of initial or uncomfortable sleep.

15. Bernard Silvester, *Commentum super sex libros Eneidos*: Per picturas vero bona temporalia que ideo pictura dicuntur quia bona non sunt, sed videntur et ideo Boetius ea 'imagines veri boni' vocat. Atque ita oculos, id est sensus, saturat in picturis, id est in mundanis bonis" [by pictures he means indeed temporal goods which are called pictures because they are not really good but seem to be, and so too Boethius calls them 'images of the true good.' And he feasts his eyes, that is his senses, on pictures, that is on worldly goods]. For the Boethius reference, see *Philosophiae consolatio* III.prose 9.

16. Fulgentius's commentary too glosses Dido as *libido* in both Books IV and VI. (Fulgentius, *Opera*, ed. Rudolf Helm [Stuttgart, 1970], pp. 94 and 99.)

17. Cf. my discussion of Fiammetta's position in *Filocolo* IV. In the *Visione* VI.30–39, the narrator *still* disagrees with her condemnation of his enthusiasm for the portrait of Dante; is she truly too severe?

18. I am using version A of this text as befits the chronological treatment of Boccaccio's works. For some of the changes in the revised version, see above pp. 116, 126–27 and nn. 36 and 39 of this chapter.

19. For historical identifications, see Branca's notes.

20. A manuscript with the first line of each terzina set out in the margin would make this acrostic easy to discover and to read. Boccaccio's own copy of Dante's *Commedia* is written this way. Ernest Hatch Wilkins, "Maria . . . Prete," *Italica* 28 (1951), 101, notes that the first five alternate lines of the acrostic sonnet also form an acrostic spelling "Maria."

21. Cf. *Comedia delle Ninfe* XXXV.32.

22. Also *Vita Nuova* 24.

23. *Physiologus Latinus*, ed. Francis J. Carmody (Paris, 1939), pp. 40–43; Hugh of St. Victor, *De bestiis* I.56, *PL* 177.69–72. Albertus Magnus, *De animalibus* and Brunetto Latini, *Li Livres dou Tresor*, ed. P. Chabaille (Paris, 1863), I.144 and 192, say much the same thing about the nature of these animals but without allegorization.

24. Job 39:27–28.

25. Rabanus Maurus, *Allegoriae in universam sacram scripturam*, *PL* 112.862.

26. Deut. 2:11.

27. Hugh of St. Victor, *De bestiis* I.56, *PL* 177.53–55.

28. Hugh cites Gregory, whose *Moralium* XXXI.cap.47–53, *PL* 76.624–30, is

very similar. Gregory glosses the eagle as sublime contemplation, rising above the earthly heights of wealth, power, honors, etc. (cf. Boccaccio's painted triumphs) toward a heavenly object of desire.

29. See also Rabanus's *Allegoriae, PL* 112.862: "Aquila est Christus, ut in cantico Deuteronomii: 'Aquila provocavit ad volandum pullos suos,' quod Christus discipulos suos, ut de virtute in virtutem proficiant, monere non cessat. . . . Aquila animam significat ut in Job: 'Elevabitur aquila, et ponet in arduis nidum suum,' quod per contemplationem exaltatur anima, et in coelis defigit desiderium suum." [The eagle is Christ, as in the verse of Deuteronomy: "The eagle has provoked her chicks to fly," because Christ does not cease to admonish his disciples that they may advance from virtue to virtue. . . . The eagle signifies the soul as in Job: "The eagle will rise and set her nest on high," because through contemplation the soul rises and fixes its desire in the heavens.]

30. On the combination of holy and erotic associations with Fiammetta, see also Hollander, *Boccaccio's Two Venuses*, pp. 88–89.

31. Time, in a dreamlike manner, expands and contracts unrealistically: XL.32, cf. XLVII.56 and 57, and see Branca's notes.

32. The description of the lady's image and her song in cantos XV–XVI occur at the point where the acrostic is spelling out Boccaccio's name, thus strengthening the connection between the lady within the vision and the Fiammetta-Maria addressed in the acrostics, as well as adding emphasis to the passage in XV–XVI.

33. Cf. XLVIII.34–39.

34. Cf. the *Caccia di Diana* I.46–47; the parallel might support Kirkham's reading of that work.

35. Cf. *Purgatorio* XVIII.136–38: "E quella che l'affanno non sofferse / fino a la fine col figlio d'Anchise, / sé stessa a vita sanza gloria offerse" [and that people who did not suffer the toil until the very end with the son of Anchises gave themselves to a life without glory].

36. The revised version of the song does not diminish the possibility of this reading. Indeed, the substitution of "vera" for "somma" in line 4, the addition of "grazia" to line 6, and the change of line 18 to "di lui'l *ristoro* ed il fin bello" all give the reading additional support. But cf. also pp. 126–27 for the revision of the final canto.

37. Cf. *Amorosa Visione* XV.61–63.

38. See Green's chapter on "Irony of the Narrator," in *Irony in the Medieval Romance*, esp. p. 220.

39. The second version reads:

> La qual s'io per terrestre e furiosa
> voglia fruire amassi, in veritate
> con dover ne saresti crucciosa;
>   anzi con quella ver integritate
> ch'ogni razionale amar si dee,
> amo ed onoro la sua gran biltate;
>   . . .
> per cui ergo la mente all'alte idee.

[Whom if I loved in order to enjoy her with earthly and furious will, in truth you would have a right to be angry about it; but with that true integrity with which every rational creature ought to love, I love and honor her great beauty . . . through whom I drive my mind to high ideas.]

40. Marcus Landau, *Giovanni Boccaccio: Sua Vita e Sue Opere*, trans. Antona-Traversi (Naples, 1881), p. 223. Cf. more recently the dissertation by Jon D. Boshart, "Giovanni Boccaccio's *Amorosa Visione:* A New Appraisal" (Ph.D. diss., Johns Hopkins University, 1974); DAI 35:7860A: "Sensual love triumphs over spiritual love. . . . Boccaccio, in the *Amorosa Visione*, is the first to place the two in direct allegorical opposition and give the winner's crown to sensual love."

41. One can, nonetheless, commit adultery with one's own spouse by an excessive lust, according to Christian doctrines.

42. Eugenio Rossi, *Dalla mente e dal cuore di Giovanni Boccaccio*, p. 85.

43. Ibid., p. 83.

44. Crescini, *Contributo*, p. 137: "C'è quindi una flagrante contraddizione tra l'ufficio ch'egli assegna alla sua donna . . . e il limite peccaminoso a cui giungono i suoi rapporti con essa." [There is thus a flagrant contradiction between the office which he assigns to his lady . . . and the sinful end at which his relations with her arrive.]

45. Boccaccio, *Esposizioni* I.alleg.150–51.

46. Hollander, *Boccaccio's Two Venuses*, p. 91, using the revised version of the text, reads the *congedo* as purely erotic.

47. Boccaccio copied from Seneca into his *Zibaldone magliabechiano:* "Sola autem nos philosophia excitavit, somnum excutiet gravem" [Moreover only philosophy shakes us and rouses us from heavy sleep].

48. Cf. the final prayer in the *Elegia di Madonna Fiammetta*.

49. Ambrose, *Psalmum XXXVIII enarratio*, PL 14.1051.

VI. *Elegia di Madonna Fiammetta*

1. Charles Muscatine, "The Emergence of Psychological Allegory in Old French Romance," *PMLA* 68 (1953), 1160–82, discusses the frequent occurrence in romances of inner debates or dialogues between Reason (or Sens or Savoir) and Amor.

2. Boccaccio, *Esposizioni* Accessus. 46–47: "'Descendant in infernum viventes,' quasi voglia dire: 'nelle miserie della presente vita.' E di questo inferno sentono i poeti co'santi, fingendo questo inferno essere nel cuore de'mortali" ["They descend into hell alive," as if to say: "into the miseries of the present life." And this is the hell that poets along with saints are talking about when they feign that this hell is in the hearts of mortals]. See also *Genealogia* I.14.

3. For further discussion, see below, p. 132.

4. The nine books of the *Elegia* may be a reminder of the number of Beatrice, whose love for Dante contrasts with the downward-leading love of Fiammetta here.

5. The question remains debatable, however, whether the *Elegia* is a serious moral warning or a comedy. Readers who did understand Boccaccio's previous works might well find in the *Elegia*, despite its title, a humorous parody of the whole lover-poet tradition as well as a comic reversal of Fiammetta's earlier responses. The exaggerations and duplicities of the rhetoric would be further comic ingredients. Hollander (*Boccaccio's Two Venuses*, pp. 46 and 169) sees the work as comic; others have usually considered it a tragedy. I think that Fiammetta herself is not a humorous figure as is, for example, the lover-poet of the *Caccia* or *Comedia delle Ninfe*. In Christian terms her fall is certainly tragic rather than funny.

The issue has been debated for the *Heroides* too: are they pathetic or funny? Jean-Marc Frécaut, *L'esprit et l'humeur chez Ovide* (Grenoble, 1972) discusses (pp. 194ff.) "dans quelle mesure celui-ci prend-il son sujet au serieux, dans quelle mesure y trouve-t-il une occasion de badiner?" Howard Jacobson, *Ovid's Heroides* (Princeton, 1974), p. 8, notes his disagreement with E. J. Winsor, "A Study in the Sources and Rhetoric of Chaucer's Legend of Good Women and Ovid's Heroides" (Ph.D. diss., Yale Univ., 1963), who claims that the work is comic. Antonio Salvatore, "Motivi poetici nelle *Heroides* di Ovidio," in *Atti del Convegno Internazionale Ovidiano* (Rome, 1958), vol. 2, p. 240, comments on a passage from the "Fedra": "sembra un facile, retorico gioco di parole, ed è una retorica che esprime, con densa rapidità e concisione, un concetto triste." The whole work is suffused, for him, with "un'atmosfera lirico-tragica." "Anzi direi che la nota poetica fondamentale delle *Heroides* consista nell' attenuarsi, nell'addolcirsi del sentimento tragico in quello elegiaco" (p. 243) [it seems a facile, rhetorical play of words, but it is a rhetoric which expresses, with dense rapidity and concision, a sad thought. . . . I would say rather that the fundamental poetic note of the *Heroides* consists in the attenuation and sweetening of the tragic sentiment into the elegiac].

6. Crescini, *Contributo*, pp. 164, 163 suggests that the work is a kind of wishful thinking: "si piaceva dunque d'imaginare, che Fiammetta, mentre egli era lontano, lo aspetasse e si struggesse di lui; ma era, ahimè, solamente un sogno, pel quale il poeta attribuiva i sentimenti propri alla sua donna" [he liked then to imagine that Fiammetta, while he was far away, was waiting for him and longing for him; but it was, ah me, only a dream, through which the poet attributed his own sentiments to his lady]. The bitter truth, according to Crescini, was that Fiammetta had ceased to care about Boccaccio even before his move. Renier, *Vita Nuova e Fiammetta*, pp. 264–66, also finds Boccaccio putting his own sentiments into Fiammetta's speeches, but observes that the reproaches against adultery are intended as a criticism against her actions. To Gigli ("Per l'interpretazione della *Fiammetta*," pp. 70–71), the *Elegia* is an act of vengeance for Fiammetta's infidelity. "Come? la infidele Fiammetta mutata in costei, vero specchio di amorosa abnegazione? . . . il tentato suicidio dovette produrre la più grande ilarità tra i lettori partenopei del romanzo. Uccidersi lei, così spensierata e desiderosa di svaghi e uccidersi per chi aveva abbandonato e forse dimenticato?" [How is this? the faithless Fiammetta changed into her, true mirror of loving self-denial? . . . the attempted suicide must have produced the greatest hilarity among the Neapolitan readers of the novel. Kill herself, she, so thoughtless and desirous of amusement? and kill herself for someone whom she had abandoned and perhaps forgotten?] Salvatore Battaglia, *La cos-*

cienza letteraria del medioevo (Naples, 1965), p. 660, takes a totally different angle: "non s'è mai scritta un'opera così nobile come l'*Elegia*, in cui il narratore intendeva esaltare unicamente la generosa dedizione della donna amata, confinando nell'oblio o al margine del racconto se stesso e le proprie vanità" [never has a work been written as noble as the *Elegia*, in which the narrator intended to exalt only the generous dedication of his beloved lady, limiting to oblivion or to the margin of the narrative himself and his own vanities]. Thus for Battaglia the book is not a criticism of Fiammetta, but rather praise for her devoted love. By putting the work into her mouth, he can surpass the humility of the earlier poets who praised their ladies because whereas they focus a large part of their attention on the poet in the act of praising, Boccaccio can leave himself out of the picture almost altogether.

7. Crescini, *Contributo*, pp. 149–64; the *Elegia* text edited by Segre (Milan, 1966) includes notes by Maria Segre Consigli and Antonia Benvenuti on the classical sources. See also Cesare Segre, "Strutture e registri nella *Fiammetta*," in *Le strutture e il tempo* (Turin, 1974), pp. 88–92.

8. This is also Hollander's interpretation, *Boccaccio's Two Venuses,* p. 42: "the *Elegia* is a stinging treatment of the religion of love." Ramat, *Scritti*, p. 12, recognizes Fiammetta's "deviazione dalla natura innocente" [deviation from an innocent nature] to "follia" and remarks: "Nel cuore di questa intuizione sta il rovesciamento del concetto cortese d'amore." [At the heart of this intuition is the overturning of the concept of courtly love.] I would add only that this overturning is not something new for Boccaccio.

9. Sapegno, *Storia letteraria*, pp. 305, 307. Cf. Ramat, *Scritti*, p. 12: "Il Boccaccio scrive il primo romanzo intimista europeo e crea il primo personaggio tragico moderno." [Boccaccio writes the first European intimate novel and creates the first modern tragic character.]

10. Cf. *Amorosa Visione* XVI.1ff. and *Decameron* song III about beauty as a sign of God's goodness.

11. Cf. the *Teseida* VII.50 gloss where Boccaccio equates Priapus with the illegitimate Venus.

12. Cf. the female readers addressed by Boccaccio at the beginning of the *Decameron;* they are alone in their rooms, brooding on love.

13. Otto Bird, "The Canzone d'Amore of Cavalcanti according to the Commentary of Dino del Garbo," *Medieval Studies* 2 (1940), 150–204 and 3 (1941), 117–60, includes the Latin text of the commentary and an English translation.

14. Cf. Brunetto Latini, *Livres dou Tresor* II.i.xvii, pp. 276–79: "concupiscence et ire, qui sont achoison de totes mauvaises oevres que on fait par volenté; car il n'est mie possible chose que on face les bones oevres par volentés et les mauvaises sanz volenté" [concupiscence and wrath, which are the occasion of all the evil works which one does by will; for it is not possible that one does good works by will and evil ones without will]. Becoming involved in passion is like throwing a stone: "avant que il la giete a il en sa volenté de giter la ou non; mais puis que ele est alée, il n'est pas en sa volenté dou repenre ne dou retenir" [before he throws it, he has it in his power to throw it or not; but once it is gone, it is not in his will to repent nor to call it back]. Thus bad choices trap us and become habit.

15. Renier's delightful protest against her character provides the basis for a

valuable comparison: "Ma questa balia ha la ciarla ed i cavilli d'un avvocato, la indifferenza d'un cinico, la sapienza boriosa di un erudito. Quale diversità dalla affettuosa, sublime nutrice del *Romeo e Giulietta* di Shakespeare!" (*Vita Nuova e Fiammetta*, p. 322) [But his nurse has the chattering and caviling of a lawyer, the indifference of a cynic, the ostentatious wisdom of a scholar. What a difference from the affectionate, sublime nurse of Shakespeare's *Romeo and Juliet!*]

16. Cf. *Teseida* III.33, where the same simile is used for the falling in love of Palemon and Arcita.

17. The gloss to the *Elegia* refers to this book of the *Georgics* later on in regard to Fiammetta's mention of Leander, who, in Vergil's poem, appears among bulls, boars, horses, and other beasts as an example of the mighty and destructive drive of sexual desire: "quid iuvenis, magnum cui versat in ossibus ignem / durus amor? nempe abruptis turbata procellis / nocte natat caeca serus freta" (258–60) [what could the young man do, in whose bones harsh love pours a great fire? late at night he swims the blind straits troubled with violent storms]. There is controversy as to whether the gloss is by Boccaccio or by someone else. Antonio Enzo Quaglio, *Le chiose all'Elegia di Madonna Fiammetta* (Padua, 1957), argues that it is not by Boccaccio; Hollander, *Boccaccio's Two Venuses*, pp. 182–84, argues that it is.

18. Even Dario Rastelli in "L'Elegia di Fiammetta (il mito mondano e la caratterizzazione della protagonista)," *Studi ghisleriani*, S. II, 1 (1950), 156, calls her "incolpevole" [innocent]. But Paulette Françoise Bayliss, "A Reassessment of Boccaccio's Fiammetta with Special Reference to Classical and Contemporary Literary Influences" (Ph.D. diss., University of Cambridge, 1978), p. 180, asserts that Fiammetta is morally responsible and guilty, not a victim.

19. On the concept "elegia" in the Middle Ages, see Pio Rajna, "Il titolo del poema dantesco," *Studi danteschi* 4 (1921), 33. Pier Vincenzo Mengaldo, "L'elegia 'umile,'" *Giornale storico della letteratura italiana* 143 (1966), 177–98. Segre, "Strutture e registri nella *Fiammetta*," pp. 89–91.

20. Segre, "Strutture e registri nella *Fiammetta*," pp. 95–96.

21. Mario Marti, introduction to his edition of the *Filocolo* (Milan, 1969), p. 45.

22. Cf. Boccaccio's gloss on Pasiphae in the *Genealogia* IV.10, discussed above in re the *Teseida*, pp. 70–71.

23. Robert Griffin, "Boccaccio's *Fiammetta*: Pictures at an Exhibition," *Italian Quarterly* 18 (1975), 79–80, suggests that she rises in the end through some process of redemption. I do not see any evidence for a redemption of any sort at the end.

24. See n. 13 of the *Amorosa Visione* chapter, and p. 105.

25. Hauvette, *Boccace*, pp. 158–59.

26. Including his own? Perhaps he felt the need to convince himself as well as others. Thus too his previous pose as someone in need of correction may be in part sincere.

27. Serafini, "Tragedie di Seneca nella *Fiammetta*." Crescini, *Contributo*, pp. 160–62; and "Il primo atto della *Phaedra* di Seneca nel primo capitolo della *Fiammetta* del Boccaccio," *Atti del R. Istituto Veneziano di Scienze, Lettere ed Arti* 70 (1920–21), 455–66. Albert Cook, "Boccaccio, *Fiammetta*, Chap. I, and Seneca, *Hippolytus*, Act I," *American Journal of Philology* 28 (1907), 200–204.

28. Renier, *Vita Nuova e Fiammetta*, p. 304.

29. Silvio Segalla, *Sentimenti religiosi nel Boccaccio* (Bern, 1909), p. 27.

30. See Segre, "Strutture e registri nella *Fiammetta*," pp. 101–3.

31. Fiammetta's "più che altra" (p. 6) may also possibly suggest that the happy and holy married life is rare.

32. Hollander, *Boccaccio's Two Venuses*, p. 166, n. 64, also notes the absence of Juno and her association with marriage.

33. Cf. Caleone's examples in defence of love in *Filocolo* IV.45 and Fiammetta's reply in 46.

34. See also Walter Pabst, *Venus als Heilige und Furie in Boccaccios Fiammetta-Dichtung* (Krefeld, 1958).

35. Battaglia, *Coscienza letteraria*, p. 668.

36. The following dedicatory letters are cited in Vincenzo Pernicone's edition of the *Elegia* (Bari, 1939), pp. 222, 225, 230. Pernicone is interested in their comments about textual corrections and does not remark on the dramatic change in interpretation.

37. The most nearly similar tactic that I can think of by an English writer is the *Delia* sonnet sequence and accompanying *Complaint of Rosamond* by Samuel Daniel in the 1590s. There too the lengthy seduction efforts of the poet-character are countered by the warning example of the fallen Rosamond told from her own ghostly mouth. The *Elegia* had been translated into English and published in London in 1587 (Patricia Gathercole, "Boccaccio in English," *Studi sul Boccaccio* 7 [1973], 357). Although Daniel was writing at the time of Filippe Giunti's misreading, he would have known better how to interpret Boccaccio's works.

VII. *Corbaccio*

1. On dating the *Corbaccio* see the edition by Pier Georgio Ricci (Milan, 1965), pp. 492–93; the edition by Tauno Nurmela (Helsinki: *Annales Academiae Scientium Fennicae* vol. 146, 1968), pp. 18–21; the translation by Anthony K. Cassell (Urbana, Ill., 1975), nn. 87 and 231; and G. Padoan, "Sulla datazione del *Corbaccio*," *Lettere italiane* 15 (1963), 1–27 and "Ancora sulla datazione e sul titolo del *Corbaccio*," *Lettere italiane* 15 (1963), 199–201. Padoan argues on behalf of a later date, 1365–66, but is opposed by the other scholars, who prefer 1355. Mario Marti, "Per una metalettura del *Corbaccio*: il ripudio di Fiammetta," *Giornale storico della letteratura italiana* 153 (1976), 60–86, esp. 63–64, aligns himself with Padoan.

2. Not only is the Maria of the *Amorosa Visione* named with a similar circumlocution and described as a fountain of mercy and sister of "pietà" but also the revision of the final lines, presumably written near the time of the *Corbaccio*, adds:

che'n voi son sempre, e come ancora in scoglio
immobil, *fissa*, sarò ognor tenace (my emph.)

[for in you I am always and always will be fixed like an anchor in an immobile rock].

3. This misogynism is in notable contrast to the *Filocolo*, where the antifeminist generalizations of Fileno and Idalagos are directly negated by Biancifiore.

4. Cf. the attitude of the servant woman in the *Decameron* VI, introduction.

5. Noted by Sapegno, *Storia letteraria*, p. 331. Isidore of Seville's *Etymologiae* XII, 43–44, (*PL* 82.465) mentions the crow's habit of eating first the eyes. Hugh of St. Victor, citing Isidore in his *De bestiis* I.35 (*PL* 177.31–33) explains that the crow signifies the devil, who puts out the eyes of the mind or the discretion of humans; it signifies also the sinner dressed in the black feathers of sin. "Similiter peccator, qui carnalibus desideriis pascitur, quasi corvus qui ad arcam non rediit, curiis exterioribus detinetur." [Similarly the sinner who feeds on carnal desires, like the crow which did not return to the ark, is detained by external concerns.] For other discussions of the title, see Anthony Cassell, "The Crow and the Fable of the *Corbaccio*," *MLN* 85 (1970), 83–91, and the introduction to Nurmela's edition, pp. 16–17, which surveys other articles. Padoan, "Ancora sulla datazione e sul titolo del *Corbaccio*," pp. 199–201, proposes that the black feathers of the crow refer to the widow's hypocritical black dress of mourning and thus to "ipocrisie e falsità" in general. See also below, pp. 158–60, on other meanings of the crow.

6. Obviously, cf. *Purgatoria* XXXI.34–36, and the *Amorosa Visione*.

7. Attilio Levi, *Il Corbaccio e la Divina Commedia* (Turin, 1889), p. 16; see also p. 8. For an opposite view, see Marti, "Per una metalettura," pp. 74–75.

8. Hauvette, *Boccace*, p. 340; Sapegno, *Storia letteraria*, p. 348; Renier, *Vita Nuova e Fiammetta*, pp. 284–85; Giuseppe Gigli, introduction to his edition of the *Corbaccio*, in *Opere minori volgari* (Florence, 1907), p. vi, and "Per l'interpretazione della *Fiammetta*," p. 71; Arnaud Tripet, "Boccace et son clerc amoureux," *Bibliotheque d'Humanisme et Renaissance* 29 (1967), 7–20; Levi, *Corbaccio*, p. 18; all assume that a real personal experience of disillusionment led Boccaccio to write this invective as his revenge against the widow who betrayed his love. Once again this is an autobiographical assumption which, although possible, is based on no known facts outside the fictional account. Nurmela, surveying the arguments for and against believing that the book is in some sense autobiographical, concludes, "diversi passi del libretto esprimono un sentimento così vivamente personale che ci pare almeno possibile che vi sia al fondo del libro un fatto qualunque realmente accaduto al poeta" (*Corbaccio*, pp. 7–8) [various passages of the little book express a feeling so lively and personal that it seems to us at least possible that there may underlie the book some fact which really happened to the poet].

9. Similarly Capellanus, in Book III of *De amore*, lists the faults of women in general in order to dissuade his nephew from love.

10. Levi, *Corbaccio*, p. 18: "lo spirito boccaccesco, che pure è avviato alla eterna gloria, si abbandona a un turpiloquio male scusato dal cavillo che questa è la fetida medicina di malattia sì fetida" [the Boccaccian spirit, which is on its way to eternal glory, abandons itself to foul language hardly excused by the cavil that this is the stinking medicine for such a stinking disease].

11. Gian Piero Baricelli, "Satire of Satire: Boccaccio's *Corbaccio*," *Italia Quarterly* 18 (1975), 104–8: "when we read at the end that our long enslaved hero feels freed, we must snicker at the thought that he has unheroically reshackled himself by substituting an exaggerated, irrational hate for an exaggerated, inordinate

love." Anthony Cassell, "An Abandoned Canvas: Structural and Moral Conflict in the *Corbaccio*," *MLN* 89 (1974), 60–70. See also his translation of the *Corbaccio*, pp. xxii–xxv. The dream is not, he claims, "ultimately a truly salutary experience."

12. Cf. Troilus's laughter at the end of Chaucer's *Troilus and Criseyde*.

13. See above, pp. 126–27.

14. Although the *corvus* of Apollo is distinguished by Ovid from the *cornix* of Athena, their two tales are intertwined, and the two birds were frequently confused in later times. See Cassell, "Crow of the Fable and the *Corbaccio*," p. 87. The *De planctu Naturae* carries on the traditional association of the crow with "vain chatter" (Prose 1.250).

15. Pliny, *Historia naturalis* X.30. Cf. Frazer's commentary on the *Fasti* (London, 1929), vol. 2, pp. 305–7.

16. Apuleius in a prefatory apology for publishing his unpolished writing at the urging of friends, contrasts the crow and swan to point out the foolish vanity of the harsh-voiced bird who thinks he can sing sweetly; "Florida," attached as a preface to *De deo Socratis* until the sixteenth century, in *Opuscules Philosophiques*, ed. with trans. into French by Jean Beaujeu (Paris, 1973), introd., p. 161; IV.108. The work was copied by Boccaccio in his own hand, it is not known exactly when; *Mostra di manoscritti, documenti e edizioni*, ed. by the Comitato Promotore (Certaldo, 1975), vol. 1, p. 152. Paolo da Perugia, in a commentary on Persius's *Satires*, similarly compares good poets to swans and bad ones to crows; Torraca, *Giovanni Boccaccio a Napoli*, p. 84.

17. "Corvus, sicut ait B. Gregorius, est doctus quisque praedicator, qui magna voce clamat, dum peccatorum suorum memoriam, quasi quamdam coloris nigredinem portat. Cui quidam nascuntur in fide discipuli, sed fortasse adhuc considerare infirmitatem propriam nesciunt, et fortasse a peccatis praeteritis memoriam avertunt, et per hoc eam, quam assumi oportet contra hujus mundi gloriam, humilitatis nigredinem non ostendunt. . . . Expectat quippe atque admonet ut a nitore vitae praesentis prius per poenitentiae lamenta nigrescant, et tunc demum congrua praedicationis subtilissimae nutrimenta percipiant." (Hugh of St. Victor, *De bestiis* I.35, "De corvo," *PL* 177.31–33) [The crow, says the blessed Gregory, is any learned preacher who calls with a great voice while he wears the memory of his sins like a black color. To him come certain disciples in the faith, but perchance they do not yet know how to regard their own infirmity, and perchance they turn away their memory from their past sins, and therefore they do not show the black of humility which one ought to wear against the glory of the world. . . . He awaits them, forsooth, and admonishes them so that first from the brightness of the present life they may grow black through the laments of penitence, and then may receive the suitable nourishment of subtlest preaching.]

18. Marti, "Per una metalettura," maintains just the opposite view: that the works up until the *Corbaccio* are basically realistic and not allegorical, whereas the *Corbaccio* is new in requiring an allegorical reading (see esp. pp. 74–76). What he considers the allegory of the *Corbaccio*, however, is so obvious as to require little interpretation; the story is *about* the moral message, not about some romance with spiritual implications. We are far from the doubleness of the *Comedia delle Ninfe*, for example. Even in the *Elegia*, which is one of the previous works that he specifi-

cally mentions, Fiammetta's text must be seen *through* because the narrator is herself in error; the *Corbaccio* narrator, on the other hand, speaks from the vantage point of his disillusioned and liberated state.

19. Cf. the *Caccia* where we discover to our surprise at the end that the narrator was an animal.

20. Hollander, *Boccaccio's Two Venuses*, pp. 99–102, points out the *Corbaccio*'s reversal of the book-as-Galeotto topos recurrent in Boccaccio's previous works.

21. Hastings, *Nature and Reason*, p. 60. Marga Cottino-Jones, "The *Corbaccio*: Notes for a Mythical Perspective of Moral Alternatives," *Forum italicum* 4 (1970), 490.

22. Nurmela, introduction to his edition of *Corbaccio*, p. 9. See also Billanovich, *Restauri*, p. 61.

23. Cottino-Jones, "*Corbaccio*," p. 506. Salvatore Battaglia, *Le epoche della letteratura italiana: Medioevo, Umanesimo, Rinascimento* (Naples, 1965), pp. 368–69: "Il *Corbaccio* segna una frattura all'interno della biografia letterario del suo autore, che rinnegava radicalmente i miti di tutta la sua opera, dal *Filocolo* al *Decameron*, almeno rispetto alla tripudiante cupidigia della natura e dei sensi. . . . è concepita come un'integrale palinodia." [The *Corbaccio* signals an internal break in the literary biography of its author, who radically renounces the myths of all his works, from the *Filocolo* to the *Decameron*, at least with respect to the reveling cupidity of nature and of the senses. . . . it is conceived as a whole palinode.] Cassell, *Corbaccio*, pp. xviii and xxvi, argues against seeing too strong a break between the *Corbaccio* and earlier works because, he says, the *Corbaccio* is not so moralizing as it seems.

VIII. *Decameron*

1. Hastings, *Nature and Reason*, p. 11, writes about repressive social laws which "cause needless frustration and suffering (for instance, the distress caused to women in love by confining them to their chambers, and depriving them of the satisfaction of their desires, at which Boccaccio protests in the *Proemio*)." Although Boccaccio certainly does protest certain kinds of social repression, such as the marriage of young girls to old men or the excessive jealousy of husbands, Hastings has entirely missed the point of the Proemio. Men are free, as women are not, to *distract themselves from love*, not to satisfy their passions. Boccaccio, freed from the demands of his own "appetito," wants to help women free themselves from their obsessive thoughts on love. His allusion to Ovid's *Remedia* is clear.

2. The plague symptom of swellings on the body matches Boccaccio's own earlier descriptions of the effects of love as a poison which swells the body (*Teseida* III.33; *Elegia* I). The association between love and plague has a model in Vergil's *Georgics* III, but the notion of love as a sickness is much too common to require a single source.

3. Cf. *Purgatorio* XXVI, esp. 84, where Guinizelli and others are suffering in flames of their own shame for "seguendo come bestie l'appetito."

4. See discussion on p. 89.

5. See the notes to Branca's edition.

6. Mario Baratto, *Realtà e stile nel Decameron* (Vicenza, 1970), p. 47: "non a caso, pur affermando di scrivere per le donne (ed è già il segno di una nuova richiesta di un pubblico più vasto), il Boccaccio sente il bisogno di difendere e di valorizzare la sua opera agli occhi dei dotti, dei litterati" [not by chance, while affirming that he writes for women (and it is already the sign of a new demand by a wider public), Boccaccio feels the need to defend and give value to his work in the eyes of the learned and the lettered]. Douglas Radcliff-Umstead, "Boccaccio's Idle Ladies," in *The Roles and Images of Women in the Middle Ages and Renaissance* (Pittsburgh, 1975), pp. 75–76, takes Boccaccio literally with regard to the audience but not with regard to Boccaccio's expressed purpose in addressing this audience: calling the *Decameron* "the western world's first major feminist text, dedicated to idle women to distract the loneliness and tedium of a sheltered and constricted existence," he claims that "the *Decameron* as a text of pleasant readings for the unoccupied women of the Tuscan middle class proclaims a revolutionary message of the rights of Love and Nature to inspire Boccaccio's public to find joy despite Fortune's cruelty and the arbitrary limitations of a male-centered society." But see my objections in n. 1 above.

7. Giorgio Padoan, "Mondo aristocratico e mondo communale nell'ideologia e nell'arte di Giovanni Boccaccio," *Studi sul Boccaccio* 2(1964), 125; Branca, "Profilo biografico," p. 180.

8. Women really were important as readers in the court society of Naples; Padoan, "Mondo," pp. 91–92, assumes that the *Decameron*'s address to women is a carry-over from that earlier context.

9. This has been pointed out by Cesare Segre in a note to his edition of the *Decameron* (Milan, 1970), p. 254, and by Marga Cottino-Jones in a paper read to the American Boccaccio Association, New York, December 1976. Lucia Marino's reading in *The Decameron "Cornice": Allusion, Allegory, and Iconology*, L'interprete 14 (Ravenna, 1979), while less literal than Radcliff-Umstead's (above, n. 6), is similar in effect, taking the amorous feminine audience to imply a defence of love by Boccaccio: "The enamoured ladies of Boccaccio's fictive readership emblematically suggest not only the refined and worldly enjoyment of natural pleasures, but also the artistic inspiration such experience gives rise to."

10. Francesco Tateo, "Poesia e favola nella poetica del Boccaccio," *Filologia romanza* 5 (1958), 295–96, writes: "Nella contrapposizione delle donne alle muse è evidente che le prime rappresentano il diletto della vita, . . . le altre una più severa ispirazione quale il Boccaccio non si sente mai di aver avuta ('le donne già mi furon cagione di comporre mille versi, dove le muse mai non mi furon di farne alcuna cagione'). Le Muse dunque non sono la elaborazione poetica, ma la guida ad una più alta ispirazione, come appare anche nell'Egl. XII, dove esse, impersonate in Calliope, guidano a *Saphos*, la poesia che 'celso se condidit antro / atque sacro lauro texit castissima vultus,' di contro a quella poesia che si accontenta dell'applauso del grosso pubblico. . . . le Muse, pur sempre garanti della serietà dell'opera, si lasciano rivestire di quel diletto che nasce dalla favola piacevole e umana e quindi si ripresentano, senza perdere dignità, nella figura leggiadra del sesso femminile." [In the contraposition of women to muses, it is evident that the former represent the pleasure of life, . . . the others a more severe inspiration which Boccaccio feels that

he has never had ("women have been already the cause of my composing a thousand verses, whereas the muses have never been the cause of my writing any"). The muses, then, are not poetic elaboration but the guide to a loftier inspiration, as appears also in Eclogue XII, where in the person of Calliope they guide one to *Saphos*, the poetry which "hid itself in a lofty cave and bound its chaste face with sacred laurel," as against that poetry which contents itself with the applause of the gross public. . . . the muses, while always assuring the seriousness of the work, let themselves be dressed in that delight which comes from a pleasing and human fable and thus they represent themselves, without loss of dignity, in the charming figure of the female sex.] In sum, Boccaccio's passage is for Tateo and others essentially a defence of the popular nature and subject matter of his work.

11. Giuseppe Mazzotta, "The *Decameron:* The Marginality of Literature," *University of Toronto Quarterly* 42 (Fall 1972), 68, 78–79.

12. Cf. Charles Singleton's reading, "On Meaning in the *Decameron*," *Italica* 21 (1944), 117–24. Millicent Marcus, *An Allegory of Form: Literary Self Consciousness in the Decameron*, Stanford French and Italian Studies 18 (Saratoga, Calif., 1979), p. 112, agrees with both Mazzotta and Singleton: "Boccaccio revels in the aesthetic abstraction from moral care that Cato punishes in Dante" but she qualifies this view on another page (p. 24): "The author's refusal to make providential claims for his work has been consistently confused with frivolity and escapism. . . . throughout the entire *Decameron*, Boccaccio reveals a serious preoccupation with questions of faith, honesty, and the status of human artifacts in the divine order." Mark Musa and Peter Bondanella, "The Meaning of the *Decameron*," in *The Decameron: 21 Novelle, Contemporary Reactions, Modern Criticism* (New York, 1977), p. 326, suggest that the address to idle ladies is an excuse by which "Boccaccio grants his creative faculty complete freedom to interpret and comment upon the state of society in his times and upon the human condition in general."

13. On this topic, see Ramat, *Scritti*, pp. 8–13; Giovanni Getto, *Vita di forme e forme di vita nel Decameron* (Turin, 1958), p. 11; Luigi Malagoli, *Il Decameron e primo Boccaccio* (Pisa, 1961), pp. 10–12; Hans-Jörg Neuschafer, *Boccaccio und der Beginn der Novelle* (Munich, 1969), pp. 125–33; Battaglia, *Giovanni Boccaccio e la riforma della narrativa*, pp. 151–54; Padoan, "Mondo," pp. 187–96; Baratto, *Realtà e stile*, pp. 15–16, 62, 150.

14. Boccaccio may be following Dante's divisions from *Purgatorio* XVII, rejecting those whose love is defective or misdirected and writing for those whose love is excessive. Marguerite de Navarre, one of Boccaccio's enthusiastic readers, returns several times in her *Heptameron* to the phrase from St. John: "par les choses visibles, on est tiré à l'amour des invisibles." Her nineteenth tale is followed by a long discussion of this idea: "Le cueur de l'homme, qui n'a nul sentiment d'amour aux choses visibles, ne viendra jamais à l'amour de Dieu par la semence de sa parolle, car la terre de son cueur est sterile, froide, et damnée." Gower too, writing as a lover in need of help, quotes from St. John 3:14: "He who does not love abides in death" (*Confessio Amantis* IV.2323–25). His context is a lesson against sloth. Again love is a necessary motive energy.

15. Cf. Calcidius, in his commentary on the *Timaeus*, ed. Jan Hendrik Waszink (London, 1962), CXCV, p. 217, quoting Plato as saying about the "perturbationes"

of the vices and passions, "quas quidem si frenarent ac subiugarent, iustam his lenemque vitam fore, sin vincerentur, iniustam et confragosam. Et victricibus quidem ad comparis stellae contubernium sedemque reditum patere acturis deinceps vitam veram et beatam, victas, porro mutare sexum atque ad infirmitatem naturae muliebris relegari secundae generationis tempore" [which if they rein or subdue, a just and smooth life will be theirs, but if they are overcome (by passions), an unjust and rough one. And the conquerors return to the dwelling and seat of a similar star to live thenceforth a true and blessed life; the conquered in the future change their sex and are relegated to the infirmity of a woman's nature in the time of their regeneration].

16. Thomas Greene, "Forms of Accommodation in the *Decameron*," *Italica* 45 (1968), 297–313, discusses the use of deceit as a means of preserving social bonds and reconciling conflicts of interest.

17. Millicent Marcus, "The Sweet New Style Reconsidered: A Gloss on the Tale of Cimone (*Decameron* V.1)," *Italian Quarterly* 81 (Summer 1980), 5–16. Day V begins and ends with false solutions: the pseudo-civilization based on concupiscent love and the illicit harmony of a homosexual ménage à trois.

18. See Battaglia, *Giovanni Boccaccio e la riforma della narrativa*, pp. 135–54.

19. Umberto Bosco, *Il Decameron: Saggio* (Rieti, 1929), p. 203. Billanovich, *Restauri*, p. 143.

20. It is already omitted in the *Elegia*, where Fiammetta, although still in Naples, is demoted from her royal connections.

21. Bosco, *Decameron*, pp. 53–55. Billanovich, *Restauri*, pp. 131–63. Ferdinando Neri, "Il disegno ideale del *Decameron*," in *Storia e poesia* (Turin, 1936), pp. 51–60. Branca, *Boccaccio medievale*, pp. 11–15. Joan Ferrante, "The Frame Characters of the *Decameron*: A Progression of Virtues," *Romance Philology* 19 (1965), 212–26. Stavros Deligiorgis, *Narrative Intellection in the Decameron* (Iowa City, 1975). Giorgio Padoan, "Sulla genesi del *Decameron*," in *Boccaccio 1975: Secoli di vita*, Atti del Congresso Internazionale: Boccaccio 1975, ed. Marga Cottino-Jones and Edward Tuttle (Ravenna, 1978), pp. 143–76, discusses the possible composition of the *Decameron* in separate pieces, days I–III and X being written earlier than the rest. This further supports the notion that Boccaccio had an overall arrangement in mind from the beginning. In any case, he presented the book finally as a whole.

22. Janet Smarr, "Symmetry and Balance in the *Decameron*," *Medievalia* 2 (1976), 159–87.

23. Kirkham, "Reckoning with Boccaccio's *Questioni d'amore*," pp. 47–59.

24. See Smarr, "Boccaccio and the Choice of Hercules."

25. See above, Chap. VI, p. 138 and n. 20.

26. The introduction to the fourth day, as an interruption in the author's own voice, has obviously received much critical attention. For a few of the many and varied interpretive comments, see: Angelo Lipari, "Donne e Muse," *Italica* 15 (1938), 132–41. Enrico de'Negri, "The Legendary Style of the *Decameron*," *Romanic Review* 43 (1952), 175–78. Getto, *Vita di forme*, p. 30. Raffaello Ramat, "L'introduzione alla quarta giornata," in *Scritti*, pp. 93–107. Neuschafer, *Boccaccio und der Beginn der Novelle*, pp. 56ff. Mazzotta, "Marginality," pp. 76–77. Baratto, *Realtà e stile*, p. 56.

27. Plutarch (*De E apud Delph.* 338c) notes that the Pythagoreans called five the marriage number because it is the sum of two and three, the first female and male numbers. Plutarch also discusses the significance of the five lights lit at a Roman wedding (*Quaest. Rom.* 264 A), saying again, "Five is above all the nuptial number." For examples of the use of five as a wedding number, see Alastair Fowler, *Triumphal Forms* (Cambridge, 1970), the chapter on "Epithalamia," pp. 148ff.

28. For the view of Boccaccio as a rebel against establishment values and champion of the "rights of nature" see: Francesco de Sanctis, *Storia della letteratura italiana*, ed. Benedetto Croce, 2 vols. (Bari, 1958), vol. 1, chap. 9. Hauvette, *Boccace*, p. 256. Erich Auerbach, *Zur Technik der Frührenaissancenovelle in Italien und Frankreich* (Heidelberg, 1921), p. 20. Auerbach, *Mimesis*, pp. 188–89, 200. Hiram Haydn, *The Counter Renaissance* (New York, 1950), pp. 66–67. Walter Pabst, *Novellentheorie und Novellendichtung* (Hamburg, 1953), pp. 27–40. Scaglione, *Nature and Love in the Late Middle Ages*, pp. 44–45, 67–68, 68–82, 97–100. Radcliff-Umstead, "Boccaccio's Idle Ladies," pp. 75–103. For the *Decameron* as a work dealing with aesthetic and *not* with moral issues, see Russo, *Letture critiche del Decameron*, pp. 40–41. Angelo Lipari, "The Structure and Real Significance of the *Decameron*," in *Essays in Honor of Albert Feuillerat*, ed. Henri Peyre, Yale Romanic Studies 22 (New Haven, 1943), pp. 43–83. And Singleton's review of Lipari's work, "On Meaning in the *Decameron*."

29. See Branca's notes, pp. 1000–1001.

30. In the *De Mulieribus Claris* where virgins are among those worthy of fame and praise, Boccaccio nonetheless writes a long and vehement protest against parents who force their daughters into nunneries before they know how to choose for themselves, so that "to console their saddened hearts, they have recourse only to thinking how they can destroy their prison and flee, or at least bring their lovers inside, trying to take furtively the pleasure which has been denied them, since they have been deprived of open marriage." (Trans. Guido Guarino [New Brunswick, N.J., 1963], p. 97.) The young son in the half-tale too has not chosen his monastic life but has been pushed into it at an early age by his father.

31. On the importance of marriage and other forms of social accord in the *Decameron*, see Greene, "Forms of Accommodation in the *Decameron*," pp. 297–313; Franco Fido, "Il sorriso di messer Torello (*Decameron* X.9)," *Romance Philology* 23 (1969), 154–71; Victoria Kirkham, "Love's Labors Rewarded and Paradise Lost," *Romanic Review* 72 (Jan. 1981), 88–89.

32. Cf. Dante's paradise, possibly described in *Paradiso* XXX as a theater, e.g., l. 115 "l'infimo grado." Such an allusion would make this place surpass the garden of day III, described as the earthly paradise.

33. See the discussion by Marino, *Decameron "Cornice,"* pp. 84ff., esp. p. 85 on six as a perfect number.

34. The stories of days III and VII have much in common. They are the days most concerned with illicit love, and many of the tales reflect one another in their theme across the two days.

35. Padoan, "Mondo," p. 138. Antonio Stäuble, "La brigata del *Decameron* come pubblico teatrale," in *Studi sul Boccaccio*, vol. 9 (Florence, 1975–76), associates Padoan's two worlds with the tendencies of the cornice and tales toward idealiza-

tion and realism respectively, producing an unresolved tension between container and contained. But the tales themselves contain both tendencies, as Padoan has pointed out.

36. Cf. *Filocolo* V.39.4 for a crown of oak leaves as a sign of victory. Also in the *Comedia delle Ninfe* XXVII.10, Lia or Faith is crowned with oak. Kirkham has suggested that Emilia, ruler of the *Decameron*'s ninth day, is similarly a representative of faith ("An Allegorically Tempered *Decameron*," *Italica* 62 [1985], 17).

37. Gordon Silber, *The Influence of Dante and Petrarch on Certain of Boccaccio's Lyrics* (Menasha, Wis., 1940), pp. 69–70.

38. That Dioneo is consciously and humorously taking the role he does is made clear by his statement at the end of the ninth day (see below, pp. 188–89).

39. The same pattern of symmetry in one through nine and correspondence between a central five and final ten has been discovered in Vergil's *Eclogues* by Ewald Krause, *Quibus temporibus quoque ordine Vergilius eclogas scripserit* (Berlin, 1884), pp. 6ff. See also P. Maury, "Le secret de Virgile et l'architecture des Bucoliques," *Lettres d'humanité* 3 (1944), 71–147; and George Duckworth, *Structural Patterns and Proportions in Vergil's Aeneid* (Ann Arbor, Mich., 1962), pp. 3–4. Perhaps Boccaccio was thinking of the *Decameron* partly as a Vergilian pastoral; the eclogues, after all, begin and end with reference to the grim results of the civil war in the real world outside, a situation comparable to the social breakdown in Florence.

40. Marguerite de Navarre probably imitated this pairing in presenting Hircan and Parlemente as a married couple. Hircan is certainly the Dioneo of her group.

41. For Lipari, "Structure and Real Significance of the *Decameron*," pp. 43–84, each narrator represents some particular aspect of Boccaccio's writing. Cf. similarly Branca, "Giovanni Boccaccio rinnovatore dei generi letterari," p. 25. For Ferrante, "Frame Characters of the *Decameron*," each lady is one of the virtues; cf. similarly Marino, *Decameron "Cornice,"* pp. 140–50, 160–79. Henri Hauvette, "Les ballades du *Décaméron*," *Journal des savants* (1905), 405–6, proposed that Boccaccio intended his narrators to represent the arts and sciences in their songs but that he gave up the idea after the third song. For other attempts to identify the narrators separately, see Adolfo Albertazzi, *Parvenze e sembianze* (Bologna, 1892), pp. 163–99. Billanovich, *Restauri*, pp. 131–63. Bosco, *Decameron*, pp. 20–25. Rossi, *Dalla mente e dal cuore di Giovanni Boccaccio*, pp. 148–79. Lipari, "Donne e Muse," pp. 132–41. But cf. Battaglia, *Giovanni Boccaccio e la riforma della narrativa*, p. 147: "Non importa quindi la individualità di un Dioneo, che tuttavia si distingue dagli altri per una più accentuata spregiudicatezza, né di una Pampinea; ma conta ciò che hanno in commune: il senso dell' evasione da una società in dissolvimento e il ricostruire un ordine nella loro esistenza e nei loro animi. A loro interessa rifugiarsi in una comune idealità idillica." [Therefore the individuality of a Dioneo is not important, although he is distinguished from the others by a more accentuated openmindedness, nor of a Pampinea; but what counts is what they have in common: the sense of escape from a dissolving society and the reconstruction of order in their life and in their souls. They are interested in taking refuge in a common idyllic ideal.] Padoan, "Mondo," p. 144, also comments on the vanity of all attempts to distinguish among the narrators, who are significant as a collective group. Russo,

Letture critiche del Decameron, pp. 20ff., also treats the narrators as a homogeneous group. Lars Peter Rømhild, "Osservazioni sul concetto e sul significato della cornice del *Decameron*," *Analecta Romana Instituti Danici* 7 (1974), 167–68, remarks that although the absence of distinct attributes renders implausible any allegorical interpretation of the individual narrators, nonetheless a completely homogeneous treatment of the group ignores essential tensions in it, and he compares the work to a *joc parti* or dialogue poem in this regard.

The most recent and convincing theory about the narrators is Kirkham's identification of the women with virtues and the men with parts of the soul ("An Allegorically Tempered *Decameron*"). Her identifications fit the symmetries of the book, pairing hope with wrath or despair, charity with concupiscence, and suitably positioning temperance at the center.

42. Billanovich, *Restauri*, pp. 138–39 and 143, pairs Dioneo with Elissa as well as with Fiammetta.

43. See below, pp. 188ff.

44. Rømhild, "Osservazioni," p. 172, also comments on this relation between I.4 and I.5.

45. Kirkham, "Love's Labors Rewarded," pp. 90–91, describes a descending pattern from the paradise garden of the introduction to the "ninferno" of III.10, and comments on the appropriateness of the tragic song at the end of this day.

46. See Segre's edition of the *Decameron*, p. 468.

47. Venus is associated with the sea from which she was born, while Mars is the fiery planet, named Pyrois by the Greeks.

48. Boccaccio cannot resist, however, introducing this happy conclusion with the admiral's cynical remark to Gianni: "Io farò sì che tu la vedrai ancora tanto, che ti rincrescerà." [I will make it so that you can see so much of her that you'll be sick of it.]

49. The very use of Latin contributes to the official quality of the phrase.

50. Marcus, "Sweet New Style Reconsidered," pp. 11–12. Boccaccio even seems to echo certain phrases or details: the overturned wedding tables, for example; or the phrase "già, a tavola erano per mangiare assettate ordinatemente," cf. Ovid's l. 211: "Nubigenasque feros positis ex ordine mensis"; or "ciascuna prese la sua," cf. ll. 224–25: "alii, quam quisque probabant / aut poterant, rapiunt."

51. Ovid reinforces the connection in l. 225: "captaeque erat urbis imago" [it was the image of a captured city].

52. See also Branca's note, p. 1265, on the plight of the Greek Efigenia evoked by Boccaccio.

53. Marcus connects Cimone's bestial nature to the centaurs, Dante's image of violence; the association is perhaps supported further by the name of Cimone's father, Aristippo, which suggests a horsey parentage.

54. Seung, *Cultural Thematics*, p. 213, views Griselda as the totally passive person necessary to live with a Faustian ego such as Gualtieri's. But it is Griselda, not Gualtieri, who is the heroic example of magnificence, and Dioneo's comment about Gualtieri's "bestialità" is far from implying Boccaccio's celebration of Gualtieri as a new kind of hero and model.

55. Boccaccio, *Decameron* VI.concl.20: "secondo che alcuna di loro poi mi ridisse" [as one of the ladies later reported to me]. This is noted by Rømhild, "Osservazioni," p. 159.

56. This aim is just the opposite of Filostrato's, who wants stories that will make the hearer weep (III.concl.6; IV.1.2; IV.2.2–3).

57. Chaucer, "Clerk's Tale," ll. 871–72, 932. Petrarch, *Seniles* XVII.3, does not name Job, but his version of Griselda's line is even closer to Job 1:21 than Boccaccio's.

58. Clearly we cannot say that Gualtieri represents God without raising serious questions about the negative image of God which that would imply; for superhuman powers are portrayed through a human figure who, as human, has no right to behave the way he does. His testing is severely condemned both by the narrator and by Griselda in her poignant request on behalf of the new bride. Dioneo's observation that Gualtieri's actions are *sub*human may be meant as a warning in this regard. What we can say, nonetheless, is that Griselda's relationship to Gualtieri, based on her willful determination to adhere to the rules established at the time of their marriage, represents the ideal relation of the human soul to God.

59. The narrators' proffered "morals" are not always seriously meant; but just as the comment can be a joke appended to a serious tale, as in X.10 or V.1, so too the comment can turn a witty tale to serious use.

60. See Robert Durling, "Boccaccio on Interpretation: Guido's Escape (*Decameron* VI.9)," in *Dante, Petrarch, and Others: Studies in Honor of Charles Singleton*, ed. Aldo Bernardo and Anthony Pellegrini (Binghamton, N.Y., 1983), pp. 273–304.

61. Marcus, *Allegory of Form*, is right to note Boccaccio's efforts to educate the reader to detect a multiplicity of meanings. She is mistaken, however, to suggest that the way to understand Boccaccio is to consider him totally apart from Dante (pp. 2, 110–12); for it is often through allusions to Dante's work that many of Boccaccio's meanings are formed. See, e.g., Durling, "Boccaccio on Interpretation: Guido's Escape," and Victoria Kirkham, "Painters at Play on the Judgment Day (*Decameron* VIII.9)," *Studi sul Boccaccio* 14 (1984–85), 256–77.

Tripet, in contrast, praises the "lecteur naif mais qui obéit sans le savoir à l'intention de Boccace et ne recherche dans la lecture du *Decameron* que le plaisir d'un moment." For him the narrators' escape to the hills is "l'évasion en un monde enchanteur qui n'obéit qu'aux lois du plus exquis hédonisme" [the naive reader who, however, obeys without knowing it the intention of Boccaccio and in reading the *Decameron* seeks nothing but the pleasure of the moment . . . the escape into a magic world which obeys only the laws of the most exquisite hedonism] ("Boccacce et son clerc amoureux," pp. 7–9).

62. Franco Fido, "L'*ars narrandi* di Boccaccio nella sesta giornata," in *Le Metamorfosi del Centauro* (Rome, 1977), pp. 43–62; also in English in *Italian Literature—Roots and Branches, Essays in Honor of Thomas G. Bergin*, ed. Giose Rimanelli and Kenneth John Atchity (New Haven, 1976), pp. 225–42. Guido Almansi, "Lettura della novella di Madonna Oretta," *Paragone letterature* 270 (Aug. 1972), 139–42.

63. The words "tacito e nascoso" do not appear in Branca's edition, but are

present in Segre's and in Singleton's, Scrittori d'Italia 97–98 (Bari, 1955), vol. 97, p. 269. Although not necessary to my argument, they do strengthen the association between Boccaccio's descriptions of his own and Giotto's humility.

64. See, for example: Auerbach, *Mimesis*, p. 202; Sapegno, *Storia letteraria*, p. 328; di Pino, *Polemica*, p. 209; Getto, *Vita di forme*, pp. 188–262; Battaglia, *Coscienza letteraria*, pp. 669–84; F. Tateo, "Il realismo del *Decameron* nella storia della critica," *Dialoghi* 1–2 (1958), 18–36.

65. Di Pino, *Polemica*, p. 209: "si realizza il trasferimento della invenzione da un piano favoloso a un altro storico, dove tutto—dall'occasione proposta dalla pestilenza, alle situazioni dei racconti—appartiene a un tempo reale di circostanza e di uomini." [A transference of invention is realized from the plane of fable to that of history, where everything—from the proposed occasion of the plague, to the situations in the tales—belongs to a real time of circumstances and men.] See also Padoan, "Mondo" pp. 105–9.

66. Mazzotta, "Marginality," pp. 65, 68–73, 79, claims that the *Decameron* is chiefly about "the essential discontinuity between literature and historical reality," and the "deception" or "inherent duplicity of language." The author, he claims, ends up by viewing literature as a joke and disclaims responsibility for the effects of the book by pointing to its garden setting, that is, to "the necessary role of the disvalued and the useless: a perennial marginality." Boccaccio is thus both playing with the deceptive possibilities of language and at the same time "unmasking the threats and seductions of his own artifact." For a similar view, see Marcus, *Allegory of Form*, esp. pp. 6–7. Rather than a total separation from reality, however, the narrators' withdrawal to the garden on the hill can be understood as a moment of objective review; for the narrators remain fascinated by the life of their own fellows in the cities below. If the garden in some sense symbolizes art, what that art offers is not so much irrelevant pleasures as a realm of the ideal or possible from which to view the real world.

67. Pabst, *Novellentheorie und Novellendichtung*, "Boccaccios Protest," pp. 27–40, asserts that Boccaccio revolutionized novelle by rebelling against the tale as moral exemplum while fooling his critics by paying lip service to the tradition at the beginning and end of the book. Cf. Marcus, *Allegory of Form*, p. 12.

68. Joan Ferrante, "Narrative Patterns in the *Decameron*," *Romance Philology* 31 (1978), 590.

69. For Boccaccio's interest in this legend, see Smarr, "Boccaccio and the Choice of Hercules."

70. See above, Chap. II, p. 55.

71. The echo was noted by Cavallari, *Fortuna di Dante*, pp. 427–28.

72. It can also be associated with the wolf which Dante encounters when similarly lost in the woods.

73. See n. 37.

74. Robert Durling, "Boccaccio on Interpretation: Guido's Escape," esp. pp. 274–86.

75. Giuseppe Mazzotta, *Dante, Poet of the Desert* (Princeton, 1979), p. 279, observes that "sanus intellectus" is a common formula to describe proper, i.e., non-heretical readings of the Bible. Thus Dante in *Convivio* IV.xv.10–16 uses "intelletti

sani" to mean those who understand according to Christian faith. Boccaccio too seeks readings which will be compatible with faith; for his numerous references to the Christian religion within the *Decameron* are not mere lip service, if one may judge by the rest of his writings both before and after.

76. Giovanni Pinelli, "La moralità nel *Decameron*," *Il propugnatore* 15 (1882), 316: "Oltre a ciò vi dice che ogni scrittore ha il suo pubblico, e il suo non può essere composto che di coloro che han già l'uso di ragione e che atti sono a tenergli dietro nel libero esame de' costumi del secolo e che possono sulle sue norme giudicare quello ch'è da fuggire e quello che è da seguitare. Per gli ipocriti e per gli adolescenti non è fatto il suo libro . . . per i secondi, che sono gli inesperti, la rappresentazione del vizio, fatta anche coll'intendimento di moralizzare, può riuscire lusinghiera ed eccitatrice a termine contrario a quello che si propone l'autore." [Besides, he says there that every writer has his public, and his own must consist of those who have already the use of reason and are apt to follow him in the free examination of the manners of the age and can with his evidence judge what is to be shunned and what followed His book is not made for hypocrites and adolescents . . . for the second, the inexperienced, the representation of vice, even when made with the intent to moralize, can turn out to be alluring and provocative to an end contrary to that set by the author.]

77. Padoan, "Sulla genesi del *Decameron*," suggests that the *Decameron* was composed in several pieces.

78. There have been various explanations of the "Galeotto" subtitle. For Mazzotta ("Marginality," pp. 68–69), the title is a sign that Boccaccio is "aware of literature as an erotic snare . . . Boccaccio seems intent on assigning to this text the role of erotic mediator, and thus unmasking the threats and seductions of his own artifact." The threat includes the seductive powers of rhetoric and fiction as well as sexual seduction. For Padoan, however, the title is a shield against just such seduction ("Mondo," pp. 124–25): "Egli era del resto pienamente consapevole di ciò che volesse significare il sopranominare il proprio libro 'Prencipe Galeotto': da questa precisa accusa infatti si difende nella Conclusione del *Decameron* affermando che la sua opera non potrà indurre al male nessuno che non vi sia naturalmente disposto." [He was, moreover, fully aware of what he wanted to signify by naming his own book "Prince Galeotto": from this very accusation, in fact, he defends himself in the conclusion of the *Decameron*, affirming that his work will not be able to lead into evil anyone who is not naturally disposed to it.] For Padoan it is a reference to *Inferno* V where Francesca, but not Dante, blames the book for her behavior; in God's view, it is the reader Francesca's fault and she is merely trying to shift the blame. (But cf. also Padoan's introduction to the *Esposizioni* and "Boccaccio" in *Enciclopedia dantesca* where Padoan says that Boccaccio misunderstood the scene of Paolo and Francesca. And see Antonio Enzo Quaglio's reply in *Al di là di Francesca e Laura* [Padua, 1973], pp. 14–26.) Segre, in the introductory note to his edition of the *Decameron*, p. 24, again in contrast, denies the connection to Dante's verse and sees the title chiefly as expressing Boccaccio's desire to please the reader; Galeotto was willing to do anything to help his friend Lancelotto. For Galletti, too, the echo from *Inferno* V is irrelevant; the word means *guide* or *mediator*, he argues, and it is the "intendimento del suo Autore di guidare l'uomo, smarrito e perduto nella peste

morale del vizio, per la via della riconquista, alla virtù" [meaning of its author to guide man, misdirected and lost in the mortal plague of vice, by the path of reconquest to virtue]. In short, it is the opposite sort of guide from Galeotto (Salvatore Galletti, *Patologia al Decameron* [Palermo, 1969], pp. 215–16). These last two explanations seem to me the weakest. It is true that Boccaccio wants to "help" the melancholy lovers, his readers, in a very different way from the way in which Galeotto helped Lancelot and the queen. But Boccaccio says "Prencipe Galeotto," not just "galeotto" as a general term. Surely Dante *is* being invoked, moreover, and the warning about the effects of reading does fit in neatly with Boccaccio's defense in the conclusion. Franco Fido, "Dante personaggio mancato del *Decameron*," *Boccaccio 1975: Secoli di vita*, pp. 180–89, has argued that the subtitle is an ambivalent acknowledgment of Dante's literary influence, signifying "insieme rispettoso omaggio e voluta deviazione semantica. Un'ammirazione e un independenza di giudizio" [at the same time a respectful homage and willful semantic deviation. An admiration and an independence of judgment]. Dante is named at the beginning of the fourth day, a day of tragic loves which could easily include the story of Paolo and Francesca. But "dobbiamo supporre fin dall'inizio una tmesi intenzionale fra denotazione e connotazione in quell'epiteto, che si referisce sì a un libro persuasore d'amore, ma di un amore molto meno cattivo di quanto altri non pensino" [we must suppose from the beginning an intentional division between denotation and connotation in that epithet, which refers indeed to a book persuasive of love, but of a love much less wicked than others think]. Hollander, *Boccaccio's Two Venuses*, pp. 102 and ff., has suggested furthermore that the title refers not only to Dante's poem but also to Boccaccio's own previous writing, his pose as narrator there, and the previous echoes of *Inferno* V such as in the dedicatory preface to the *Teseida* or in the reading scene of Florio and Biancifiore. A reader who knew at least some of those earlier works and who saw in the title an allusion to their authorial pose, might well have been surprised by and attentive to the author's new state as exlover and might therefore have launched into the tales wondering what this new attitude could mean.

79. Mazzotta, "Marginality," p. 80.

IX. The *Rime* and Late Writings

1. Billanovich, *Restauri*, pp. 87–88.

2. König, *Begegnung*, p. 84: "Fiammetta enthült sich tatsächlich, und zuallererst durch ihr Auftreten in der Kirche, als 'minore sorella di Laura.'" [Fiammetta reveals herself in fact, and above all through her appearance in church, as "younger sister of Laura."]

3. Branca, "Profilo biografico," p. 37. Giuseppe Billanovich, *Petrarca letterato* (Rome, 1947), pp. 62–63, and *Restauri*, p. 88.

4. Ernest Hatch Wilkins, "Notes on Petrarch," *MLN* 32 (1917), 196–98. The connection is between *Canzoniere* 112 and *Filostrato* V.54–55. See also Paolo Savj-Lopez, "Il *Filostrato* di Boccaccio," *Romania* 27 (1898), 465; Francesco Mango, "Note," *Propugnatore* 16 (1883), part 1, 437–52.

5. Gordon Silber, "Alleged Imitations of Petrarch in the *Filostrato*," *Modern Philology* 37 (1939), 113—24.

6. See Chap. I, n. 13.

7. Wilkins, *Making*, pp. 81—82, 146. The collection, dated by Petrarch as he copied it out in its finished form between 1336—37, is described by Wilkins in "Petrarch's First Collection of His Italian Poems," *Speculum* 7 (1932), 169—80.

8. Wilkins, *Making*, p. 34.

9. Carlo Calcaterra, *Nella selva del Petrarca* (Bologna, 1942), pp. 74—75. Aldo S. Bernardo, *Petrarch, Laura and the "Triumphs"* (Albany, 1974), pp. 26—60. Wilkins, *Making*, pp. 95, 81—82.

10. Angelo Solerti, *Le Vite di Dante, Petrarca e Boccaccio scritte fino al secolo decimosesto* (Milan, n.d.), p. 262.

11. Wilkins, *Making*, p. 26.

12. Branca, introduction to his edition of the *Rime* (1958), pp. vi—viii, xviii—xix.

13. Bernardo, *Petrarch, Laura*, p. 27.

14. Boccaccio, *Rime*, ed. Branca (1939), p. 313. Branca, to avoid confusion among critics and scholars, has followed the order of the poems invented by Massèra (1914) in imitation of Petrarch's arrangement. He warns, however, "Ogni coerenza psicologica e ogni svolgimento artistico è nelle *Rime*, come già dimostrai, chiaramente inconciliabile con quell'ordinamento biografico." *Neubert*, p. 13. [Any psychological coherence and any artistic development in the *Rime* is, as I already demonstrated, clearly irreconcilable with that biographical ordering.]

15. Boccaccio, *Rime*, ed. Branca (1958), pp. vi—viii, xviii—xix.

16. Di Pino, *Polemica*, pp. 10—13, compares *Rime* VI and XXVI to passages in the *Elegia;* Rosario Ferreri, "Studi sulle *Rime*," *Studi sul Boccaccio* 7 (1973), 215—16, does the same for VI and LXV. Massèra, ed., *Rime*, pp. 66—67, observes that some of the women from LXIX reappear in the *Comedia delle Ninfe* and *Amorosa Visione*. IV presents a scene like that of the *Comedia delle Ninfe*, where Ameto follows an angelic song and discovers a group of ladies. Branca's notes to the *Rime* often point out such echoes as a means of establishing Boccaccio's authorship.

17. Cf. Caleone's vision in the *Filocolo*, IV.43, where a flame seems to play on Fiammetta's head as a divine omen. See also Chap. II, n. 31, for the parallel between the Exodus pillar of fire and the Pentecostal flame.

18. Poems CVIII and XCI are both possibly by Petrarch rather than by Boccaccio; however, Branca (1939) considers them probably Boccaccio's. See also Billanovich's review of Branca's edition of the *Rime*, *Giornale storico della letteratura italiana* 116 (1940), 146.

19. The phrase has a different meaning in Boccaccio's letter "Sacre famis": "Et cum in recthorice sermonum generibus ingenioso venabulo peragrares, tuorum fervens amor habendi, te invito, de pio sinu Rachelis ad Lie gremium transtulerunt. Heu! humanarum mentium cecitas, et insatiabilis acervos auri congregandi cupiditas!" [And when you wander through the kinds of styles in rhetoric with your witty spear, the fervent love of possessions of your family will, to your displeasure, draw you from the bosom of Rachel to the lap of Lia. Alas! the blindness of human minds, and the insatiable cupidity for collecting heaps of gold!] Might XXII

too be not about writing "per donna" but rather about being compelled to turn from his literary passion to more mundane work? But then neither "unde" nor "dolce voglia" would make much sense. It is Amor himself who forces the poet to serve Lia in order ultimately to attain the higher goal.

20. Ferreri, "Ovidio e le Rime di Giovanni Boccaccio." Ussani, "Alcune imitazioni ovidiane del Boccaccio."

21. Rosario Ferreri, "Sulle *Rime* del Boccaccio," *Studi sul Boccaccio* 8 (1974), 185–96.

22. Ibid., pp. 190–96.

23. More than twenty poems have been somewhere attributed to Petrarch from the first part of the *Rime* (1–126), and another twenty-five from the second part (1–41). Branca has divided the two parts according to the more and less probable authorship of Boccaccio.

24. Boccaccio, *Rime*, ed. Branca (1939), p. 363.

25. However, the myth is used in quite another way in the letter to Durazzo: "Utinam tamen rude desultoriumque eloquium sic in vestri conspectu se prebeat, prout Athlantiadis fistula in auribus custodis iunonii se locavit." [Yet would that my rough and scattered speech might offer itself to your view as the pipe of Atlantiades (i.e., Mercury) placed itself in the ears of the Junonian guard.]

26. See Chap. III, n. 14; not only do Arcita and Palemon come from Thebes, but already in the *Filocolo* (II.32) the royal hall where the king falsely incriminates Biancifiore is decorated with scenes of Theban history and the destruction of Troy.

27. E.g., *Filostrato* IV.164. In contrast to Mary's humility, it is "gli atti tuoi altieri e signorili" and "tuo sdegno donnesco" [your lofty and signorial gestures, your ladylike scorn] which attract Troiolo to Criseida.

28. As many lines and phrases from the *Caccia* are repeated closely in the *Amorosa Visione* (see Branca's notes on the *Caccia*), and as the *Corbaccio* repeats scenes and images from the *Amorosa Visione*, one can think of these three pieces as rewritings much the way the poems to Mary or God redo poems to Fiammetta or whoever the unnamed lady of other poems may be.

29. Etienne Gilson, "Poésie et vérité dans la *Généalogie*," *Studi sul Boccaccio* 2 (1964), 260, suggests that Books XIV and XV may have been written much later than the rest of the *Genealogia*, sometime after 1370; however, Pier Giorgio Ricci, "Contributi per un'edizione critica della *Genealogia deorum gentilium*," *Rinascimento* 2 (1951), 142–44, argues against this, and Giuseppe Billanovich, "Pietro Piccolo da Monteforte fra il Petrarca e il Boccaccio," *Medioevo e Rinascimento: Studi in onore di Bruno Nardi* (Florence, 1955), vol. 1, p. 35, accepts Ricci's argument.

30. See Vittore Branca, "Per il testo del *Decameron*: La prima diffusione del *Decameron*," *Studi di filologia italiana* 8 (1950), 43, concerning Boccaccio's shift from Italian to Latin under the influence of Petrarch's humanism.

31. Both Lauretta's song in the *Decameron* and the comment which follows it may indicate that Petrarch's poems too, although correctly read by some, were being misunderstood by superficial readers. See above, p. 180.

32. Tateo, "Poesia e favola," p. 302; Billanovich, "Pietro Piccolo da Monteforte," p. 19.

33. Re Crisis see Eclogue XIII, "Laurea," and Zumbini, "Ecloghe," p. 142. And see Chap. I, n. 21.

Conclusion

1. Branca, "Profilo biografico," pp. 124–26.
2. Boccaccio, *Trattatello in laude di Dante*, p. 521.

INDEX

Index

A Note on the Author

Janet Levarie Smarr received her doctorate in comparative literature from Princeton University and is a member of the comparative literature faculty of the University of Illinois. She has published on Boccaccio, Petrarch, and Dante, as well as on poets of the English Renaissance, and her recent *Italian Renaissance Tales* won the American Association of Italian Studies 1984 Presidential Award for the Best Translation of Classical Texts.